REDISCOVERING
PASTORAL
MINISTRY

REDISCOVERING
PASTORAL MINISTRY

SHAPING CONTEMPORARY MINISTRY
WITH BIBLICAL MANDATES

JOHN MacARTHUR, JR.
AND THE MASTER'S SEMINARY FACULTY

John MacArthur, Jr., Editor
Richard L. Mayhue, Associate Editor
Robert L. Thomas, Associate Editor

WORD PUBLISHING
Dallas·London·Vancouver·Melbourne

REDISCOVERING PASTORAL MINISTRY

Library of Congress Cataloging-in-Publication Data

    MacArthur, John 1939–
    Rediscovering pastoral ministry: shaping contemporary ministry with biblical mandates / John MacArthur, Jr. and The Master's Seminary Faculty.
      p. cm.
    Includes bibliographical references and index.
    ISBN 0-8499-1092-7
    1. Pastoral theology.   2. Clergy—Office.   I. Title.
BV4011.M34   1995
253-dc20   95-6452
                                                CIP

Printed in the United States of America

5 6 7 8 9 1 2 3 4 BVG 9 8 7 6 5 4 3 2 1

Dedicated to undershepherds around the world
who obediently labor for the Chief Shepherd
in fulfilling His promise,
"I will build my church."

Contents

Preface

In keeping with the purposes of The Master's Seminary, the goal of this volume is to encourage and instruct this and the next generation of pastors, missionaries, and teachers to provide the kind of shepherd leadership for the church that God's Word requires. In a highly condensed form, *Rediscovering Pastoral Ministry* provides much of the pastoral theology curriculum of The Master's Seminary, the goal of which is to prepare men for pastoring the church, giving pastoral leadership on the mission field, and assuming pastoral functions in institutional teaching responsibilities. This work joins the previously published volumes, *Rediscovering Expository Preaching*[1] and *Introduction to Biblical Counseling*,[2] to provide a three-volume pastoral resource library.

Rediscovering Pastoral Ministry targets both seasoned pastors and young men preparing for or just beginning ministry. It calls pastors back to the Scriptures as the authoritative basis for developing a philosophy of ministry. Since many of our generation's pastors have fallen prey to the consumer approach or market-driven philosophy of ministry, this volume purposes to recover, reaffirm, and restore a biblical approach to pastoral ministry. In this regard *Rediscovering Pastoral Ministry* is both prescriptive of guidelines to follow and proscriptive of dangers to avoid.

This is *not* an unabridged treatment of pastoral ministry. We have left many particulars such as church growth, church discipline, church membership, church polity,[3] and the details of specialized ministries (e.g., youth ministry, adult ministry) to be dealt with in other forums. Further, no single chapter exhausts its subject but rather furnishes a suggestive general treatment. The broad

---

1. John MacArthur, Jr., et al., *Rediscovering Expository Preaching* (Dallas: Word, 1992).

2. John F. MacArthur, Jr., and Wayne A. Mack, et al., *Introduction to Biblical Counseling* (Dallas: Word, 1994).

3. This work assumes the presbyterian type of church polity with its plurality of elders in each local church (Acts 14:23; 20:17). For a detailed description of this type of church organization, see John F. MacArthur, Jr., *The Master's Plan for the Church* (Chicago: Moody, 1991), 87–94, 179–213, and Alexander Strauch, *Biblical Eldership*, 2nd ed. (Littleton, Colo.: Lewis and Roth, 1988).

sweep of this work is its intended strength, as it deals with the biblical nature of what a pastor is to be personally and how he is to minister in the church.

More specifically, the threefold aim of *Rediscovering Pastoral Ministry* is:

1. To *validate* the biblical absolutes required by God for pastoral ministry, i.e., to answer the question, "What is one's authority for establishing a philosophy of ministry?"

2. To *elucidate* the biblical qualifications for church pastors, i.e., to answer the question, "Whom has God authorized to be undershepherds of Christ's flock?"

3. To *delineate* the biblical priorities for pastoral ministry, i.e., to answer the question, "What does a scripturally based pastoral ministry involve?"

President John MacArthur, Jr., who has pastored Grace Community Church for over twenty-six years and has had a worldwide impact to the glory of God, has contributed a significant portion of this book. His colleagues on The Master's Seminary faculty, with an average of more than twenty years experience each in pastoring and in the seminary training of pastors, have also contributed from the treasury of their particular expertise. The reader will quickly appreciate their varied but united affirmations on pastoral ministry that emerge amidst an abundance of individual expressions.

The reader will also note a diversity in the levels of style in treating the different topics. At one extreme are the chapters whose documentation is extensive, and at the other are those in which documentation is minimal. To some extent, this diversity is a consequence of the nature of individual subjects, and to a lesser degree, the choice of each contributor. Each has handled his phase of pastoring in the manner he deemed wisest.

The book outlines four broad categories that move from the biblical to the practical. They include: (1) the biblical character and essence of pastoral ministry, (2) the biblically required preparation of a man who would pastor, (3) the personal qualifications of a man biblically qualified to pastor, and (4) the biblical priority of activities involved in pastoral ministry. The underlying reason for this undertaking is the strong desire to answer the question, "How does today's pastor build a contemporary ministry in line with biblical mandates?" The hoped-for result of applying the ideas in *Rediscovering Pastoral Ministry* will be a pastoral ministry that majors in spiritual relevance to the body of Christ.

Because of the extreme importance of prayer in pastoral ministry, the section on "personal qualifications" has two chapters to emphasize that phase of the pastor's life. One deals primarily—though not exclusively—with the pastor's own prayer life, the other predominantly with prayer in the life of the church. Of course, it is impossible to make a complete distinction between these two types of prayer, but the dual treatment serves to give added attention to a very important subject.

In the "Additional Reading" section at the end of the volume, we avoided listing hundreds of books on pastoring that are no longer in print or do not make a significant contribution; instead, we have selected a sampling of the best available and affordable volumes on pastoral ministry. The inclusion of a work in this list does not constitute an endorsement of everything in that work but reflects the faculty's favorable impressions of its general thrust. Conversely, the exclusion of a title does not necessarily reflect negatively on that work. We encourage the reader to make the listed works his first acquisitions in supplementing the material in *Rediscovering Pastoral Ministry*.

The footnotes document extensive literature related to pastoral ministry. For the reader who chooses to utilize it, this information can be a gold mine for further study. Those who prefer may, of course, read just the body of the text. The "Index of Authors" will be useful in locating all the references to a particular writer. The addition of an "Index of Scriptures" and an "Index of Subjects" provides for ready reference to two more categories.

We are deeply indebted to a number of individuals who have assisted in the production of *Rediscovering Pastoral Ministry*. Please accept our appreciation: Professors Ben Awbrey, Keith Essex, Paul Felix, and Milton Vincent, for reading and offering suggested improvements; librarian Dennis Swanson, for compiling the indexes at the end of the volume; Cindy Gehman, Susan Hansen, Janice Hatter, Pam Leopold, Amy Osmus, and Pat Rotisky, for contributing immensely in the secretarial phase of the work; and Dave Enos, Phil Johnson, John Metcalf, and Allacin Morimizu, for rendering indispensable computer and editorial assistance throughout the project.

The Master's Seminary faculty offer *Rediscovering Pastoral Ministry* with the simple prayer that the Lord Jesus Christ will be pleased to use it to encourage fellow pastors and to groom a new generation of shepherds who will feed and lead Christ's flock—the church—with the same passion as the apostles had.

John MacArthur, Jr.

Richard L. Mayhue

Robert L. Thomas

Introduction[1]

Ministering in the church constitutes the highest privilege. Nothing could be more honorable or have greater eternal significance than serving our Christ in His church. This privilege is also the most serious responsibility a person can undertake. Fulfilling this privilege and discharging this responsibility demands a comprehension of the church and its ministries that is correct according to God's Word. In order to grasp the issues of the church and establish that understanding as a foundation for ministry, we need to understand a few basic truths:

1. The church is the only institution that our Lord promised to build and to bless (Matt. 16:18).

2. The church is the gathering place of true worshipers (Phil. 3:3).

3. The church is the most precious assembly on earth since Christ purchased it with His own blood (Acts 20:28; 1 Cor. 6:19; Eph. 5:25; Col. 1:20; 1 Pet. 1:18; Rev. 1:5).

4. The church is the earthly expression of the heavenly reality (Matt. 6:10; 18:18).

5. The church will ultimately triumph both universally and locally (Matt. 16:18; Phil. 1:6).

6. The church is the realm of spiritual fellowship (Heb. 10:22–25; 1 John 1:3, 6–7).

7. The church is the proclaimer and protector of divine truth (1 Tim. 3:15; Titus 2:1, 15).

8. The church is the chief place for spiritual edification and growth (Acts 20:32; Eph. 4:11–16; 2 Tim. 3:16–17; 1 Pet. 2:1–2; 2 Pet. 3:18).

9. The church is the launching pad for world evangelization (Mark 16:15; Titus 2:11).

10. The church is the environment where strong spiritual leadership develops and matures (2 Tim. 2:2).

---

1. Adapted from John MacArthur, Jr., "Wanted: A Few Good Shepherds," *Masterpiece* (November-December 1989): 2–3, and MacArthur, "Ten Reasons I Am a Pastor," *Masterpiece* (November-December 1990): 2–3.

The ten items above are precisely why I love the church and have devoted my life to it. Understanding those truths is the foundation of effective ministry. Unless spiritual men devoted to these realities lead the church, the next generation of churches will not be without blemish. I am concerned over a growing trend to produce strong natural leaders who know how to manage a business or enterprise but do not understand the church from Christ's perspective. Their leadership style and substance is earthly, not biblical and spiritual.

Some contemporary church leaders fancy themselves to be businessmen, media figures, entertainers, psychologists, philosophers, or lawyers. Those notions contrast sharply with the tenor of the symbolism Scripture employs to depict spiritual leaders.

In 2 Timothy 2, for example, Paul uses seven different metaphors to describe the rigors of leadership. He pictures the minister as a teacher (v. 2), a soldier (v. 3), an athlete (v. 5), a farmer (v. 6), a workman (v. 15), a vessel (vv. 20–21), and a slave (v. 24). All such images evoke ideas of sacrifice, labor, service, and hardship. They speak eloquently of the complex and varied responsibilities of spiritual leadership. Not one of them makes leadership out to be glamorous.

That is because it is not supposed to be glamorous. Leadership in the church—and I am speaking of every facet of spiritual leadership, not just the pastor's role—is not a mantle of status to be conferred on the church's aristocracy. It is not earned by seniority, purchased with money, or inherited through family ties. It does not necessarily fall to those who are successful in business or finance. It is not doled out on the basis of intelligence or talent. Its requirements are blameless character, spiritual maturity, and above all, a willingness to serve humbly.

Our Lord's favorite metaphor for spiritual leadership, one He often used to describe Himself, was that of a shepherd—a person who tends God's flock. Every church leader is a shepherd. The word *pastor* itself means "shepherd." It is appropriate imagery. A shepherd leads, feeds, nurtures, comforts, corrects, and protects—responsibilities that belong to every churchman.

Shepherds are without status. In most cultures, shepherds occupy the lower rungs of society's ladder. That is fitting, for our Lord said, "Let him who is the greatest among you become as the youngest, and the leader as the servant" (Luke 22:26).

Under the plan God has ordained for the church, leadership is a position of humble, loving service. Church leadership is ministry, not management. The calling of the ones whom God designates as leaders is not to a position of governing monarchs, but humble slaves; not slick celebrities, but laboring servants. Those who would lead God's people must above all exemplify sacrifice, devotion, submission, and lowliness.

Jesus Himself gave the pattern when He stooped to wash His disciples' feet, a task that was customarily done by the lowest of slaves (John 13). If the Lord of the universe would do that, no church leader has a right to think of himself as a pastoral elitist.

Shepherding animals is semiskilled labor. No colleges offer graduate degrees in shepherding. It is not that difficult a job; even a dog can learn to guard a flock of sheep. In biblical times, young boys—David, for example—herded sheep while the older men did tasks that required more skill and maturity.

Shepherding a spiritual flock is not so simple. It takes more than a wandering bumpkin to be a spiritual shepherd. The standards are high, the requirements hard to satisfy (1 Tim. 3:1–7). Not everyone can meet the qualifications, and of those who do, few seem to excel at the task. Spiritual shepherding demands a godly, gifted, multiskilled man of integrity. Yet he must maintain the humble perspective and demeanor of a shepherd boy.

With the tremendous responsibilities of leading God's flock comes the potential for either great blessing or great judgment. Good leaders are doubly blessed (1 Tim. 5:17), and poor leaders are doubly chastened (v. 20), for "from everyone who has been given much shall much be required" (Luke 12:48). James 3:1 says, "Let not many of you become teachers, my brethren, knowing that as such we shall incur a stricter judgment."

People often ask me what I think is the secret to Grace Community Church's development over the past twenty-six years. I always point out, first of all, that God sovereignly determines the membership of a church, and numbers alone are no gauge of spiritual success. In the midst of tremendous numerical growth, however, the spiritual vitality of our church has been remarkable. I am convinced God's blessing has been on us primarily because our people have shown a strong commitment to biblical leadership and biblical ministry.

The leaders of Grace Church have endeavored to withstand the preoccupation some churches seem to have with self-esteem and the selfishness of our contemporary society. Our elders desire both to model and to proclaim Jesus' call to discipleship: "He who does not take his cross and follow after Me is not worthy of Me. He who has found his life shall lose it, and he who has lost his life for My sake shall find it" (Matt. 10:38–39).

I love being a pastor. I love the work of ministry for a number of reasons:

1. *Preaching is the chief human means God uses to dispense His grace.* The apostle Paul commanded Timothy to "preach the word" (2 Tim. 4:2). I have the privilege each Sunday of proclaiming God's message to His people—a message of grace, by which God saves people and transforms lives.

2. *I can be consumed with study and communion with God.* There is a public side to me that the congregation sees, but there is a private side to me that only God knows. Though I may preach only three hours a week, I study thirty. Those hours spent each week in God's presence are a high and holy privilege.

3. *I am directly responsible to God for the lives of the people He has given me to shepherd.* As a radio teacher, I am not as personally accountable for how people apply God's Word. However, as the pastor-teacher of a congregation, I have a relationship with my people like that of a shepherd and his sheep. I watch over their souls as one "who will give an account" (Heb. 13:17).

4. *I am also accountable to the people in my church.* Everything is exposed to them: my life and family, my personal strengths and weaknesses—everything. I cherish that accountability. It is a constant encouragement for me to reflect Christ in everything I say and do.

5. *I love the challenge of building an effective leadership team from the people God has put in the church.* When someone starts a business, he can hire anyone he wants. It is another thing entirely to build with the people God has called, few of whom are wise, mighty, or noble by the world's standards (1 Cor. 1:26). God reveals the greatness of His power by demonstrating that the world's nobodies are His most precious resources.

6. *The pastorate embraces all of life.* I share the joy of parents over the birth of a child, as well as the pain of children over the death of a mother or father. I help celebrate at a wedding; I also offer comfort at a funeral. There is an inevitable unpredictability that accompanies my calling—an incredible adventure may begin at any given moment. It is at those times that the pastor goes beyond his sermon to stand in the gap for God in the lives of His people.

7. *The rewards in this life are marvelous.* I feel loved, appreciated, needed, trusted, and admired—all a result of being an instrument God has used in the spiritual progress of His people. I know my people pray for me and care deeply about me. I owe a debt of gratitude to God for

that. I am honored to be a channel through which the grace of God, love of Christ, and comfort of the Holy Spirit can become real to people.

8. *I am afraid not to be a pastor.* When I was eighteen, the Lord threw me out of a car traveling seventy miles an hour. I landed on my backside and slid 110 yards on the pavement. By the grace of God I wasn't killed. As I stood up on that highway, having never lost consciousness, I committed my life to serving Christ. I told Him I would no longer resist what He wanted me to do, which was to preach His Word.

The purpose of this volume is the equipping of those who understand and love the church so that they may serve that body with blessing and power by doing ministry biblically.

John MacArthur, Jr.

Part I

Biblical Perspectives

1

Rediscovering Pastoral Ministry

Richard L. Mayhue

Current changes beginning to overtake the church could distinctively mark the twenty-first century church. A growing number of respected evangelicals believe that the present redirection of the church toward being less biblical and more acceptable to man will ultimately lead to a Christ-condemned church. By using Scripture to answer the questions "What is a pastor to be and do?" and "How can contemporary ministry be shaped by biblical mandates?" the church can obediently realign herself with God's revealed purposes for the bride of Christ. In this manner, it is possible to achieve a biblically balanced, complementary relationship between understanding God's will for the church, engaging in pastoral ministry as defined by Scripture, and preparing a new generation of pastors for ministry as outlined by God's Word.

Crossroads. Transition. Crisis. Uncertainty. Restlessness. These words express the perception by many evangelicals regarding the status of the church and pastoral ministry. Few disagree that a call for redirection has come to the evangelical church as the twenty-first century rapidly approaches.

For example, consider John Seel's 1992 survey of twenty-five prominent evangelical leaders.[1] The leaders expressed their views on the general state of evangelicalism at the end of the twentieth century. Eight dominant themes emerged from their responses:

---

1. John Seel, *The Evangelical Forfeit* (Grand Rapids: Baker, 1993), 48–65.

1.   Uncertain identity—a widespread confusion over what defines an evangelical.

2.   Institutional disenchantment—a perceived ministry ineffectiveness and irrelevance.

3.   Lack of leadership—a lament over the paucity of leadership in the church.

4.   Pessimistic about the future—a belief that the future of evangelicalism hangs in the balance.

5.   Growth up, impact down—a confusing paradox without immediate, clear explanations.

6.   Cultural isolation—the post-Christian era has fully arrived.

7.   Political and methodological response provides the solution— unbiblical approaches to ministry are emerging.

8.   Shift from truth-orientation to market-response ministry—a redirection from preoccupation with the eternal to concern for the temporal in an effort to be viewed as relevant.

We acknowledge these alarming trends, believing that decisions made in this decade will reshape the American evangelical church for much of the century to come. Thus, the future direction of the contemporary church is a legitimate, preeminent consideration. Unquestionably, the late twentieth-century church faces a defining moment.[2] The real contrast in competing ministry models is not the traditional versus the contemporary, but rather the *scriptural* compared to the *unscriptural*.

THE MOMENT OF DECISION

Having arrived at the proverbial "fork in the road," evangelicals must decide between two alternatives. The first is an approach to ministry that

---

2.   Four of the top five books in *Christianity Today's* "Reader's Choice" Book-of-the-Year survey addressed these issues with a strong call for a return to a God-centered, biblically based ministry ("1994 Book Awards," *Christianity Today* 38, no. 4 [April 4, 1994]: 39). These four books are Charles Colson, *The Body* (Dallas: Word, 1992); David F. Wells, *No Place for Truth or Whatever Happened to Evangelical Theology* (Grand Rapids: Eerdmans, 1993); John MacArthur, Jr., *Ashamed of the Gospel: When the Church Becomes Like the World* (Wheaton: Crossway, 1993); Hank Hanegraaff, *Christianity In Crisis* (Eugene, Oreg: Harvest House, 1993).

is characteristically—but not necessarily exclusively—need-based, man-centered, consumer-driven, and culturally defined. These emphases generally depend on and change with the latest directions in psychology and sociology, which after attempted integration as coequals with Scripture, supposedly provide a scientifically validated, relevant ministry for the contemporary computer/media-oriented atmosphere.

The second option features a redemptively centered, God-focused, biblically defined, and scripturally prioritized ministry. In this book we champion this latter model, which looks to the sufficiency of Scripture as the revelation of past, present, and future works of God the Father, God the Son, and God the Holy Spirit that have the utmost relevance—now and forever. The church must look to the Scriptures and address the challenge of shaping contemporary ministry with biblical mandates.

Arguably, no time in church history has more closely approximated the first-century beginnings of the church than now. Our ancient brethren faced a pagan, pre-Christian, and premodern culture. Similarly, the contemporary church encounters a pagan, post-Christian, and postmodern world. The essential biblical model of ministry of the first century has never been more appropriate than it is today.

Rediscovering Pastoral Ministry attempts to balance the tensions between temporal and eternal considerations and between divine and human factors in ministry. God's character, God's revelation, and God's will have not changed although time and culture have. How should a balanced ministry reconcile the two sides? We reason that the timeless should define any particular moment in time, not the reverse. Christ has been and will remain the Chief Shepherd (1 Pet. 5:4), the Good Shepherd (John 10:11, 14), and the Great Shepherd (Heb. 13:20). Pastors will always be His undershepherds and laborers in the church that He purchased with His own precious blood (Acts 20:28) and continues to build (Matt. 16:18).

Pastors assume a huge responsibility when they accept the unequaled task of exhorting and reproving on Christ's behalf (Titus 1:9). Paul's word about this stewardship to the Corinthian church almost two thousand years ago is sobering:

> Let a man regard us in this manner, as servants of Christ, and stewards of the mysteries of God. In this case, moreover, it is required of stewards that one be found trustworthy. But to me it is a very small thing that I should be examined by you, or by any human court; in fact, I do not even examine myself. I am conscious of nothing against myself, yet I am not by this acquitted; but the one who examines me is the Lord. Therefore do not go on passing judgment before the

time, but wait until the Lord comes who will both bring to light the things hidden in the darkness and disclose the motives of men's hearts; and then each man's praise will come to him from God (1 Cor. 4:1–5).

The late twentieth-century church in general and pastors in particular face the following crucial questions:

What is the pastor to be and do?

How should the church respond to a rapidly changing culture?

What does God consider relevant?

How concerned is Christ with the traditional and/or the contemporary?

Are the Scriptures an adequate basis of ministry today?

What are a pastor's ministry priorities?

Under whose authority does a pastor stand?

How shall we distinguish between the God-called pastor and the counterfeit?

Who defines the need for ministry—God or men?

What direction does Christ want for His church in the twenty-first century?

And foremost of all, when we stand before the Lord of glory and give account of our stewardship, What will we say? and, far more importantly, What will He say?

We submit that God will use His Word as the benchmark by which He commends or condemns our labors in His church. He will not inquire whether a ministry was traditional or contemporary, but He will ask, "Was it biblical?" Our ministry will either be in accord with His will or in opposition to it, as Scripture expresses it: "All Scripture is inspired by God and profitable for teaching, for reproof, for correction, for training in righteousness; that the man of God may be adequate, equipped for every good work" (2 Tim. 3:16–17).

THE CHURCH ON THE WRONG WAY

A reasonable expectation would be that after two thousand years of existence, the church should know and understand exactly what God intended her to be. Yet just the opposite seems to be true.[3]

It appears that the way of religion in American culture has become the way of the church—a wrong way. Sheler concludes that culture is having its way with Christianity instead of Christianity having an influence on culture:

> The social critics among us, and the consciences within us, increasingly wonder if we have lost our moral compass and forsaken our spiritual heritage. Yale professor Stephen Carter, in his recent book *The Culture of Disbelief*, blames this cultural decay on what he believes has been a growing exclusion of religion from public life. "We have pressed the religiously faithful . . . to act as though their faith does not matter," Carter argues.[4]

Francis Schaeffer called this phenomenon "the great evangelical disaster." He succinctly summarized the situation:

> Here is the great evangelical disaster—the failure of the evangelical world to stand for truth as truth. There is only one word for this—namely *accommodation*: the evangelical church has accommodated to the world spirit of the age. First, there has been accommodation on Scripture, so that many who call themselves evangelicals hold a weakened view of the Bible and no longer affirm the truth of all the Bible teaches—truth not only in religious matters but in the areas of science and history and morality. As part of this, many evangelicals are now accepting the higher critical methods in the study of the Bible. Remember, it was these same methods which destroyed the authority of the Bible for the Protestant church in Germany in the last century, and which have destroyed the Bible for the liberal in our

---

3. This confusion is not as apparent when one reads standard theology offerings or specific volumes dealing with the theology of the church, such as Gene A. Getz, *Sharpening the Focus of the Church* (Chicago: Moody, 1974); Alfred F. Kuen, *I Will Build My Church* (Chicago: Moody, 1971); John MacArthur, Jr., *Body Dynamics* (Wheaton: Victor, 1982); Earl D. Radmacher, *What the Church Is All About* (Chicago: Moody, 1978). The problem arises in volumes dealing with translating one's theology into contemporary practices in the church.

4. Jeffery L. Sheler, "Spiritual America," *U.S. News and World Report* 116, no. 13 (April 4, 1994): 48.

own country from the beginning of the century. And second, there has been accommodation on the issues, with no clear stand being taken even on matters of life and death.[5]

Encouragingly, the 1990s have seen a rash of books calling the church back to the primacy of God and Scripture. They strongly warn that the church is slowly but surely being culturalized.

David F. Wells, the Andrew Mutch Professor of Historical and Systematic Theology at Gordon-Conwell Theological Seminary, has recently written a landmark analysis of American evangelicalism in the 1990s. He notes,

> The disappearance of theology from the life of the Church, and the orchestration of that disappearance by some of its leaders, is hard to miss today but, oddly enough, not easy to prove. It is hard to miss in the evangelical world—in the vacuous worship that is so prevalent, for example, in the shift from God to self as the central focus of faith, in the psychologized preaching that follows this shift, in the erosion of its conviction, in its strident pragmatism, in its inability to think incisively about the culture, in its reveling in the irrational.[6]

Wells argues that it was the influential and liberal preacher, Harry Emerson Fosdick, who popularized the ministry philosophy that begins with man's needs rather than God's will.[7] He traces the lineage forward to Norman Vincent Peale and then to Robert Schuller.[8] It appears that Schuller has significantly influenced Bill Hybels, the most visible current evangelical

---

5. Francis A. Schaeffer, *The Great Evangelical Disaster* (Westchester, Ill: Crossway, 1984), 37. Also see Harold Lindsell, *The New Paganism* (San Francisco: Harper and Row, 1987), 211–32, where he asserts that the west is now in a post-Christian era of paganism, and then discusses the role of the church in this type of culture. For a decisive analysis of the battle between fundamentalism and liberalism in the early 1900s see J. Gresham Machen, *Christianity and Liberalism* (reprint, Grand Rapids: Eerdmans, 1992). George Marsden, *Understanding Fundamentalism and Evangelicalism* (Grand Rapids: Eerdmans, 1991), provides a historical background to Machen's era. James Davison Hunter, *Evangelicalism: The Coming Generation* (Chicago: University of Chicago, 1987), discusses the profile of late twentieth, early twenty-first century evangelicalism. For further reading consult John Fea, "American Fundementalism and Neo-Evangelicalism: A Bibliographic Survey," *Evangelical Journal* 11, no. 1 (spring 1993): 21–30.

6. Wells, *No Place*, 95.

7. Ibid., 178. It is most interesting that Leith Anderson et al., *Who's in Charge?* (Portland, Oreg.: Multnomah, 1992), 100, identifies Fosdick as his mentor. Anderson, who is widely read and respected by a large segment of evangelicalism, also points to Fosdick as a model in preaching in *A Church for the 21st Century* (Minneapolis: Bethany, 1992), 213–14.

8. Ibid.

proponent of a "church the unchurched" philosophy of ministry.[9] In a sense, Fosdick's philosophy of ministry lives on long after his death.

Noted historian George Marsden warns evangelicals of the encroachments of humanism on the church. He concludes that "while fundamentalists and their evangelical heirs have erected doctrinal barriers against theological liberalism, more subtle versions of similar sub-Christian values have infiltrated behind their lines."[10]

John MacArthur, Jr., sees the church becoming like the world.[11] In a positively provocative fashion, he compares the many similarities between the decline of the church in England during Spurgeon's day a century ago and the faltering American church in our day. MacArthur notes the parallel path and common distinction of spiritual deadness shared by the liberal modernists of a century ago and evangelical pragmatists today. They both have an unhealthy aversion to doctrine.

Os Guinness provides several probing analyses of the modern church and evangelicals.[12] They include *The Gravedigger File*, *No God but God*, and *Dining with the Devil*. In these three works he writes about the secularization of the church, idolatry in the church, and the modern church growth movement, respectively.

"Selling Out the House of God?" a recent *Christianity Today* interview of Bill Hybels, illustrates the tensions existing in today's church.[13] This article was occasioned by the increase in probing questions that pastors want to ask this highly visible, consumer-oriented church pastor about his ministry basis and style. Many fear that if the next generation takes the path

---

9. Bill Hybels on several occasions has been a prominent speaker at Robert Schuller's institutes for pastors. Like Fosdick, Hybels has a penchant for needs-based preaching to reach the consumer in the pew as is evident in Bill Hybels et al., *Mastering Contemporary Preaching* (Portland, Oreg.: Multnomah, 1989), 27.

10. George Marsden, "Secular Humanism Within the Church," *Christianity Today* 30, no. 1 (January 17, 1986): 141–51. A Christianity Today Institute included this article under the title of "In the Next Century: Trends Facing the Church."

11. MacArthur, *Ashamed of the Gospel*. Almost two decades before this book, MacArthur wrote of the dangers then facing the church in "Church Faces Identity Crisis," *Moody Monthly* 79, no. 6 (February 1979): 123–26.

12. Os Guinness, *The Gravedigger File* (Downers Grove, Ill.: InterVarsity, 1983); Os Guinness and John Seel, eds., *No God but God* (Chicago: Moody, 1992); Os Guinness, *Dining with the Devil* (Grand Rapids: Baker, 1993).

13. Michael G. Maudlin and Edward Gilbreath, "Selling Out the House of God?" *Christianity Today* 38, no. 8 (July 18, 1994): 20–25. Contrast Hybels' approach with the far more biblical course recommended by Bill Hull, *Can We Save the Evangelical Church* (Grand Rapids: Revell, 1993).

Hybels now travels, it, too, will arrive at the same destination as the modernist movement did earlier this century.

Consider this recent warning:

> Evangelical pastors and theologians can learn from the mainline experience of placing relevance above truth. We must avoid the lure of novelty and soft sell, which, we are told, will make it easier for moderns to believe. Methods may change, but never the message. . . . We are called to be faithful stewards of a great and reliable theological heritage. We have truths to affirm and errors to avoid. We must not try to make these truths more appealing or user friendly by watering them down. We must guard against a trendy "theological bungee-jumping" that merely entertains the watching crowd.[14]

Interestingly, this clear call to a biblically bound ministry does not come from the conservative wing of evangelism. Rather, it is a warning to evangelical churches from one who is attempting to bring revival within the liberal, mainline United Methodist Church. He cautions the church to avoid the user-friendly route of church ministry because the end is predictable: within a generation or at the most two generations, churches will lose their spiritual direction and life.

IDENTITY CRISIS

As the church succumbs to cultural and secular pressures, it is not surprising that biblically defined pastoral roles and the scripturally oriented content of ministerial training have experienced a serious challenge also.

Pastoral Identity

This confusion is not entirely new to the church. As early as the first century, Paul felt compelled to articulate carefully the role of the pastor. All succeeding generations have felt this tension with the corresponding need to reaffirm the biblical absolutes of ministry. Culbertson and Shippee notice this ongoing tension:

> Pastoral theology is for the most part a field without a clear definition: its precise meaning and component parts seem to vary widely

---

14. James V. Heidinger II, "Toxic Pluralism," *Christianity Today* 37, no. 4 (April 5, 1993): 16–17.

from one denomination to the next and from one seminary to the next. The how-to of pastoral care and the component elements in the process of clergy character formation seem to be equally slippery. In all three fields, however, constitutive material seems to be taught either from a strictly scriptural base, or from a base of modern psychological and sociological theory as it has been appropriated by the church, or through a combination of Scripture and modern scientific insight—but rarely does the teaching of pastoral formation make direct reference to the fascinating history and tradition of the early church.[15]

H. Richard Niebuhr documents the confusion that prevailed during the early and middle twentieth century.[16] Thomas Oden updates the dilemma into the 1980s.[17] He laments that the entire twentieth century has evidenced confusion over the role of the church and the pastor.[18] Oden strongly calls for a return to Scripture in order to understand the pastoral office and role:

> Scripture provides the primary basis for understanding the pastoral office and its functions. We will treat Scripture as the church's book, rather than as the exclusive turf of the historian or social theorist. Pastoral wisdom has lived out of the key *locus classicus* texts that have enjoyed a rich history of interpretation long before the advent of modern historical research. We are free to learn from and use that research without being handcuffed by some of its reductionist assumptions.
>
> Pastoral theology lives out of Scripture. When the pastoral tradition has quoted Scripture, it has viewed it as an authoritative text for shaping both its understanding and its practice of ministry. We do not put Scripture under our examination, according to criteria alien to it, in order to understand ministry. Rather, Scripture examines our prior understandings of ministry. It puts them to the test.[19]

---

15. Philip L. Culbertson and Arthur Bradford Shippee, *The Pastor: Readings from the Patristic Period* (Minneapolis: Fortress, 1990), xi.

16. H. Richard Niebuhr, *The Purpose of the Church and Its Ministry* (New York: Harper and Brothers, 1956), 51.

17. Thomas C. Oden, *Pastoral Theology: Essentials of Ministry* (San Francisco: HarperCollins, 1983).

18. Ibid., x–xii.

19. Ibid., 11.

Ministerial Training

Redefining the church leads inevitably to redefining the pastoral role. The latter then spills over into pastoral training at the seminary level. Predictably, a seemingly endless flood of current literature is calling for radical restructuring of seminary education.

In 1990 *The Atlantic* published a striking general assessment of American seminaries. This comprehensive study concluded,

> If they are to succeed, this generation of seminarians must, of course, be educationally and spiritually sound, politically aware, as conversant with demography as they are with morality. They must be sensitive to race, ethnicity, gender, and sexuality, but they must not drive us up still another wall with their convictions. We have been flogged enough; we know our shortcomings. When our future clerics speak, we want to hear powerful yet measured voices bringing out the moral dimension of life, and not only the politics of the left wing of the Democratic Party or the right of the Republican, masquerading as religious belief.
>
> We want them to be people who in some tiny way reflect the mercy and goodness of God we want to know, not only His judgment. We want them to be people who see the goodness in us that we have yet to unleash, the potential within us to transcend our differences. In the end, I think, we are looking for those who will help us find that voice deep within us which is not our own, but calls us to do what is right.[20]

Consumer appeal in both ministry and pastoral training clearly marks the conclusion to this article and reflects much of the current literature.

A 1993 study commissioned by seven well-known American seminaries concluded, "The church, in order to maintain relevancy to its constituency, has had to devise new ways of 'doing' ministry or be faced with closing the doors.... This report ... calls for a major restructuring of the seminary—form and function."[21]

---

20. Paul Wilkes, "The Hand That Would Shape Our Souls," *The Atlantic* 266, no. 6 (December 1990): 59–88.

21. Carolyn Weese, *Standing on the Banks of Tomorrow* (Granada Hills, Calif.: Multi-Staff Ministries, 1993): 3, 53. Other recent pieces include Michael C. Griffith, "Theological Education Need Not Be Irrelevant," *Vox Evangelica* XX (1990): 7–19; Richard Carnes Ness, "The Road Less Traveled; Theological Education and the Quest to Fashion the Seminary of the Twenty-First Century," *The Journal of Institute for Christian Leadership* 20 (winter 93/94): 27–43; Bruce L. Shelly, "The Seminaries' Identity Crisis," *Christianity Today* 37, no. 6 (May 17, 1993): 42–44.

If we carry the consumer paradigm to its logical conclusion, it will be brilliantly consistent with prevailing contemporary theories but sadly unscriptural. In effect it reasons, "What the people want, the church should provide. What the church provides, pastors should be trained to deliver." Taking it one step further, the ultimate result will be that "What pastors are trained to deliver, the church will provide. When the church provides what the people want, people will want more." This eventually will create a virtually unbreakable cause-and-effect cycle that will render the American church impotent and condemned by Christ.

However, before seminaries capitulate, they should study the history of seminaries and seminary education in America. Notable among many are Andover Seminary and Princeton Seminary, founded in 1807 and 1812 respectively.[22] Both started strong, with seemingly unshakable biblical foundations, but with time and for various reasons, each succumbed to the demand to go beyond the Scriptures for both their doctrine and their practice. Conservatives agree that they long ago outlived their usefulness to the gospel ministry because they shifted from their initial high view of God and the Scriptures.

Any given seminary might change many things to make itself more useful to the church and ultimately the cause of Christ, but its emphasis upon biblical truth as the core of the curriculum should never change. David Dockery, Vice President for Academic Administration at Southern Seminary, recently summed up seminary education in a new century like this:

> We want to be able to teach the Scriptures in a creative and relevant way that models for our students that the Bible is normative and authoritative for the contemporary church—for their lives individually and for the church corporately. The Bible is an ancient document that is written to specific people in specific times in specific context. It nevertheless transcends those times and contexts because it is inspired by the Spirit of God, so it is both a divine and human document. It is a time-related document as well as an eternal document. Therefore, it speaks beyond its context and we want faculty who live out of deep commitment to the full truthfulness and complete authority of God's inspired word.
>
> Biblical authority is a much maligned and misunderstood concept in our contemporary world. People ask how can you believe that a

---

22. Steven Meyeroff, "Andover Seminary: The Rise and Fall of an Evangelical Institution," *Covenant Seminary Review* 8, no. 2 (fall 1982): 13–24, and Mark A. Noll, "The Princeton Theology," in *The Princeton Theology*, ed. David F. Wells (Grand Rapids: Baker, 1989), 14–35, present convincing accounts of these two institutions.

book written 2,000 years ago has authority and relevance where we are now? The answer is because of its source. Its source is not just in the prophets and the apostles; it is in God Himself, who has actually breathed out this Word to us to study, to believe, and obey.[23]

Taking a Biblical Approach

We believe Paul made an absolute assertion with undeniable implications when he wrote to Timothy, "All Scripture is inspired by God and profitable for teaching, for reproof, for correction, for training in righteousness; that the man of God may be adequate, equipped for every good work" (2 Tim. 3:16–17). This passage teaches not only a high view of Scripture's authority but also its sufficiency, especially in formulating ministry plans and priorities. It demands that we begin with God and the Bible rather than man and culture in order to understand God's will in ministry.

The ministry tensions, problems, and questions that our generation faces are not new. Malachi indicted Israel because they exchanged the glory of God for the way of the culture. Paul confronted the Corinthians. Jeremiah and Ezekiel warned against the proliferation of false shepherds in the Old Testament, as did Peter and Jude in the New Testament. The contemporary pastor must pay close attention to the lessons of biblical history, for they will surely be repeated in his generation. Therefore when we ask, "What is a pastor to be and do?" we must look to God's Word for answers and not to the latest fads or theories that find their source in society rather than in Scripture, or in culture but not in Christ.

God has given several defining passages explaining who a pastor is to be and what a pastor is to do (e.g., 1 Tim. 3:1–7; Titus 1:6–9; 1 Pet. 5:1–5), which the following chapters will discuss. But perhaps the most explicit books in the New Testament regarding the work of the ministry are 1 and 2 Thessalonians. A careful analysis of these pastoral epistles leads to this basic ministry description. A pastor's primary activities include:

1.   Praying   1 Thess. 1:2–3; 3:9–13
2.   Evangelizing   1 Thess. 1:4–5, 9–10

---

23. David Dockery, "Ministry and Seminary in a New Century," *The Tie: Southern Seminary* 62, no. 2 (spring 1994): 20–22.

3.	Equipping	1 Thess. 1:6–8
4.	Defending	1 Thess. 2:1–6
5.	Loving	1 Thess. 2:7–8
6.	Laboring	1 Thess. 2:9
7.	Modeling	1 Thess. 2:10
8.	Leading	1 Thess. 2:10–12
9.	Feeding	1 Thess. 2:13
10.	Watching	1 Thess. 3:1–8
11.	Warning	1 Thess. 4:1–8
12.	Teaching	1 Thess. 4:9–5:11
13.	Exhorting	1 Thess. 5:12–24
14.	Encouraging	2 Thess. 1:3–12
15.	Correcting	2 Thess. 2:1–12
16.	Confronting	2 Thess. 3:6, 14
17.	Rescuing	2 Thess. 3:15.

Paul exemplifies the *character* of a pastor and how that character relates to ministry *conduct* (1 Thess. 2:1–6). He describes the *nature* of pastoral leadership in terms of a mother (2:7–8), a laborer (2:9), a family member (2:10), and a father (2:11–12). Though these texts do not exhaust the subject, they do point to Scripture as the appropriate source from which to draw answers to questions about ministry.

Christ's letters to the seven churches in Revelation 2–3 raise the relevant question, "If Christ were to write a letter to the American church in 1995, what would He say?" This inquiry is purely hypothetical and will not happen because the time of written divine revelation has passed. However, the timeless truths of Revelation 2–3, revealed in the first century, are applicable to the twentieth-century church because they represent the unchanging mind of Christ in regard to His church. We know what He would *commend* and what He would *condemn*.

The bottom line is simply this: Will we seek to be fruitful in ministry by depending on the power of God's Word (Rom. 1:16–17; 1 Cor. 1:22–25; 1 Thess. 2:13) and God's Spirit (Rom 15:13; 2 Tim 1:8) or on the power of man's wisdom? Consider how Paul instructed the Corinthian church, whose curious preoccupation with their culture parallels the contemporary evangelical church's comparable fascination:

For consider your calling, brethren, that there were not many wise according to the flesh, not many mighty, not many noble; but God has chosen the foolish things of the world to shame the wise, and God has chosen the weak things of the world to shame the things which are strong, and the base things of the world and the despised, God has chosen, the things that are not, that He might nullify the things that are, that no man should boast before God. But by His doing you are in Christ Jesus, who became to us wisdom from God, and righteousness and sanctification, and redemption, that, just as it is written, "Let him who boasts, boast in the Lord" (1 Cor. 1:26–31).

REDISCOVERING PASTORAL MINISTRY

We remain convinced that God's Word provides the timeless defining paradigm for the nature and particulars of pastoral ministry. Scripture outlines what God wants a pastor to be and what God wants a pastor to do. Contemporary ministry in any generation needs to be shaped by biblical mandates.

We set before our peers the assertion that Christ must build His church His way (Matt. 16:18).[24] If we desire to see God-pleasing fruit in our ministry, it must come from planting the good seed of God's Word in the rich soil of diligent pastoral labor according to the Scriptures.

The statements of this chapter are *not* a call for a user-*unfriendly* church, a culturally *ignorant* church, or a seeker *insensitive* church. We have no desire to "unchurch the unchurched" or to promote an irrelevant dinosaur of a church. On the other hand, neither do we want to substitute the latest theories in sociology and psychology for the truth of theology. We do not want to confuse the common sense benefit of demographic statistics and analysis of culture with the far more important understanding of God's will for the church—both for Christians and non-Christians. We ardently desire to let the important consideration of God and His revealed will in Scripture be the major focus.

A significant segment of evangelical churches and a growing proportion of evangelical literature seems to be distancing itself from biblical priorities. Unbiblical imbalances among contemporary evangelicals are showing up in growing tendencies toward:

---

24. John MacArthur, Jr., "Building His Church His Way," *Spirit of Revival* 24, no. 1 (April 1994): 21–24.

1. overemphasis on man's reasoning—and a corresponding under-emphasis on God's revelation in Scripture

2. overemphasis on human need as defined by man—and a corre-sponding underemphasis on God's definition of man's need

3. overemphasis on earthly relevance—and a corresponding under-emphasis on spiritual relevance

4. overemphasis on the temporal side of life—and a corresponding underemphasis on the eternal.

5. overemphasis on contemporary culture—and a corresponding underemphasis on the Bible

Because of these escalating trends, the church is increasingly in dan-ger of equating religion with Christianity and "going to church" with salvation. The church increasingly substitutes human power for God's power and peripheral talk about God for talk that centers on Him directly. The church increasingly confuses emotion with worship in Spirit and truth and the cleverness of man's words with the power of the gospel. If the evan-gelical church remains on its present course, we fear that by popular demand the next generation may replace true Christianity with an impotent, idola-trous religion.

The remainder of this book could expand on these present dangers and deceits facing the evangelical church and ministry. Instead, however, it urges all of Christendom, both in America and around the world, to redis-cover pastoral ministry as outlined in Scripture. Here you will find ministry that is biblically based, not demographically defined; Spirit led, not market driven; Christ centered, not man directed; and God focused, not consumer oriented.

Being About the Father's Business

As Jesus engaged in His Father's work, so must we. An anonymous writer vividly captured the essence of pastoral stewardship before the Lord with his exhortation to do God's work God's way according to God's Word:

Stick with your work. Do not flinch because the lion roars; do not stop to stone the devil's dogs; do not fool away your time chasing the devil's rabbits. Do your work. Let liars lie, let sectarians quarrel, let critics malign, let enemies accuse, let the devil do his worst; but see to it nothing hinders you from fulfilling with joy the work God has given you.

He has not commanded you to be admired or esteemed. He has never bidden you defend your character. He has not set you at work to contradict falsehood (about yourself) which Satan's or God's servants may start to peddle, or to track down every rumor that threatens your reputation. If you do these things, you will do nothing else; you will be at work for yourself and not for the Lord.

Keep at your work. Let your aim be as steady as a star. You may be assaulted, wronged, insulted, slandered, wounded and rejected, misunderstood, or assigned impure motives; you may be abused by foes, forsaken by friends, and despised and rejected of men. But see to it with steadfast determination, with unfaltering zeal, that you pursue the great purpose of your life and object of your being until at last you can say, "I have finished the work which *Thou* gavest me to do."

2

What Is a Pastor to Be and Do?

John MacArthur, Jr.

First Peter 5:1–3 expresses the foundational principles of pastoral leadership: Be humble and do the work of shepherding the flock. John the Baptist and Paul were good New Testament examples of humility. The keys to humility include confidence in God's power, commitment to God's truth, a commission by God's will, a compulsion by God's omniscience, and a consuming passion for God's glory. The primary objective in shepherding God's flock is to feed them. Besides this, a shepherd must exercise oversight of the flock and provide them with an exemplary life to look to. He cannot do his job with an unwilling spirit, neither can he do it for the sake of monetary gain. Furthermore, he must obey scriptural commands to be faithful to biblical truth, bold in exposing and refuting error, exemplary in godliness, diligent in ministry, and willing to suffer in his service.

A vast amount of material is available to advise pastors on how to conduct their ministries. Books, tapes, journals, and seminars abound. In fact, so much material is available that a pastor could easily spend all his time absorbing it—and have no time left for actual ministry! How can a pastor sift through this mountain of information to discern what is really important in ministry? Can what a pastor is to be and do be boiled down to a few basic principles?

The apostle Peter read no books or journal articles on pastoral leadership. He attended no seminars and heard no tapes. However, with the wisdom of long years of experience, Peter distilled the essence of pastoral leadership into two simple admonitions: be humble, and do the work of shepherding the flock. He expressed these foundational principles in 1 Pet. 5:1–3:

Therefore, I exhort the elders among you, as your fellow elder and witness of the sufferings of Christ, and a partaker also of the glory that is to be revealed, shepherd the flock of God among you, exercising oversight not under compulsion, but voluntarily, according to the will of God; and not for sordid gain, but with eagerness; nor yet as lording it over those allotted to your charge, but proving to be examples to the flock.

Peter modeled the humility he enjoined for pastors. Although the acknowledged leader of the twelve apostles, he humbly described himself as "your fellow elder." He refused to lord his exalted position over the other elders. And in verse 2 he gave the pastor's calling, to "shepherd the flock of God" entrusted to his care. Humble shepherds are what God requires to lead His flock.

A Pastor Should Be Humble

We live in a world that neither values nor desires humility. Whether in politics, business, the arts, or sports, people work hard to achieve prominence, popularity, and fame. Sadly, that mind-set has spilled over into the church. Personality cults exist, because pastors and Christian leaders strive for celebrity status. The true man of God, however, seeks the approval of his Lord rather than the adulation of the crowd. Humility is thus the benchmark of any useful servant of God. Spurgeon reminds us that "if we magnify ourselves, we shall become contemptible; and we shall neither magnify our office nor our Lord. We are the servants of Christ, not lords over His heritage. Ministers are for churches, and not churches for ministers. . . . Take heed that you be not exalted above measure, lest you come to nothing."[1]

Examples of Humility

Until his time, John the Baptist was the greatest man who had lived (Matt. 11:11; Luke 7:28). He was the last of the Old Testament prophets, privileged to be no less than the immediate forerunner of the Messiah. Yet he was a humble man and expressed that humility when he said of Christ, "He must increase, but I must decrease" (John 3:30). Except for Jesus Christ, the apostle Paul is the greatest spiritual leader the world has known, but he

---

1. C. H. Spurgeon, *An All-round Ministry* (reprint, Pasadena, Tex.: Pilgrim, 1973), 256–57.

described himself as "the least of the apostles" (1 Cor. 15:9), "the very least of all saints" (Eph. 3:8), and the foremost of sinners (1 Tim. 1:15–16).

Five marks of Paul's humility are identified in 1 Corinthians 4. First, he was content to be a servant: "Let a man regard us in this manner, as servants of Christ, and stewards of the mysteries of God" (v. 1). The word he used for "servants" is *huperetes*, which refers literally to an under rower, one who rowed in the lower tier of a war galley. Such rowers were unknown, unheralded, and unhonored. "When all is said and done," Paul says, "let it be said of me that I pulled my oar."

A second mark of Paul's humility was his willingness to be judged by God. In 1 Cor. 4:4 he wrote, "The one who examines me is the Lord." Paul did not seek the accolades of men, nor did he care what they thought of him. God was the audience before whom he executed his ministry; God was the one he sought to please, whatever the cost. Any human evaluation of his ministry, whether by others or himself, was meaningless.

Third, Paul was content to be equal with other servants of God. In 1 Cor. 4:6 he cautioned the Corinthians not to compare him with Apollos. He did not want his readers to presume to elevate one over the other. Paul and Apollos were not in competition with each other, nor did Paul consider himself better than Apollos. The Puritan Walter Cradock's description of a humble man fits Paul perfectly:

1. When he looks upon another that is a sinner, he considereth that he has been worse than he.

2. A humble heart thinks himself to be worse still.

3. It is God that hath made it and not anything in himself.

4. He considereth that the vilest sinner may be, in God's good time, better than he.[2]

Fourth, Paul was willing to suffer (1 Cor. 4:12–13). He suffered for the cause of Christ as few men in history have suffered, thus fulfilling the Lord's prediction at his conversion (Acts 9:16). Paul details some of that suffering in his letters to the Corinthians (1 Cor. 4:9–13; 2 Cor. 11:23–33). His exhortation to Timothy to "suffer hardship with me, as a good soldier of Christ Jesus" (2 Tim. 2:3) is his challenge to every pastor, for all will face suffering. As Sanders notes, "No one need aspire to leadership in the work of God

---

2. Cited by I. D. E. Thomas, *A Puritan Golden Treasury* (Edinburgh: Banner of Truth, 1977), 148–49.

who is not prepared to pay a price greater than his contemporaries and colleagues are willing to pay. True leadership always exacts a heavy toll on the whole man, and the more effective the leadership is, the higher the price to be paid."[3] Spurgeon gives a reason pastors may expect suffering: "It is of need be that we are sometimes in heaviness. Good men are promised tribulation in this world, and ministers may expect a larger share than others, that they may learn sympathy with the Lord's suffering people, and so may be fitting shepherds of an ailing flock."[4]

Finally, Paul was content to sacrifice his reputation. A pastor's goal is not to be popular with the world. Those who preach boldly against sin and live godly lives will sacrifice their public reputation and prestige. They will suffer rejection, face opposition, and endure slander. Paul described his own loss of reputation when he wrote, "For, I think, God has exhibited us apostles last of all, as men condemned to death; because we have become a spectacle to the world, both to angels and to men. We have become as the scum of the world, the dregs of all things, even until now" (1 Cor. 4:9, 13).

Keys to Humility

True humility flows from a correct view of God. How a pastor lives his life and functions in the ministry relates directly to his view of God. A humble man, with a proper view of God, will be confident in God's power, committed to God's truth, commissioned by God's will, compelled by God's knowledge, and consumed with God's glory.

A humble pastor will be confident in God's power. In 1 Thess. 2:2, Paul reminded the Thessalonians that "after we had already suffered and been mistreated in Philippi (see Acts 16:19–24), as you know, we had the boldness in our God to speak to you the gospel of God amid much opposition." Paul's humble confidence in God's power translated into boldness and courage in his ministry. He was confident that God was more powerful than any opposition he would face. That gave his ministry strength and tenacity. It enabled him to speak out no matter what the response and consequences were.

In the ministry, pressure to compromise, to mitigate the message, and to avoid offending sinners will always exist. However, the preacher's job is to expose sin, to confront the lost with the hopelessness of their condition,

---

3. J. Oswald Sanders, *Spiritual Leadership*, rev. ed. (Chicago: Moody, 1980), 169.

4. C. H. Spurgeon, *Lectures to My Students: First Series* (reprint, Grand Rapids: Baker, 1972), 168.

and to offer the cure for their wretchedness in the saving gospel of Jesus Christ. Doing those things will lead to confrontation and opposition. The courage to stand firm derives from a humble dependence on God's power. It comes from being "strong in the Lord, and in the strength of His might" (Eph. 6:10).

A humble pastor will be committed to God's truth. We live in a day when most are ignoring Paul's exhortation to Timothy to "preach the word" of God. Instead of the Word of God, all too often from the pulpit come the uncertain sounds of political rhetoric, social commentary, and pop psychology. Such "persuasive words of [human] wisdom" (1 Cor. 2:4) are a prostitution of the preacher's true calling.[5] The pulpit is not a place for the pastor to express his opinion, demonstrate his erudition, or browbeat those who oppose him. Such prideful exaltation of self is the antithesis of humility. John Stott believes that

> the less the preacher comes between the Word and its hearers, the better. What really feeds the household is the food which the householder supplies, not the steward who dispenses it. The Christian preacher is best satisfied when his person is eclipsed by the light which shines from the Scripture and when his voice is drowned by the Voice of God.[6]

A man committed to God's truth is a man dedicated to "handling accurately the word of truth" (2 Tim. 2:15). His greatest fear in preaching is that he might present that Word inaccurately to his flock and so mislead them. Paul stressed the importance in his own ministry of handling the Word accurately in 1 Thess. 2:3. In that passage, he gave a threefold response to the charge of teaching false doctrine.

First, he declared that "our exhortation does not come from error." *Plane* (error) comes from a verb meaning "to wander or roam." From it the English word *planet* is derived, since the planets appear to wander through space. To be in error is to wander from the truth, to roam from the divine standard and be out of control. Paul's teaching was not in error. He was neither deceived nor a deceiver. He guarded the truth of the Word of God, even as he twice exhorted Timothy to do (1 Tim. 6:20; 2 Tim. 1:14). That concept of guarding the truth has largely been lost today. Yet pastors *are* guardians of the truth, responsible for keeping it pure and handing it on to

---

5. For a further discussion of this point, see chapter 15, "Preaching."

6. John R. W. Stott, *The Preacher's Portrait* (Grand Rapids: Eerdmans, 1979), 30.

the next generation. The measure of a pastor, then, is not how clever or interesting he is, but how well he guards the truth. Anyone who fails to do so "advocates a different doctrine, and does not agree with sound words, those of our Lord Jesus Christ, and with the doctrine conforming to godliness" (1 Tim. 6:3). Such a man "is conceited and understands nothing" (v. 4). He has failed in the most important aspect of his ministry.

One of the most provocative verses in all the Pauline literature is 2 Cor. 2:17, where the apostle declares, "We are not like many, peddling the word of God, but as from sincerity, but as from God, we speak in Christ in the sight of God." *Peddling* is from *kapeleuo*. It describes the activity of those spiritual hucksters and con men who peddle the Word of God insincerely for their own enrichment. Unfortunately, they are as common today as they were when Paul wrote. False prophets, spiritual phonies, and assorted cultists, crackpots, and swindlers abound, unceasingly laboring "to make crooked the straight ways of the Lord" (Acts 13:10). To combat this onslaught of false teaching, the church needs pastors humbly committed to proclaiming the truth of God's Word.

Merely proclaiming the Word is not enough, however, the pastor must live out its truths in his life. Paul declares that his teaching was free of *akatharsia* (impurity, 1 Thess. 2:3). While that word can refer to uncleanness in general, it often refers to sexual uncleanness. That sexual uncleanness and false doctrine go hand in hand is evident from the many scandals that have rocked the church in recent years.

In his classic work *The Reformed Pastor*, Richard Baxter addressed pastors with some of the most pointed words ever penned regarding living the truths they preach:

> Take heed to yourselves, lest your example contradict your doctrine, and lest you lay such stumbling-blocks before the blind, as may be the occasion of their ruin; lest you unsay with your lives, what you say with your tongues; and be the greatest hinderers of the success of your own labours. It much hindereth our work, when other men are all the week long contradicting to poor people in private, that which we have been speaking to them from the Word of God in public, because we cannot be at hand to expose their folly; but it will much more hinder your work, if you contradict yourselves, and if your actions give your tongue the lie, and if you build up an hour or two with your mouths, and all the week after pull down with your hands! This is the way to make men think that the Word of God is but an idle tale, and to make preaching seem no better than prating. *He that means as he speaks, will surely do as he speaks.* One proud, surly,

lordly word, one needless contention, one covetous action, may cut the throat of many a sermon, and blast the fruit of all that you have been doing. . . .

It is a palpable error of some ministers, who make such a disproportion between their preaching and their living; who study hard to preach exactly, and study little or not at all to live exactly. All the week long is little enough, to study how to speak two hours, and yet one hour seems too much to study how to live all the week. . . . Oh how curiously have I heard some men preach; and how carelessly have I seen them live! . . .

Certainly, brethren, we have very great cause to take heed what we do, as well as what we say: if we will be the servants of Christ indeed, we must not be tongue servants only, but must serve him with our deeds, and be "doers of the work, that we may be blessed in our deed." As our people must be "doers of the word, and not hearers only"; so we must be doers and not speakers only, lest we "deceive our own selves." . . .

Maintain your innocency, and walk without offence. Let your lives condemn sin, and persuade men to duty. Would you have your people more careful of their souls, than you are of yours? . . .

Take heed to yourselves, lest you live in those sins which you preach against in others, and lest you be guilty of that which daily you condemn. Will you make it your work to magnify God, and, when you have done, dishonor him as much as others? Will you proclaim Christ's governing power, and yet contemn it, and rebel yourselves? Will you preach his laws, and wilfully break them? *If sin be evil, why do you live in it? if it be not, why do you dissuade men from it?* If it be dangerous, how dare you venture on it? if it be not, why do you tell men so? If God's threatenings be true, why do you not fear them? if they be false, why do you needlessly trouble men with them, and put them into such frights without a cause? Do you "know the judgment of God, that they who commit such things are worthy of death"; and yet will you do them? "Thou that teachest another, teachest thou not thyself? Thou that sayest a man should not commit adultery," or be drunk, or covetous, art thou such thyself? "Thou that makest thy boast of the law, through breaking the law dishonourest thou God?" What! shall the same tongue speak evil that speakest against evil? Shall those lips censure, and slander, and backbite your neighbour, that cry down these and the like things in others? Take heed to yourselves, lest you cry down sin, and yet do not overcome it; lest, while you seek to bring it down in others, you bow to it, and become its slaves yourselves: "For of whom a man is overcome, of the same is he brought into bondage." "To whom you yield yourselves servants to obey, his servants ye are to

whom ye obey, whether of sin unto death, or of obedience unto righteousness." *O brethren! it is easier to chide at sin, than to overcome it.*[7]

The preacher who wants his words taken to heart by his congregation must
first take them to heart himself.

Finally, in 1 Thess. 2:3, Paul's preaching was free of deceit. He moves
from preaching to living to motive, and now asserts that his motives were
not deceitful. Paul had no hidden agendas and did not seek to trick or en-
snare anyone. He was not like the false teachers, who had lust or profit as
their motive (2 Pet. 2:15–18; Jude 11). He was like David, who "shepherded
[Israel] according to the integrity of his heart" (Ps. 78:72).

It is humble men, men of integrity, whom God desires to shepherd
His flock.

A humble pastor is commissioned by God's will. All believers have the
right and the duty to share the gospel wherever and whenever they can.
However, no one should hold the office of pastor who has not received a call
to that ministry from God (see chapter 6, "The Call to Pastoral Ministry").
Those who pridefully exalt themselves to that position will not have God's
blessing. God will say of them what He said of the false prophets of
Jeremiah's day: "I did not send these prophets, but they ran. I did not speak
to them, but they prophesied" (Jer. 23:21).

Paul certainly did not exalt himself to the ministry. Indeed, becoming a minister of the gospel was the last thing he expected to do with his life.
But on the Damascus Road, God redeemed him and called him to the
ministry. No doubt that incident was in his mind when he wrote to the
Corinthians, "If I preach the gospel, I have nothing to boast of, for I am
under compulsion; for woe is me if I do not preach the gospel. For if I do
this voluntarily, I have a reward; but if against my will, I have a stewardship
entrusted to me" (1 Cor. 9:16–17). Unlike the false teachers who dogged his
steps and unlike their present-day counterparts, he did not appoint himself
to the ministry. Instead, Paul was "approved by God to be entrusted with
the gospel" (1 Thess. 2:4).

The knowledge that we did not earn the right to preach through our
own efforts or abilities should humble us. God called us to the ministry,
God trusted us to proclaim His Word, and God chose us to lead His
flock. To forget that is to take the first step toward disqualification from
the ministry.

---

7. Richard Baxter, *The Reformed Pastor* (Edinburgh: Banner of Truth, 1979), 63, 64,
65, 67–68 (emphasis added).

A humble pastor is compelled by God's knowledge. God's omniscience is a further key to and motive for humility. While it is possible to fool others by an outward facade of piety, God knows the secrets of the heart. "What [a] minister is on his knees in secret before God Almighty," wrote John Owen, "that he is and no more."[8] God's omniscience means accountability in the ministry. It keeps a man focused on pleasing God, not men. God scrutinizes the desires, motives, and intentions of the heart, and He knows what is done to please others and what is done to please Him.

Paul was quite aware of the implications of God's knowledge about his life. To the Thessalonians he wrote, "Just as we have been approved by God to be entrusted with the gospel, so we speak, not as pleasing men but God, who examines our hearts. For we never came with flattering speech, as you know, nor with a pretext for greed—God is witness" (1 Thess. 2:4–5). He knew he was commissioned by God to preach the gospel of God, not by men to preach a man-pleasing gospel. In Gal. 1:10 he added, "For am I now seeking the favor of men, or of God? Or am I striving to please men? If I were still trying to please men, I would not be a bond-servant of Christ." Remembering God's omniscience kept Paul from seeking to be a man-pleaser.

A humble pastor is consumed with God's glory. This key achieves the epitome of humility, for it is impossible to seek self-glory and God's glory at the same time. It is the New Covenant that is glorious (2 Cor. 3:7–11), not its ministers (2 Cor. 4:7). If all that rank-and-file believers do is to be for God's glory (1 Cor. 10:31), how much more the work of the ministry?

In 1 Thess. 2:6 Paul wrote, "nor did we seek glory from men, either from you or from others, even though as apostles of Christ we might have asserted our authority." Paul was no Diotrephes (3 John 9), seeking preeminence; he did not seek esteem, honor, or praise. His preoccupation was the glory of God (2 Cor. 4:5).

What marks a man effective in the ministry?

tenacity—he trusts totally in God's power

integrity—his life is consistent with his doctrine

authority—he receives his commission from God, not himself

accountability—he is constantly aware of the implications of God's omniscience

---

8. Cited by Thomas, *Golden Treasury*, 192.

humility—he is consumed not with himself, but with the glory of God.

Only such a man is humble enough to shepherd God's flock.

A Pastor Has to Shepherd the Flock of God

Of all the titles and metaphors used to describe spiritual leadership, the most fitting is that of shepherd. As shepherds, pastors are to guard their flocks from going astray, lead them to the green pastures of God's Word, and defend them against the savage wolves (Acts 20:29) that would ravage them. The shepherd metaphor is the one chosen by Peter in 1 Pet. 5:1–3. There he discusses the primary objective of shepherding, and gives wise counsel on how to shepherd and how not to shepherd.

The Primary Objective of Shepherding

A shepherd who fails to feed his flock will not have a flock for long. His sheep will wander off to other fields or die of starvation. Above all, God requires of His spiritual shepherds that they feed their flocks. In fact, the one ability that distinguishes an elder from a deacon is that an elder must be "able to teach" (1 Tim. 3:2; Titus 1:9). Charles Jefferson writes,

> That the feeding of the sheep is an essential duty of the shepherd-calling is known even to those who are least familiar with shepherds and their work. Sheep cannot feed themselves, nor water themselves. They must be conducted to the water and the pasture. . . . Everything depends on the proper feeding of the sheep. Unless wisely fed they become emaciated and sick, and the wealth invested in them is squandered. . . . When the minister goes into the pulpit, he is the shepherd in the act of feeding, and if every minister had borne this in mind, many a sermon would have been other than it has been. The curse of the pulpit is the superstition that a sermon is a work of art and not a piece of bread or meat.[9]

Jesus forcefully drove home the importance of feeding the sheep to Peter in His encounter with him described in John 21. Twice in His

---

9. Charles Jefferson, *The Minister as Shepherd* (Hong Kong: Living Books For All, 1980), 59, 61.

command to Peter, Jesus used the term *bosko*, which means "I feed" (vv. 15, 17). The shepherd's goal is not to please the sheep, but to feed them—not to tickle their ears, but to nourish their souls. He is not to offer light snacks of milk, but substantial meals of solid biblical truth. Those who fail to feed the flock are unfit to be shepherds (cf. Jer. 23:1–4; Ezek. 34:2–10).

How to Shepherd

Besides feeding them, the shepherd has two primary duties to his flock. He must exercise oversight of them and must lead them by the example of his life. Peter challenged his fellow elders to "shepherd the flock of God among you" by "exercising oversight" (1 Pet. 5:2). God entrusted them with the authority and responsibility of leading the flock. Shepherds are accountable for how they lead, and the flock for how they follow (Heb. 13:17).

However, being a shepherd does not mean merely getting the overall picture from a distance; it requires getting right in among the flock and leading by example. It is not leadership from on high so much as leadership from within. An effective shepherd does not herd his sheep from the rear but leads them from the front. They see him before them and imitate his actions. The most important asset of spiritual leadership is the power of an exemplary life.[10]

How Not to Shepherd

In his exhortation to his fellow shepherds, Peter warns them of two pitfalls. First, they must avoid doing what they do unwillingly. A good shepherd does his work "not under compulsion, but voluntarily" (1 Pet. 5:2). Sheep can be disagreeable, dirty, stubborn, exasperating animals. Former sheep rancher W. Phillip Keller observes that "No other class of livestock requires more careful handling, more detailed direction, than do sheep."[11] A lazy shepherd is an ineffective shepherd. The temptation that Peter cautions against is merely going through the motions—i.e., merely doing the work of the ministry only when under compulsion. Shepherding God's flock

---

10. See the discussion of this principle earlier in this chapter and in chapter 16, "Modeling."

11. W. Phillip Keller, *A Shepherd Looks at Psalm 23* (Grand Rapids: Zondervan, 1979), 71.

must be done spontaneously, voluntarily, with eagerness, and with a knowledge of its vital importance.

Another more sinister pitfall to avoid is doing the work of the ministry for sordid gain. "I have coveted no one's silver or gold or clothes," Paul said to the Ephesian elders (Acts 20:33). "No one can serve two masters," Jesus declared, "for either he will hate the one and love the other, or he will hold to one and despise the other. You cannot serve God and mammon" (Matt. 6:24). That is doubly true of pastors, whom God requires to be "free from the love of money" (1 Tim. 3:3). It is the false prophets who engage in the furious pursuit of monetary gain (see Isa. 56:11; Jer. 6:13; 8:10; Mic. 3:11; 2 Pet. 2:3).

It is not wrong for a pastor to be paid; in fact, Scripture commands it. "Let the elders who rule well be considered worthy of double honor," Paul wrote to Timothy, "especially those who work hard at preaching and teaching" (1 Tim. 5:17).[12] What *is* wrong is allowing financial gain to be one's motivation in the ministry. That not only produces insincere, ineffective leaders but also degrades the ministry in the eyes of the world. I'll never forget the time when, as a young pastor, a woman (not realizing I was a pastor) advised me to go into the ministry. "You don't have to work hard," she informed me, "and you can make lots of money at it." One can only wonder what sort of pastors she had encountered that made her develop that view of the ministry.

A humble man, dedicated to shepherding the souls God has entrusted to his care, "will receive the unfading crown of glory" in that day "when the Chief Shepherd appears" (1 Pet. 5:4).

THE OBEDIENT SHEPHERD

If Peter were still alive, I would like to ask him, "Could you be more specific as to what the humble shepherd should do?" Though we do not have Peter's specific response, we do have God's thorough answer to the question through the pen of Paul in the two epistles to Timothy in the New Testament. Paul had personally mentored the young pastor, but Timothy encountered severe trials when assigned the task of leading the church at Ephesus out of sin and error. He struggled with fear and human weakness. He apparently experienced the temptation to soften his preaching in the face of persecution. At times he seemed ashamed of the gospel.

---

12. For Paul's defense of his own right to be paid for his ministry, see 1 Cor. 9:6–14.

Paul had to remind him to stand up for the faith with boldness, even if it meant suffering: "Do not be ashamed of the testimony of our Lord, or of me His prisoner; but join with me in suffering for the gospel" (2 Tim. 1:8). The two rich epistles from Paul to Timothy outline a ministry philosophy of being and doing that challenges the prevailing practice of today.[13] Paul instructed Timothy in the first letter that he must:

Correct those teaching false doctrine and call them to a pure heart, a good conscience, and a sincere faith (1 Tim. 1:3–5).

Fight for divine truth and for God's purposes, keeping his own faith and a good conscience (1:18–19).

Pray for the lost and lead the men of the church to do the same (2:1–8).

Call women in the church to fulfill their God-given role of submission and to raise up godly children, setting an example of faith, love, and sanctity with self-restraint (2:9–15).

Carefully select spiritual leaders for the church on the basis of their giftedness, godliness, and virtue (3:1–13).

Recognize the source of error and those who teach it, and point these things out to the rest of the church (4:1–6).

Constantly be nourished on the words of Scripture and its sound teaching, avoiding all myths and false doctrines (4:6).

Discipline himself for the purpose of godliness (4:7–11).

Boldly command and teach the truth of God's Word (4:12).

Be a model of spiritual virtue that all can follow (4:12).

Faithfully read, explain, and apply the Scriptures publicly (4:13–14).

Be progressing toward Christlikeness in his own life (4:15–16).

Be gracious and gentle in confronting the sin of his people (5:1–2).

Give special consideration and care to those who are widows (5:3–16).

Honor faithful church leaders who work hard (5:17–21).

Choose church leaders with great care, seeing to it that they are both mature and proven (5:22).

Take care of his physical condition so he is strong to serve (5:23).

---

13. The following is adapted from John MacArthur, Jr., *Ashamed of the Gospel: When the Church Becomes Like the World* (Wheaton: Crossway, 1993), 24–27.

Teach and preach principles of true godliness, helping his people discern between true godliness and mere hypocrisy (5:24–6:6).

Flee the love of money (6:7–11).

Pursue righteousness, godliness, faith, love, perseverance, and gentleness (6:11).

Fight for the faith against all enemies and all attacks (6:12).

Instruct the rich to do good, to be rich in good works, and to be generous (6:17–19).

Guard the Word of God as a sacred trust and a treasure (6:20–21).

In his second epistle, Paul reminded Timothy to:

Keep the gift of God in him fresh and useful (2 Tim. 1:6).

Not be timid but powerful (1:7).

Never be ashamed of Christ or anyone who serves Christ (1:8–11).

Hold tightly to the truth and guard it (1:12–14).

Be strong in character (2:1).

Be a teacher of apostolic truth so that he may reproduce himself in faithful men (2:2).

Suffer difficulty and persecution willingly while making the maximum effort for Christ (2:3–7).

Keep his eyes on Christ at all times (2:8–13).

Lead with authority (2:14).

Interpret and apply Scripture accurately (2:15).

Avoid useless conversation that leads only to ungodliness (2:16).

Be an instrument of honor, set apart from sin and useful to the Lord (2:20–21).

Flee youthful lusts, and pursue righteousness, faith, and love (2:22).

Refuse to be drawn into philosophical and theological wrangling (2:23).

Not argue, but be kind, teachable, gentle, and patient even when he is wronged (2:24–26).

Face dangerous times with a deep knowledge of the Word of God (3:1–15).

Understand that Scripture is the basis and content of all legitimate ministry (3:16–17).

Preach the Word—in season and out of season—reproving, rebuking, and exhorting with great patience and instruction (4:1–2).

Be sober in all things (4:5).

Endure hardship (4:5).

Do the work of an evangelist (4:5).

To sum it all up in five categories, Paul commanded Timothy (1) to be faithful in his preaching of biblical truth, (2) to be bold in exposing and refuting error, (3) to be an example of godliness to the flock, (4) to be diligent and work hard in the ministry, and (5) to be willing to suffer hardship and persecution in his service for the Lord.

3

Pastoral Ministry in History

James F. Stitzinger

The biblical pattern for pastoral ministry derives from both testaments of the Bible. Deviations from that pattern crept into the church during the second century A.D. and continued, becoming increasingly severe into the Medieval period of the church. Nevertheless, a faithful few continued to follow the biblical pattern. These included Chrysostom and Augustine in the early church and the Paulicans, Waldenses, as well as Wycliffe and Huss during the Medieval period. The Reformation period witnessed a broader return to the biblical pattern through the magisterial reformation of Luther, Calvin, and through the Anabaptist reformation. During the modern period, Puritan leaders such as Baxter, Perkins, and Edwards have led a return to biblical principles in pastoral ministry. Bridges, Morgan, and Spurgeon were nineteenth-century examples of biblical ministers. The late twentieth century has produced others, including Lloyd-Jones, Adams, and MacArthur.

In God's gracious sovereignty, He chose to reconcile believers to Himself through Christ. In His marvelous plan He has committed to them the ministry of reconciliation (2 Cor. 5:18), based upon His Word of reconciliation (5:19). The office and function of the pastor has a key role in this ministry to proclaim the mystery of godliness. His functions are associated with the church, the pillar and support of the truth (1 Tim. 3:15–16).

The duty and privilege of pastoral ministry has resulted in the development of the discipline of pastoral theology within the broader framework of practical theology.[1] It has also produced a long procession of individuals who have filled the pages of church history in responding to God's call to be faithful pastors and ministers of the truth. Sadly, traditions[2] not measuring up to the standards of biblical scrutiny have skewed and embellished much of what has been called ministry.

A plethora of mind-sets and often conflicting traditions emerge in a study of pastoral ministry in history, though all traditions claim a lineage going back to the apostolic age. In every generation some have sought to return to the basic fundamentals of primitive biblical ministry. This pursuit of the true church or "primitivism" has led Littell and others to speak of the concept of the "Believers' Church."[3] Such a church included people of various ages and regions who followed the same principles of commitment to apostolic truth. These are believers who "gathered and disciplined a 'true church' upon the apostolic pattern as they understood it."[4] The truth for

---

1. Thomas C. Oden notes, "Pastoral theology is a special form of practical theology because it focuses on the practice of ministry, with particular attention to the systematic definition of the pastoral office and its function" (*Pastoral Theology, Essentials of Ministry* [San Francisco: HarperCollins, 1983], x).

2. In early church history Christians understood tradition as "revelation made by God and delivered by Him to His faithful people through the mouth of His prophets and apostles." It was something handed over, not something handed down, and was thus in accord with divine revelation. In the period since the early church, "tradition means the continuous stream of explanation and elucidation of the primitive faith, illustrating the way in which Christianity has been presented and understood in past ages. It is, that is, the accumulated wisdom of the past" (Tradition," in *The Oxford Dictionary of the Christian Church*, 2d ed., ed F. L. Cross and E. A. Livingstone [Oxford: University Press, 1983], 1388). The latter approach to tradition has allowed much deflection from simple, primitive, biblical ministry.

3. In Franklin Hamlin Littell, "The Concept of the Believers' Church," in *The Concept of the Believers' Church*, ed. James Leo Garrett, Jr. (Scottdale, Pa." Herald, 1969), 27–32, the author delineates at least six basic principles or marks of the "Believers' Church" that represent common themes in various churches. They include (1) the Believers' Church, although outwardly constituted by volunteers, is Christ's church and not theirs; (2) membership in the Believers' Church is voluntary and witting (done deliberately); (3) the principle of separation from the world is basic, although it has often been misinterpreted; (4) mission and witness are key concepts for the Believers' Church, and all members are involved; (5) internal integrity and church discipline are stressed; and (6) the proper concept of the secular in relationship to the sacred. The primary example of an application of this last theme is to a state church in which government attempts to control all ideology and thinking, thus limiting human liberty.

4. Franklin Hamlin Littell, *The Origins of Sectarian Protestantism* (New York: Macmillan, 1964), xvii.

these people was an ongoing pursuit, not a closed book in a sectarian sense. It was one that "wanted fellowship with all who bore the Name and lived the covenant of a good conscience with God."[5]

Other committed believers like these within the wider framework of church history have sought above all else the true, pure, primitive church. They have sought a church and a ministry patterned after the theology and practice of the book of Acts and the New Testament Epistles. Such individuals and churches have appeared in various forms and have come from various settings, but all display a desire to return to a vibrant, biblical church and ministry. Some have journeyed further in their plans than in their practice. Some have advanced further than others in their quest for biblical ministry.

This chapter focuses on a history of those who have sought to teach and practice biblical pastoral ministry. Examinations of efforts to follow biblical ministry patterns rather than accepted tradition and recurring ministry practices can serve as a helpful guide to a future generation with the same goals. Such historical study provides valuable insights through enabling Christians and churches to learn from the past. Though history is not the unfolding of an unalterable tradition or a hermeneutical principle for interpreting ministry, "the flow of time bears divine sovereignty and providence on its wings and constitutes a general, not special, revelation of God himself."[6] Only the Bible can teach the true theology of pastoral ministry, but the working of the Holy Spirit in the hearts of church leaders through the centuries can inform this theology and its practical implementation. The following historical material will provide such information.

The Biblical Period

Many have noted the elusive and complex nature of pastoral theology that makes the discipline hard to define. As Tidball points out, part of this "elusiveness stems from the multitude of labels which exist in this area and which seem to be used without any agreement as to their exact meaning or relationship." As a further reason, he points out that the difficulty "stems from the fact that so many sub-disciplines of practical theology are spoken

---

5. Littell, "Concept," 25–26.

6. Marc Mueller, "What Is History" (unpublished chapel lecture, The Master's Seminary, Sun Valley, Calif., February 16, 1989), 5.

of as if they are pastoral theology."[7] The historical development of the doctrine of the church in general and of practical theology in particular, have no doubt contributed to this elusiveness, since tension has surrounded this whole subject from the outset of church history.[8]

Thomas C. Oden, in expanding his definition of pastoral theology, observes, "Pastoral theology is that branch of Christian theology that deals with the office, gifts, and functions of the pastor. As theology, pastoral theology seeks to reflect upon that self-disclosure of God witnessed to by Scripture, mediated through tradition, reflected upon by critical reasoning, and embodied in personal and social experience."[9] Throughout history, it is precisely when the weight of tradition, critical reasoning, and experience have come to bear upon pastoral theology that it has been most likely to drift from its biblical moorings. In reality, it is impossible to say that one has no tradition or critical thinking on this subject. It is, therefore, imperative that one begin, continue, and end with the Scriptures in a study of true pastoral ministry.

The place to begin is with an investigation of the various aspects of primitive biblical ministry as they relate to the office and functions of pastors. A brief summary of the biblical data can serve as the basis for identifying historic efforts to reproduce that kind of ministry.

Old Testament

A history of pastoral ministry must begin in the Old Testament. The theme, "The Lord is my shepherd" (Ps. 23:1), expresses the pastoral role of God with His people. Tidball describes this image as "the underlining paradigm of ministry," and points out that it contains "references to the authority, tender care, specific tasks, courage and sacrifice required of the pastor."[10] Many passages, including Gen. 49:24; Isa. 53:6; Ps. 78:52–53; 80:1, contribute to the development of this theme. The Old Testament often describes Israel as sheep who need a shepherd (Ps. 100:3; see also Ps. 44:22; 119:176; Jer. 23:1; 50:6).

---

7. Derek J. Tidball, *Skillful Shepherds: An Introduction to Pastoral Theology* (Grand Rapids: Zondervan, 1986), 18.

8. Note the divergence of views as reflected in Louis Berkhoff's development of the doctrine of the church (*The History of Christian Doctrines* [Edinburgh: Banner of Truth, n.d.], 227–41).

9. Oden, *Pastoral Theology*, 311.

10. Tidball, *Skillful Shepherds*, 54.

The theme of God's love also contributes to the shepherd theme: "I have loved you with an everlasting love; therefore I have drawn you with lovingkindness" (Jer. 31:3). God demonstrates His love for Israel in vivid imagery with Hosea's marriage to a harlot (Hos. 1:2). Though Israel spurned His love, God continues loving, as He says in Hos. 11:1: "When Israel was a youth I loved him, and out of Egypt I called My son." In the end, God is there to "heal their apostasy . . . [and] love them freely" (Hos. 14:4). The Old Testament abounds with statements of God's love for His people. Another is in Isa. 43:4–5: "Since you are precious in My sight, since you are honored and I love you . . . do not fear, for I am with you."[11]

Associated with the love of God is His disciplining of those He loves (Prov. 3:11); His holding accountable of those whom He loves (Ps. 11:7); and His command that men love Him in return (Deut. 6:5). Also associated with the divine pastoral concern is the profound theme of God's mercy (i.e., loyal love, Ps. 62:12; Isa. 54:10; 55:3,)[12] God's compassion (Ps. 145:9), and His delight (2 Sam. 22:20). Combined with this are numerous examples of servant leaders—including Abraham, Joseph, Moses, Samuel, and David—who demonstrated the faithfulness of God as they accomplished His work through faith (Hebrews 11).

Thus the Old Testament provides an important basis for understanding the office and function of the pastor. The Shepherd Himself displays his Fatherly care, love, mercy, discipline, compassion, and delight toward His people whom He desires to love and fear Him with a pure heart. The image of a shepherd also demonstrates God's authority, faithfulness, as well as the necessity and implications of obedience to Him. Servant leaders exemplify both strengths and weaknesses as God uses them to carry out His sovereign plan in human history.

New Testament

The New Testament builds on this Old Testament foundation as it reveals the Chief Shepherd, Christ, in all His wisdom, glory, power, and

---

11. See Leon Morris, *Testaments of Love: A Study of Love in the Bible* (Grand Rapids: Eerdmans, 1981), 8–100; also Norman Snaith, *The Distinctive Ideas of the Old Testament* (New York: Schocken, 1964), 131–42.

12. The Hebrew word חֶסֶד (*hesed*) has been variously translated with meanings such as "mercy, love, loyal love, unfailing love, constant love, strong, faithful love, lovingkindness" (Morris, *Testaments of Love,* 66–7). The *hesed* or mercy of God as He covenants with His people to love them and to be faithful to that love always is a rich and profound study that furnishes important insight into true pastoral activity (see Nelson Glueck, *Hesed in the Bible* [New York: KTAV, 1975]; see also Snaith, *Distinctive Ideas,* 94–130).

humility (John 10:11, 14; 1 Pet. 5:4). The person and work of the Great Shepherd culminates in His death (i.e., the blood of the eternal Covenant, Heb. 13:20; 1 Pet. 2:25) and resurrection. The Good Shepherd gave His life for His sheep whom he calls to Himself (John 10:11–16). These "called out" ones are His church. Christ, as Head of the church, leads His church (Eph. 1:22; 5:23–25) and shepherds it. He calls pastors as undershepherds to function and give oversight under His authority (1 Pet. 5:1–4).

Both as a doctrine (1 Corinthians 12) and through living example, the New Testament reveals the nature of the church and all its members and activities. It also furnishes clear teaching about church officers and their functions. The role and duties of a pastor as presented in the New Testament are the basis of all future biblical ministry in history.

Five distinct terms refer to the pastoral office:

1. *elder (presbyteros)*, a title highlighting the administration and spiritual guidance of the church (Acts 15:6; 1 Tim. 5:17; James 5:14; 1 Pet. 5:1–4)

2. *bishop* or *overseer (episkopos)*, which emphasizes guidance, oversight, and leadership in the church (Acts 20:28; Phil. 1:1; 1 Tim. 3:2–5; Titus 1:7)

3. *shepherd* or *pastor (poimen)*, a position denoting leadership and authority (Acts 20:28–31; Eph. 4:11) as well as guidance and provision (1 Pet. 2:25; 5:2–3)

4. *preacher (kerux)*, which points to public proclamation of the gospel and teaching of the flock (Rom. 10:14; 1 Tim. 2:7; 2 Tim. 1:11)

5. *teacher (didaskalos)*, one responsible for instruction and exposition of the Scriptures whose teaching is both instructive (1 Tim. 2:7) and corrective (1 Cor. 12:28–29)

Scripture is quite clear that these descriptive titles relate to the same pastoral office. The terms *elder* and *bishop* are synonymous in Acts 20:17 and Titus 1:5–7. The terms *elder, bishop,* and *shepherd* are synonymous in 1 Pet. 5:1–2. The leadership role of elders is also evident in the shepherdly activity of James 5:14. As clearly noted by Lightfoot, in biblical times *elder* and *bishop* were synonymous terms.[13]

---

13. J. B. Lightfoot, "The Christian Ministry," in *Saint Paul's Epistle to the Philippians* (reprint, Grand Rapids: Zondervan, 1953), 196–201. Though Lightfoot himself became Bishop of Durham in 1879 and remained strongly committed to the Anglican tradition, his work remains of primary significance in understanding primitive church ministry and subsequent embellishments in church history.

It was not until the rise of apostolic succession in the second century that bishops took the places of the apostles and presided over groups of elders.[14]

First Timothy 5:17 and Heb. 13:7 associate the terms *teacher* and *preacher* with each other. Ephesians 4:11 connects shepherds (pastors) with teachers, as do 1 Tim. 5:17 and Heb. 13:7. These last two passages furnish no exegetical grounds for separating the work of governing from that of teaching.[15] Consequently, the conclusion must be that pastoral leadership in the church included preaching, teaching, oversight, and shepherding. The parity of the titles look to a single role, the office of pastor.

In addition to these five terms, a number of descriptive words shed light on biblical pastoral ministry:

ruler	1 Thess. 5:12; 1 Tim. 3:4–5; 5:17
ambassador	2 Cor. 5:20
steward	1 Cor. 4:1
defender	Phil. 1:7
minister	1 Cor. 4:1
servant	2 Cor. 4:5
example	1 Tim. 4:12, 1 Pet. 5:3

The New Testament also tells the pastor to:

preach	1 Cor 1:17
feed	1 Pet. 5:2
build up the church	Eph. 4:12
edify	2 Cor. 13:10
pray	Col. 1:9
watch for souls	Heb. 13:17
fight	1 Tim. 1:18
convince	Titus 1:9

---

14. Ibid., 95–99, 193–96. Both biblical and early patristic data support this conclusion (see John Gill, *Body of Divinity* [reprint, Atlanta: Lassetter, 1965], 863–64; A. E. Harvey, "Elders," *Journal of Theological Studies* ns 25 [1974]: 326.

15. See Lightfoot, *Philippians*, 195.

comfort	2 Cor. 1:4–6
rebuke	Titus 1:13
warn	Acts 20:31
admonish	2 Thess. 3:15
exhort	Titus 1:9; 2:15

The Scriptures are clear regarding the office and functions of the pastor. The biblical pattern, describes a Spirit-filled man who gives oversight, shepherds, guides, teaches, and warns—doing all with a heart of love, comfort, and compassion. All of these functions were evident in the first-century church. The church at this early stage was marked by purity (including church discipline), primitivism (New Testament simplicity), voluntarism (no compulsion to join), tolerance (no persecution of those who disagreed), evangelistic zeal (missionary activity), observation of biblical ordinances (baptism and the Lord's Supper), emphasis on the Holy Spirit, and dynamic ministry (involving both pastor and people)—not tradition, hierarchy, and corruption.

In time, however, a more complex and embellished church doctrine and practice replaced this early church simplicity.[16] This development had direct bearing on the nature of pastoral ministry as it reflected a similar change in scope and complexity of the pastoral role. The remainder of this chapter will identify major examples of those who approached biblical pastoral ministry following the pattern of the first-century church.

The Early Christian Church
(A.D. 100–476)

From its earliest days, the Christian church has moved from simplicity to complexity as it has drifted from a spontaneous living organism to a more settled institution.[17] This ever dangerous institutionalism arose simulta-

---

16. Adolph Harnack, *History of Dogma* (Boston: Roberts, 1897), 2:77.

17. William A. Clebsch and Charles R. Jaekle, *Pastoral Care in Historical Perspective* (New York: Harper, 1967), 11–31; cf. also Carl A. Volz, "The Pastoral Office in the Early Church," *Word and World* 9 (1989): 359–66; Theron D. Price, "The Emergence of the Christian Ministry," *Review and Expositor* 46 (1949): 216–38; B. H. Streeter, *The Primitive Church* (New York: Macmillan, 1929); T. W. Manson, *The Church's Ministry* (Philadelphia: Westminster, 1948).

neously in the second generation of many widely separated churches. No more vivid example exists than that of the second-century church, which developed strong ecclesiastical traditions[18] as it came to view the bishop as the successor to the apostle.[19] This trend progressed into the fourth century, causing the church to enter more and more into an era of "speculation on the law and doctrine of the church."[20] The rise and development of sacerdotalism with its elevation of clergy to the status of priests, in effect, made the minister an instrument of the saving grace of God as he participated with God in the salvation of human beings.[21] This development of the threefold ministry of bishops, elders, and deacons represented a serious departure from simple New Testament ministry.

In contrast to this general trend, several strong proponents of biblical ministry existed during this period. Polycarp (ca. A.D. 70–55) wrote,

> And the presbyters also must be compassionate, merciful towards all men, turning back the sheep that are gone astray, visiting all the infirm, not neglecting a widow or an orphan or a poor man: but providing always for that which is honorable in the sight of God and of men. . . . Let us therefore so serve Him with fear and all reverence, as He himself gave commandment and the Apostles who preached the Gospel to us and the prophets who proclaimed beforehand the coming of the Lord.[22]

The spirit here is one of humble and loving service, with no seeming regard for the hierarchical relationship of bishops and elders. Clement of Alexandria (ca. A.D. 155–220) has written in a similar vein, emphasizing that ministers are those who are chosen to serve the Lord, who moderate their passions, who are obedient to superiors, and who teach and care for sheep as

---

18. Hans Von Campenhausen, *Ecclesiastical Authority and Spiritual Power in the Church of the First Three Centuries* (Stanford, Calif.: Stanford Press, 1969), 149–77. He describes this process as the apostolic teaching and traditional teaching "taking in more and more material, historical, legal, and dogmatic" (151).

19. The hierarchy of bishop, presbyter, and deacon became known as the "threefold ministry." As an endorsement of the doctrine of "apostolic succession," these layers of authority furnished the groundwork for the Papacy (see Dom Gregory Dix, "The Ministry in the Early Church," in *The Apostolic Ministry*, ed. Kenneth E. Kirk [London: Hodder and Stoughton, 1946], 183–304, esp. 186–91).

20. Ibid., 177. See also Fenton John Anthony Hort, *The Christian Ecclesia* (London: Macmillan, 1914), 224.

21. See Benjamin B. Warfield, *The Plan of Salvation* (Grand Rapids: Eerdmans, 1955), 52–68.

22. Polycarp, "Epistle of Polycarp to the Philippians," para. 6, in *The Apostolic Fathers*, ed. J. B. Lightfoot (London: Macmillan, 1926), 179.

a shepherd.[23] He also observed that "bishops, presbyters, deacons . . . are imitations of the angelic glory, and of that economy which, the Scriptures say, awaits those who follow the footsteps of the apostles, having lived in perfection of righteousness according to the Gospel."[24] Origen (ca. A.D. 185–254), his pupil, assigned a similar role to the one representing Christ and his house (the church) and teaching others of these truths.[25] This emphasis contrasts sharply with that of Cyprian (ca. A.D. 200–258), the well-known Bishop of Carthage, who apparently limited his discussion of pastoral theology to the elevation of the bishop to the level of an apostle.[26]

The powerful pen of John Chrysostom (ca. A.D. 347–407) contributed significantly to the early church's understanding of the pastoral position.[27] He developed the role and functions of a pastor both in his commentaries on the Pastoral Epistles and in his Treatises. His statements about the nature of ministry are very biblical:

> There is but one method and way of healing appointed, after we have gone wrong, and this is, the powerful application of the Word. This is the one instrument, the finest atmosphere. This takes the place of physic, cautery and cutting, and if it be needful to sear and amputate, this is the means which we must use, and if this be of no avail, all else is wasted: with this we both roust the soul when it sleeps, and reduce it when it is inflamed; with this we cut off excesses, and fill up defects, and perform all manner of other operations which are requisite for the soul's health.[28]

To this Chrysostom adds the necessity of living by example with the ambition that the Word of Christ would dwell in men richly.[29] His statements

23. Clement of Alexandria, "The Stromata, or Miscellanies," vi:xiii, vii:vii, in *The Ante-Nicene Fathers*, ed. Alexander Roberts and James Donaldson (Grand Rapids: Eerdmans, 1983), 2:504, 535.

24. Ibid., vi:xiii, 505. Although Clement mentions the threefold ministry, he does not emphasize it or call attention to a special authority of bishop.

25. "Origen against Celsus," v:xxxiii, in *The Ante-Nicene Fathers*, ed. Alexander Roberts and James Donaldson (Grand Rapids: Eerdmans, 1982), 4:557–58.

26. Cyprian, "The Epistles of Cyprian," Epistle lxviii: 8, in *The Ante-Nicene Fathers*, ed. Alexander Roberts and James Donaldson (Grand Rapids: Eerdmans, 1981), 5:374–75; cf. also Cyprian, "The Treatises of Cyprian," *Treatises*, i:5–6, ibid., 5:5–6.

27. St. Chrysostom, "Treaties Concerning the Christian Priesthood," in *A Select Library of the Nicene and Post-Nicene Fathers of the Christian Church*, ed. Philip Schaff (Grand Rapids: Eerdmans, 1983), FS IX:25–83.

28. Ibid., 64.

29. Ibid., 64–65. See Tidball's excellent description of John Chrysostom in *Skillful Shepherds*, 154–63.

warm the heart as perhaps the most useful expression of pastoral ministry during the period, but they also reveal signs of the monastic stranglehold fast coming upon the organized church of his day.[30] The monastic understanding of pastoral ministry was soon to have a profound effect upon church leadership.

Another important spokesman from this period is Augustine of Hippo (A.D. 354–430). Often best known as a theologian and preacher, Augustine devoted his life to pastoral ministry. Soon after his ordination he wrote to Valerius, his superior,

> First and foremost, I beg your wise holiness to consider that there is nothing in this life, and especially in our own day, more easy and pleasant and acceptable to men than the office of bishop or priest or deacon, if its duties be discharged in a mechanical or sycophantic way; but nothing more worthless and deplorable and meet for chastisement in the sight of God: and, on the other hand, that there is nothing in this life, and especially in our own day, more difficult, toilsome, and hazardous than the office of bishop or priest or deacon; but nothing more blessed in the sight of God, if our service be in accordance with our Captain's orders.[31]

Augustine's ministry included many well-articulated biblical functions, including those of apologist, administrator, minister to the afflicted, preacher and teacher, judge, and spiritual leader.[32] Much to his credit, he spent considerable time and energy in personal biblical ministry. Pastoral interaction and ministry appear to be at the heart of his book, *The City of God*, as he deals with those who challenge God's divine city with an earthly city.[33] At the same time, however, Augustine brought into the church a leprosy of monastic tradition involving both men and women (nunnery), thereby laying the groundwork for the Augustinian Rule.

Independent groups are a final source of biblical ministry patterns during this period. As Gunnar Westin points out, "The process of development which transformed the original Christian congregations to a sacramental, authoritarian Church took place during the latter portion of the second cen-

---

30. Note Chrysostom's statements about reclusion, ibid., 74–77. Monasticism began with Antony of Egypt just before Chrysostom's time.

31. Augustine, "Letters of Saint Augustine," Letter xxi:1, *A Select Library*, ed. Schaff, FS 1:237.

32. See Joseph B. Bernardin, "St. Augustine the Pastor," in *A Companion to the Study of St. Augustine*, ed. Roy W. Battenhouse (New York: Oxford, 1955), 57–89.

33. Augustine, *The City of God*, vol. 1, *A Select Library*, ed. Schaff, 2:1.

tury. . . . This change did not take place without protest."[34] Many church historians have dismissed as heretics those churches that opposed the institutionalized church—a campaign often called "The Free Church Movement."[35] Though some of these groups struggled with doctrinal purity, a closer look reveals that the heretical label in most cases was primarily due to their un-willingness to be loyal to the received tradition of the fathers,[36] not to significant doctrinal weakness. A thorough investigation of these independents is difficult, because, for the most part, only the works of those who wrote against them have survived. So some sensitivity in examining these writings is necessary. Such groups include the Montanists (ca. A.D. 156), Novatians (ca. A.D. 250), and Donatists (ca. A.D. 311), all of whom left the official church of their day to pursue the pure church.[37] An inclusion of these groups in the present discussion is not an attempt to demonstrate their consistent soundness of doctrine, but to point to their common commitment to the gospel and a primitive church with a primitive biblical ministry.

It is beyond the scope of this survey to explore these groups in depth, but the comments of Philip Schaff regarding the Donatists—a group strongly opposed by Constantine after A.D. 325—are noteworthy: "The Donatist controversy was a conflict between separatism and catholicism; between ecclesiastical purism and ecclesiastical eclecticism; between the idea of the church as an exclusive community of regenerated saints and the idea of the church as the general Christendom of state and people."[38] The critical issue for the Donatists was the purity of the church and the holiness of its pastors. This resulted in a more biblical ministry.[39]

---

34. Gunnar Westin, *The Free Church through the Ages* (Nashville: Broadman, 1958), 9.

35. Ibid., 1–8.

36. Jaroslav Pelikan (*The Growth of Medieval Theology [600–1300]*, vol. 3 of *The Christian Tradition* [Chicago: University of Chicago Press, 1978], 3:17–18) writes, "The quality that marked Augustine and the other orthodox fathers was their loyalty to the received tradition. The apostolic anathema pronounced against anyone, even 'an angel from heaven,' who preached 'a gospel contrary to that which you have received' by tradition was, as in the East so also in the West, a prohibition of any kind of theological novelty. . . . One definition of heretics could be 'those who now take pleasure in making up new terminology for themselves and who are not content with the dogma of the holy fathers.' "

37. See the discussion by Westin, *Free Church*, 9–23; see also, E. H. Broadbent, *The Pilgrim Church* (London: Pickering and Inglis, 1931), 10–48; Donald F. Durnbaugh, *The Believers' Church* (New York: Macmillan, 1968), 3–40.

38. Philip Schaff, "Nicene and Post-Nicene Christianity," in *History of the Christian Church* (Grand Rapids: Eerdmans, 1968), 3:365, cf. also 366–70.

39. See W. H. C. Frend, *The Donatist Church, A Movement of Protest in Roman North Africa* (Oxford: Clarendon, 1952), 315–32.

As the church of the New Testament passed through its early centuries and became the official or organized church, it frequently departed from simple New Testament patterns. Nonetheless, strong voices both inside and outside this church called for a biblical ministry.

THE MEDIEVAL PERIOD (A.D. 476-1500)

The general structure of the western medieval church focused on the authority and celibacy of its clergy. Many leaders had retreated to the ascetic life of the monastery to escape the worldliness of the Christianity of their day. The pattern of authority centered in Rome with the first pope, Gregory the Great (540-604), assuming power in 590.

Though Gregory's papacy plunged the church into deeper political involvement and corruption, he also contributed a positive influence on the pastoral ministry of its clergy. In his *Book of Pastoral Rule*, he discussed many issues, including qualifications and duties of ministers as well as listing thirty types of members with rules of admonition for each.[40] He addressed the poor, the sad, the foolish, the sick, the haughty, the fickle, and many others. This monumental work became a textbook of medieval ministry,[41] yet Gregory's own preoccupation with political implications of the papacy caused him to neglect the souls of men while caring for his estates.[42]

The rise of the papacy produced complete corruption as popes, in their devotion to an increasingly pagan agenda, resorted to any available means to reach their goals. The monastic church, now fully developed, experienced tremendous corruption as well. In balance, however, Payne points out, "Though there was widespread spiritual famine in many nominally Christian lands and notorious corruption in high places, the theologians, the mystics and the reformers of the Middle Ages are further evidence of the Holy Spirit within the Church. They came, almost without exception, from the ranks of the clergy."[43] During the thousand-year period from Nicea to Wycliffe, ministry took place in spite of the church more than because of the official church.

---

40. Gregory the Great, "The Book of Pastoral Rule," in *A Select Library of Nicene and Post-Nicene Fathers of the Christian Church*, ed. Philip Schaff and Henry Wace (Grand Rapids: Eerdmans, 1983), SS 12.

41. Roland H. Bainton, "The Ministry in the Middle Ages," in *The Ministry in Historical Perspectives*, ed. Richard Niebuhr and Daniel D. Williams (New York: Harper, 1956), 98.

42. Ibid., 86.

43. Ernest A. Payne, "The Ministry in Historical Perspective," *The Baptist Quarterly* 17 (1958): 260-61.

Even more than in the early period, biblical ministry occurred among elements of the Free Church, which were and are commonly regarded as heretics.[44] Groups such as the Paulicans (ca. 625), Cathari (ca. 1050), Albigenses (1140), and Waldenses (1180) demonstrated a strong passion for a pure church with biblical ministry. As Bainton notes, these "very definitely were not heretics but only schismatic, and schismatics only because [they were] cast out against their will."[45] The Paulicans, in their important manual *The Key of Truth*, speak of a simple church, built on "repentance and faith" and refer to what was "learned from the Lord" about the church. "Good shepherds," whose responsibilities included ruling, shepherding, preaching, caring, and administration of the sacraments were its leaders.[46] The following prayer offered at the time of an elder's election to office reflects the nature of Paulician ministry:

> Lamb of God, Jesus, help us and especially this thy newly-elected servant, whom thou hast joined unto the number of thy loved disciples. Establish him on thy Gospel vouchsafed to thine universal and apostolic Church, the sure and immovable rock at the gate of hell. And bestow on him a goodly pastorship, to tend with great love thy reasonable flock. . . . Keep this thy servant with thine elect; that no unclean spirit of devils may dare to approach him.[47]

The Waldenses, who by 1184 had separated from the Church of Rome and formed their own church and ministry, exhibit a similar theme of simple biblical ministry. Allix notes that "their ministers exercised these holy functions, extraordinarily to the edification of their people."[48] Their long history of pre-Reformation Christianity in the Piedmont reflects a relatively pure and uncorrupted form of primitive Christianity.[49]

---

44. Note the easy use of the term heretic even by evangelical historians, e.g., J. D. Douglas, *The New International Dictionary of the Christian Church*, rev. ed. (Grand Rapids: Zondervan, 1978). The issue of perspective is always relevant when charging someone with being a heretic.

45. Bainton, "Ministry in the Middle Ages," 108.

46. Fred C. Conybeare, ed., *The Key of Truth, a Manual of the Paulican Church of Armenia* (Oxford: Clarendon, 1898), 76–77, 106–11.

47. Ibid., 112.

48. Peter Allix, *Some Remarks upon the Ecclesiastical History of the Ancient Churches of Piedmont* (Oxford: Clarendon, 1891), 238 f.

49. See "Waldenses" in *Dictionary of Sects, Heresies, Ecclesiastical Parties and Schools of Religious Thought*, ed. John Henry Blunt (London: Longmans, 1891), 616–21.

The beliefs and practices of the Albigenses, whose church was in southern France by 1190, also exemplified this theme of purity. They experienced heavy persecution and frequent misunderstanding from others. Commenting on their ministry, Allix writes,

> It appears therefore that the discipline of the Albigenses was the same that had been practiced in the primitive Church: they had their Bishops, their Priests, and their Deacons, whom the Church of Rome at first held for schismatics, and whose ministry she at last absolutely rejected, for the same reasons that made her consider the ministry of the Waldenses as null and void.[50]

Perhaps the greatest voices for biblical ministry were those of the pre-Reformation reformers. These called for true biblical ministry in a day when such convictions often required men to die for their views.

John Wycliffe (1324–1384), the leading Oxford scholar of his day, clearly addressed the issue of biblical ministry in his Forty-Three Propositions.[51] His writings "restrict the charter of the preacher to the expounding of Scripture," and state that "priests should exercise their primary function, namely, pastoral care. They should not lurk in cloisters."[52] His most powerful statements are in his book *On the Pastoral Office*, where he states,

> There are two things which pertain to the status of pastor: the holiness of the pastor and the wholesomeness of his teaching. He ought to be holy, so strong in every sort of virtue that he would rather desert every kind of human intercourse, all the temporal things of this world, even mortal life itself, before he would sinfully depart from the truth of Christ. . . . Secondly, [he] ought to be resplendent with righteousness of doctrine before his sheep.[53]

John Huss (1373–1415) followed Wycliffe's rich emphasis on biblical ministry by calling for a pure church and ministry. In his writings are many examples of this teaching. He said, "The church shines in its walls, but

---

50. Peter Allix, *Remarks upon the Ecclesiastical History of the Ancient Churches of the Albigenses*, new ed. (Oxford: Clarendon, 1821), 207.

51. John Wycliffe, cited in *Documents of the Christian Church*, ed. Henry Bettenson (London: Oxford, 1963), 173–75.

52. Herbert E. Winn, ed. *Wyclif, Select English Writings* (London: Oxford, 1929), 41, 68.

53. John Wycliff, "On the Pastoral Office," in *The Library of Christian Classics: Advocates of Reform*, ed. Matthew Spinka (London: SCM, 1953), 32, 48. In this discussion Wycliffe speaks of the primitive church and its importance on several occasions (e.g., 40).

starves in its poor saints; it clothes its stones with gold, but leaves its children naked."[54] Gillett summarizes his teaching: "In the early church there were but two grades of office, deacon and presbyter; all beside are of later and human invention. But God can bring back his church to the old pattern, just as the apostles and true priests took oversight of the church in all matters essential to its well-being, before the office of pope was introduced."[55] He further taught, "Not the office makes the priest, but the priest the office. Not every priest is a saint, but every saint is a priest."[56] Spinka offers his summary of Huss' position: "His reform program may be summarized by defining it as restitutionalism—the return of Christ and His apostles as exhibited in the primitive Church. He contrasts the Church militant with the true spiritual Church—the body of Christ."[57]

The writings of William Tyndale (1494–1536) reveal a similar commitment to primitive biblical ministry.[58]

In summary, the Middle Ages, though dominated by a powerful and corrupt institutional church, was a period when many rose up to challenge that body because of their pursuit of the truth. This should encourage present-day servants in their quest to rediscover true pastoral ministry. The effort may be extremely difficult in the face of strong traditions, but it is both necessary and possible.

THE REFORMATION PERIOD (1500–1648)

The Protestant Reformation was of great importance in the history of the church and the development of its ministry. Flowing out of late-medieval piety, mysticism, and scholarship,[59] its focus was upon reforming the

---

54. John Huss, cited by E. H. Gillett, *The Life and Times of John Huss; or the Bohemian Reformation of the Fifteenth Century* (Boston: Gould, 1864), 1:285.

55. Ibid., 1:248.

56. Ibid.

57. Matthew Spinka, *John Huss, A Biography* (Princeton, N.J.: Princeton University Press, 1968), 19. See also, Matthew Spinka, *John Huss' Concept of the Church* (Princeton, N.J.: Princeton University Press, 1966). *On Simony* (1413), and *On the Church* (1415) are among Huss' own works.

58. See S. L. Greenslade, *The Works of William Tyndale* (London: Blackie, 1938), 181–96. Tyndale's statements are in sharp contrast to those of his late-medieval contemporaries; see Dennis D. Martin, "Popular and Monastic Pastoral Issues in the Later Middle Ages," *Church History* 56 (1987): 320–32.

59. See Steven Ozment, *The Age of Reform 1250–1550, an Intellectual and Religious History of Late Medieval and Reformation Europe* (New Haven: Yale, 1980), xi–xii, 1–21;

existing church according to biblical principles. It was more accurately the "Magisterial Reformation," since the reformers retained the mind-set of the magistrate who compelled individuals in matters of faith. This state-church concept contrasted sharply with the Free-Church thinking of true Anabaptists (distinguished from a larger group of Anabaptists), who attempted to build a new church based on the Bible.[60] This important difference has led an increasing number of historians to focus on the "Radical Reformation" as "a major expression of the religious movement of the sixteenth century."[61] Williams identifies this Radical Reformation as the "fourth" Reformation in distinguishing it from Lutheranism, Calvinism, and Anglicanism.[62] Although acknowledging doctrinal differences within the fourth Reformation, Williams observes,

> Though Anabaptists, Spiritualists, and Evangelical Rationalists differed among themselves as to what constituted the root of faith and order and the ultimate source of divine authority among them . . . all three groups within the Radical Reformation agreed in cutting back to that root and in freeing church and creed of what they regarded as the suffocating growth of ecclesiastical tradition and magisterial prerogative. Precisely this makes theirs a "Radical Reformation."[63]

In seeking an understanding of the contribution of the Reformation to biblical ministry, one must look to both the magisterial reformers (Luther, Bucer, Calvin, and Knox) and the Free Church (true Anabaptists). The former

---

Heiko A. Oberman, *The Harvest of Medieval Theology* (Grand Rapids: Eerdmans, 1967); Oberman, *The Dawn of the Reformation* (Grand Rapids: Eerdmans, 1992), 1–83.

60. Littell has a good development of this important distinction in *Sectarian Protestantism*, xvii–xviii, 65–66, 73. Philip Schaff writes, "The Reformers aimed to reform the old Church by the Bible; the Radicals attempted to build a new Church from the Bible. The former maintained the historic continuity; the latter went directly to the apostolic age, and ignored the intervening centuries as an apostasy. The Reformers founded a popular state-church, including all citizens with their families; the Anabaptists organized on the voluntary principle, select congregations of baptized believers, separated from the world and from the State" (*History of the Christian Church, Modern Christianity, The Swiss Reformation* [reprint, Grand Rapids: Eerdmans, 1969], 8:71).

61. George Huntston Williams, *Spiritual and Anabaptist Writers*, vol. XXV of *The Library of Christian Classics* (London: SCM, 1957), 19.

62. Ibid., 19. This distinguished Harvard scholar further develops the same distinction and the term "Magisterial Reformation" in George Hunston Williams, *The Radical Reformation* (Philadelphia: Westminster, 1962), xxiii–xxxi. See also Roland Bainton, "The Left Wing of the Reformation," *Journal of Religion* 21 (1941): 127.

63. Ibid., 22. See also Philip Schaff, *History of the Christian Church, Modern Christianity, The German Reformation* (reprint, Grand Rapids: Eerdmans, 1967), 7:607.

worked under the banner of *reformatio* (reformation) while the latter had *restitutio* (restitution) as its banner. Both offer important insight.

The Magisterial Reformation

An examination of the reformations of Martin Luther (1483–1546) and John Calvin (1509–1564) reveals that they differed in degrees of progress toward the biblical pattern of church ministry. In the final analysis, both maintained a magisterial church-state system, believing that any reformation should ultimately result in a Christian state.[64] The two distinguished between the visible and the invisible church, viewing the invisible as the church made up of the elect only.[65] Their view of the visible church, created by a magisterial church-state, precluded a simple doctrine of church and ministry. The difference between the two men was that Luther tended to retain in the church the traditions not specifically condemned on Scripture, and Calvin tended to include only what Scripture taught explicitly about church ministry.[66] This difference is evident in the corresponding traditions of worship emerging from these founders: Lutheran worship being very embellished and incorporating ritual, and the Reformed mind-set reflecting more simple church settings.

According to general recognition, Martin Luther's doctrine of the church and ministry was complex and changed progressively throughout his life.[67] In his "Open Letter to the Christian Nobility of the German Nation" (1520), Luther called for the pulling down of the three walls of Romanism, and offered proposals including reform to establish a simple national church with parish priests of godly character.[68] The implementation of that church was more complex than Luther first envisioned,[69] but contained the key elements of the preaching of the Word, the sacraments of baptism and the

---

64. Williams, *Radical Reformation*, xxiv; cf. also, Timothy George, *Theology of the Reformers* (Nashville: Broadman, 1988), 98.

65. See R. L. Omanson, "The Church," *Evangelical Dictionary of Theology* (Grand Rapids: Baker, 1984), 231.

66. Williams notes this regulatory principle in *Radical Reformation*, xxvii. See also: Francois Wendel, Calvin (New York: Harper and Row, 1963), 301–2.

67. Gordon Rupp, *The Righteousness of God, Luther Studies* (London: Hodder, 1953), 310–28.

68. Martin Luther, "An Open Letter to the Christian Nobility of the German Nation Concerning the Reform of the Christian Estate," in *Three Treatises* (Philadelphia: Muhlenberg, 1947), 9–44, 47, 98.

69. George, *Theology*, 86–98.

altar, the keys of Christian discipline and forgiveness, a called and conse-crated ministry, public thanksgiving and worship, and suffering, i.e., the possession of the Holy Cross.[70] He stressed ministry of the Word as the duty of pastors and of all believers. In particular, the functions of pastors included the ministry of the Word, baptizing, administration of the sacred bread and wine, binding and loosing sin, and sacrifice.[71] He put great em-phasis on pastoral care, which always related directly to the ministry of the Word.[72]

Martin Bucer (1491–1551), an important disciple of Luther and a teacher of Calvin, had an important ministry in Strasbourg. Tidball rightly calls him the "Pastoral Theologian of the Reformation"[73] because of his extensive work in developing the office and work of the pastor. In his "*De Regno Christi,*" Bucer identified three duties of a pastor: (1) a diligent teacher of the Holy Scriptures, (2) an administrator of the sacraments, and (3) a partici-pator in the discipline of the church. The third duty had three parts: life and manners, penance (involving serious sin), and sacred ceremonies (worship and fasting). A fourth duty was care for the needy.[74] Bucer wrote,

> Those pastors and teachers of the churches who want to fulfill their office and keep themselves clean of the blood of those of their flocks who are perishing should not only publicly administer Christian doc-trine, but also announce, teach and entreat repentance toward God and faith in our Lord Jesus Christ, and whatever contributes toward piety, among all who do not reject this doctrine of salvation, even at home and with each one privately. . . . For the faithful ministers of Christ should imitate this their master and chief shepherd of the churches, and seek most lovely themselves whatever has been lost, in-cluding the hundredth sheep wandering from the fold, leaving behind the ninety-nine which remain in the Lord's fold (Matt 18:12).[75]

Calvin's contribution to a biblical understanding of pastoral ministry is

---

70. Rupp, *Righteousness of God*, 322.

71. Martin Luther, "Concerning the Ministry" (1523), in *Luther's Works, Church and Ministry*, ed. Conrad Bergendoff, gen. ed. Helmut T. Lehmann (Philadelphia: Fortress, 1958), 40:21–29.

72. Martin Luther, "Instructions for the Visitors of Parish Pastors in Electoral Saxony" (1528), in *Luther's Works, Church and Ministry*, 40:269–320.

73. Tidball, *Skillful Shepherds*, 184.

74. Martin Bucer, "*De Regno Christi,*" *Melanchthon and Bucer*, in *The Library of Chris-tian Classics*, ed. Wilhelm Pauck (London: SCM, 1969), 19:232–59.

75. Ibid., 235.

tremendous. Though often viewed as primarily a theologian and exegete, Calvin was also a pastor and churchman.[76] He devotes the fourth book of his *Institutes* to the church, speaking of the necessity of the church's function: "In order that the preaching of the Gospel might flourish, He deposited this treasure in the church. He instituted 'pastors and teachers' [Eph 4:11] through whose lips He might teach His own; he furnished them with authority; finally, He omitted nothing that might make for holy agreement of faith and for right order."[77]

He used the title "mother" to illustrate the importance and place of the church:

> For there is no other way to enter into life unless this mother conceive us in her womb, give us birth, nourish us at her breast, and lastly, unless she keep us under her care and guidance until, putting off mortal flesh, we become like the angels [Matt. 22:30]. Our weakness does not allow us to be dismissed from her school until we have been pupils all our lives.[78]

Calvin found the duties of a pastor throughout the Bible. Specifically, he observed that "the teaching and example of the New Testament set forth the nature and work of the pastorate in the calling and teaching of the apostles." This, he said, makes a delineation of ministerial work in the church an important aspect of theology.[79]

Previous writings have described the fourfold office of pastor, teacher, elder, and deacon in Calvin's Geneva.[80] Calvin placed strong emphasis on the preaching, governing, and pastoring: "A pastor needs two voices, one for gathering the sheep and the other for driving away wolves and thieves. The Scripture supplies him with the means for doing both."[81] Furthermore,

---

76. For an excellent development of this side of Calvin, see, W. Stanford Reid, "John Calvin, Pastoral Theologian," *The Reformed Theological Review* 42 (1982): 65–73. Cf. also Jim van Zyl, "John Calvin the Pastor," *The Way Ahead* (a paper read to the 1975 Carey Conference, Haywards Heath: Carey, 1975), 69–78.

77. John Calvin, *Institutes of the Christian Religion*, in *The Library of Christian Classics*, vols. 20–21, ed. John T. McNeill, trans. and index. Ford Lewis Battles (Philadelphia: Westminster, 1960), iv:1:1 (21:1011–12).

78. Ibid., iv:1:4 (21:1016).

79. Reid, "John Calvin," 65–66.

80. See George, *Theology*, 235–49; cf. also, John T. McNeill, *The History and Character of Calvinism* (New York: Oxford, 1954), 214–21; John Calvin, *Calvin's Ecclesiastical Advice*, trans. Mary Beaty and Benjamin W. Farley (Louisville: Westminster/John Knox, 1991).

81. John Calvin, *The Epistle of Paul to Titus*, in Calvin's *New Testament Commentaries*, ed. David W. Torrance (Grand Rapids: Eerdmans, 1964), 361.

"Paul assigns to teachers the duty of carving or dividing the Word, like a father dividing the bread into small pieces to feed his children."[82]

Calvin's concern was the profit and edification of the hearer. To this he added the important tasks of administration of the sacraments and visitation of the sick. This philosophy developed into a church polity in Geneva that was difficult and complex due to Calvin's understanding of the visible church and a Christian magistracy.[83] It resulted in a kind of Christian theocracy in Geneva because of the intersection of religious and civil authorities in implementing the polity.

The most biblical of the outworkings of Calvin's ecclesiastical and civil views did not emerge until much later, since Calvin never rose above the magisterial state-church he inherited from Romanism. Woolley observes, "Calvin was influenced by Rome even while helping to counteract Rome," and, "The greater fruitage of Calvin's ideas elsewhere than in Geneva is due to the fact that in other areas they were not subjected to implementation by the civil state to the same degree as was true in Geneva."[84] It was the issue of civil intolerance, brought about by the state-church such as existed at Geneva, that caused the Anabaptists to seek a more primitive and biblical church and ministry than what the Magisterial Reformers provided. This was an unfortunate flaw in the otherwise profound efforts of Calvin to purify, clarify, and systematize the truth of scriptural teaching regarding the ministry and other areas.

One cannot consider the Reformation period without describing the legacy of biblical ministry from John Knox (1514–1572). Following Calvin's lead, Knox developed a manual for the English-speaking church of Geneva, which he pastored from 1556 to 1559.[85] In addition, his letters and pastoral records reflect a rich understanding of commitment to preach the Word with great passion, deep interest, and care for the spiritual welfare of men.[86]

---

82. John Calvin, *The First and Second Epistles of Paul the Apostle to Timothy*, in *Calvin's New Testament Commentaries*, ed. Torrance, 314.

83. Note the excellent work of Harro Hopfl, *The Christian Polity of John Calvin* (Cambridge, England: Cambridge University Press, 1982).

84. Paul Woolley, "Calvin and Toleration," in *The Heritage of John Calvin* (Grand Rapids: Calvin College and Seminary, 1973), 138, 156.

85. John Knox, "The Form of Prayers and Ministration of the Sacraments, Used in the English Congregation at Geneva, 1556," in *The Works of John Knox*, ed. David Laing (Edinburgh: James Thin, 1895), 4:141–216.

86. W. Stanford Reid, "John Knox, Pastor of Souls," *Westminster Theological Journal* 40 (1977): 20–21.

The Anabaptist Reformation

Anabaptism draws heavily on the work and influence of Luther and Zwingli in its contribution to biblical understanding of the church and its ministry. As hinted above, within the larger number known as Anabaptists was a smaller group whose root of faith was the Scripture, constituting them as the "true Anabaptists."[87] This included men like Conrad Grebel (1495–1526), Michael Sattler (1490–1527), Balthasar Hubmaier (1480–1528), and Menno Simons (1496–1561). Though influenced by the theology of the magisterial reformers, these men went further in their efforts to reinstitute a primitive, biblical church and ministry. In describing the nature of their ecclesiology, Bender remarks, "The Anabaptist idea of the church is derivative, based on the deeper idea of discipleship, which of course also implies an active covenanting into a brotherhood, without which discipleship could not be realized."[88]

As a general rule, the Anabaptists rejected the idea of an invisible church, viewing the church as a voluntary association of regenerated saints. They sought to restore the idea of a primitive, New Testament church free from magisterial entanglements. This allowed the practice of church discipline, but meant that the church did not have a right to force its views on anyone or persecute those who opposed it. Friedmann identifies the following characteristics of the Anabaptist church:.[89]

1. a visible covenantal community of believers

2. a shared brotherhood practicing brotherly love

3. a commitment to exclusion (ban) as an act of brotherly love

4. a church of order where members submit to authority

5. a suffering church under the cross

6. a church practicing voluntarism or the liberty of conscience

7. a church practicing the two ordinances of baptism and the Lord's Supper

---

87. Note the classifications of Littell, *Sectarian Protestantism*, 163, and Williams, *Spiritual and Anabaptist Writers*, 28–31.

88. Harold S. Bender, "The Anabaptist Theology of Discipleship," *Mennonite Quarterly Review* 23 (1950): 26; see also Bender, *The Anabaptist Vision* (Scottdale, Pa.: Herald, 1944).

89. Robert Friedmann, *The Theology of Anabaptism* (Scottdale, Pa.: Herald, 1973), 122–43.

Within this primitive church structure, Anabaptism taught a simple ministry style. Michael Sattler described this ministry as follows:

> This office [of Pastor] shall be to read, to admonish and teach, to warn, to discipline, to ban in the church, to lead out in prayer for the advancement of all the brethren and sisters, to lift up the bread when it is broken, and in all things to see to the care of the body of Christ, in order that it may be built up and developed, and the mouth of the slanderer be stopped.[90]

Conrad Grebel held a similar position in his brief but important work,[91] as did Balthasar Hubmaier, the scholar and pastor of Waldshut and Nikolsburg, in his major contribution.[92] The "Discipline of the Church," an Anabaptist document from 1528, summarizes their position: "The elders and preachers chosen for the brotherhood shall with zeal look after the needs of the poor, and with zeal in the Lord according to the command of the Lord extend what is needed for the sake of and instead of the brotherhood (Gal. 2; II Cor. 8, 9; Rom. 15; Acts 6)."[93] Timothy George reports that Menno Simons[94] said on his deathbed that nothing on earth was as precious to him as the church.[95] This well summarizes the Anabaptist commitment to the primitive church and its ministry. Many paid the ultimate price for this love.[96]

---

90. "The Schleitheim Confession, 1527," in William Lumpkin, *Baptist Confessions of Faith* (Valley Forge, Pa.: Judson, 1969), 22–30.

91. Harold S. Bender, *Conrad Grebel c. 1498–1526* (Goshen, Ind.: Mennonite Historical Society, 1950), 204–8.

92. *Balthasar Hubmaier, Theologian of Anabaptism*, trans. and ed. H. Wayne Pipkin and John H. Yoder (Scottdale, Pa.: Herald, 1989), 386–425. A careful study of these writings reveals his deep commitment to sound preaching as well as strong pastoral commitment.

93. "Discipline of the Church: How a Christian Ought to Live (October, 1527)," in *Anabaptist Beginnings (1523–1533)*, ed. William R. Estep (Nieuwkoop, Netherlands: De Graaf, 1976), 128.

94. In a letter to Gellius Faber on the church and its ministry, Simons offers the following signs of the church: (1) the unadulterated doctrine of the divine Word, (2) the scriptural use of the sacraments, (3) the obedience to the Word of God, (4) the unfeigned love of one's neighbor, (5) the confident confession of Christ, and (6) the bearing of Christ's testimony in persecution (Menno Simons, "Reply to Gellius Faber," *The Complete Writings of Menno Simons* [Scottdale, Pa.: Herald Press, 1956], 739–41).

95. George, *Theology*, 285.

96. William R. Estep (*The Anabaptist Story* [Nashville: Broadman, 1963]) gives a fair account of many Anabaptists persecutions.

The above discussion reveals that the Reformation era refocused the church on a biblical structure for the ministry. The Magisterial Reformers made significant progress in their reformation of the church. Among the Radical Reformers are those who carried through this commitment in seeking to reinstitute a consistent biblical ministry.

THE MODERN PERIOD (1649–PRESENT)

The modern era has many examples of those who have sought a biblical church ministry. Some of them have drawn on the heritage of progress toward a biblical ministry by the Magisterial Reformers. The survey of this chapter can cite only a few outstanding examples of biblical ministry.

One such pastor was Richard Baxter (1615–1691), the early Puritan divine. He is best known for the book *The Reformed Pastor*, which he wrote in 1656 during a nineteen-year pastorate in Kidderminister, England. The book concentrates on Acts 20:28 in developing his philosophy of ministry. He deals with the pastor's labors, confessions, motives, constraints, and dedication. The work is profoundly deep and intensely spiritual as it flows from the heart of a humble pastor to other pastors: "I do now, in the behalf of Christ, and for the sake of his Church and the immortal souls of men, beseech all the faithful ministers of Christ, that they will presently and effectually fall upon this work. . . . This duty hath its rise neither from us, but from the Lord, and for my part . . . tread me in the dirt."[97]

The larger Puritan movement advanced the church through its clear focus on the Word of God. Though never becoming a distinct and unified denomination, the Puritans nevertheless exerted considerable influence on many others. Anglicanism labeled most English Puritans nonconformists, yet the British Puritans were unable to establish their own churches as American Puritans were able to. Even in America, though, they identified with various denominations rather than forming their own church. Leland Ryken concludes, "There was, to be sure, a theoretical Puritan consensus on most issues involving worship and the theory of what a church is. Puritanism also bequeathed at least one permanent legacy, the phenomenon of a 'gathered church' separate from the state and with an accompanying proliferation of independent churches."[98]

---

97. Richard Baxter, *The Reformed Pastor* (London: Epworth, 1939), 58.

98. Leland Ryken, *Worldly Saints, The Puritans As They Really Were* (Grand Rapids: Zondervan, 1986), 112.

Ryken identifies several important aspects of the Puritan concept of the church:[99]

1.   Calling the extravagance and elaborate tradition in the church an inadequate authority for religious belief, Puritans reasserted the primacy of the Word, resorting to the "strongest control at their disposal, the Bible. They vowed to limit all church polity and worship practices to what could be directly based on statements or procedures found in the Bible."

2.   Puritans viewed the church as a "spiritual reality." "It is not impressive buildings or fancy clerical vestments. It is instead the company of the redeemed," dissociated from any particular place. Certain activities and relationships—including preaching, sacraments, discipline, and prayer—define the church.

3.   The Puritans elevated the lay person's role in the church and participation in worship. Many Puritans gravitated toward either Presbyterian or Congregational polity, which provided for lay responsibility within each congregation in choosing ministers.

4.   The Puritans embraced simplicity in various parts of worship. These included orderly and clear organization, curbed ceremony and ritual, simplified church architecture and furnishings, simplified church music, simplification of the sacraments, and a clearly defined goal of worship.

In this very biblical church setting, the teaching and practice of true ministry was commonplace. The Puritan pastor was to preach, to minister the sacraments, and to pray. Preaching was primary, but closely associated was a godly life.[100] In his "Of the Calling of the Ministry," William Perkins (1558–1602) describes the minister as first, an *angel* or "Messenger of God"— that is, the "Messenger of the Lord of Hosts" to the people. He is, second, an *interpreter*—that is, "one who is able to deliver aright the reconciliation, made betwixt God and man." "Every minister is a double Interpreter, God's to the people and the people's to God."[101] To this he adds the necessity of

---

99.   Ibid., 112–13, 115–16, 119, 121–24.

100.   Puritans associated theology with spirituality. See J. I. Packer, *A Quest for Godliness, the Puritan Vision of the Christian Life* (Wheaton: Crossway, 1990), 11–17.

101.   William Perkins, *The Workes of That Famous and Worthie Minister of Christ in the Universitie of Cambridge, M. W. Perkins*, 3 vols. (Cambridge, England: Universitie of Cambridge, 1608–1609), 3:430–31.

being a "godly minister," and urges men to dedicate their sons to this, the highest office:

> For the Physician's care for the body, or the Lawyer's care for the cause, are both inferior duties to this of the Minister. A good Lawyer may be one of ten, a good Physician one of twenty, a good man one of 100, but a good Minister is one of 1000. A good Lawyer may declare the true state of thy cause, a Physician may declare the true state of the body: No calling, no man can declare unto thee thy righteousness, but a true minister.[102]

This same pastoral perspective of Perkins characterized many future Puritans after him. "The great names of the Puritan era, John Owen, Thomas Brooks, Richard Sibbes, Robert Bolton, Thomas Manton, Thomas Goodwin and William Gurnal, all adopted this pastoral perspective in their writing of theology."[103] The colorful ministry of William Tennent and his Log College in Neshaminy, Pennsylvania, is also worthy of note.[104]

Jonathan Edwards (1703–1758), known so well as a profound philosopher and theologian, was also a pastor. He wrote,

> More especially is the uniting of a faithful minister with a particular Christian people as their pastor, when done in a due manner, like a young man marrying a virgin. . . . The minister joyfully devoting himself to the service of his Lord in the work of the ministry, as a work that he delights in, and also joyfully uniting himself to the society of the saints that he is set over . . . and they, on the other hand, joyfully receiving him as a precious gift of their ascended Redeemer.[105]

Westra states that Edwards knew that his biblical name, Jonathan, meant "Jehovah's gift" and "prayerfully dedicated himself to being 'Jehovah's gift' to the souls of his care; he did so wholeheartedly convinced that a faithful minister as a means of grace can be 'the greatest blessing of anything in

---

102. Ibid., 435–36.

103. Tidball, *Skillful Shepherds*, 200. See also P. Lewis, *The Genius of Puritanism* (Haywards Heath: Carey, 1975).

104. See Archibald Alexander, *The Log College* (reprint, London: Banner of Truth, 1968); Archibald Alexander, comp., *Sermons of the Log College* (reprint, Ligonier, Pa.: Soli Deo Gloria, n.d.).

105. Jonathan Edwards, *The Works of Jonathan Edwards*, 2 vols. (reprint, Edinburgh, England: Banner of Truth, 1974), 2:19–20.

the world that ever God bestows on a people.' "[106] One needs only to read the Puritans to see that they provide some of the finest pastoral theology of the modern period.

After the Puritan era, Charles Bridges (1794–1869), a pastor in England for fifty-two years, wrote his respected *The Christian Ministry*. He combined a deep and accurate knowledge of Scripture with great spirituality and humility to produce a classic work worthy of careful reading. In a word, he felt that the "sum of our whole labor in this kind is to honor God, and to save men."[107]

Charles Spurgeon (1834–1892), primarily known for his preaching rather than his daily functions in the pastorate, taught his students the principles of preaching;[108] nevertheless, he viewed the ministry as centered around serving the spiritual needs of his people. He wrote, "Ministers are for churches, and not churches for ministers."[109] Significantly, the controversies surrounding Spurgeon's ministry have everything to do with the application of his theology to pastoral duties, such as to evangelism in particular or philosophy of ministry in general.[110]

Nineteenth-century pastors, including G. Campbell Morgan (1863–1945)[111] and missionary Roland Allen (1868–1947), provided other important examples of faithful ministry.[112] The long teaching ministry of Benjamin B. Warfield (1851–1921) at Princeton Theological Seminary (1887–1921) was a great positive influence in promoting biblical ministry.[113]

---

106. Helen Westra, "Jonathan Edwards and the Scope of Gospel Ministry," *Calvin Theological Journal* 22 (1987): 68; cf. also Edwards, *Works*, 2:960.

107. Charles Bridges, *The Christian Ministry* (reprint, London: Banner of Truth, 1959), 8.

108. C. H. Spurgeon, *Lectures to My Students* (reprint, Grand Rapids: Zondervan, 1954).

109. C. H. Spurgeon, *The All Around Ministry* (reprint, Edinburgh: Banner of Truth, 1960), 256.

110. Iain H. Murray, *The Forgotten Spurgeon* (Edinburgh: Banner of Truth, 1966), 45–46, 99–101, 153–65.

111. G. Campbell Morgan, *The Ministry of the Word* (London: Hodder and Stoughton, 1919), and Jill Morgan, *A Man of the Word, Life of G. Campbell Morgan* (New York: Revell, 1951).

112. He is especially known for his works on indigenization of missions, see Roland Allen, *The Spontaneous Expansion of the Church* (London: World Dominion, 1960).

113. Benjamin B. Warfield, "The Indispensableness of Systematic Theology to the Preacher," in *Selected Shorter Writings of Benjamin B. Warfield—II*, ed. John E. Meeter (Nutley, N.J.: Presbyterian and Reformed, 1973), 280–88. He writes, "Systematic Theology is, in other words, the preacher's true text-book" (228).

Since the twentieth century began, theological liberalism has found its way into every major denomination and replaced the passion for biblical ministry in many instances with an agenda of the social gospel.[114] The rise of New Evangelicalism[115] in 1958, with it intentional accommodation of error, along with its subsequent tributaries[116] into pragmatic ministry, was another step away from biblical ministry.[117] Much true biblical ministry in recent years occurs in smaller denominations or churches that have continued the Free Church tradition.[118] The nature of such ministry is obscure and often difficult to identify because of a lack of adequate documentation.

During the last half of the twentieth century, several prominent examples of biblical ministry are worthy of note. The unusual way God has used these men is the reason for citing them. It is not that they have been the only ones.

One prime example is D. Martyn Lloyd-Jones (1939–1981). Lloyd-Jones was well respected as an expository preacher, but he was also a devoted and faithful pastor. His biography is full of examples of both preaching and shepherding.[119] He was first a preacher, advocating the irreplaceability of biblical preaching, a right relationship with the congregation (the pew is never to dictate the message, but the preacher must listen to his people), and an adequate preparation of the preacher in all areas.[120] He also had a reputation as a pastoral counselor. Murray records, "Next to the pulpit,

---

114. See B. J. Longfield, "Liberalism/Modernism, Protestant (c. 1870s–1930s)," in *Dictionary of Christianity in America*, ed. Daniel G. Reid (Downers Grove, Ill.: InterVarsity Press, 1990), 646–48.

115. Edward John Carnell, *The Case for Orthodox Theology* (Philadelphia: Westminster, 1959), and Roland Nash, *The New Evangelicalism* (Grand Rapids: Zondervan, 1963), 13–17.

116. See Richard Quebedeaux, *The Young Evangelicals, Revolution in Orthodoxy* (New York: Harper and Row, 1973), and Quebedeaux, *The Worldly Evangelicals* (New York: Harper and Row, 1977).

117. See John MacArthur, Jr., *Ashamed of the Gospel: When the Church Becomes Like the World* (Wheaton: Crossway, 1993). See also MacArthur, *Our Sufficiency in Christ* (Dallas: Word, 1991).

118. See Ernest A. Payne, *Free Churchmen, Unrepentant and Repentant* (London: Carey, 1965).

119. Iain H. Murray, *David Martyn Lloyd-Jones, The First Forty Years, 1899–1939* (Edinburgh: Banner of Truth, 1982), and Murray, *David Martyn Lloyd-Jones, The Fight of Faith, 1939–1981* (Edinburgh: Banner of Truth, 1990).

120. D. Martyn Lloyd-Jones, *Preaching and Preachers* (Grand Rapids: Zondervan, 1971), 26, 143, 165.

Dr. Lloyd-Jones throughout his ministry was constantly engaged in seeking to help individuals." Interestingly, he viewed people as in need of spiritual rather than psychological help. Lloyd-Jones was also a pastor to pastors as he sought to instill in them what God had taught him.[121]

Another example of biblical ministry is that of Jay Adams, longtime professor at Westminster Theological Seminary and often a pastor. Adams has contributed greatly to current understanding of biblical ministry in several areas. In each case he has built his understanding of pastoral theology firmly on his biblical and exegetical theology. His first major focus was counseling, where he developed a biblical model of nouthetic counseling (note the Greek word *noutheteo*), and emphasizing the need to confront sin with biblical teaching.[122] He has also developed a series of textbooks on pastoral theology, covering pastoral life, pastoral counseling, and pastoral leadership. The foundation of all these is his firm commitment to sound biblical theology. He has written, "The directions that one's practical activities take, the norms by which he operates and the motivation behind what he does must emerge from a biblical theological study of the Scriptures. The pursuit of Practical Theology, therefore, must be seen as the study and application of the biblical means of expressing one's theology."[123]

In recent years, Adams has devoted his thinking to biblical preaching and its importance in ministry.[124] All his teachings have had a profound effect in redirecting ministry toward the biblical pattern.

Another important example of biblical ministry is John MacArthur, Jr. MacArthur defines the term *shepherdology* as (1) the study of shepherding, (2) the science of leading a flock, (3) a method of biblical church leadership. He develops this term by understanding all ministry to flow from the teaching of Scripture.[125] His essay, "The Anatomy of the Church" represents a significant contribution to a biblical philosophy of ministry in defining the church as (1) the skeletal structure—unalterable doctrines or nonnegotiable

---

121. Ibid., 697–713.

122. Jay Adams, *Competent to Counsel* (Grand Rapids: Baker, 1970), 41–50. Behind this approach is a solid theological foundation, xi–xxii. Adams also draws from the presuppositional apologetics of Cornelius Van Til, *The Defence of the Faith* (Philadelphia: Presbyterian and Reformed, 1955).

123. Jay Adams, *Shepherding God's Flock* (Grand Rapids: Zondervan, 1986), 1–2.

124. Jay Adams, *Preaching with Purpose* (Grand Rapids: Zondervan, 1982), xiii, 114.

125. John MacArthur, Jr., *Shepherdology: A Master Plan for Church Leadership* (Panorama City, Calif.: The Master's Fellowship, 1989), 3–5, rev. ed., *The Master's Plan for the Church* (Chicago: Moody, 1991).

truths; (2) the internal systems—proper spiritual attitudes; (3) the muscles—spiritual activities, which include preaching and teaching, worship, discipleship, shepherding, and fellowship; and (4) the head—the person and work of Christ.[126] This model has become the basis for biblical ministry in many churches. MacArthur is continuing to contribute significant works challenging the church not to drift away from the truth. The most significant of these compares the Down-Grade Controversy of Spurgeon's day to the pragmatism of many contemporary evangelical churches.[127]

John MacArthur's contribution is most valuable because he is a committed expositor, a theologian, and a pastor. He is one who has chosen to write and address significant issues in a way that the entire church can understand. In the tradition of Charles Spurgeon, God has used him to build a significant church with a widely published preaching ministry, to start schools for the training of a future generation of servants and preachers, and to author significant works dealing with important theological issues faced in his day.

A FINAL THOUGHT

This is but a brief history of biblical, pastoral ministry. Such accounts are often based on those ministries whose record remains for future generations to examine. There are many faithful ministers who have also sought a biblical ministry and whose accomplishments only heaven has recorded. The future examination of each man's ministry (1 Cor. 3:13–15) and the recounting of faithful ministry for God's glory will be a time of great rejoicing in heaven. Today's pastors can find great encouragement and receive great challenges by examining the lives and convictions of faithful ministers of the past. May this and future generations of Christ's servants commit themselves to the purest form of primitive, biblical ministry so that when history records their efforts, they may say with Paul, "I *have* fought the good fight, I *have* finished the course, I *have* kept the faith" (2 Tim. 4:7, emphasis added).

---

126. Ibid., 9–64.

127. MacArthur, *Ashamed of the Gospel*, xi–xx. See also MacArthur, *Our Sufficiency in Christ*, 25–43.

4

Approaching Pastoral Ministry Scripturally

Alex D. Montoya

The sensible approach to pastoral ministry is to formulate a biblical phi-losophy or a statement of purpose for that ministry. This philosophy is dependent on the biblical purposes of the church, which are exalting the Lord, evangelizing the world, and edifying the church's members. The pastor plays the leading role in helping the church implement these purposes. Eph. 4:7-16 and Col. 1:28-29 provide good guidelines for accomplishing these goals in a local church. The seven ministries through which the pastor can see these purposes realized in the church he leads are the ministry of the Word, the ministry of fellowship, the ministry of the Lord's Supper, the ministry of prayer, the ministry of outreach, the ministry of missions, and the ministry of interchurch fellowship.

Pastoral ministry is a unique divine calling bestowed upon God's elect ministers of His Word and servants of His church. Men called to such a work feel both unworthy (1 Tim. 1:12–17) and unqualified (2 Cor. 3:4–6) for such a precious task. Yet to those set aside for this ministry, the claim of the apostle Paul applies: "We have this treasure in earthen vessels, that the sur-passing greatness of the power may be of God and not from ourselves" (2 Cor. 4:7).

The sinfulness of man and the schemes of the evil one complicate the task of pastoral ministry, but our own ignorance of the basic purposes of the ministry add to the confusion. All too often no awareness exists regarding what the minister is to do in his calling. Such ignorance can lead him to embark on erroneous and dangerous courses.

An understanding of the biblical philosophy of pastoral ministry can serve as a means of helping the minister enter into his vocation properly and in addition can facilitate the proper execution of that vocation. This chapter will deal with two basic tenets: first, the definition and benefits of a basic biblical philosophy of ministry, and second, biblical discussions on the purposes of the church, in the execution of which it is the pastor's function to lead. Some may wonder why we have a discussion of the purposes of the church in connection with a pastor's philosophy of ministry. The answer is in the question, how can a pastor minister effectively if he cannot identify, clarify, simplify, and execute the purposes of the church he leads? He will be serving in a fog unless he fully understands the importance of biblical purposes.

A BIBLICAL PHILOSOPHY OF MINISTRY

Every profession needs a mission statement that answers the questions: "Why am I in this role?" "What am I supposed to be doing?" and, "How am I to accomplish this task?" Like one on a journey, a pastor needs to know where he is going. The formulation of a statement of purpose is another way of referring to a philosophy of ministry. For the pastor, a philosophy of ministry must come from the mandates addressed to Christ's church.

We need to stress here the importance that every pastor know and own the biblical philosophy of pastoral ministry. No variety in philosophies of ministry exists. There is only one! It comes from the Scriptures and applies to all pastors.

Some today endeavor to have churches adopt a particular purpose, such as "a church for the families," "a church for the poor," etc. These may be proper, but they must be part of a larger context of the overall purpose of the church. As we shall see, the church has a purpose, and every minister is called into service to help accomplish this purpose. We dare not enter His service with our preconceived ideas or our personal agenda or a new theory on church ministry. As God said to Moses, so He says to us: "See . . . that you make all things according to the pattern which was shown you on the mountain" (Heb. 8:5).

Definition

What then is a philosophy of ministry? As already noted, it is a statement of purpose. It spells out exactly what we are to accomplish in ministry. It identifies the reason for the existence of the church and, thus, the reason for the existence of Christian ministry. The ministry does not exist independent of the church but rather as the means for fulfilling the purpose of the church. Paul reminds Timothy of this when he writes, "I am writing these things to you, hoping to come to you before long; but in case I am delayed, I write so that you may know how one ought to conduct himself in the household of God, which is the church of the living God, the pillar and support of the truth" (1 Tim. 3:14–15). He tells Timothy his role in the purpose of the church.

For this reason, a pastor's philosophy of ministry becomes a guide for his personal ministry. Once established and understood, it will guide the pastor's ministry accordingly. It becomes the map to keep him on track, a guide for his course of action—to correct him when blown astray by the hazards of ministry—and an encouragement to his life when the weight of the task burdens and almost overcomes him.

Benefits

Many benefits accrue from having a biblical philosophy of ministry. Five are worthy of emphasis. First, *it forces us to be biblical*. When we look to the Scriptures themselves for our reasons for ministering, it keeps us on a biblical track. The church drifts from its biblical foundation when its leaders abandon the biblical course. Ministers can apostatize by degrees, hardly noticing the slippage. They need constant reminders of the grave responsibility to keep the church firmly rooted and grounded upon the Word. The biblical writers and founding apostles have made clear the divine instructions as to the church's pattern, purposes, and practices. Even its power is to be from God. Hence we read of traditions (1 Cor. 11:2; 2 Thess. 2:15; 3:6) and practice(s) (1 Cor. 11:16). The earliest churches of God held the same philosophy of ministry (1 Cor. 14:33, 40). Any attempt to abandon that philosophy was a sign of apostasy, either in doctrine or in practice (2 Thess. 3:6; 3 John 9).

A biblical philosophy of ministry includes the means as well as the goals. A shallow and flippant understanding of the divine purposes for the church will lead to pragmatic, carnal, and even sinful approaches to the accomplishment of these ends. The winds of social change, the currents of liberal theology, and the influence of carnal stowaways will surely take the ship off course unless its captain stays faithful to the divine course.

A second advantage to a philosophy of ministry is that *it makes practical sense*. We must have a definite goal; there must be an aim to what we do. Paul said it best: "Therefore I run in such a way, as not without aim"

(1 Cor. 9:26). He would not spend his life shadow-boxing (1 Cor. 9:26). Ministerial burn out usually lies at the feet of a lack of direction.

Efficiency is a third reason for a philosophy of ministry. Knowing his course of action will allow the pastor to concentrate his resources on accomplishing those aspects of ministry that are most essential. Too often, issues, programs, and efforts that have little or nothing to do with the church's overall purpose consume the pastor's resources as well as the church's. The temptation to waste its apostolic energies on social issues came to the early church but was averted through the wisdom of church leaders (Acts 6:1–7).

Fourth, the most obvious result of efficiency is *effectiveness*. He who aims at nothing hits it every time. A clearly delineated battle plan, architectural blueprint, or work detail ensures success. Ministers laboring under the hit-and-miss philosophy will have little to show after a lifetime of faithful service. Even those with meager personal resources and on difficult ground will have something to show for their labors if they toil under the guidance of a divine blueprint. This undoubtedly was the secret to the church's success in the first century. The church knew what it had to do and went about doing it. In a short while the church had gained a reputation of upsetting the world (Acts 17:6).

The fifth benefit of holding to a biblical philosophy of ministry applies to a minister's *personal call to be faithful* (1 Cor. 4:2). We must one day give an account to the Lord for the ministry entrusted to us. How can we stand before Him and plead ignorance and ask for pardon for a blundering ministry? How can we claim a reward when we have not followed the charted course? Faithfulness includes the wise execution of our work. Men do not reward failure, no matter how much effort goes into it. Neither does God. Only those like Paul achieve the prize (Acts 20:24, 27; 1 Cor. 9:24; 2 Tim. 4:7).

Using another framework, Johnson has summarized eight advantages for having a philosophy of ministry.[1] He said that a church that can articulate its philosophical foundations:

1. can determine the scope of its ministry

2. can continuously reevaluate its corporate experience in the light of its message

3. can evaluate its ministry in the light of thoughtful criteria rather than on the basis of a program's popularity

---

1. Rex Johnson, "Philosophical Foundations of Ministry," in *Foundations of Ministry*, ed. Michael J. Anthony (Wheaton: Victor, 1992), 55–59.

4. is more likely to keep its ministry balanced and focused on essentials

5. can mobilize a greater proportion of its congregation as ministers

6. can determine the relative merits of a prospective ministry

7. can be a clear, attractive alternative community to people seeking relief from systematic failure

8. can choose to cooperate or not cooperate with other churches and parachurch ministries.

The Purpose of the Church

The biblical philosophy of ministry must be rooted in biblical ecclesiology. To understand one's role as a minister, one needs to understand the role of the church. Getz puts it this way:

> Anyone who attempts to formulate a biblical philosophy of the ministry and develop a contemporary strategy, a methodology that stands foursquare on the scriptural foundations, must ask and answer a very fundamental question. Why does the church exist? Put in another way, what is its ultimate purpose? Why has God left it in the world in the first place?[2]

Upon discovering the answers to these questions, the minister can then answer the question, "What is *my* purpose in the overall purpose of the church?"

Prior to His death, our Lord predicted the establishment of His church, which would be victorious over all foes (Matt. 16:18) and would consist of all believers becoming His body (Eph. 1:22–23). The church replaces Israel as God's people in the present dispensation and becomes a community of believers, redeemed by Christ's precious blood, with a threefold function. The church is a *worshiping* community, a *witnessing* community, and a *working* community. In other words, the church is to *exalt* the Lord, it is to *evangelize* the world, and it is to *edify* its members. Everything the New Testament commands the church to do falls under these headings. Only an understanding of these functions can enable an individual believer to fill his or her role in the body of Christ. Only as the minister comprehends the mission of Christ's church can he properly serve

---

2. Gene Getz, *Sharpening the Focus of the Church* (Chicago: Moody, 1974), 21.

his Lord and execute the pastoral ministry. We shall examine these three purposes in further detail.

A Worshiping Community

The ultimate purpose of mankind is to worship God and to enjoy His creation. The greatest commandment is to love God with your total being and then to love your neighbor as you love yourself (Matt. 22:36–40). The church's foremost calling is to exalt the Lord, to magnify His character, and to glorify Him before all creation. Saucy states, "Worship is central in the existence of the church. The words of the apostle Paul that God has chosen and predestined sons unto Himself in Christ 'to the praise of the glory of His grace' (Eph. 1:4–6) suggests that the ultimate purpose of the church is the worship of the one who called it into being."[3]

Hence we understand the words of Peter as identifying the express purpose of Christ's church to be the exaltation of God through word and deed:

> You also, as living stones, are being built up as a spiritual house for a holy priesthood, to offer up spiritual sacrifices acceptable to God through Jesus Christ. But you are a chosen race, a royal priesthood, a holy nation, a people for God's own possession; that you may proclaim the excellencies of Him who has called you out of darkness into His marvelous light (1 Pet. 2:4, 9).

The church is a redeemed community of sinners set apart to worship God in Christ. The minister is himself a worshiper of God. He must worship and then assist the community in the worship.

What is worship? "Worship is the honor and adoration directed to God," says MacArthur.[4] Martin says, "Worship is the dramatic celebration of God in His supreme worth in such a manner that his 'worthiness' becomes the norm and inspiration of human living."[5] Hence, "to worship God is thus to ascribe Him the supreme worth to which He alone is worthy." We are worshiping God when we give ourselves "completely to God in the actions and attitudes of life." [6]

3. Robert L. Saucy, *The Church in God's Program* (Chicago: Moody, 1972), 166.

4. John MacArthur, Jr., *The Ultimate Priority* (Chicago: Moody, 1983), 14.

5. Ralph R. Martin, *The Worship of God* (Chicago: Moody, 1982), 4.

6. Saucy, *The Church*, 166.

The New Testament minister must see the clear distinction between worship patterns of Israel and those of the church. A dramatic change transpires between the delineated pattern of worship in Israel and that in the new order in which God is worshiped "in spirit and in truth" (John 4:24). The church has no prescribed format, no temple or holy place, no sacrificial system, and no priesthood. Any attempt to institute any of these old features into the church faces the danger of trying to turn the church back into Israel.

The church is spiritually a temple in that it is the habitation of God and is called a "spiritual house" (1 Cor. 3:16; 1 Pet. 2:5). The church does not contain a priesthood but rather *is* a priesthood, which in turn offers up spiritual sacrifices to God (Rom. 12:1–2; 1 Pet. 2:5; Rev. 1:6). The New Testament writers, though employing similar terminology in describing the worshiping function of the church, were careful not to impose upon the church the "old wine" that was intended for the "old wine skins."

The absence of a prescribed order introduces some unique and particular ways in which the church offers worship to God. These spiritual sacrifices become the Christian's ministry to the Lord. The New Testament speaks of these sacrifices, often employing sacrificial terminology, but with an obvious distinction from the Old Testament system implied. The Christian is to be involved in the ministry of the gospel (Acts 6:5; Rom. 15:16; 2 Tim. 4:6), the ministry of holy living (Rom. 12:1–2; 1 Pet. 1:12–16), the ministry of prayer (Acts 6:6; 13:2–3; 1 Tim. 5:5; Rev. 4:8, 10–11), the ministry of serving others (Rom. 12:1–8; Phil. 2:17, 30; Heb. 13:16), the ministry of gratitude (Eph. 5:19–20; Col. 3:16–17; Heb. 12:28; 13:15), and the ministry of giving (Rom. 15:27; 2 Cor. 9:12; Phil. 2:4.; 4:18; Heb. 13:16).

A casual glance at these aspects of New Testament worship reinforces what has been true since the beginning of time—that all of life is to be an act of worship. Moule offers this distinct summary: "All Christian life is worship, 'liturgy' means service, all believers share Christ's priesthood, and the whole Christian church is the house of God (1 Cor. 3:16; Eph. 2:22)."[7]

The New Testament presents but a sketchy picture of any particular type of the actual corporate worship experience in the early church. Here and there, we have a brief glimpse at the meetings of New Testament believers. We know they were "continually devoting themselves to the apostles' teaching and to fellowship, to the breaking of bread and to prayer" (Acts 2:42). They came together for seasons of prayer (Acts 4:31; 12:5). The best

---

7. C. F. D. Moule, *Worship in the New Testament* (London: Lutherworth, 1961), 85.

glimpse of a church service is in Paul's correction of the Corinthian catastrophe over the use of tongues (1 Cor. 12–14). Believers obviously met to exalt God both in prayers and prophecies, as well as in singing (see 1 Cor. 14:26). The intent of all was the worship of God (14:16, 25) and with the purpose that all be edified (14:26).

The function of the pastor is to lead the church in the attainment of this grand design, the worship of God. Obviously, the minister himself must be a true worshiper of God. He must practice in a personal and authentic way the worship of God. Then he must assist the congregation in the worship of God by helping them to understand the New Testament aspects of worship for the believer and to lead in the corporate worship of God during the various gatherings of the Christian community. He must teach the church to worship, lead them in worship, and join them in worship.

A Witnessing Community

It is not unusual to view the second and third grand purposes of the church as extensions of the first. Witnessing and ministering to one another are in a sense individual acts of worship. Hence two more ways to worship God are to win lost people and to help God's people. At times "only a few things are necessary, really only one" (Luke 10:42), the simple worship of God! Yet we have chosen for the sake of simplicity and development to keep the next two purposes distinct from the first.

The second grand purpose of the church is to evangelize a lost world. The church is to be a community witnessing to the saving grace of Christ. The Gospels are unanimous regarding the Great Commission given to the church by Christ (Matt. 28:18–20; Mark 16:15–16; Luke 24:46–47; John 17:18). The book of Acts not only concurs with this commission (1:8) but records the church's obedience to the Great Commission, from Jerusalem to the remotest part of the earth.

Evangelism is not an option to be accepted or rejected by the church. Outreach is a command. Evangelism is not limited to the gifted or to the church leadership. It is the mission of the entire church. To the truly faithful, evangelism is not merely a command but a compulsion (Acts 5:42; Rom. 1:14–17; 1 Cor. 9:16–18). Evangelism is the heart and soul of the New Testament church. The mandate is clear "that repentance for forgiveness of sins should be proclaimed in His name to all the nations, beginning from Jerusalem" (Luke 24:47–48).

Carrying out this purpose follows two approaches in Acts. The first is contact with the lost in the immediate surroundings, whether it be the person next to us (Acts 2), the house next door (Acts 5:42), the next town (Acts 8:5), or people of a different ethnic makeup (Acts 10). The early church did not understand the Great Commission as a mandate to do specialty evangelism. There was but one church composed of all peoples (see Rev. 7:9).

The second approach was to reach out to those in the regions beyond (cf. Rom. 15:18–29), which involved commissioning special men with the mission of taking the gospel to the remotest parts of the earth (Acts 13:1–3). The church was not negligent in obeying the Lord's command, either in soul winning or in planting churches in other communities.

The purpose of the church has not changed today. The Great Commission still stands. Modern technology has not annulled it. Pressing social needs have not abrogated it. Spiritual problems in the church have not surpassed its importance. Neither Christ nor Paul would stay longer than necessary in one particular place. They moved on so that others might hear the gospel.

In our biblical approach to pastoral ministry, the pastor must see his role in leading the congregation in fulfilling the Great Commission. The minister is by Christ's design himself a missionary. His church is to be a missionary church to those across the street or around the world. He is to be a world-class leader. He must have a vision beyond the pews in his facility. He should lead the way in praying for new fields, praying for God to thrust out laborers (Matt. 9:37–38), praying over the selection of missionaries (Acts 13:1–3), and supporting missionaries and the evangelistic enterprise. If he is a faithful minister, he can do no less and he dare not do otherwise.

A Working Community

The third purpose of the church is to build itself up through the interworking of various members of the Body of Christ. The function of the Christian is to edify or spiritually build up fellow members in the Body of Christ. Getz states, "The church is to become a mature organization through the process of edification so that it will honor and glorify God."[8]

The New Testament contains a number of references to this vital but neglected purpose of the church (Matt. 28:18–20; Acts 20:17–35; Rom. 12:1–8; 1 Cor. 12–14; Eph. 4:7–16; Col. 1:24–29; 1 Pet. 4:10–11). A summary of these texts is that God expects the church, which is a living organism, to grow spiritually in Christlikeness and that God has given every believer a unique

---

8. Getz, *Sharpening the Focus*, 53

spiritual gift that is intended not for self-growth but to enhance the spiritual development of fellow Christians. The role of the pastor, himself gifted for his task, is to help believers discover and utilize their gifts for the growth of the Body of Christ. A mature church can thus remain united, firm in its devotion to Christ, functioning according to the purpose of God, and able to stand against the attacks of Satan.

Paul understood his pastoral ministry well, as he states in Col. 1:28–29: "And we proclaim Him, admonishing every man and teaching every man with all wisdom, that we may present every man complete in Christ. And for this purpose also I labor, striving according to His power, which mightily works with me." This passage serves well in pointing out the express purpose of a Christian minister. Consider these observations from this text:

1.　*The purpose*—"That we may present every man complete in Christ." Paul makes clear that the purpose of every pastor is not to fill the auditorium with people, nor is it to preach wonderful sermons or entertain a congregation or collect a salary. The minister's task is to help every believer become Christlike, to prepare every child of God for meeting the Lord and Savior on that great day (see 1:22). "A glorious aim," states Eadie, ". . . the noblest that can stimulate enthusiasm, or sustain perseverance in suffering or toil."[9]

2.　*The plan*—"We proclaim Him, admonishing every man, . . . teaching . . . with all wisdom" (1:28). Paul's plan was simple, direct, complete, and effective. Paul preached Christ and Christ alone! (See 1 Cor. 1:23; 2:2.) His goal was to present Christ to every man, exhorting men to repent from their sins and to understand the totality of what a believer has in Christ. Paul felt "the necessity of employing the highest skill and precedence in discharging the duties of his office."[10] By warning and teaching Paul sought to bring about this maturity.[11]

3.　*The pain*—"For this purpose also I labor, striving . . ." (1:29). Paul's purpose was all-consuming, taxing. As an athlete, he strove for a

---

9. John Eadie, *Commentary on the Epistle of Paul to the Colossians* (reprint, Minneapolis: James and Klock, 1977), 104.

10. Ibid., 103. Eadie also gives an earnest admonition here.

11. "The two words νουθετεῖν (*nouthetein*, "to warn") and διδάσκειν (*didaskein*, "to teach") present complementary aspects of the preacher's duty and are related to each other, as μετάνοια (*metanoia*, "repentance") is to πίστις (*pistis*, "faith"): "*warning* to repent, *instructing* in the faith" (J. B. Lightfoot, *Saint Paul's Epistles to the Colossians and to Philemon* (reprint, Grand Rapids: Zondervan, 1968), 170.

perfect mission.[12] "It was no light work, no pastime; it made a demand upon every faculty and every moment," explains Eadie.[13] The work of winning and discipling believers is not easy, nor is it for the fainthearted. The motivation must be the all-consuming goal of presenting mature believers to Christ (see. Eph. 5:26–27).

4. *The power*—"According to His power, which mightily works . . ." (1:29). No minister is adequate for such a task. There must be absolute dependence upon the strength that only Christ can and will supply to those whom He calls and who humbly depend upon His strength, grace, and effective power. Paul elsewhere states that "our adequacy is from God" (2 Cor. 3:5).

Thus we see that Paul saw his role as a minister of the Word to bring about the maturity of every person. His was not an exclusive gospel, but an all-encompassing message.

Another text to consider in discussing the purpose of the church as a working community is Eph. 4:11–16. This passage is important not only in understanding the purpose of the church, but also because it is one of the few places that explicitly tells the role of the pastor in relation to that purpose.

Paul's epistle to the Ephesians is *the* epistle on ecclesiology. Chapter 4 treats the relationship believers should have with one another, namely harmonious loving unity. A means of promoting unity in the church is the gracious giving and exercise of these gifts. Paul proceeds in verses 7–16 to expound on this truth. Four observations are apropos.

1. *The distribution of gifts* (vv. 7–11). Paul first speaks of the divine distribution of gifts whereby each member of Christ's church receives a spiritual gift. The gifts vary in nature and effect but have one goal: the benefit or the common good, that is, the building up of one another (see 1 Cor. 12:1–11; Rom. 12:3–8). The distribution of these gifts to the church in general (v. 7) also includes gifts to a particular group of people who fill the offices of apostles, prophets, evangelists, and pastors and teachers (or pastor-teacher).[14] The intent of the

---

12. Paul uses κοπιάω (*kopiaō*, "I labor") and ἀγωνίζω (*agōnizō*, "I strive"). Κοπιάω "is used especially of the labor undergone by the athlete in his training, and therefore introduces the metaphor of ἀγωνιζόμενος" (Lightfoot, *Colossians*, 176).

13. Eadie, *Colossians*, 104

14. Some regard the office of pastor and teacher as one, namely that of pastor-teacher. See William Hendriksen, *New Testament Commentary, Exposition of Ephesians* (Grand Rapids: Baker, 1967), 196; see also John Eadie, *Commentary on the Epistle to the Ephesians* (reprint, Minneapolis: James and Klock, 1977), 304–5.

apostle Paul is to highlight the specific nature of these gifts so as to indicate the part they play among the rest of the gifted brethren.

2. *The destination of the gifts.* Paul states that the purpose of the gifted men is "the equipping of the saints for the work of service, to the building up of the body of Christ" (v. 12). The plain order of the phrases and the arrangement of the prepositions yield the simple sense "for the perfecting of the saints unto all that variety of service which is essential unto the edification of the church."[15] The role of the pastor-teacher is to mature the saints, to mend them, to instruct them in the Word of God. These matured saints are then duly qualified and fit to perform the work of ministry, to exercise their spiritual gifts to serve one another. The purpose of the work of the minister to the saints is that the body of Christ be built up. Eadie states, "The spiritual advancement of the church is the ultimate design of the Christian pastorate."[16]

God did not design the pastor to be the church's errand boy. Nor is the pastor the only one gifted to do the ministry. In fact, he does not possess all the gifts necessary for the proper and complete building up of the body. His gifts are equipping gifts, whereas the other members of the body have the useful gifts for a well-rounded ministry to the whole body. It is foolish for a church to expect its pastor to do all the ministry, as it is equally foolish for a minister to see himself as the only one capable of serving the saints. His job is to equip. Theirs is to minister to one another. The end result is an edified church.

3. *The description of edification.* Paul goes on to explain what building up the body means by giving three parallel descriptions (v. 13). The goal of the church is to be united in the faith and in the full knowledge of the Lord Jesus. A partial comprehension of Christ obviously breeds disunity as history so well testifies. The church is to grow in stature, to move from infancy to manhood, from childhood to maturity. Finally, it is to fill up the measure of Christ's fullness, to be all that Christ is and that Christ expects the church to be.

No doubt, this is a big order for the pastor. No one can expect to accomplish this goal fully this side of heaven. Yet we are to strive to bring Christ's church to maturity. Hendriksen comforts the minister with this thought: "Marvelous growth in maturity, nevertheless, is

---

15. Eadie, *Ephesians*, 308. See his commentary for the different views on the interpretation of this verse.

16. Ibid., 309.

certainly obtainable through human effort springing forth from, and sustained from start to finish by, the Holy Spirit."[17]

4.   *The designs of edification.* Paul shows what will be the ultimate result of a mature church (vv. 14–16). It will no longer be a church resembling an easily deceived child with an unstable personality. The church will not be carried about by differing doctrines and glaring error. Nor will it be susceptible to the tricks of Satan, but because of its full knowledge of Christ, it will detect, deter, and defend itself against the wiles of the devil.

While upholding the truth in love, the church will grow into all the aspects of Christ. It will become like Christ, or as Hodge states, "We are to grow so as to be conformed to him. . . . We are to be conformed to our head—because he is our head, i.e. because of the intimate union between him and us."[18]

Christ is really the ultimate source of all power and energy for the accomplishment of the growth of the body (see 4:16). The ultimate goal is a loving community united by the strongest bond of all—God's divine love.

The pastor, then, has the special duty of equipping the members of his congregation so that they will discover and utilize their respective gifts for the spiritual maturity of one another. Some use the analogy of a coach and his team. The coach teaches the team the fundamentals of the game, and the team plays the game. The church is designed to be a working community where each individual member is faithfully serving the Lord by ministering to the rest.

The apostle Peter concurs with Paul and exhorts the pilgrims in his Epistle:

> As each one has received a special gift, employ it in serving one another, as good stewards of the manifold grace of God. Whoever speaks, let him speak, as it were, the utterances of God; whoever serves, let him do so as by the strength which God supplies; so that in all things God may be glorified through Jesus Christ, to whom belongs the glory and dominion forever and ever. Amen (1 Pet. 4:10–11).

---

17. Hendriksen, *Ephesians*, 200.

18. Charles Hodge, *A Commentary on the Epistle to the Ephesians* (reprint, Grand Rapids: Eerdmans, n.d.), 240.

The New Testament picture of a shepherd and his sheep provides an excellent model for the church and its leadership. Just as the shepherd leads, feeds, equips, encourages, protects, and multiplies the flock, so the pastor is to view his role with his flock. The parallels are marvelous and illustrative. In modern terms, the church's leaders must provide direction to Christians by pointing them toward the truth. The leader is to teach the congregation the whole counsel of God as it is revealed in Scripture by a faithful exposition of the whole Bible (see Acts 20:27; 2 Tim. 4:1–5). The pastor must see to it that every member of his flock is growing in Christlikeness by providing the necessary means for the fulfillment of this goal. He is to encourage the sheep as the flock moves through a harsh environment. Because of many dangers from the world, the flesh, and the devil, the minister must protect the flock (Acts 20:28). His watchfulness for wolves and snares ensures a safe and maturing flock. The obvious goal of the pastor is that the church grows both in numbers and in Christlikeness. He will not be content with a few sheep or with a flock so decimated by sin and Satan that they resemble "sheep without a shepherd" (Matt. 9:36).

The pastor plays a vital role in the establishment of a working community. Although the church is an organism, God sees to it that the church has direction and protection by providing a godly leadership for Christ's body. The minister's task is obviously never done, but he can see his flock progressing in maturity as it functions together, ministering to the needs of one another.

PRACTICAL APPLICATION

Having proposed a definition and suggested some benefits for a biblical philosophy of pastoral ministry, and having summarized the basic purpose of the church, we can now offer a general statement of the biblical purpose of Christian leadership: The role of the pastoral leadership, composed of a select group of men from the church of redeemed believers, is to provide guidance, care, and oversight for the church so that it fulfills its Christ-ordained mandate of evangelizing the entire world, growing into the likeness of Christ, and existing for the exaltation and worship of God.

The question remains as to how this biblical philosophy fleshes out in the practical ministry of the local church. What programs or practices should the pastor implement in his church to bring about the fulfillment of the church's purpose? Again, the New Testament is silent on rigidly specifying regulations, rituals, and practices that are to be the pattern for every congregation. The early churches were not clones of one another. Rather than precise patterns, the Lord gave the purpose of the church and the basic means by which the purpose was to be accomplished. We should look for principles rather than patterns. In some instances the apostles are specific (see 1 Cor. 14.); in most cases, they present the ministry of the church in generalities, thus leaving room for each church to adapt its ministry in its own culture and context.

Though the New Testament does not furnish specific programs to implement, it is not lacking in illustrations of how the early church functioned so as to accomplish its goal. Some concepts and practices are quite adaptable and furnish a bare minimum by way of New Testament examples of what should be taking place in every local assembly. The Scriptures indicate seven ministries for accomplishing the three basic purposes of the church: exaltation, evangelism, and edification.

The Ministry of the Word

Acts 2:41–42 provides the first hint of the practice of the early disciples: "So then, those who had received his word were baptized; and there were added that day about three thousand souls. And they were continually devoting themselves to the apostles' teaching and to fellowship, to the breaking of bread and to prayer."

Entrance into the church came through repentance and baptism accompanied by the gift of the Holy Spirit (Acts 2:38). The newly formed church then devoted itself to a number of activities that resulted in numerical and spiritual growth (see 2:47; 4:32–35). First on the list of practices was continuance in the apostles' teaching. The Christians learned the Word of God or doctrine of the apostles, and they not only heard it but put the Word into practice. The preaching and teaching of the Word was central to the ministry of the apostles. The Word is the primary means of bringing a Christian to maturity (2 Tim. 3:16–17; cf. Ps. 19:7–11) and must not be neglected (Acts 6:2).

The pastor, then, is responsible for the teaching of the Word of God to the local church. Whether this is done through a preaching service, a Sunday school class, a discipleship group, cell groups, or home Bible studies does not matter ultimately. What is important, however, is that the Word of God be taught. If the Word of God is taught, the church will grow in faith and love (Rom. 10:17). Yet to introduce innovative programs for the sake of change and excitement without actually concentrating on teaching the Word of God is to change dinner plates without concern for the actual food that is served on those plates. The church leader must see to it that

God's people continually devote themselves to the study and practice of the Word of God.

The Ministry of Fellowship

Luke mentions a second practice of the church. They devoted themselves to the fellowship—to the oneness and the commonality of the body of Christ. Rackham states,

> This fellowship was begun by our Lord, when he called the apostles to leave all and follow Him. So they formed a fellowship, living a common life and sharing a common purse. When the Lord was taken up, the common life continued: and the most characteristic words in the early chapters of the Acts are *all, with one accord, together*.[19]

The job of the leadership is to incorporate new believers into the local body of Christ by visible acceptance into the membership of the church, to develop the use of their spiritual gifts, to place them in a useful spiritual function in the church, and to care for their spiritual welfare (see Acts 2:44–45; 4:32–37; 6:1). The focus of the Christian community is a continual devotion to caring for one another. "Christians," adds Getz, "cannot grow effectively in isolation! They need to experience each other."[20]

Leaders need to get Christians involved with one another. They should create meetings, occasions, ministry opportunities, and structures and funnel social patterns so that Christians are involved with one another. The church is not to be a theater, a lecture hall, or a spectator event. Rather, it is to be a community, a body, a mutual sharing of lives (see 1 Cor. 12:14–27). MacArthur gives these insights into fellowship:

> Fellowship involves being together, loving each other, and communing together. Fellowship includes listening to someone who has a concern, praying with someone who has a need, visiting someone in the hospital, sitting in a class or a Bible study, even singing a hymn with someone you've never met. Fellowship also involves sharing prayer requests.[21]

---

19. R. B. Rackham, *The Acts of the Apostles* (reprint, London: Methuen and Co., 1957), 35.

20. Getz, *Sharpening the Focus*, 117.

21. John MacArthur, Jr., *Shepherdology: A Master Plan for Church Leadership* (Panorama City, Calif.: The Master's Fellowship, 1989), 54; rev. ed., *The Master's Plan for the Church* (Chicago: Moody, 1991).

There are no gimmicks to fellowship, nor can it be artificially maintained. Either Christians care for one another or they do not. They have a sense of belonging or they do not. True maturity in Christlikeness does not develop adequately in assemblies filled with anonymous, noncommitted spectators. Pastors must strive for the opposite and look for ways to make it happen.

The Ministry of the Lord's Supper[22]

The early church participated regularly in "the breaking of bread," which may be taken in the general sense of eating meals together or in the specific sense of partaking of the Lord's Supper. We take it as the latter, although there is evidence that the Lord's Supper as practiced by the early church was accompanied by a common meal (see 1 Cor. 11:17–34).[23]

The Lord's Supper, like the ordinance of baptism, is no trivial practice, but is one that lies at the heart of the Christian message (1 Cor. 11:23–26). The symbolism, solemnity with celebration, and the sanctity required by all participants makes it one of the most inspirational and worshipful services of the Christian community. Lindsay, speaking of the early church and its practice of observing the Lord's Supper, recalls its importance as an act of worship: "And the Holy Supper, the very apex and crown of all Christian public worship, where Christ gives Himself to His people, and where His people dedicate themselves to Him in body, soul and spirit, was always a sacrifice as prayers, praising and alms-giving were."[24]

If the church's worship service never or seldom includes the Lord's Supper, it falls short of the intentions of the Lord (1 Cor. 11:23) and the practices of the early church (Acts 2:42). Great spiritual benefit comes to the church when the Lord's Supper is properly observed and is not trivialized as an appendix to a sermon or musical celebration. Pastors must teach and encourage the congregation to celebrate the Lord's Supper in a way that will be meaningful, uplifting, and edifying to the soul.

---

22. "The marks of the church that follow are the chief outward manifestations of this inner unity, and they may be briefly summed up as—a common life, with common eating (whether of bodily or spiritual food) and common worship" (Rackham, *Acts of the Apostles*, 35).

23. Thomas M. Lindsay, *The Church and the Ministry in the Early Centuries* (reprint, Minneapolis: James Family, 1977), 50–52.

24. Ibid., 37.

The Ministry of Prayer

We observe in Acts 2:42 that the church was devoted not just to prayer, but to "*the* prayers."[25] The expression probably refers "to their own appointed seasons for united prayer within the new community."[26] Rackham says that "the expression *the Prayers* almost implies that there were regular hours of prayer, corresponding to the Jewish synagogue prayers, but we have no information on the subject."[27] Prayer was an important part of the church's life (Acts 1:14; 3:1; 4:23–31; 6:4; 10:9; 12:5, etc.). The church prayed for its leaders (6:6), its missionaries (13:3), its sick (James 5:14–18), governing authorities (1 Tim. 2:1–2), and just about anything one could think of (Phil. 4:5–7).

Prayer moves God; prayer changes things. Effective prayer accomplishes much. A praying church will be a victorious, growing, maturing community. The wonder of today's church is that so much goes on with so little praying. The answer to many of the church's problems is not more seminars, programs, and promotional gimmicks but more intercession on the part of God's people, both as a group and in the closet.

The Ministry of Outreach

Another aspect of the ministry that needs incorporation into the life of the church is educating, involving, and motivating the church to reach out to the lost community around them. Early believers were concerned for the unsaved and made it a lifestyle to testify about the gospel of Jesus Christ. Luke makes this observation about the church's leadership: "And every day, in the temple and from house to house, they kept right on teaching and preaching Jesus as the Christ" (Acts 5:42). The record of the Acts of the Apostles is a description of the spread of the gospel as Christ had commanded.

Evangelism is expected of the believer, and especially of the local church. The church today commits two grave errors when it comes to evangelism. The first is the notion that the pastor's role is to teach the people and then the church will naturally go about the business of evangelism. The other fallacy is that evangelism is the task of the pastor or church leadership.

---

25. Note the Greek article: ταῖς προσευαῖς (*tais proseuchais*).

26. F. F. Bruce, *Commentary on the Book of the Acts* (Grand Rapids: Eerdmans, 1970), 80.

27. Rackham, *Acts of the Apostles*, 41.

They are the "hired ones," paid to do evangelism. More recently, some have suggested that evangelism is a gift held by some who in turn are to do the work of evangelism for the church.

We contend that evangelism is both caught and taught. Pastors must practice personal soul winning as well as teach evangelism to their congregations. A church that does not know how to reproduce and does not reproduce is in reality an immature congregation, regardless of its intellectual comprehension of Scripture or the sophistication of its corporate programs. (The matter of outreach is addressed in more detail in chapter 18, "Outreaching.")

The Ministry of Missions

The obvious result of attempting to fulfill the Great Commission will be the incorporation of a missions program into the local church. Faithfulness to the Lord's command to disciple all the nations will include a directed effort, regardless of the magnitude, at reaching the regions beyond the local church's immediate locality. The local church will have a missions program where they participate in selecting, sending, supporting, and interceding for special Christians who are sent out from them to reach the lost in other places.

The pastor will lead the way in establishing and maintaining the missions program. It is not a task to leave to the women's missionary society or the missions committee. Missions is world-class work and needs top-level guidance and support. The early church considered missions a matter of extreme importance (Acts 13:1–3; 14:27; 15:36–40). It was not a secondary or minor program. Every church, large or small, should have its own involvement in the great missionary enterprise of the body of Christ.

The Ministry of Interchurch Fellowship

New Testament churches were autonomous congregations under the supervision of their own eldership or leadership. They shared in similar traditions and practices, while being distinct congregations. Yet there was a great amount of interdependence. They shared in discipleship efforts (Acts 11:26), in common relief efforts (Acts 11:27–30), and in general ecclesiastical decisions (Acts 15:1–31; 16:4). They maintained an active relationship with one another so that each church saw itself as a part of the whole.

The same needs to be true today; churches should belong to a larger group of churches for mutual support and cooperative efforts. This may be done by belonging to a denomination, an association of churches, or a fellowship of like-minded ministries. The result will be the same.

The pastor should be careful not to become the proverbial lone ranger, isolating himself and his congregation from the rest of the body of Christ. This will result in his own loss and the diminished ministry of his congregation. The minister must lead the church in these cooperative efforts and implement the programs that will sustain and invigorate these fellowships.

As one can see, there is no end to specific ways that the pastor can flesh out the purposes of the biblical church in his particular congregation. Yet he must make sure that he begins with the Scriptures. The Holy Spirit in His sovereign wisdom gave biblical principles that can be applied during all ages to all cultures. The rest is up to Christian ministers.

Part II

Preparatory Perspectives

5

The Character
of a Pastor

John MacArthur, Jr.

In Titus 1, Paul provides a good opportunity to discuss the character traits necessary for one who holds the pastoral office in a local church. He must be a man with the highest of morals in his sexual behavior, including a wholesome relationship with his wife. Second, he must also be one who has proven his leadership capabilities in his own family. He must be successful in ministering to his own children spiritually as well as otherwise. Third, he must demonstrate nobility in his attitude and conduct by being free from self-will, quick temperedness, addiction to wine, pugnaciousness, and a fondness for sordid gain. He must have the positive qualities of hospitality, a love for the good, sensibleness, justice, purity, and self-control.

There are many trends in the church today, and I have tried to address them often from the pulpit and in the books I write.[1] The book of Titus addresses one of the most disturbing trends I've noticed: the disregard of God's guidelines for what kind of man He wants shepherding His sheep. Titus 1:9 tells what God wants the pastor to do, but first and foremost, verses 6–8 tell who he is to be:

---

1. For example, in *Ashamed of the Gospel: When the Church Becomes Like the World* (Wheaton: Crossway, 1993); *Our Sufficiency in Christ* (Dallas: Word, 1991); *Reckless Faith* (Wheaton: Crossway, 1994); and *The Vanishing Conscience* (Dallas: Word, 1994).

> Above reproach, the husband of one wife, having children who be-
> lieve, not accused of dissipation or rebellion. For the overseer must
> be above reproach as God's steward, not self-willed, not quick-
> tempered, not addicted to wine, not pugnacious, not fond of sordid
> gain, but hospitable, loving what is good, sensible, just, devout,
> self-controlled.[2]

That is God's standard for any pastor's character and is thus the primary consideration in preparing for pastoral ministry.[3]

"Above reproach" (ἀνέγκλητος, *anengklētos*) twice describes the effect of a godly life (1:6–7). Literally, the pastor will "not be called in" or, in other words, the pastor will be "blameless" or "above reproach." It should be consistently characteristic of his life as one who assumes the stewardship of God's ministry (1:7). This term applies to deacons in 1 Tim. 3:10, thus bringing it into close association with ἀνεπίλημπτος (*anepilēmptos*), the word used of overseers in 1 Tim. 3:2.[4]

"Above reproach" cannot refer to sinless perfection, because no human being could ever qualify for the office in that case,[5] but it is a high and mature standard that speaks of being a consistent example. It is God's demand that His steward live in such a holy manner that his preaching would never be in contradiction of his lifestyle, that the pastor's indiscretions never bring shame on the ministry, and that the shepherd's hypocrisy not undermine the flock's confidence in the ministry of God.

"Above reproach" is the overarching quality of the pastor. The remainder of the list is a detailed examination of each component of that characteristic, developing what it means to be above reproach. The components fall into three groups: sexual morality, proven family leadership, and nobility in attitude and conduct.

SEXUAL MORALITY

One contemporary trend that is cause for great concern is the shock-

---

2. For an in-depth discussion of 1 Tim. 3:1–7, see John F. MacArthur, Jr., *The Master's Plan for the Church* (Chicago: Moody, 1991), 215–33.

3. See Alexander Strauch, *Biblical Eldership*, 2d ed. (Littleton, Colo.: Lewis and Roth, 1988), 166–206, for an exposition of 1 Tim. 3:1–7 and Tit. 1:5–9.

4. H. Währisch, "ἀνέγκλητος," *IDNTT*, 3:923–25.

5. The term does refer to ultimate blamelessness when applied to the eternal character of Christians after death (see 1 Cor. 1:8; Col. 1:22).

ing moral sins pastors commit only to step back into ministry as soon as the publicity cools down. I have received inquiries from other churches wondering if our church has written guidelines or a workbook for restoring fallen pastors to their pulpits. We have to tell people we do not have any such thing because we believe the Bible clearly teaches that once a man fails in the area of sexual morality, he is unqualified for pastoral ministry any longer. Certainly we want him restored to the Lord and to the fellowship, but biblical qualifications for one who preaches God's Word and is identified as pastor, overseer, or elder exclude him from that role in a church that is pleasing God.

For the most part, evangelical Christianity during this century has focused on the battle for doctrinal purity—and it should—but we are losing the battle for moral purity. We have people with the right theology who are living impure lives. God's standard cannot be lowered for the sake of sympathy. It does not need to be, because we can be loving, forgiving, gracious, merciful, and kind without compromising what God says about the character of the men He wants leading His church. All battles for the integrity of Scripture are ultimately in vain if the church's preachers are corrupt and the sheep no longer follow their shepherds as models of holiness. The church must have leaders who are above reproach. Anything less is an abomination to God and spells disaster for the life of the church.

The first character qualification in Titus that spells out what it means for a pastor to be above reproach is that he be "the husband of one wife" (Titus 1:6). A literal translation of the Greek expression is "a one-woman man." This is not talking about polygamy, a sin that is forbidden for everyone—not just pastors.

Some people think "the husband of one wife" means that if the pastor has been widowed and remarried, he is disqualified. Romans 7:1-6 makes it clear, however, that if a man's wife dies, he is no longer bound by that union. So that cannot be the meaning here. Others therefore conclude "the husband of one wife" means the pastor must be married, not single. The emphatic position of the word for *one* argues against that, though. If Paul wanted to talk about being married as opposed to being single, he could have said pastors have to be married or be the husband of *a* wife.

Paul, through inspiration of the Holy Spirit, deliberately used the phrase meaning "a one-woman man." I think there are two aspects to it, the first having implications with regard to divorce. The Word teaches that the Lord hates divorce (Mal. 2:16), even though He makes provision for it in certain circumstances. It is never God's ideal, however, and it could be that a pastor was to be chosen from men who even before their salvation had not been divorced, so that their lives were the proper model of God's marital ideal. Prior wives or offspring would, then, have no opportunity to compromise, confuse, or attack the credibility of the highest office in the church and destroy the reputation of the man by saying things about him.

Certainly the task of building godly marriages and strong families in the church necessitated the most impeccable marriage history in the pastor's life. A man who had never been divorced but had been married singularly to the same woman would be the kind of premium example God would want of one man and one woman together in harmony for life.

That is just a starting point, however. There are a lot of men who have had only one wife but are not one-woman men (Matt. 5:27–28). They are the husband of one but the lover of two or three more. In its primary aspect, a one-woman man simply means a man who is devoted to the woman who is his wife. His eyes and heart remain focused on her. The issue is not just to avoid getting a divorce at all costs. It is that of continuing faithfulness to one's wife.

This world overflows with sexual sin, and Paul directs the church to find as leaders men who have impeccable reputations. Is the man under consideration without blame in that he has been and now is loyal to the woman who is his wife? Does he have a sexual career in his past that has perhaps come to a screeching halt lately, but most everybody around town knows about it? This is not a man who can stand up and say, "Here, beloved, is God's divine model." The issue is moral character, not marital status.

The pastor must have a reputation of being sexually pure. If he is married, he is devoted to his one wife, not scandalized by past mistresses, illegitimate children, or present adulteries. He loves and desires only one woman and has been faithful to her.

This is the kind of man God is looking for to set up as the model in His church. That does not mean such men are better than others—that they are more spiritual, more gifted, or more used of God than other men. It does mean, however, that they fit the unique role. No one else is suitable according to God's Word.

Many would ask, "What about David and Solomon?" First Kings 15:5 says, "David did what was right in the sight of the Lord, and had not turned aside from anything that He commanded him all the days of his life, *except* in the case of Uriah the Hittite" (emphasis added). That was when he committed sexual sin with Bathsheba, Uriah's wife. Of David's son, who followed his father's lead in that area, Scripture says, "Among the many nations there was no king like him, he was loved by his God, and God made him king over all Israel, *nevertheless* the foreign women caused even him to sin" (Neh. 13:26, emphasis added). There was an exception clause in the lives of both kings. They were qualified as kings, but not as pastors.

Sexual sin disqualifies any man from being a pastor. The apostle Paul remained keenly aware of that fact, saying, "I buffet my body and make it my slave, lest possibly, after I have preached to others, I myself should be disqualified" (1 Cor. 9:27). That is strong terminology. Paul maintained rigorous self-discipline to avoid being disqualified from pastoral ministry. He knew that any kind of sexual sin brings lifelong reproach.

PROVEN FAMILY LEADERSHIP

Sexual sin defiles the flock of God. The pastor or shepherd, far from defiling the flock, is to care for it with the love of a mother and father. That is the pastoral portrait Paul painted: "We proved to be gentle among you, as a nursing mother tenderly cares for her own children . . . just as you know how we were exhorting and encouraging and imploring each one of you as a father would his own children" (1 Thess. 2: 7, 11). Since the pastor is to be a leader of the Lord's church and a loving parent to the family of God, what better way can he qualify than by proving his spiritual leadership in his own family?

If you want to know whether a man lives an exemplary life, whether he is consistent, whether he can teach and model the truth, and whether he can lead people to salvation, to holiness, and to serve God, then look at the most intimate relationships in his life and see if he can do it there. Look at his family and you will find the people who know him best, who scrutinize him most closely. Ask them about the kind of man he is.

There are many fathers who work hard. Some also manage their households well but do not lead their children to Christ and a life of godliness. These men are not potential candidates as pastors. Since spiritual leadership is a parenting process where the pastor or elder must be able to lead his people by his life as well as his precepts, the church needs to look at some proving ground where they can see that kind of leadership already visible in his life. That proving ground is the home.

It is important to clarify three points:

1.   It may be that you as a father have made a good and righteous effort to lead your children to faith in Christ, but you have not seen the fruit that you would desire. You are not responsible for your child's rejection of the truth, but neither would you be qualified to be a pastor.

2.   Scripture does not bar a single man from being a pastor. The apostle Paul was probably single as best we can tell.

3.   There is nothing in Scripture that would prevent a childless man from being a pastor.

When there is not a marriage or children, the church must look at other experiences as evidences of a man's spiritual leadership. If indeed he has been faithful as a spiritual leader in other arenas, the virtue of his life being abundantly evident, then he should be considered for pastoral ministry.

For most men, however, the family is the arena in which spiritual leadership can be evaluated. If a man has children who believe and who are not involved in dissipation and rebellion, they will not bring scandal upon his good name and the integrity of God's church. Imagine the shame if a man stood in the pulpit and said, "Thus says the Lord: This is how to live; this is God's high standard; this is what God expects of you; this is how to pass godliness from one generation to the next," but people could look at his life and say, "Wait a minute, you've got wild, uncontrolled children who live in rebellion and reject the gospel. Why are *you* telling us how to please God?" It questions the integrity of his message. It minimizes the credibility of his ministry and thus reduces its impact.

Paul says that you want to make sure you select men who have a good reputation outside the church as well as inside, who will never be discredited by an unbelieving, wayward child. Some people question this interpretation, saying, "Titus 1:6 can't mean a pastor has to have converted children because that's up to God's sovereignty. If God doesn't choose to elect your children, then you're in real trouble." Frankly, that is an unbiblical and fatalistic approach that fails to consider the impact of a godly life or the believer's personal responsibility for evangelism. Scripture repeatedly teaches that a godly life leads people to salvation. Election is God's own business and something for which we give Him glory, but it is not a consideration in our spiritual living and witness.

If in my home I am committed to living a godly, virtuous life of integrity, and by it to proclaim the truth of the saving gospel, there is every reason to believe God in His grace will use that to redeem my children. It may not always happen, but for the man who would stand in the pulpit as a model and not be scandalized by some activity on the part of his children, it is necessary. And God, who calls the pastor to ministry in the first place, makes it possible.

Another footnote regarding the home relates to the pastor's wife. Although Titus 1 mentions the pastor's children, it does not mention his wife. I think it is fair to assume she also is a believer. In 1 Cor. 9:5 Paul, speaking about himself and fellow pastors, says, "Do we not have a right to take along a believing wife?" Anyone in Christian ministry has the right to be married, but not to just anyone. Scripture is unequivocally specific that a believer is to marry only another believer. That is the main point of 2 Cor. 6:14, "Do not be bound together with unbelievers; for what partnership have righteousness and lawlessness, or what fellowship has light with darkness?" In marriage where the two partners are a believer and an unbeliever, the harmony does not exist that can create the spiritual power and energy of a godly family. It just is not there.

So the text in Titus assumes a believing wife to whom the pastor is totally devoted and children who also follow along in the faith. A truly godly life is the most powerful tool God has in saving sinners. How can a pastor lead people to faith in Christ and holiness unless he can show them the power of his faith in his life? One of the principal missions of the pastor is to teach the church how to raise a godly generation. How can he teach this if he cannot do it himself?

The man whom God calls to pastoral ministry must have "children who believe, not accused of dissipation or rebellion" (Titus 1:6). Context suggests that Paul was speaking of adult children—there aren't too many dissipated, debauched young children. The terms more accurately reflect adult life.

Further, elders by definition were older men who tended to have older children. If Paul wanted to talk about little children, he could have used the specific Greek term *teknion*. If he wanted to talk about babies, he could have used *brephos*. Instead he used a general word for sons and daughters.

The New American Standard Bible speaks of "children who believe." The King James Version, however, translates the same phrase "faithful children." Some therefore conclude that all Titus 1 is saying is that pastors' children must be faithful in the sense of being obedient to their parents, but not necessarily believers in Christ. That, however, is not an accurate understanding of the text, since it is only small children who are under their parents' authority. As we have just surmised, this text speaks about adult children. More specifically, Paul refers to faithful adult children who are not going to scandalize their father's ministry by their unruly lifestyle.

What if your children don't fit into this category because they're not old enough to believe? Another section of Scripture describing pastors covers younger children: 1 Tim. 3:4 says the pastor "must be one who manages his own household well, keeping his children under control with all dignity." In context, that is a reference to small children, not adult children. A pastor can have children of any age, but whatever age they are, they must not bring reproach on him if he is to remain qualified for pastoral ministry.

The Greek word translated "believe," (*pista*) means exactly that. Its opposite, *apistos*, means not to believe, disbelief, or unbelief. So from the simplicity of the word, it is best to see Titus 1:6 as a reference to believing children, not faithful children.

The word translated "dissipation" is *asotia*. It is used in association with drunkenness, revelry, and pagan festivals in Eph. 5:18. It literally means "saving nothing," just throwing oneself away in an indulgent lifestyle. The second term describing the opposite of believing children is "rebellion," which characterizes those who are out of control, wild, and unruly. The pastor's children are to live obediently under their father's control when they are small, following their father's faith until it emerges as their own faith. At that point they must live a faithful Christian life, not a wild, rebellious, out-of-control, wasteful life. If they do not, besides the damage they do to themselves, they disqualify their father from pastoral ministry.

In summary, a man qualified to be a pastor exhibits the leadership and integrity of life to lead people to salvation and service to God by having done it or being in the process of doing it in his own home. He should be known as having children who believe as they are able to comprehend the truths of Scripture and who live according to its principles, having a simple faith that emerges into a saving faith at some point. Those children become important proof of his spiritual leadership.

I think back on my little ones as they were growing up. Their initial faith was a simple affirmation of the things precious to father and mother, and it later matured into saving faith. That is God's ordained pattern for the pastor's family. Such a man is not necessarily better than other Christian men, but he is uniquely suited to the ministry. Other godly, faithful, loyal men may have children who are wayward. That does not hinder their relationship to the Lord, because they are not ultimately responsible for what their children choose to do, but neither does it qualify them for the role of pastoral leadership.

Those who do qualify as pastors have received a special and abundant portion of God's grace because of the uniqueness of their task. To God alone belongs the glory and credit for whatever has happened in their lives to qualify them for their ministry.

NOBILITY IN ATTITUDE AND CONDUCT

This is the third and final aspect of what it means for a pastor to be above reproach as God's steward. Titus 1:7–8 gives two lists of general characteristics, one list of five negatives and the other of six positives. They speak of nobility in attitude and conduct, nobility in the sense of being above the world's standards. The implication is that the pastor is a cut above the rest in attitude and conduct and worthy of being imitated. The man marked by these qualities has the character you'd expect of one who possesses a high sexual morality and is a proven family leader. As a result he will have power—not only the power of God because of the holiness of his life—but credibility, honor, respect, admiration, and love that will endow him with respect as a leader. *This* is the kind of man who will effectively lead the church.

The Negatives

Not Self-Willed. The term used in the Greek text is particularly strong. It means the *opposite* of having a self-loving arrogance, of being consumed with yourself, seeking your own way, satisfaction, and gratification to the point of disregarding others. A pastor should not be a person who could be called headstrong or stubborn.

False teachers are described as: "Daring, self-willed, they do not tremble when they revile angelic majesties" (2 Pet. 2:10). They are so bold in their arrogance that they venture where angels fear to tread. They do not have the sense to realize the forces they are dealing with. Their egotism makes them so arrogant that they will let nothing stand in their way. They have no regard for the power and authority of any other.

In the world's system, the first thing people look for in a leader is someone who is a strong and aggressive natural leader. However, that is opposite of the kind of person who is effective in leading the church. This is not to imply that the godly pastor is not strong or without convictions. The point is that the church who selects a man because of his strong natural leadership ability will find that what drives him is not a concern for God and His truth but a sense of ego fulfillment and a need to be in charge. When things do not go the way he wants them to go, it is very frustrating for him and everyone else in the church.

No one dominated by self is fit for pastoral ministry. I think Jesus said it best in Matthew 20:25–26: "You know that the rulers of the Gentiles lord it over them, and their great men exercise authority over them. It is not so among you, but whoever wishes to become great among you [as a leader] shall be your servant." The man who is chosen for pastoral leadership must not be self-willed. He has to give space for other people's ideas and direction. Most of all, he needs to seek out the mind and heart of God and to do only what God wants done in His church.

Not Quick Tempered. Recently I was talking with people who were telling me the problems with their church. After listening to them I said, "You're obviously very upset with your pastor. What is it about him that causes you such concern?" They responded that he gets angry all the time. I asked them to give me an example. They said, "In a meeting he's apt to blow up and then stomp out of the room. What should we do?"

The obvious answer in light of Titus 1:7 is they should get another pastor, because the one they have is not qualified. The word translated "quick tempered" (orgilon) comes from *orge*, which refers to wrath or anger. This is the only place the word is used in the New Testament. It speaks of a smoldering anger that resides under the surface. Everyone is going to lose it now and then and get upset about something, but this is different. It characterizes a person with what we would call a temper. It is a nurtured hostility maintained in the heart that frequently erupts. Paul probably had something like this in mind when he said, "The Lord's bondservant must not be quarrelsome, but be kind to all . . . [and] patient when wronged" (2 Tim. 2:24). When things do not go the way the pastor wants them to, he should retain his composure inside and out.

James 1:20 sums up the matter: "The anger of man does not achieve the righteousness of God." Anger produces nothing of value in spiritual leadership. The man God ordained to pastoral ministry will not be angry, hostile, quarrelsome, or fuming on the inside, because he is not getting his way. He is a man who can take *no* for an answer. He is willing to let another man's decision preempt his. He can turn responsibilities over to people who do them in ways that he might not think best. He can allow people around him to fail until they learn to succeed, because he does not tie up his ego in everything they do. As a result, he maintains an attitude of joy in his heart and is consistently kind and patient.

Not Addicted to Wine. This third point translates the Greek word *paroinon*, which literally means "to be alongside wine." This pastoral requirement is repeated in 1 Tim. 3:3, as well as in Titus 2:3, where it gives a qualification of older women who assist younger women in an official capacity in the church. Anyone in any kind of Christian leadership needs to be alert and clearheaded.

Does this mean that pastors in New Testament times never drank any wine at all? No, wine was the common drink back then. You could not drink the water without risking infection. Even today in countries where adequate refrigeration and water purification do not exist, the first thing you are told when you visit is, "Don't drink the water."

Any kind of juice standing in the heat will ferment. People of ancient times were well aware of that, so they took a number of precautions to avoid intoxication. The first was to mix wine with water, as much as eight parts of water to one part of wine. This served more as a disinfectant for the water than a recipe for a tasty drink, because mixed eight to one, there was not much taste there. You could not get drunk on it because your stomach could not hold what it would take to intoxicate you since the combination included so much water.

The second thing they commonly did was to boil the wine. That kind of wine is probably associated with the Hebrew word *yayin*, the main word for wine in the Old Testament. Within the very word itself is the concept of bubbling up, perhaps more a commentary on the preparatory process of boiling rather than the bubbly that is characteristic of some wines. When the wine was boiled down, the alcohol would evaporate, and what was left was a thick paste. Often the people would spread it on bread to use as a jam, as we do today. This thick paste was stored in animal skins and could be squeezed out in its concentrated form and remixed with water to produce a reconstituted, nonalcoholic grape juice.

People in biblical times took serious precautions to avoid producing a highly intoxicating wine. Things are different today. Wine today is made straight out of the fruit and is purposely fermented. Mixing wine with water would be a cardinal sin to any wine connoisseur. Therefore, the biblical injunction for the pastor not to be addicted to wine has more relevance than ever.

Alcohol is not to be a part of the pastor's life or have an impact on his thinking. He is not to be a drinker, one who goes to the tavern, inn, or bar—places associated with drinking where there is a potential for drunkenness and other indiscretions. He is at risk of losing control of himself and saying or doing things that are inappropriate. Especially in ancient times, taverns and inns were places of debauchery and iniquity. No man whose life centers around places of drunkenness is fit to be a pastor or an elder.

Apparently, in the early church those who knew the Lord drank wine mixed with water or the reconstituted grape juice. In addition, Paul had to tell Timothy to take a little wine for medicinal purposes (1 Tim. 5:23), because some Christians evidently avoided anything having to do with wine. They certainly did not drink what the Bible calls "strong drink," a term for intoxicating beverages that are not mixed at all. They did everything they could to avoid being inebriated.

The same should be true of Christians today. When you consider the purification and refrigeration techniques prevalent today, most people have no need to drink any alcoholic beverage. That is why at Grace Church, the pastors and elders avoid alcohol altogether. Beyond recognizing that it is not necessary to drink, we realize it could be harmful to more than just ourselves if we did.

In Romans 14 and 1 Corinthians 8, Paul warns against doing anything that will cause another believer to stumble. I am certain that if people thought I drank wine, they would say, "Since John MacArthur drinks wine, then certainly I can." Some of those people may lose control, do something irresponsible that hurts other people, or even become alcoholics. I do not want that to happen, and I do not want the fear of that weighing on my conscience.

Now there may be the rare occasion when you are in a Third World country enjoying a communion service where you are served real wine. It would be appropriate to have a sip of it since it is the necessary thing to do in that environment. That is an obvious exception to the general principle of avoiding alcohol. What Paul is saying in Titus 1 is that no man who is at all irresponsible with that which can lead to drunkenness has any business being in spiritual leadership.

Leviticus 10:9 instructs priests to abstain from alcoholic beverages. Proverbs 31:4–5 gives the same instruction to princes or rulers. The principle is that anyone in a position to make significant decisions that affect a wide range of people should not be operating without full comprehension. Think how much better our churches and government would run if more leaders took this biblical injunction seriously.

Not Pugnacious. This fourth term occurs only here and in 1 Tim. 3:3. It basically speaks of someone who uses his hand, fist, a stick, or a rock to hit someone else. That was a common way people dealt with conflict in ancient times. It is not unheard of today, but most of us are more dignified than that. Perhaps people now are prone to use a more subtle means of vengeance.

In 2 Cor. 11:19 Paul says, "Bear with the foolish gladly." He goes on to illustrate what foolish people are inclined to do to you: "If he enslaves you, if he devours you, if he takes advantage of you, if he exalts himself, *if he hits you in the face*" (v. 20, emphasis added). Some people will hit you in the face if they are upset at you, and that is the way it is. It is something we all need to learn to live with. It is certainly something a pastor must to be prepared to endure, but—perish the thought—never to *inflict* on anyone else. He who goes around punching people obviously does not belong in spiritual ministry.

Second Timothy 2:24–25 says that the servant of the Lord must seek to make peace, not disruption, while ministering. A spiritual leader is to resolve conflict peacefully in a godly, gentle, and humble manner.

Not Fond of Sordid Gain. This is the fifth and last negative describing what a pastor must not be. The Greek term is a compound of the words *aischros* (shameful) and *kerdos* (which refers to personal gain). It describes someone who does not care how he makes money. He lacks honesty and integrity.

This qualification does not imply there is anything wrong with paying the preacher. First Corinthians 9:14 says that "the Lord directed those who proclaim the gospel to get their living from the gospel." First Timothy 5:17 says that those who work hard in preaching and teaching should "be considered worthy of double honor," an expression referring to compensation.

Preachers have a right to be paid and it is right to pay them, but those whom God calls to the ministry will not preach for that purpose. First Peter 5:2 says that true shepherds of God's flock do not function "for sordid gain," the same expression used in this text from Titus.

In contrast, Paul warns that false shepherds will be in it for the money. They

> suppose that godliness is a means of gain. . . . Those who want to get rich fall into temptation and a snare and many foolish and harmful desires which plunge men into ruin and destruction. For the love of money is a root of all sorts of evil, and some by longing for it have wandered away from the faith, and pierced themselves with many a pang (1 Tim. 6:5, 9-10).

The man of God will not pursue such things. He will flee from them (1 Tim. 6:11).

Any man who is enamored by money will compromise himself and will gain somehow in a sordid way. The man who is in spiritual leadership must not be greedy or self-indulgent, because he can be so easily corrupted. He handles God's money, therefore, he should use only the holiest of hands.

The Positives

After his list of what a pastor should not be, Titus includes a comparable list of what he must be.

Hospitable. The compound word translated "hospitable" means literally "a lover of strangers." It is an oft-repeated attribute of Christian character (Rom. 12:13; 1 Tim. 5:10; Heb. 13:2; 1 Pet. 4:9). The basic principle it teaches is to make himself and his resources available to people he does not know. In the context of the early church, it referred primarily to other Christians.

As I mentioned earlier, taverns and inns during biblical times were despicable dens of sin and debauchery. They were very dangerous. Robbers as well as prostitutes preyed on vulnerable travelers. Yet many believers were obliged to travel for business or ministry. Some of them were on the road because they had been kicked out of their city under persecution, driven from their homes, and dispossessed of all they had. There was plenty of opportunity in the early church to open one's home to fellow believers and meet a significant need, providing a haven from sin and perhaps even death.

Hospitality in the biblical sense is not to have your friends over for dinner. That is a kind thing to do, but note what Jesus said to those who seek to minister:

> When you give a luncheon or a dinner, do not invite your friends or your brothers or your relatives or rich neighbors, lest they also invite you in return, and repayment come to you. But when you give a reception, invite the poor, the crippled, the lame, the blind, and you will be blessed, since they do not have the means to repay you; for you will be repaid at the resurrection of the righteous (Luke 14:12–14).

A pastor is to be a generous man. Far from loving gain, he sees whatever he has as a means for meeting the needs of those he does not even know.

Loving What Is Good. A pastor is also to be a lover of good men and good things. You can tell a lot about a man by looking at his friends and what he surrounds himself with. With whom does he associate? What does he do in his leisure time? What is precious to him? Some of the answers should be found in Phil. 4:8—whatever is true, honorable, right, pure, lovely, of good repute, excellent, and worthy of praise. The pastor's heart responds to what is excellent.

Sensible. This third positive trait is another one of those compound words: a combination of *phroneo* (which refers to the thinking process) and *sozo* (I save). This describes a man who has saving thoughts. He is in control of his mind, and his thoughts are redeemed thoughts. They are delivered from the mundane, earthy, and base. Such a man rescues his mind out of the gutter, you might say. He also lifts his mind above what is trivial and passing. He is not a clown or a jokester, but a man with a sure and steady wisdom. He is dispassionate, careful in judgment, thoughtful, wise, and profound. Such is the fruit of a disciplined mind. This is the kind of man to be a pastor.

Just. This describes the conduct of a man who meets God's standard. It is a legal term indicating that the divine verdict on his life is positive. He is known as a man whom God approves of, because he lives according to divine standards.

Devout. This could also be translated "holy." It means "pure, unpolluted, free from any stain of sin." This returns to the concept of being above reproach. In every area of the pastor's life, what you see is exemplary. You will find no stain of sin there.

Perhaps you have been wondering, "Is anybody really like this?" Of course, no one is free from sin, but sin can be confessed and dealt with, and it does not have to scandalize the church. All Christians can live like that by God's grace and mercy in the power of the Holy Spirit. The pastor is to be a living reminder of that great possibility.

Self-Controlled. This is the sixth and last qualification. A pastor is to have control of his life. Well-meaning people who hear of a pastor falling into sin will often say, "The poor man must not have had any accountability. If he had been accountable to others, he would have been all right." There is a place for spiritual accountability. We all need friends, partners, and co-laborers in ministry to help us to walk before the Lord as we should. However, if a man cannot control his life when he is alone, he does not belong in the pastorate. If he is the kind of person who needs to have a committee to keep him in line, he will end up bringing grief to the church. Be assured: If a man wants to sin, he can find the time and place to do it, no matter what other humans he may be accountable to.

You cannot follow me around twenty-four hours a day. If I am so fragile that I have to have people looking over my shoulder all day, then I should not be anyone's pastor. If there is no commitment to godliness on the inside that holds my life in check, it is fruitless for you to control me from the outside and expect me to minister to you as if I were controlled from the inside. The character of a pastor comes from the inside. I cannot think of a better ending note than that, for that is how the Spirit of God concluded the matter in this text from Titus 1:6–8.

6

The Call to
Pastoral Ministry

James M. George

The call of God to vocational ministry is different from God's call to salvation and His call to service issued to all Christians. It is a call to selected men to serve as leaders in the church. To serve in such leadership capacities, recipients of this call must have assurance that God has so selected them. A realization of this assurance rests on four criteria, the first of which is a confirmation of the call by others and by God through the circumstances of providing a place of ministry. The second criterion is the possession of abilities necessary to serve in leadership capacities. The third consists of a deep longing to serve in the ministry. The final qualification is a lifestyle characterized by moral integrity. A man who fulfills these four qualifications can rest in the assurance that God has called him to vocational Christian leadership.

I often receive calls from men who for various reasons are interested in seminary training. Most of these men believe God is directing them into the ministry as a full-time vocation. This inclination has often been termed "the call." This chapter will explain what is involved with the call and will seek to alleviate the misunderstandings surrounding this unique experience.

The call of God to vocational ministry has several different dimensions. First, there is the call to salvation. This must be the starting point for any call to service or ministry. The one seeking to identify his call to vocational ministry must first be sure he is called to Christ (2 Cor. 13:5). One dare not contemplate a ministry of the gospel of grace to God's people until he has experienced God's grace in his own life through saving faith in Jesus Christ.

The calling to salvation also entails a call to serve (Eph. 2:10). God not only predestined us to salvation, but He also predestined us for a life of service. Service is every Christian's privilege and obligation. This calling to service means that we as Christians constitute "a royal priesthood" (1 Pet. 2:9). Our privilege is to "proclaim the excellencies of Him who has called [us] out of darkness into His marvelous light" (1 Pet. 2:9). Käsemann sees this as referring to the duty of one who has personally experienced the gracious power of God to publicly acknowledge that fact.[1] Thus, all believers should engage in the ministry of service as priests of God. To accomplish this, they have the Holy Spirit through whom God has given them spiritual abilities (1 Cor. 12:11). These spiritual gifts are for the express purpose of service for the common good of the church (1 Cor. 12:7). The apostle Paul wrote the Ephesians, "To each one of us grace was given according to the measure of Christ's gift" (Eph. 4:7). First Corinthians 12:8–10, 28–30 and Rom. 12:6-8 list these gifts. Christians are stewards of these gifts and will give an accounting of their stewardship (1 Pet. 4:10).

Beyond the call of all Christians to use their spiritual gifts, God extends a call to the vocational ministry of leadership. Realizing that every believer should be involved in ministry, we will use the term *the ministry* in the present context to refer to a specific type of service rendered to the church by a particular group of leaders.

The call to leadership involves gifted men given to the church by the Lord of the church (Eph. 4:12). This responsibility is both general—providing leadership in worship, preaching, teaching, shepherding, and evangelism—and specific—discipling and counseling.

God used Charles Haddon Spurgeon greatly during the latter part of the nineteenth century. He preached to thousands of people weekly in London at the Metropolitan Tabernacle. Besides his strong passion for preaching, he had a great desire to develop young men for the ministry. This yearning spurred him to institute what he called the "Pastor's College" as a part of the ministry of the church. His book *Lectures to My Students*, a compilation of lectures to students of the college, gives keen insight into the serious nature of the call to vocational ministry. In the early pages of his book, he asks,

> How may a young man know whether he is called or not? That is a weighty enquiry, and I desire to treat it most solemnly. O for divine guidance in so doing! That hundreds have missed their way, and stumbled against a pulpit is sorrowfully evident from the fruitless

---

1. Ernst Käsemann, "Ministry and Community in the New Testament," *Essays on New Testament Themes* (Philadelphia: Fortress, 1964), 80–81.

ministries and decaying churches which surround us. It is a fearful calamity to a man to miss his calling, and to the church upon whom he imposes himself, his mistake involves an affliction of the most grievous kind.[2]

Spurgeon continues by stressing the importance of recognizing the call when he says, "It is imperative upon him not to enter the ministry until he has made solemn quest and trial of himself as to this point."[3]

William Gordon Blaikie also ministered in London about the same time as Spurgeon. He too saw the importance of a call to the ministry and gave six criteria for evaluating a call: salvation, desire to serve, desire to live a life conducive to service, intellectual ability, physical qualifications, and social elements.[4]

Calvin divided the call into two parts when he stated, "If one is to be considered a true minister of the church, it is necessary that he consider the 'objective or external' of the church and the secret inner call 'conscious only to the minister himself.' "[5]

Oden concludes his chapter on "The Call to Ministry" with a discussion on the correspondence between these internal and external aspects of the call, when he concludes,

> The internal call is a result of the continued drawing or eliciting power of the Holy Spirit, which in time brings an individual closer to the church's outward call to ministry. The external call is an act of the Christian community that by due process confirms that inward call. No one can fulfill the difficult role of pastor adequately who has not been called and commissioned by Christ and the Church. This is why the correspondence between inner and outer call is so crucial for both the candidate and the church to establish from the outset with reasonable clarity.[6]

---

2. C. H. Spurgeon, *Lectures to My Students* (reprint of 1875 ed., Grand Rapids: Baker, 1980), 22.

3. Ibid., 23.

4. William Gordon Blaikie, *For the Work of the Ministry: A Manual of Homiletical and Pastoral Theology* (London: J. Nisbet, 1896), 18–25.

5. John Calvin, *Institutes of the Christian Religion* (reprint, Grand Rapids: Eerdmans, 1962), 2:326.

6. Thomas C. Oden, *Pastoral Theology: Essentials of Ministry* (San Francisco: HarperCollins, 1983), 25.

Why is it so necessary that a person experience internal and external compulsion to ministry? In his classic volume on ministry, Bridges has stated the reason why a call was so important:

> To labour in the dark, without an assured commission, greatly obscures the warrant of faith in the Divine engagements; and the Minister, unable to avail himself of heavenly support, feels his "hands hang down, and his knees feeble" in his work. On the other hand, the confidence that he is acting in obedience to the call of God— that he is in His work, and in His way—nerves him in the midst of all difficulty, and under a sense of his responsible obligations, with almighty strength.[7]

As Bridges has stated so eloquently, the issue is with the man himself and with his confidence before God. The man is confident that God has commissioned him for a task that only the power of God can sustain. Criswell speaks of this confidence: "The first and foremost of all the inward strengths of the pastor is the conviction, deep as life itself, that God has called him to the ministry. If this persuasion is unshakable, all other elements of the pastor's life will fall into beautiful order and place."[8]

Answering the question, "How important is the assurance of a special call?" Sugden and Wiersbe say, "The work of the ministry is too demanding and difficult for a man to enter it without a sense of divine calling. Men enter and then leave the ministry usually because they lack a sense of divine urgency. Nothing less than a definite call from God could ever give a man success in the ministry."[9]

The minister of today, like the prophets of the Old Testament, are under constant attack and pressure as they speak of the things of God. Lutzer has spoken of the difficulty of ministry as follows:

> I don't see how anyone could survive in the ministry if he felt it was just his own choice. Some ministers scarcely have two good days back to back. They are sustained by the knowledge that God has placed them where they are. Ministers without such a conviction often lack

---

7. Charles Bridges, *The Christian Ministry* (reprint of 1830 ed., London: Banner of Truth, 1967), 101.

8. W. A. Criswell, *Criswell's Guidebook for Pastors* (Nashville: Broadman, 1980), 345.

9. Howard F. Sugden and Warren W. Wiersbe, *When Pastors Wonder How* (Chicago: Moody, 1973), 9.

courage and carry their resignation letter in their coat pocket. At the slightest hint of difficulty, they're gone.[10]

Believing in the importance of the call as these men do, I suggest four questions that a man can use to evaluate whether he has a call to the ministry. The acrostic CALL summarizes the four steps outlined by the questions: Confirmation, Abilities, Longings, and Life.

Is There Confirmation?

Confirmation is of two types: confirmation by others and confirmation from God.

Confirmation by Others

Acts 16:1–2 gives a good idea of how important public recognition is in confirming the call to leadership and the ministry. Timothy was probably a convert of Paul on his first missionary journey (see Acts 14:6). Paul called him "my true child in the faith" (1 Tim. 1:2). As Paul started his second journey, he traveled through the regions he had visited on his first journey "strengthening the churches" (Acts 15:41). He arrived in Timothy's hometown where he found that Timothy was "well spoken of by the brethren who were in Lystra and Iconium" (Acts 16:2). The result was, "Paul wanted this man to go with him" (Acts 16:3). Timothy's public confirmation made him a desirable asset to Paul's missionary team. Later as Paul wrote to Timothy, he reminded him of this public confirmation by referring to the "laying on of hands by the presbytery" (1 Tim. 4:14). Both Paul and the leadership in the local community had seen how God had blessed and used Timothy in local service, so they recognized and commissioned him to serve God in the ministry on a broad scale.

Spurgeon agrees that public confirmation is a necessary step beyond the internal feeling that a man has concerning his call to the ministry. He concludes, "The will of the Lord concerning pastors is made known through the prayerful judgment of his church. It is needful as a proof of your vocation that your preaching should be acceptable to the people of God."[11]

---

10. Erwin W. Lutzer, "Still Called to the Ministry," *Moody Monthly* 83, no. 7 (March 1983): 133.

11. Spurgeon, *Lectures*, 29.

Many men who have the internal compulsion to enter the ministry are hesitant to subject this feeling to a church for confirmation. For whatever reason, they do not trust the church with this important area of their lives. Spurgeon told his students,

> Churches are not all wise, neither do they all judge in the power of the Holy Ghost, but many of them judge after the flesh; yet I had sooner accept the opinion of a company of the Lord's people than my own upon so personal a subject as my own gifts and graces. At any rate, whether you value the verdict of the church or no, one thing is certain, that none of you can be pastors without the loving consent of the flock; and therefore this will be to you a practical indicator if not a correct one.[12]

Bridges also gives sound advice when he speaks of the counsel of others, especially friends and experienced ministers: "[They] . . . might be useful in assuring the mind, whether or not the desire for the work be the impulse of feeling rather than a principle, and the capacity be self-deceiving presumption."[13]

The Bible says much about seeking advice and wise counsel. Proverbs is especially excellent in this area: "Where there is no guidance, the people fall, but in abundance of counselors there is victory" (11:14); "the way of a fool is right in his own eyes, but a wise man is he who listens to counsel" (12:15); "through presumption comes nothing but strife, but with those who receive counsel is wisdom" (13:10); "without consultation, plans are frustrated, but with many counselors they succeed" (15:22).

Besides the advice and counsel of others is the procedure of ordination, which is the step of publicly recognizing one set apart for the ministry (see chapter 8 , "Ordination to Pastoral Ministry"). The Bible indicates that the early church had a specific process whereby bodies of Christians chose and set apart leaders for service. Paul's instruction that Titus appoint elders (Titus 1:5) exemplifies a number of passages that point to the idea of an ordaining process. The basis of the appointments was the recognition of qualified men in each of the cities. A good definition of ordination is the public confirmation of an inner qualification and giftedness.[14] It is a public testimony of a man's gifts, his education, and his ministry experience.

---

12. Ibid., 30.

13. Bridges, *Ministry*, 100–101.

14. Clifford V. Anderson, *Worthy of the Calling* (Chicago: Harvest, 1968), 56–57.

Even though the man being ordained is no different than other members of the congregation, public ordination provides a visible affirmation that God has called an individual to use his unique abilities and gifts for the whole church.

Confirmation from God

Newton found three indications of a call to the ministry: desire, competence, and the providence of God. He termed the third indication "a correspondent opening in providence, by a gradual train of circumstances pointing out the means, the time, the place, of actually entering upon the work."[15]

This factor covers all we have discussed thus far. God's sovereignty provides for the calling of certain men for leadership in the local church. God gives them the gifts to carry out the functions of the ministry, gives them the desire to serve in this capacity, and then orchestrates the circumstances to provide for the place of ministry.

All this speaks of open doors and God's blessing. Paul said in 1 Cor. 16:8–9, "But I shall remain in Ephesus until Pentecost; for a wide door for effective service has opened to me." He then proceeds to balance the opportunity with the obstacles: "and there are many adversaries."

These adversaries are a constant element in the ministry and sometimes cause frustration and limit results. Results are not the final indicator of God's blessing, however. Many have labored throughout their ministries with little or no visible fruit. Jeremiah prophesied for more than forty years (Jer. 1:2–3) without much, if any, response from the people. Adoniram Judson labored seven years in Burma before having his first convert, but he still saw God's hand of providence in his ministry. The ministry is never easy nor are the results always positive, but a sense of God's confirmation of the work should always be present.

Besides asking if there is confirmation from God, the man seeking to know whether he has the call must ask himself several practical questions:

Do others recognize my gifts and leadership abilities?

Do they ask me to serve in a leadership capacity?

Am I asked to communicate the truths of God through teaching or preaching?

---

15. John Newton, cited by Spurgeon, *Lectures,* 32.

Are there those who have suggested that I should consider the ministry?

Answers to these questions come only through active involvement in a local church ministry. Receiving public confirmation requires public ministry. This public ministry involves the use of gifts and abilities that others can identify, help develop, and encourage. Without these abilities, confirmation will be missing. So abilities are an integral part in the process of determining the call.

ARE THERE ABILITIES?

Ephesians 4:11 is the background of this second question, which deals with giftedness. In part, the verse says that Christ "gave some as . . . pastors and teachers, for the equipping of the saints." Pastor-teachers are God-appointed gifts to the church.

Just as God called out men for specific tasks in the Old Testament, so in the New Testament God has His chosen ones to accomplish specific tasks during this church age. The task is that of "equipping of the saints for the work of service" (Eph. 4:12). Fulfilling this responsibility entails an equipping of the called man. Formal and informal education by other men can achieve part of this equipping, but spiritual giftedness from God has the major role in a man's call to the ministry. Bridges says, "The ability for the sacred office is very distinct from natural talent, or the wisdom and learning of this world."[16]

Many a man has thought himself a prime candidate for the ministry, because he loved God and was the debate champion in college. As important as these assets are, unless God has selectively gifted the man for the ministry, he labors in vain who builds the house (Ps. 127:1).

Besides the speaking gifts of preaching and teaching, usually considered essential for the ministry, Spurgeon also suggested several other qualifications:

> I should not complete this point if I did not add, that mere ability to edify, and aptness to teach is not enough; there must be other talents to complete the pastoral character. Sound judgment and solid experience must instruct you; gentle manners and loving affections must

---

16. Bridges, *Ministry*, 98.

sway you; firmness and courage must be manifest and tenderness and sympathy must not be lacking. Gifts administrative in ruling well will be as requisite as gifts instructive in teaching well.[17]

Many men who want to be ministers go to a seminary or Bible school to get the gifts necessary for the ministry. This is a mistake. Since each Christian at the time of conversion has received all the gifts that he will need for ministry (1 Cor. 12:11), training cannot furnish the necessary gifts, but if the gifts are already there, training can develop what God has previously given.

What are the abilities needed for the ministry? The quotation just cited from Spurgeon alludes to them. Basically the functions of a minister are three types: instructional, pastoral, and administrative.

Instructional. In Eph. 4:11–12 the pastor-teacher's responsibility is "the equipping of the saints for the work of service, to the building up the body of Christ." The word *equipping* is the Greek word καταρτίζώ (*katartizō*). This word, translated "mending" in Matt. 4:21, occurs in the description of Christ's call to James and John. He summoned them while they were "mending their nets," that is, equipping their nets for fishing. This suggests that a major function of a leader is a figurative mending of the saints—getting them ready for service.

In 1 Thess. 3:10 the translation of this word is "complete." The apostle Paul wanted to return to the Thessalonians to "complete what is lacking in your faith," that is, to finish what he had started earlier. Galatians 6:1 also has *katartizō*, this time in the sense of restoring a sinning brother. Abbott-Smith gives the meaning of this word as "to furnish completely; complete; prepare."[18] Stedman suggests the nearest modern equivalent is "to shape up."[19]

How does this instruction occur? The two major avenues for instruction are preaching and teaching. In 1 Tim. 5:17 Paul refers to certain elders at Ephesus as "those who work hard at preaching and teaching." The NASB has correctly translated the Greek phrase οἱ κοπιῶντες ἐν λόγῳ (*oi kopiōntes en logō*) by "those who work hard at preaching."[20] "Since *en logō* ("in preaching") is *anarthrous*, it should not be identified as the word of God . . . ,"[21]

---

17. Spurgeon, *Lectures*, 28.

18. George Abbott-Smith, *A Manual Greek Lexicon of the New Testament*, 3d ed. (Edinburgh: T. and T. Clark, 1968), 238.

19. Ray C. Stedman, *Body Life* (Glendale, Calif.: Gospel Light, 1972), 82.

20. BAGD, 477.

21. Marvin Edward Mayer, "An Exegetical Study on the New Testament Elder" (Th.D. diss., Dallas Theological Seminary, 1970), 129 (translation added).

although the foundation for these discourses was the Word of God. Basically, *en logō* referred to any general form of oral discourse given in some kind of public assembly. It probably included exhortation, admonition, and comforting, as well as the proclamation of the gospel.[22]

The second avenue of instruction in 1 Tim. 5:17 is "teaching" (διδασκαλία, *didaskalia*). Teaching overlaps the function of preaching to some degree. Since preaching is more of a public ministry, teaching is the explanation and application of that which is proclaimed.[23] It can be either public or private, as Paul described his teaching ministry in Ephesus (Acts 20:20).

According to 1 Tim. 3:2 a leader must be "able to teach." In Titus 1:9 he must "be able both to exhort in sound doctrine and to refute those who contradict." In Heb. 13:7 the writer describes leaders as those "who spoke the word of God to you," thus implying that leaders are communicators.

Shepherding. Both Acts 20:18 and 1 Peter 5:2 have commands for church leadership to feed the flock of God. Feeding the flock relates to the function of teaching. In fact, shepherding duties link closely with teaching duties. In Eph. 4:11 Paul combines the two in the title "pastor-teacher." Yet the Bible makes a distinction between shepherding and teaching. Teaching imparts a body of knowledge, but shepherding imparts a life more broadly. Paul shows this distinction in 1 Thess. 2:8 where he says, "Having thus a fond affection for you, we were well-pleased to impart to you not only the gospel of God [teaching] but also our own lives [shepherding]."

In Acts 20:28 Paul admonished the Ephesian elders "to shepherd the church of God." He did not command these elders to take care of their own flock but to take care of God's flock, the church. First Peter 5:2 notes the same stewardship when Peter tells his fellow elders to "shepherd the flock of God among you." The church leader is an under shepherd who will give an account to God (Heb. 13:17), so he must shepherd with utmost care.

How is he to do this shepherding? Paul tells the Ephesian elders in Acts 20 to face the reality of enemy attacks (v. 29). Attacks will come through the efforts of "savage wolves" who will arise from within the flock (v. 30). The enemy will try to divide the flock, necessitating constant watchfulness by the church's leaders (note the command "be on the alert," v. 31). Leaders must "admonish" and intimately involve themselves with the people "with tears" (v. 31). Ultimately, they must entrust the flock to God through prayer, with the assurance of growth in the flock through study of the Word (v. 32).

---

22. Homer A. Kent, Jr. *The Pastoral Epistles* (Chicago: Moody, 1958), 181.

23. Robert H. Mounce, *New Testament Preaching* (Grand Rapids: Eerdmans, 1960), 41–42.

Administrative. The basic function of a New Testament leader is overseeing.[24] Acts 20:28 calls the Ephesian elders "overseers." First Peter 5:2 tells the leadership to "exercise oversight."

Oversight involves ruling, a function to which 1 Tim. 5:17 refers when Paul instructs Timothy to "let the elders who rule well be considered worthy of double honor." Also, the writer of Hebrews refers to ruling in his reference to leading: "Remember those who led you" (Heb. 13:7). Two other verses in Hebrews 13 refer to the ruling function: "Obey your leaders, . . . for they keep watch over your souls" (v. 17); "Greet all of your leaders" (v. 24).

How are leaders to rule? Jesus told His disciples in Matt. 20:25–26 that they were to be servants, not lords. As an obedient disciple, Peter gave the same advice in 1 Pet. 5:3: "Nor yet as lording it over those allotted to your charge, but proving to be examples to the flock." As Christ was a servant (Matt. 20:28; John 13:1–16), so leaders are to follow His example and be servants of the church.

How is your ability to teach and preach? Do you enjoy communicating God's Word in a preaching or teaching environment? How are your leadership skills? Do you take the initiative or are you a follower? How would you rate yourself as a shepherd? Do you have a heart for people? Do you love to care for those "lost and without a shepherd?"

Is There a Longing?

In 1 Tim. 3:1 the apostle Paul has written, "If any man aspires to the office of overseer, it is a fine work he desires to do." The word translated "aspires" is ὀρέγομαι *(oregomai)*, a word occurring only three times in the New Testament. It means "to stretch oneself out in order to touch or to grasp something, to reach after or desire something."[25] It pictures a runner lunging for the finish line. The second time the word appears is in 1 Tim. 6:10 where it is translated "longing"—related to money, which is the object of so much love as to make it the very foundation for "all sorts of evil." The third usage is in Heb. 11:16 where it is rendered "desire," with the object of desire being a "better country." So each context determines how legitimate the stretching and reaching is.

---

24. Harvey E. Dana, *Manual of Ecclesiology* (Kansas City: Central Seminary, 1944), 254.

25. Henry J. Thayer, *Greek English Lexicon of the Greek New Testament* (reprint of 1868 ed., Edinburg: T. and T. Clark, 1955), 452.

The second word speaking of inner compulsion in 1 Tim. 3:1 is ἐπιθυμέω (*epithumeō*), a verb meaning "to set one's heart upon, desire, lust after, covet."[26] The noun form of this verb usually has a bad sense, but the verb has primarily a good or neutral sense, which expresses a particularly strong desire.[27] This aspiration for the ministry is therefore an inward impulse that releases itself in outward desire.

Sanders notes that it is not the office but the work that is the object desired.[28] It must be a desire for service, not for position, fame, or fortune. So this aspiration is good as long as it is for the right reasons.

Spurgeon gives the following warning concerning the desire for the ministry:

> Mark well, that the desire I have spoken of must be thoroughly disinterested. If a man can detect, after the most earnest self-examination, any other motive than the glory of God and the good of souls in his seeking the bishopric, he better turn aside from it at once; for the Lord will abhor the bringing of buyers and sellers into his temple: the introduction of anything mercenary, even in the smallest degree, will be like the fly in the pot of ointment, and will spoil it all.[29]

This inner desire should be so single-minded that the aspiring leader cannot visualize himself as pursuing anything else except the ministry. "Do not enter the ministry if you can help it," was the wise advice of an old preacher to a young man when asked his judgment regarding pursuing the ministry.[30] Bicket said, "If you can be happy outside the ministry, stay out. But if the solemn call has come, don't run."[31] Bridges calls the "constraining desire . . . a primary ministerial qualification."[32]

Do you long for the ministry? Is it impossible for you to function in any other vocation? Do you see yourself only in the ministry? If your answers to these questions are yes, one more area is critical for determining your call to the ministry.

---

26. Abbott-Smith, *Manual Greek Lexicon*, 170.

27. H. Schönweiss, "*epithumeō*," *NIDNTT*, ed. Colin Brown (Grand Rapids: Zondervan, 1971), 1:456–58.

28. J. Oswald Sanders, *Spiritual Leadership* (Chicago: Moody, 1967), 13.

29. Spurgeon, *Lectures*, 25.

30. Ibid., 23.

31. Zenas J. Bicket, ed., *The Effective Pastor* (Springfield, Mo.: Gospel, 1973), 1.

32. Bridges, *Ministry*, 94.

Is There a Lifestyle of Integrity?

The Bible says much about a leader's character. It is interesting that it says more about what a leader is to be than it does about what he is to do. This is a good clue as to what God thinks about this important prerequisite. It does not matter how much education or how much experience a person has. If he does not meet qualifications of biblical morality, he is unfit to be a leader in God's church. Phillips Brooks, a prominent clergyman during the nineteenth century, says of this important subject: "What the minister *is* is far more important than what he is able to do, for what he is gives force to what he does. In the long run, ministry is what we *are* as much as what we *do*."[33]

Paul told Timothy, "Pay close attention to yourself" (1 Tim. 4:16). Why is this so important? The Old Testament priests had to practice elaborate washing and cleansing procedures, as well as sacrificing offerings for their own sins, before they could minister in behalf of the people (Heb. 5:3). How could they intercede for others when their own sin had not been covered? So it is for the New Testament leader. Spiritual leadership without character is only religious activity, possibly religious business or, even worse, hypocrisy.

Henry Martyn wrote in his journal, "Let me be taught that the first great business on earth is the sanctification of my own soul."[34] Peter commands every Christian to be "holy as your father in heaven is holy" (1 Pet. 1:15–16) and exhorts the leaders "to be examples to the flock" (1 Pet. 5:3). As those who are to assist the people in worship and be examples, New Testament leaders must have lives that set a standard for the rest of the church. The standard for conduct and character to guide the leader as he guides God's people is the Word of God. The qualified leader is a man of the Book, using it not just to prepare sermons and teaching notes but, first and foremost, to prepare himself. The Bible is not a textbook but a manual for transforming the life of one who aspires to leadership.

Within the covers of the Bible, certain sections are particularly relevant to the qualifications for leadership. First Timothy 3:1–7 and Titus 1:6–9 are key passages that deal with a leader's qualifications. Certainly no man claims that his life measures up to these standards perfectly as a model for what the rest of the church should be, but the Bible gives the standards as an ideal to

---

33. Cited in David Wiersbe and Warren W. Wiersbe, *Making Sense of the Ministry* (Chicago: Moody, 1983), 32.

34. Ibid., 33.

strive for. As an added safeguard, God usually also provides a core of godly men in each church to supervise and hold one another accountable to ful-filling these standards.

These, then, are the four major questions for a person to ask when considering the ministry. Is there confirmation? Is there appropriate gift-edness? Is there an insatiable longing for the ministry? Finally, is there a life of integrity? If a man can answer these questions in the affirmative, he can in all confidence say he has the call of God to pursue ministerial options. He can proceed with joy, for God has an exciting and rewarding—but also an incredibly demanding—life waiting for him. To cope with the incredible demands, he has the assurance of God's help and empowerment.

7

Training for Pastoral Ministry

Irvin A. Busenitz

Training for pastoral ministry is a specialized form of the mandate given to all Christians to make disciples. Three essential parts of that training are godly character, biblical knowledge, and ministry skills. Godly character needs development in the trainee's moral life, home life, maturity, and reputation. Primary focus in Bible knowledge is upon linguistic facility, theological framework, and bibliographical familiarity. The four areas of leading with conviction, teaching with authority, preaching with passion, and shepherding with care comprise the major part of developing ministry skills. In this whole process it is important to combine the academic part with experience in ministry.

At the very core of the Christian life is the mandate to make disciples. Whether in the home or in the church, whether institutional or personal, passing the baton to another generation is the sacred task of every believer. Near the close of his life, the apostle Paul exhorted Timothy, his child in the faith, "And the things which you have heard from me in the presence of many witnesses, these things entrust to faithful men, who will be able to teach others also" (2 Tim. 2:2). But later he cautioned Timothy by adding, "For the time will come when they will not endure sound doctrine; but wanting to have their ears tickled, they will accumulate for themselves teachers in accordance to their own desires" (2 Tim. 4:3).

Paul solemnly reminded Timothy that in passing the baton, he must follow principle (i.e., the dictates of the doctrine of the church clearly defined in Scripture) not expediency in expediting the process. In other words, training for the pastoral ministry cannot be market-driven; it must be Bible-driven. Pastoral training cannot capitulate to the whims of the pew[1] nor bow to the latest church-growth methodology. Rather, an education that reflects the biblical mandates for the church and its leadership must dominate pastoral training. This principle is crucial, for one's view of the ministry will influence and ultimately dictate his philosophy of training for that service.

The constricting influence of tradition and the inflating pressures of expediency upon churches are enormous, misdirecting them into thinking they want a certain kind of pastoral model that will make their church relevant or place it on the cutting edge. The mandate of seminaries and church leaders is to teach first the *what* and *why* of church leadership before the *how*.[2] As long as a century ago, Warfield rightfully noted, "A low view of the functions of the ministry will naturally carry with it a low conception of the training necessary for it. . . . And a high view of the functions of the ministry on evangelical lines inevitably produces a high conception of the training which is needed to prepare men for the exercise of these high functions."[3]

Pastoral trainers are faced with the challenge of determining what the *biblical* role of an elder is and how to best prepare a man for eldership. Such a road will not be popular and may foster accusations of being old-fashioned and out-of-tune with today's market. But just such an education is the requirement—the health of the church requires it.

Preparing for the pastoral ministry is a multifaceted journey, a process consisting of diverse elements occurring over an extended time. Contrary to expectations of some seminarians, three or four years is not long enough to complete the process. Rather, it is a pilgrimage that never ends, requiring commitment to an endless quest. The etymological significance of the word *seminary*, for example, includes the idea of "seedbed." That is what training for ministry must embody, whether the setting is formal or informal,

---

1. This is not to suggest that the laity should have no influence with the clergy or on the nature of their training. The training process can be a two-way street. But Scripture clearly places the responsibility for guarding and passing on the truth squarely on the shoulders of the spiritual leaders. Else the church falls prey to the dangers enunciated in 2 Tim. 4:3.

2. This is not to advocate an education of the trainee without any consideration of the contemporary scene. But it does contend that the New Testament prescriptions for the functions of the church are timeless principles and must be implemented accordingly. The drift of evangelical churches away from the New Testament model is due, at least in part, to the lack of a biblically defensible philosophy of ministry on the part of its leaders. This deficiency is traceable only to the doorstep of the seminary.

3. B. B. Warfield, "Our Seminary Curriculum," *Selected Shorter Writings*, ed. J. E. Meeter (Phillipsburg, N.J.: Presbyterian and Reformed, 1970), 1:369.

whether within the structure of a seminary or incorporated into the on-going life of a pastor or local church.[4] In either situation there must be a careful and systematic watering, nurturing, cultivating, pruning, and pro-tecting of the seed. Only then will fruit result.

Specifically, training for ministry demands the pursuit of at least the three phases of training noted in Paul's exhortation to Timothy (1 Tim. 4:12–16): godly character (what a man should be), biblical knowledge (what a man should know), and ministry skills (what a man should be able to do).[5] Before one begins to serve officially in a pastoral role, he must attain a cer-tain level of development in each of these three, with an ongoing zeal for further growth as that service continues.

GODLY CHARACTER

Give me a man of God—one man,
  Whose faith is master of his mind
And I will right all wrongs
And bless the name of all mankind.

Give me a man of God—one man,
Whose tongue is touched with heaven's fire,
And I will flame the darkest hearts
  With high resolve and clean desire.

Give me a man of God—one man,
  One mighty prophet of the Lord,
And I will give you peace on earth,
  Bought with a prayer and not a sword.

Give me a man of God—one man,
  True to the vision that he sees,
And I will build your broken shrines
  And bring the nations to their knees.[6]

---

4. The principles embraced herein are not restricted to either setting. Each setting brings with it certain advantages and disadvantages, but the principles remain unchanged.

5. The order suggested here is not accidental. Scripture clearly marks godly character as the *sine qua non* of qualification for ministry. Biblical knowledge becomes the founda-tion of ministry skills, providing the student with the understanding that is then fleshed out in active service.

6. George Liddell, cited by J. Oswald Sanders, *Spiritual Leadership* (Chicago: Moody, 1986), 23.

In 1 Tim. 4:7 Paul exhorts Timothy to "Discipline yourself for the purpose of godliness." He concludes the chapter by admonishing the young pastor to "Pay close attention to yourself and to your teaching; persevere in these things; for as you do this you will insure salvation both for yourself and for those who hear you" (1 Tim. 4:16). The focal point of any ministry is godliness. Ministry is, and always must be, an overflow of a godly life. Paul understood its importance in the ministry: "I buffet my body and make it my slave, lest possibly, after I have preached to others, I myself should be disqualified" (1 Cor. 9:27; see also 1 Tim. 4:8; 6:3; 2 Tim. 2:3–5).

An abundance of biblical knowledge or the dexterity of ministry skills is not the first test of the validity of one's desire for the pastoral ministry. Rather, Scripture makes the primary test that of godly character (1 Tim. 3; Titus 1). It is with this area that training for such a high and holy calling must commence. To begin elsewhere is to focus on the ability of natural talent or personality and to forget that shepherding the flock of God rests on a different foundation and has a different power source. The muscles of the true spiritual leader respond to the impulses of the Spirit of God, who then uncovers the treasures of the Word, ignites the fires of passion, and sharpens the eye of visionary leadership.

"Spiritual leadership is a matter of superior spiritual power, and that can never be self-generated. There is no such thing as a self-made spiritual leader. He is able to influence others spiritually only because the Spirit is able to work in and through Him to a greater degree than in those whom he leads."[7]

Paul introduces the qualifications for the pastor by extolling the ambition to pursue the office and function of an elder. In fact, he speaks of pursuing that office with intense desire (1 Tim. 3:1, *epithumeo*).[8] It is true that ambition, when selfishly motivated, is dangerous. At these times restraint and caution should prevail. However, ambition not motivated by eagerness for prestige or power but rather by a passion to serve the Master is right. Desire for positional prestige corrupts because it originates from impure motives (see Jer. 45:5). Yet desire for service purifies, because it seeks only the service of the one who has been called to service (Rom. 12:1; Mark 10:42–44). "The true spiritual leader is concerned infinitely more with the service

---

7. Sanders, *Spiritual Leadership*, 37.

8. Literally, the verb means "to long for, to desire" (BAGD, 293). The New Testament employs the term more often in a negative sense than a positive one, but the latter usage is obvious here. When used in a good sense, the verb expresses a particularly strong desire (H. Schönweiss, "Desire, Lust, Pleasure," *NIDNTT*, 1:457).

he can render God and his fellowmen than with the benefits and pleasures he can extract from life."[9]

In Paul's day the office of elder often entailed considerable hardship, danger, ridicule, and rejection. The demands of a New Testament elder were great, requiring significant self-sacrifice. Thus, the divinely bestowed desire was both foundational and motivational. "Truly, in *such* a time and amid *such* circumstances an *incentive to overseership and a word of implied praise* for the man who indicated a willingness to serve in this high office were not at all out of place."[10]

Today some may mistakenly view Christian leadership solely as a position of status, honor, and prestige, but when one carries out the leadership function biblically, the results described by these words are not at all out of place. Because neither the pastoral ministry itself nor the preparatory process leading to it are known for their relative ease, such desire can be advantageous, assisting the pursuant to weather the rigors and not lose sight of the goal.

Godly Character as a Goal

Speaking at the ordination of a young pastor, the Scottish minister Robert Murray McCheyne remarked:

> Do not forget the culture of the inner man—I mean the heart. How diligently the cavalry officer keeps his sabre clean and sharp; every stain he rubs off with the greatest care. Remember you are God's sword, His instrument—I trust a chosen vessel unto Him to bear His name. In great measure, according to the purity and perfections of the instrument, will be the success. It is not great talents God blesses so much as great likeness to Jesus. A holy minister is an awful weapon in the hand of God.[11]

It is well known that admission to a seminary or the satisfactory completion of academic requirements is not a guarantee of success in the ministry. Without certain spiritual, moral, and personal qualifications, any attempt to serve or fill a role in a ministry of the gospel can result in noth-

---

9. Sanders, *Spiritual Leadership*, 20.

10. William Hendriksen, *1 and 2 Timothy and Titus* (London: Banner of Truth, 1957), 118.

11. Andrew A. Bonar, ed., *Memoirs of McCheyne* (reprint, Chicago: Moody, 1978), 95.

ing but tragedy. Thus, godly character becomes the foundation upon which the other two areas rest. Without it they ultimately terminate in ruin.

Although godliness is often difficult to measure ("man looks at the outward appearance, but the LORD looks at the heart" [1 Sam. 16:7]), it must still be the goal and must be pursued passionately by every mentor and trainee. It is the cornerstone of effective ministry and the trademark of every true shepherd.

Areas of Godly Character

The cultivation of Christian character qualities and living skills that are essential for godly living, for leadership in ministry, and for effective service to others require special attention. The following spheres need growth in Christlikeness:

1. *Moral life* (1 Tim. 3:2–3). At the ground level of godly character in all areas of life is the matter of morality. Through the rigors of strong discipline and repetitive practice in the gymnasium of life, the leader must train his senses to discern good and evil (Heb. 5:14). "The intellectual vanguard of the Christian movement needs today, as in the Early Church, to be the moral vanguard also. In a day when discipline has virtually disappeared from the churches, and when pastors and televangelists become victims of a carnal culture, we need to embrace truth and piety by living a Godly life."[12]

2. *Home life* (1 Tim. 3:4–5). A would-be minister must pursue most vigorously a high morality in the home. He must take great care to cultivate a continually growing relationship with his wife, to build big cisterns and dig deep wells, so that he may "be intoxicated always with her love" (Prov. 5:19 NRSV). The rearing of sons and daughters who also embrace the faith is equally foundational. The demands of ministry will often tend to erode the time needed with his children, to properly "bring them up in the discipline and instruction of the Lord" (Eph. 6:4).

3. *Maturity* (1 Tim. 3:6). Maturity is not a gift with which one is born. Rather, a person learns it over a period of time, by applying the principles of the Word when walking through the valleys and shadows of life.

---

12. Carl F. H. Henry, "The Renewal of Theological Education," *Vocatio* 1, no. 2 (summer 1989): 4.

4. *Reputation* (1 Tim. 3:7–8). While learning maturity in the school of life, a person earns a reputation through the pursuit of a godly moral life, home life, and maturity.

Avenues toward a Godly Character

The route taken in pursuit of a godly character is not a short one. Nor is there any single path that inevitably leads to it. While a mentor may be able to lead to the water, only the student himself can initiate the drinking. Yet there are some steps to assist the man who desires to be truly qualified and trained for the pastoral ministry.

Reading and meditating on the Word is where this training begins. Scripture clearly enunciates the prescriptions for holy living. With these directives the man of God must saturate himself, letting "the word of Christ richly dwell within you" (Col. 3:16). Other books that can also stimulate growth toward godliness include *Spiritual Leadership,* by J. Oswald Sanders (Moody, 1980); *Keys to Spiritual Growth,* by John F. MacArthur, Jr. (Revell, 1976); and *Spiritual Maturity,* by Richard Mayhue (Victor, 1992).

Rubbing elbows with other godly men and spiritual leaders can also promote spiritual accountability, growth, and maturity. As "iron sharpens iron, so one man sharpens another" (Prov. 27:17). Even reading biographies of men whom God greatly used in past generations promotes the molding of a person's life and the shaping of his understanding of how God works, both individually and corporately.

BIBLICAL KNOWLEDGE

Biblical knowledge is an indispensable part of the training process. Without it one cannot enjoy personal spiritual growth in godly character, nor can effective and meaningful ministry to others ensue if it is not present. *Sola Scriptura* and *sola fide* provide the mortar binding together the building blocks of ministry. Quoting S. Miller's 1812 address at the inauguration of A. Alexander as the first professor at Princeton Theological Seminary, Hafemann observes, "He argued that in addition to piety and ability those called to the pastoral ministry must have a 'competent knowledge,' without which 'both piety and talents united are inadequate to the official work.'"[13]

---

13. Scott J. Hafemann, "Seminary, Subjectivity, and the Centrality of Scripture: Reflections on the Current Crisis in Evangelical Seminary Education," *Journal of the Evangelical Theological Society* 31, no. 2 (June 1988): 142.

No movement can impact a society with its creed if its leaders are ignorant of or continually undermining the veracity and applicability of its charter documents. As Carl Henry rightly contends,

> The one book above all others in which a twentieth century scholar should be learned remains the Bible; among all the great books with which one should be familiar, the Bible stands tallest. . . . The churches today need nothing so much as a vital recovery of the authority and comprehensive truthfulness of Scripture and its application to all dimensions of life.[14]

Nor should this aspect of training for the ministry be taken lightly. The influence of the teacher upon the pupil is enormous, not only in *what* is taught but also in *how* it is taught (Luke 6:40). Consequently, biblical and theological mentors must pass the scrutiny of 1 Timothy 3 and Titus 1 if they are to prepare others effectively. The ministry qualifications and pastoral experience of the teacher are vital factors in the educational equation.

Biblical Knowledge as a Goal

The goal of acquiring biblical knowledge is not personal recognition or academic respectability. Beginning with the dawn of the Age of Enlightenment and especially over the last two centuries, there has come a bloated emphasis on the academic at the expense of biblical and theological integrity. Wanting desperately to impact the universal world of academics and gain the recognition of secular scholars, many training institutions and their mentors have become victims of academic intoxication.[15]

Being biblically knowledgeable and theologically accurate should derive its motivation *first and foremost* from a yearning to know God intimately (Phil. 3:8–10). Says Packer,

> To be preoccupied with getting theological knowledge as an end in itself, to approach Bible study with no higher a motive than a desire to know all the answers, is the direct route to a state of self-satisfied self-deception. . . . There can be no spiritual health without doctrinal knowledge; but it is equally true that there can be no spiritual health

---

14. Henry, "Renewal," 4.

15. The situation is not unlike the intrusion of Greek and Jewish allegorism into the early church. Eagerness to gain acceptance within academic circles induces hermeneutical and thus biblical and theological capitulations with dire consequences.

with it, if it is sought for the wrong purpose and valued by the wrong standard. . . . We must seek, in studying God, to be led to God. It was for this purpose that revelation was given, and it is to this use that we must put it.[16]

Out of that zeal, then, flows the passion to handle the Word of Truth accurately (2 Tim. 2:15), to wield a sharp sword capably (Eph. 6:17; Heb. 4:12;), and thereby to contend for the foundational doctrines of Scripture once-for-all delivered to the saints powerfully (Jude 3).

Areas of Biblical Knowledge

Debate has waged over the areas and extent of biblical knowledge needed, especially in light of the more market-driven "let's-be-relevant" philosophies that dominate the current scene. Yet if the aims delineated above are to become realities, then the path of training must include three stepping stones: a functional facility with the original languages, a theological framework or grid forged by the fires of exegesis, and a familiarity with the theological positions of contemporary and historical authors.

Linguistic Facility. The first and most foundational of these steps is a working knowledge of the languages in which the Spirit-moved authors penned the inspired words (2 Pet. 1:21). Propelled by the knowledge that every translation to some extent is an interpretation, every pastoral trainee must vigorously pursue a basic knowledge of Greek and Hebrew. The only other alternative for the pastor-preacher is to study and expound the Word at the mercy of the commentaries, never certain of the veracity of his sources and never able to find a source that answers all the questions. A knowledge of the original languages does not guarantee accuracy, but it does promote it.

While the rewards of such a pursuit are endless, the path is not always smooth, nor is the choice without its detractors.

A commitment (requirement) to study the Scriptures historically and a seminary's demand that theology, ethics, mission, preaching and pastoral care all flow out of sound exegetical conclusions, won through grinding work of reading the Bible in its original languages and historical contexts, will appear to many to be elitist, filled with the pride of intellectualism. . . . To others it will appear too time-consuming, impractical and irrelevant in the face of serious issues that surround us. Still others will argue that such a Scripture-centered curriculum

---

16. J. I. Packer, *Knowing God* (Downers Grove, Ill.: InterVarsity, 1993), 22–23.

strikes at the very heart of an egalitarianism that many falsely equate with the gospel and our cherished Protestant heritage. . . . Only those seminaries that can communicate their unpopular convictions clearly and persuasively with prospective students and with the Church in a sort of "pre-education" will be able to overcome the initial shock of such a rigorous and old-fashioned approach to theological studies.[17]

But the church and its training institutions must overcome these obstacles, for the alternative is to interpret the Bible subjectively, according to how one feels and in a relativistic what-does-it-mean-to-me manner. Unless pastor-trainers are willing to grasp this task (2 Tim. 2:2) and to reassert (not only verbally but also in practice) the centrality of Scripture, God's propositional revelation of Himself will become devoid of any authority to compel obedience.

Theological Framework. *Theology* is defined as that which is known about God through the self-disclosure of Himself, primarily through the Scriptures (special revelation) but also in creation (general revelation). Three rudimentary elements comprise a proper theological framework or grid through which to filter what one reads and hears: historical theology, biblical theology, and systematic theology.

Historical theology provides invaluable insight into the issues, debates, councils, and creeds in church history. It demonstrates how the teachings of Scripture have been formulated and shaped into dogmas, creeds, and confessions of faith. It reveals the constant struggle against error and unmasks the heresies against which the church has battled and out of which every important dogma has emerged. Because "there is nothing new under the sun" (Eccl. 1:9) and with heresies of antiquity resurfacing repeatedly under the guise of "something new," the study of historical theology assists in understanding the current scene and prevents falling into old traps. Lloyd-Jones states, "Church history is invaluable to the preacher. . . . I would say that Church history is one of the most essential studies for the preacher were it merely to show him this terrible danger of slipping into heresy, or into error, without realizing that anything has happened to him."[18]

Biblical theology, in a narrow sense, provides the student with a basic understanding of each biblical author, book, or group of books. Quality training must include a study of these elements, providing an essential pic-

---

17. Hafemann, "Seminary, Subjectivity," 140–41.

18. D. Martyn Lloyd-Jones, *Preaching and Preachers* (Grand Rapids: Zondervan, 1971), 117.

ture of the pieces that make up the whole. Warfield notes the significance of such a study:

> Its exegetical value lies just in this circumstance, that it is only when we have thus concatenated an author's theological statements into a whole, that we can be sure that we understand them as he understood them in detail. A light is inevitably thrown back from Biblical Theology upon the separate theological deliverances as they occur in the text, such as subtly colors them, and often, for the first time, gives them to us in their true setting, and thus enables us to guard against perverting them when we adapt them to our use.[19]

Systematic theology collects the pieces and puts them together into a whole. It is an outgrowth of historical and biblical theology, being fed, tested, and corrected by a constant infusion of exegesis as exhibited in biblical theology.[20] It provides an ordered summary or synopsis of important themes in biblical teaching, assembled in such a way as not to violate the contexts of the individual parts. It is not, as some would assert, a man-made skeleton, dominated by philosophy or dead orthodoxy devoid of practical relevance. Rather, it is a structure forged in the fires of exegesis and hammered out on the anvil of centuries of intense study, debate, and understanding. According to Lloyd-Jones, "It is not enough merely that a man should know the Scriptures, he must know the Scriptures in the sense that he has got out of them the essence of biblical theology and can grasp it in a systematic manner. He must be so well versed in this that all his preaching is controlled by it."[21]

The importance of collating and integrating the full breadth of one's theology into a cohesive unit should not be underestimated. Since the Scriptures are the product of divine inspiration, the whole will not disagree with the parts. One must view the entire corpus, through the eyes of each constituent part, as an undivided whole. The preaching of the individual parts is strengthened when, welded together with the whole, their role in the overarching scheme and purpose is clearly visible.

---

19. B. B. Warfield, "The Idea of Systematic Theology," in *The Necessity of Systematic Theology*, ed. John Jefferson Davis (Washington D.C.: University Press, 1978), 112–13.

20. Ibid., 113. He adds, "It uses the individual data furnished by exegesis, in a word, not crudely, not independently for itself, but only after these data have been worked up into Biblical Theology and have received from it their final coloring and subtlest shades of meaning—in other words, only in their true sense, and after Exegetics has said its last word upon them" (113).

21. Lloyd-Jones, *Preaching and Preachers*, 117.

We cannot know what God has revealed in his Word unless we understand, at least in some good measure, the relation in which the separate truths therein contained stand to each other. . . . We have no other choice in this matter. If we would discharge our duty as teachers and defenders of the truth, we must endeavor to bring all the facts of revelation into systematic order and mutual relation. It is only thus that we can satisfactorily exhibit their truth, vindicate them from objections, or bring them to bear in their full force on the minds of men.[22]

Warfield appropriately notes the practical purpose:

If such be the value and use of doctrine, the systematic theologian is preeminently a preacher of the gospel; and the end of his work is obviously not merely the logical arrangement of the truths which come under his hand, but the moving of men, through their power, to love God with all their hearts and their neighbors as themselves; to choose their portion with the Saviour of their souls; to find and hold Him precious; and to recognize and yield to the sweet influences of the Holy Spirit whom He has sent.[23]

Bibliographical Familiarity. Another area of valuable ministry training occurs in exposure to and evaluation of a broad range of books and authors. A rudimentary acquaintance with the writings of major Christian leaders, thinkers, and writers throughout church history allows the trainee to be familiar with their hermeneutical and theological premises. The contemporary proliferation of books, periodicals, and magazines makes a general knowledge of authors and publishers imperative. Familiarity of this sort will save time and will provide a better understanding of each author in the reading of his works.[24]

Avenues to Biblical Knowledge

Many have attempted to provide pastoral students with in-depth biblical training through correspondence courses or independent-study environments, away from the more formal classroom setting. Biblical knowledge is generally more difficult to achieve that way, however. Sometimes self-

---

22. Charles Hodge, *Systematic Theology* (Grand Rapids: Eerdmans, 1970 reprint), 1:2–3.

23. Warfield, "Idea of Systematic Theology," 129.

24. Book reviews in periodicals and journals provide quick access to this type of information.

education may be the only option, but the required preparation time is considerably longer that way. Formal classroom instruction is of great benefit in imparting capability in the biblical languages and significant comprehension in matters of theology. The wisdom of skilled teachers, men who have given themselves to a lifetime of study and training others, together with the direct interaction of fellow students can shorten the learning curve, enhance the comprehension, strengthen the retention, and facilitate the process from biblical languages to exegesis to theology to teaching and preaching.

No shortcuts are advisable here. Biblical knowledge and theological understanding will inevitably impact the way a person lives (godly character) and the way he serves (ministry skills). In equal measure, it will reverberate in the lives of the people to whom he ministers. Attempts to streamline the learning process by reducing it inevitably lead to a weakened understanding and loss of productivity. Both godly character and pastoral skills are essentials available virtually anytime and anywhere in the world, but the advantage of skilled instruction and supervision in gaining biblical knowledge is not so readily available or easily obtained. When the opportunity presents itself, it must be one's highest priority to seize it.

MINISTRY SKILLS

Ministry Skills as a Goal

The assumption that scholastic achievement and academic success in the seminary classroom are equivalent to full preparation for pastoral ministry is obviously naive. Though most training institutions claim to prepare their students for spiritual leadership in the local church, sadly many of them do not. Effective preparation goes beyond the classroom to include on-the-job training, without which many students will not know whether they will sink or swim as they enter the ministry.

Areas of Ministry Skills

Four primary areas exist for honing one's ministry skills. The prepared pastor is one who, through the pursuit of godly character and the rigors of comprehensive biblical and theological studies, in addition learns to lead with conviction, to teach with authority, to preach with passion, and to shepherd with care.

Leading with Conviction. Competent leadership is anchored securely to strong biblical convictions and is an absolutely essential quality for effectiveness in ministry. Titus 1:9 says that an elder should be "holding fast the faithful word which is in accordance with the teaching, that he may be able both to exhort in sound doctrine and to refute those who contradict." Spiritual convictions that undergird strong leadership do not originate in a vacuum; rather, they emerge as the residue from the impact of the Word of God upon the individual made by the Spirit of God. Conviction, in turn, generates the discipline, vision, and courage necessary for the task. A firm grasp of the Word of God and an ever-growing absorption of its truthfulness into the fabric of one's life are the underpinning upon which convictions rest—convictions that are worth dying for.

Teaching with Authority. The preacher is under divine commission and authority. "He is an ambassador, and he should be aware of his authority. He should always know that he comes to the congregation as a sent messenger."[25] At the close of Jesus' sermon on the mount, Matthew summarizes, "The multitudes were amazed at His teaching; for He was teaching them as one having authority, and not as their scribes" (Matt. 7:28–29). Likewise, Paul instructed his trainees to teach with authority. He commands Timothy to "prescribe and teach these things" (1 Tim. 4:11). He reminds Titus, "These things speak and exhort and reprove with all authority. Let no one disregard you" (Titus 2:15).

It is important that authority is not self-based or self-generated. Authoritative teaching derives solely from a knowledge and understanding of the Word of God.

> Our authority has a foundation. First, you must know what you believe about the Bible. If you're not sure it's the Word of God, you won't be authoritative. Next you have to know what God's Word says. If you're not sure what it means, you can't be authoritative. Then you must be concerned about communicating it properly because you care that His Word is upheld. Finally, you should care about the people's response to His Word.[26]

The mandate is clear. The faithful servant is to be bold in his teaching, speaking forth God's Word and letting it do its work.

---

25. Lloyd-Jones, *Preaching and Preachers*, 83.

26. John MacArthur, Jr., *Shepherdology: A Master Plan for Church Leadership* (Panorama, Calif.: The Master's Fellowship, 1989), 139; rev. ed., *The Master's Plan for the Church* (Chicago: Moody, 1991).

Preaching with Passion. Preaching with passion intimates personal appropriation of what is preached. The preacher himself has enthusiastically embraced the content of his message to others. The message's substance has impacted his own heart, and he is eager to involve others in sharing its wealth and feeling its impact.

> A preacher must always convey the impression that he himself has been gripped by what he is saying. If he has not been gripped nobody else will be. So this is absolutely essential. He must impress the people by the fact that he is taken up and absorbed by what he is doing. He is full of matter, and he is anxious to impart this. He is so moved and thrilled by it himself that he wants everybody else to share in this. . . . So he does it with energy, with zeal, and with this obvious concern for people.[27]

Training a student to preach this way is difficult. Outwardly, enthusiasm and zeal for the message reflect passion, and these can be taught. But true passion goes beyond outward enthusiasm. Passion derives from the veins of a changed heart and an enlightened mind, from a spirit stirred by the impact of the Word rightly divided and energized by its personal application. Human effort can generate outward enthusiasm, but not passion. Rather, passion oozes—often nonverbally—out of the preacher, providing a strong adhesive to bind structural parts of the sermon together. It visibly demonstrates that the two-edged sword, the Word, has found its mark in the life of the pastor.

It is at this point that the ministry skills of a preacher most closely intertwine with his pursuit of godliness. To preach with passion, he must first study the biblical text for his own spiritual enrichment and growth, applying the truths personally, before he is ready to preach passionately to others. Lloyd-Jones said, "If a man's heart is not engaged I take leave to query and to question whether he has really understood with his head, because of the very character of the Truth with which we are dealing. . . . Do we believe it, have we been gripped and humbled by it, and then exalted until we are 'lost in wonder love and praise.' "[28]

Shepherding with Care. Leadership and rulership are often mistakenly equated. Although being in a position of oversight will require making decisions that affect others, biblical shepherding calls for ministry, not

---

27. Lloyd-Jones, *Preaching and Preachers*, 87–88.
28. Ibid., 90.

monarchy. The key to effective leadership is service, as the apostle Paul makes clear: "But we request of you, brethren, that you appreciate those who diligently labor among you, and have charge over you in the Lord and give you instruction, and that you esteem them very highly in love *because of their work*" (1 Thess. 5:12–13, emphasis added).

The caring shepherd must learn to be vigilant, watching over and guarding his flock. In his parting instructions to the Ephesian elders, Paul said, "Be on guard for yourselves and for all the flock, among which the Holy Spirit has made you overseers, to shepherd the church of God which He purchased with His own blood" (Acts 20:28). Heb. 13:17 echoes the same thought, noting that leaders "keep watch over your souls." By the foresight of the shepherd the sheep find protection; by his courage they receive defense.

The caring shepherd must learn to guide his sheep to green pastures and still waters. Jesus said of the shepherd, "When he puts forth all his own, he goes before them, and the sheep follow him because they know his voice" (John 10:4). The spiritual leader must know where he is going and encourage others to follow. "Be imitators of me, just as I also am of Christ" (1 Cor. 11:1). Spiritual nourishment to bring growth through the Word are his responsibility to prescribe and dispense.

The caring shepherd must learn how to provide for the welfare of his flock. He needs time with the sheep to become familiar with their needs. When queried as to why He ate and drank with taxgatherers and sinners, Jesus replied, "It is not those who are well who need a physician, but those who are sick" (Luke 5:31).

> The true leader regards the welfare of others rather than his own comfort and prestige as of primary concern. He manifests sympathy and concern for those under him in their problems, difficulties, and cares, but it is a sympathy that fortifies and stimulates, not that softens and weakens. He will always direct their confidence to the Lord. He sees in each emergency a new opportunity for helpfulness.[29]

The caring shepherd is one who loves the sheep. He has affection for them. The Good Shepherd carries His sheep in His bosom (Isa. 40:11), calls them by name, and lays down His life for them (John 10:3, 11).

> To love to preach is one thing, to love those to whom we preach is quite another. The trouble with some of us is that we love preaching,

---

29. Sanders, *Spiritual Leadership*, 153–54.

but we are not always careful to make sure that we love the people to whom we are actually preaching. If you lack this element of compassion for the people you will also lack the pathos which is a very vital element in all true preaching. Our Lord looked out upon the multitudes and "saw them as sheep without a shepherd," and was "filled with compassion." And if you know nothing of this you should not be in a pulpit.[30]

To try to practice the role of a caring leader apart from love is legalism. Love is the glue that holds all these things together. "And beyond all these things put on love, which is the perfect bond of unity" (Col. 3:14).

Avenues to Ministry Skills

One learns ministry skills, first of all, in the classroom. And it is probably more often caught than it is taught. Students admire their teachers and therefore emulate them, many times unintentionally. Whether it is handling the Word, responding to difficult questions, or demonstrating a genuine interest in the lives of others, students find themselves imitating their teachers. In general, they embrace the philosophy and follow the example of their mentors.

As a consequence, it is imperative that would-be pastors choose a training institution/setting where professors and mentors are pastorally trained and pastorally "brained." Instructors must bleed pastoral ministries and missions in their classes, in their own local church ministries, and in their relationships. The impact will be phenomenal.

Practical ministry preparation should also include on-the-job training. Leadership is partly a gift and partly learned. Therefore, training must include the practice of ministry in concert with the academics, preferably in an arena where praxis occurs alongside the formal training.

Training for pastoral ministry is a demanding, lifelong pursuit. It requires a man to give himself to the pursuit of godliness, to subject himself to the disciplines of learning biblical languages, doing exegesis, and formulating and understanding theology, and to hone his ministry skills through years of ministry and humble service.

Of utmost importance is the interrelatedness of experience and learning. Effective preparation demands that one not remove praxis from

---

30. Lloyd-Jones, *Preaching and Preachers*, 92.

academia, or vice versa. The church gave birth to the seminary and needs the seminary; the seminary was born for the purpose of assisting and serving the church and thus needs the church. Training that occurs exclusively within the local church will often produce a weakness in the area of biblical knowledge and theology. Training that occurs exclusively within the academic arena will produce a weakness in the area of ministry skills. The two must blend together throughout the preparation process. The lifeblood of effective training depends on this vital linkage.

> To assume that successful scholarship in theology, history, and Bible is equivalent to preparation for ministry is naive. To assume that the addition of a course in Practical Theology or a fieldwork requirement would resolve the matter is no less naive. Somehow theological education and preparation for ministry must occur in a place and time and context in which individuals are living the questions, dealing with people.[31]

Of equal importance is the need for a preparation rooted and grounded in the biblical *sine qua non*s for the church. Students must capture a clear understanding of the scriptural mandate for the church—what it is and what it is to do—and seize an unwavering commitment to carry out that mandate, whatever the cost. In an ecclesiastical world that is embracing the market-driven philosophy at an alarming rate, the task will not be easy. It is definitely the road less traveled, but the rewards are great.

Finally, there is a price of preparation to pay. No shortcuts exist in training for the pastoral ministry. Only persistent prayer, hard work, and focused perseverance will do—an undying commitment to be a man of God, equipped for every good work.

---

31. John M. Buchanan, "Basic Issues in Theological Education," *Quarterly Review* 13, no. 3 (fall, 1993): 52. "Something less than the desired, holistic pattern of church/seminary relationships will prevail if either church or seminary does not have an integrated program of reflecting upon and developing a vital and mutual interrelationship between church and seminary" (Robert P. Meye, "Toward Holistic Church/Seminary Relations," *Theology, News and Notes*, 40, no. 3 (October 1993): 15.

8

Ordination to Pastoral Ministry

Richard L. Mayhue

Ordination describes the biblical concept of God's appointment of men to full-time ministry.[1] Today, the church recognizes ordained men when their ministerial desires, godly life, and giftedness for ministry match the biblical standards (both subjective and objective) that identify a man whom God has called to ministry. Scripture does not specify the detailed procedure by which a man qualifies for ordination; therefore, liberty prevails when outlining a practical plan. One proven method used effectively by a local church illustrates how to carry out the ordination process according to biblical milestones.

Adam, God made out of dust
But thought it best to make me first
So I was made before man.
To answer God's most holy plan
A living being I became—
And Adam gave me my name.
I from his presence then withdrew
And more of Adam never knew.

---

1. For additional discussions regarding ordination, consult Robert C. Anderson, *The Effective Pastor* (Chicago: Moody, 1986), 57–67; D. Miall Edwards, "Ordain, Ordination," in *International Standard Bible Encyclopedia*, ed. James Orr (Grand Rapids: Eerdmans, 1939), 4:2199–200; Homer A. Kent, Sr., *The Pastor and His Work* (Chicago: Moody, 1963), 194–202; Robert L. Saucy, *The Church in God's Program* (Chicago: Moody, 1972), 161–65.

I did my maker's law obey
Nor ever went from it astray.
Thousands of miles I go in fear
But seldom on earth appear.
For purpose wise which God did see
He put a living soul in me.
A soul from me God did claim
And took from me the soul again.
So when from me the soul had fled,
I was the same as when first made.
I am without hands or feet or soul;
I travel on from pole to pole.
I labor hard by day, by night
To fallen man give great light.
Thousands of people, young and old,
Will by my death great light behold.
No right or wrong can I conceive;
The Scripture I cannot believe.
Although my name therein is found,
They are to me an empty sound.
No fear of death doth trouble me;
Real happiness I'll never see.
To heaven I shall never go
Or to hell below.
Now when these lines you slowly read,
Go search your Bible with all speed.
For that my name is written there
I do honestly to you declare.
If my kind you can identify,
You for ministry will qualify.
Who am I? [2]

Ordination candidates frequently fear embarrassment when facing obscure, Gordian-knot type questions—like the riddle just cited[3]—from mean-spirited pastors and seminary professors. Congregations often perceive ordination as nothing more than a postseminary inquisition inflicted

---

2. Author unknown.

3. See note 16 for solution to the riddle.

through irrelevant questions, designed to make the prospective pastor squirm just one more time.

Does ordination equate to a final moment of ecclesiastical hazing just prior to a man's admission to the ministry? Or, does it entail more noble, biblical purposes? What is ordination? Why should a man[4] be ordained? Who needs ordination?[5] How should ordination be conducted? These and other questions need solid biblical answers to make the ordination process stand for something more than a mere torturous final exam.

THE BIBLICAL CONCEPT OF ORDINATION

The overarching concept of ordination to ministry appears in both the Old and New Testaments. Ordination is the process of godly church leaders affirming the call, equipping, and maturity of new leaders to serve God's purposes in the next generation. Ordination validates/authenticates God's will for a fully qualified man to serve God and His people.

Old Testament

Moses "ordained" (יד מלא, *ml᷾ yd*, "filled the hand of") Aaron and his sons to the priesthood of Israel (Exod. 29:9, 29, 35). He symbolically represented God's will for Aaron to serve as high priest by laying hands on him, thus authenticating or ordaining Aaron for priestly ministry. This same procedure appears also in Lev. 16:32 and Num. 3:3.

---

4. This discussion will assume the biblical teaching that God calls only men as pastors/elders of the church. Therefore, only men should be candidates for ordination. The following treatments carefully outline the biblical basis for this conclusion. Gleason Archer, "Ordination Is Not for Women," *Moody Monthly* 87, no. 6 (February 1987): 8; Elisabeth Elliot, "Why I Oppose the Ordination of Women," *Christianity Today* 19, no. 6 (June 6, 1975): 12–16; George W. Knight III, "The Ordination of Women: No," *Christianity Today* 25, no. 4 (February 20, 1981): 16–19; Douglas Moo, "What Does It Mean Not to Teach or Have Authority over Men?" in *Recovering Biblical Manhood and Womanhood*, ed. Wayne Grudem and John Piper (Westchester, Ill.: Crossway, 1991), 179–93; J. I. Packer, "Let's Stop Making Women Presbyters," *Christianity Today* 35, no. 2 (February 11, 1991): 18–21; and Paige Patterson, "The Meaning of Authority in the Local Church," in *Recovering Biblical Manhood and Womanhood*, ed. Wayne Gruden and John Piper (Westchester, Ill.: Crossway, 1991), 248–59.

5. In this discussion, those ordained to Christian ministry are distinguishable from the congregation as a whole by their divine calling and giftedness for ministry, not by any inherent personal superiority to other Christians in the body of Christ. I will avoid using the misleading *clergy* and *lay people* terminology.

Put another way, ordination recognizes God's appointment of a man to ministry and is the leadership's way of commending him to the congregation. For example, the high priest of Israel was appointed (καθίσταται, *kathistatai*, "put in place") by God to minister on behalf of men in the things pertaining to God (Heb. 5:1; 8:3). Moses recognized this fact and communicated it to Israel by laying his hands on Aaron.

New Testament

The divine side of appointment to ministry comes first. Paul was "ordained" (ἐτέθην, *etethēn*) by God to the ministry (1 Tim. 2:7). Paul told the Ephesian elders that the Holy Spirit had "made" (ἔθετο, *etheto*) them overseers to shepherd the church of God (Acts 20:28). Yet God used godly human leaders to communicate to the people His appointment of these men. Both the divine and the human side of the process are necessary.[6] God sets leaders apart so that the current leadership can assimilate them into the developing order of leadership.

Humanly speaking, Jesus "appointed" (ἔθηκα, *ethēka*, "set/placed") His disciples (John 15:16). He "appointed" (ἐποίησεν, *epoiēsen*, "made") the twelve to be with Himself to preach (Mark 3:14).

The apostles affirmed a new group of leaders in ministry at Jerusalem by laying hands on them (Acts 6:6). On Paul's first missionary journey, he and Barnabas "appointed" (χειροτονήσαντες, *cheirotonēsantes*, "stretching out the hand to") elders in every church (Acts 14:23). He also instructed Titus to "appoint" (καταστήσῃς, *katastēsēs*, "put in place") elders in every city (Titus 1:5).

Understanding the biblical idea of ordination is a partial answer to the question, "Who should be added to existing ministry leadership?" But it also raises a related question: "How do we recognize God's appointed leaders?"

THE PRACTICAL ESSENCE OF ORDINATION

From the biblical examples cited, it is obvious that ordination involves God's appointment of men to ministry, which appointment godly men who are already leaders subsequently recognize and authenticate according to God's Word. Appointment to ordained ministry in the church does not

---

6. Saucy, *Church in God's Program*, 164, defines the two sides succinctly: "Ordination is the recognition by the church of those whom God has called and equipped for a regular ordained ministry in the church."

come by way of family inheritance, apostolic succession, or some sacerdotal investiture of authority by men. Rather, each generation of leadership receives its appointment from God through godly leaders, on the basis of whose recommendation the church can then verify the appointment.

Ordination is to church leadership as the bar exam is to the legal profession, the C.P.A. exam to accounting, or state board examinations to medical practice. All these examinations serve to verify genuine qualifications for service in the respective fields. More specifically, the ordination process serves to:

1. identify and certify men truly called and equipped by God for full-time pastoral ministry

2. eliminate men seeking ministry credentials who are not called by God

3. give a congregation great confidence that their leaders are genuinely appointed by God

4. furnish a standard of accountability for the church concerning a man's ministry

5. commend a man publicly to the ministry wherever God's will takes him

One of the most explicit aspects of the ordination process is the determination of the humanly discernible biblical qualifications in the life and abilities of a man whom God has appointed to ministry. These identifying elements are both subjective and objective. The subjective or internal aspect relates to the ordination candidate's self-perspective of God's will for him to be in the ministry. The balancing external or objective side looks at the possibility of ordination in relation to the standards of Scripture.

The Internal/Subjective Aspect

What a man desires and what he believes about the ministry God intends for him begins the ordination process at the subjective level: "It is a trustworthy statement: if any man *aspires* to the office of overseer, it is a fine work he desires to do" (1 Tim. 3:1, emphasis added). This initial step, humanly speaking, begins with the one who believes it to be God's will for him to engage in full-time ministry. This call presupposes a man's *genuine conversion* to Christ and God's subsequent *call* in his life to the ministry.[7]

---

7. See chapter 6, "The Call to Pastoral Ministry."

MacArthur explains the intent of 1 Tim. 3:1 regarding this subjective phase of the ordination process:

> In other words, we are not to go out and recruit men to become elders. One who is qualified to be an elder will be eager to teach the Word of God and lead the flock of God, without any thought of gain at all. He will desire the office, pursue being set apart, and devote himself to the Word. No one will have to talk him into it; it is his heart's passion.
>
> Furthermore, he serves "voluntarily, *according to the will of God*." His service as an elder is a calling from God. The desire to serve as an elder is in his heart because God put it there.[8]

Let the reader be warned. Many a man has falsely claimed a call to the ministry. Frequently, a counterfeit desire has come from human pride, the aspirations of others, misunderstanding God's will, or substituting formal education only for God's complete ordination process. That is why the objective or external part of the ordination process is indispensable in confirming God's will for a man's life. The objective process will affirm or negate the less measurable subjective side.

The External/Objective Aspect

"And let these also first be tested; then let them serve as deacons if they are beyond reproach" (1 Tim. 3:10). The immediate context of this instruction to Timothy deals with deacons (3:8–9). But the *also* refers back to the qualifications of overseers[9] in 3:1–7. Overseers "also" need testing. This allows the church to validate the subjective impressions of the one seeking ordination by using God's criteria as a basis for testing.

Scripture gives five major testing grounds: character, conduct, capabilities, creed, and commitment. First, a man's *character* must be consistent with his call in that he models the message he preaches. First Timothy 3:2–7 lists ten features that fall into four major categories according to the following grouping:[10]

---

8. John MacArthur, Jr., *The Master's Plan for the Church* (Chicago: Moody, 1991), 192 (emphasis added).

9. The New Testament uses the terms *pastor*, *elder*, and *overseer* interchangeably to denote the ordained man. See MacArthur, *Master's Plan*, 183–85, for a full biblical explanation.

10. For an in-depth discussion of 1 Tim. 3:1–7, see MacArthur, *Master's Plan*, 215–33. See chapter 5, "The Character of a Pastor," for a related discussion of Titus 1:5–9.

1. his devotion/dedication (3:2)

   "husband of one wife"

2. his personal discipline (3:2)

   "temperate"

   "prudent"

   "respectable"

3. his direction in life (3:2)

   "hospitable"—toward people

   "able to teach"—toward God's Word

4. his desires (3:3)

   "not addicted to wine"

   "not pugnacious but gentle"

   "uncontentious"

   "free from the love of money"

Second, a man's *conduct* must be consistent with his character. Three elements of life are proving grounds for his conduct:

1. his domestic excellence (3:4–5)
2. his spiritual maturity (3:6)
3. his community reputation (3:7)

Third, his *capabilities* must be in accord with his call. First Timothy 3:2 clarifies that he must be "able to teach." Titus 1:9 amplifies this: "Holding fast the faithful word which is in accordance with the teaching, that he may be able both to exhort in sound doctrine and to refute those who contradict." As a result of a man's understanding of and ability to teach the Word, including the refutation of error, he is to

1. shepherd the flock of God (Acts 20:28; 1 Pet. 5:2)
2. provide spiritual oversight (Acts 20:28; Titus 1:7)
3. lead as a mature man of God (Acts 20:17; Titus 1:5; 1 Pet. 5:1)
4. be faithful as a steward of God's ministry (Titus 1:7)

Fourth, his *creed* must join with his capabilities as God's Word says it should. He is to minister in accord with sound doctrine (Titus 1:9).[11]

Fifth, his *commitment* must demonstrate consistency in all four of the above categories by being tested over a sufficient period (1 Tim. 3:10). This allows the objective aspect of ordination to verify the subjective side as being real and not staged. Thus a man's overarching quality of life is to be "blameless." This does not equate with sinless perfection in the life of a pastor. Yet it does presuppose that his life is at such a high level of spiritual maturity that he is exempt from any valid charge of persistent sin.

MOVING FROM ESSENCE TO PRACTICE

The biblical grounds treated thus far have been fairly specific. The Bible speaks clearly about men appointing or ordaining other men to ministry according to God's will. God has provided both subjective and objective features to help the church determine God's will for a man's life. The basic criteria for objective testing in 1 Tim. 3:1–7 and Titus 1:5–9 are beyond debate. Apart from these basics, however, Scripture says little else to explain the how-to's of ordination.[12] Therefore, the church has a God-given liberty to design a practical process leading to ordination, so long as the process includes what the Scripture does dictate.

Some reject formal ordination altogether, because they believe that God, not man, ordains. Insofar as they have their life and ministry validated by the biblical standard, Scripture does not fault this approach, if it includes the biblical basis for testing/certification.

With equal liberty, others focus only on a direct ordination process. Still others follow a more indirect route, using the licensure[13] period as part

---

11. Does a man have to have a seminary degree in order to be ordained? We respond emphatically, "No!" However, he must have a firm grasp of biblical content and theological thought. Normally, but not always, seminary training provides this capability at the highest level of excellence. However, seminary is not the only practical means to reach the goal of being able to teach truth and refute error (Titus 1:9).

12. Paige Patterson, "Meaning of Authority," 249–51, discusses this observation concerning ordination in more detail.

13. Kent, *Pastor*, 187-93, thoroughly discusses the concept of licensure. The licensing period serves as a time of testing in the ordination process, during which the church appoints the candidate to perform all of the duties of an ordained man. While ordination is for life (assuming the ordained man does not disqualify himself), licensure lasts only for a given period, usually one year, and is subject to renewal if necessary. If we compare the ordination process to the driving permit process, licensure is comparable to the learner permit and ordination to the final driving permit.

of the process leading to ordination. Scripture allows for either, assuming it incorporates the essence of ordination into the process.

Therefore, the remainder of this chapter will not lay out an exclusive ordination process. Rather, it will explain how one church, with a matured and proven process developed over the past twenty years, integrates the Scriptural elements into an ordination procedure.

OVERVIEW OF THE ORDINATION PROCESS OF GRACE COMMUNITY CHURCH[14]

I.   Constitution

Ordination by Grace Community Church constitutes the formal, local church affirmation of a man's call, his biblical qualifications, and his recognized capabilities for Christian ministry. The latter includes the ability to preach and teach. Our ordination is recognized by most independent, evangelical churches. The State of California and the Internal Revenue Service also accept our ordination.

II. Definitions

The following definitions differentiate between ordination, licensure, and commissioning.

A.   *Ordination.* Ordination refers to the unanimous recognition by the Board of Elders of a man's call to the ministry, preparation as a shepherd, and qualification to serve. Ordination shall be conferred for life, so long as the man continues to manifest the qualifications of the office.

B.   *Licensing.* The license is issued by the Board of Elders and is given in recognition of a man's admission to the ordination process. Its aim is to allow a man to perform the ecclesiastical duties and functions of the church. Licenses will be evaluated and issued on a yearly basis.

C.   *Licensing/Commissioning.* When local church certification is

---

14. Adapted from "Ordination Process" (Sun Valley, Calif.: Grace Community Church, 1993), 11–24. This manual is available through the Grace Book Shack, 13248 Roscoe Blvd., Sun Valley, CA 91352 (818/909-5555).

required for ministry where ordination would be unnecessary or inappropriate, a person may be either licensed or commissioned by the Board of Elders to minister. This authorization continues as long as the opportunity to minister remains in effect and as long as the person maintains the qualifications for ministry.

III. Oversight

The ordination process will be overseen by a lay elder and an ordained pastoral elder who comprise the Ordination Facilitating Group (OFG). OFG will be selected by the Board of Elders.

IV. Applicants

Applicants for ordination by Grace Community Church will be limited to men who:

A. Currently are members of Grace Community Church.

B. Currently minister at Grace Community Church with at least two previous years of ministry experience at Grace Community Church. The most recent year should be, under normal circumstances, in the ministry overseen by the elder and staff pastor who recommend the applicant to be considered.

C. Believe that God has called and gifted them for a ministry of the Word under the authority of the local church.

V. Preliminary Steps

The ordination process (illustrated in figure 1) begins with these preliminary steps:

A. An elder and his staff counterpart recommend the candidate to OFG for consideration of admission to the ordination process. This assumes that the applicant has been reviewed by the pastoral staff with comment.

B. The applicant has read *What We Teach*[15] and has signed the "Affirmation of Doctrinal Convictions" (see Appendix 1) and sub-

---

15. *What We Teach* is a 1986 publication of Grace Community Church and can be obtained from the Grace Book Shack, 13248 Roscoe Blvd., Sun Valley, CA 91352.

mitted it to the OFG. The applicant will also identify/clarify any disagreements.

C.   The "Ordination Applicant Profile" (see appendix 2) has been completed and submitted to the OFG.

D.   Three elders have been selected by OFG to serve on the first council to consider the applicant for possible ordination candidacy.

Application Phase	*Licensure Phase* (usually one year, not more than two years)	*Ordination Phase* (lifetime or until biblically disqualified)
Preliminaries	Second Council Examination in:	Elders' Affirmation
First Council Review:		Public Recognition
	• General Bible	
	• Pastoral Ministries	
• Conversion	• Theology	
• Call		
• Character	Ordination Council	
• Conduct	Questioning in and	
• Capabilities	affirmation of:	
Elders' Approval	• Theology	
	• Bible	
	• Ministry	
	• Personal Life	

Fig. 1

VI.   First Council

The first council reviews the candidate's conversion, giftedness, call to the ministry, character, conduct, former/current ministries, biblical qualification relative to an elder in 1 Tim. 3:1–7 and Titus 1:5–9, and marital/parenting history. Prior to this first council, the first council elders must hear the candidate in a preaching/teaching situation either by tape or in person, as well as have an intimate knowledge of his personal character and ministry.

If the candidate is affirmed by the first council, he will be recommended to the Board of Elders by the first council elders as a candidate for the ordination process and formal licensure at a regular Board of Elders' meeting. When the applicant is affirmed for admission to ordination candidacy, then the three elders on his first council will become the elders serving on the second and ordination councils.

At this point, the request could also be denied. If denied, appropriate steps leading to further pursuit of ordination by the applicant shall be given.

VII.   Second Council

When approved, the second council must be completed within one calendar year. The one-year licensure can be extended upon request if unusual circumstances prevent timely progress. However, the candidate must successfully complete the second council within two years after the first council. If he fails to do so, then he must drop out of the ordination process and start again fresh at a later date.

The second council is primarily focused on the doctrinal preparation of the candidate for ministry and is designed to assess the candidate's strengths and weaknesses. The three elders over-seeing the candidate's ordination process will also continue to review the candidate's progress in ministry capabilities, especially in his teaching/preaching and leading. The candidate will be expected to initiate and maintain close contact with those elders on his council.

The doctrinal areas in which the candidate will be quizzed are presented in the "Ordination Comprehensive Questions." (See appendix 3.)

If the second council is not satisfied with the current progress of the licensee and cannot recommend that he continue as a candidate for ordination, the licensee will be given appropriate instructions to correct the situation, and the council will report back to the Board of Elders. The candidate may: (1) be removed from the process, (2) be required to repeat the second council, or (3) receive a directed study assignment as a prelude to repeating the second council.

If the second council concurs that the ordination candidate should progress to an ordination council, they will recommend to the Board of Elders that an ordination council be held within one to three months.

VIII.   Ordination Council

The ordination council, to be held during a regularly scheduled elders' meeting, will follow a questioning and affirming format relative to all pertinent areas of theology, biblical knowledge, church ministry, and spiritual life. The three ordination council elders will report on the candidate's progress. Questioning and affirming will then be received from all the elders on his life, his ministry, and his doctrine. The council session can be open to non-elders including the candidate's family members unless otherwise requested by the candidate. The purpose of this council is to finalize confirmation of the licensee's readiness for the work of the ministry.

The ordination council will, after careful consideration, recommend to the Board of Elders whether the licensee should be ordained. If approval is not granted, the licensee will be instructed as to why he was refused ordination and what steps he needs to take to remedy the situation.

IX.   Approval

When ordination is approved, the candidate will receive a certificate of ordination. He will also receive "the laying on of hands" by the elders in a subsequent public service.

Demanding but Attainable

The Grace Community Church "Ordination Process" manual begins with the following letter from pastor-teacher John MacArthur, Jr. It eloquently exalts the noble nature of the process that leads to an ordination appointment of God's man by the church to the gospel ministry for a lifetime of sacred service as a steward of God's ministry (Titus 1:7).[16]

---

16. "Whale" or "a great fish" is the answer to the riddle posed at the beginning of this chapter.

Dear Ordination Candidate,

You are about to enter the arena of preparation for the highest calling in the world—a minister of the Lord Jesus Christ, a steward of the household of God, a special agent of the King to advance His glorious Kingdom, a colaborer with Christ in building His church. It is not your choice to so serve; it is God's.

It was said of John Knox, prince of Scottish preachers, that when he was called to this holy task he was broken in his spirit and continually in tears over the awesomeness of such a calling and his unworthiness. And God used him to influence his nation and beyond.

If you sense the calling of God, if you feel a strong desire to pursue this life, and if you desire the affirmation of the church, then when you give evidence of that calling and readiness, it will be our high privilege to examine you for ordination.

Ordination is a confirmation by the church of a man's call, spiritual preparedness, ministry proficiency, and Bible knowledge. It allows a man to earn the full support of the Grace Community Church elders as he embarks on ministry. Grace Church certifies the man's suitability for ministry to the church at large.

Because we believe that the calling is holy and the task challenging, we desire that men be fully readied before they are ordained. Thus, the preparation is demanding but attainable. Our Lord is to be given the best we have to offer.

May God bless you as you pursue this most eminent calling.

Yours for the Master,

John MacArthur, Jr.
Pastor-Teacher

Part III

Personal Perspectives

9

The Pastor's Home

Richard L. Mayhue

As families in America grow weaker, so do an alarming number of pastors' families. However, Scripture establishes a strong, exemplary family as a prerequisite to pastoral ministry. Even though the pressure in contemporary ministry is admittedly enormous, a marriage and family relationship characterized by the fruit of the Spirit and the love of Christ will be able to withstand the inevitable assaults of a pagan, postmodern culture and the intense demands of today's pastoral ministry. The pastor's home must be a top priority in his ministry.

One recent bestseller on pastoral ministry contained a chapter entitled "Warning: Ministry May Be Hazardous to Your Marriage."[1] As shocking as that title is, it accurately reflects the potential reality in pastoral ministry today. A 1992 pastoral survey published in a prominent journal discovered the following significant difficulties that led to marital problems in the parsonage:[2]

81%	insufficient time together
71%	use of money
70%	income level

---

1. H. B. London, Jr. and Neil B. Wiseman, *Pastors At Risk* (Wheaton: Victor, 1993), 70–94.

2. David Goetz, "Is the Pastor's Family Safe at Home?," *Leadership* 13, no. 2 (fall 1992): 39.

64%	communication difficulties
63%	congregational expectations
57%	differences over use of leisure
53%	difficulty in raising children
46%	sexual problems
41%	pastor's anger toward spouse
35%	differences over ministry career
25%	differences over spouse's career

No one today questions the obvious fact that most pastors and their families are experiencing a growing pressure because of the climate of ministry during the 1990s.[3] When one ponders the nature of the ministry, it is not surprising. Consider these pressure points in the pastorate:

1. The pastor engages in the humanly impossible—dealing with sin in people's lives.

2. The pastor fills a never-ending role—solving one problem only to be faced with multiplied more.

3. The pastor serves with increasingly questioned credibility in the eyes of society.

4. The pastor remains on call 168 hours each week.

5. The pastor is expected to perform excellently with the widest range of skills—to be at any given time a scholar, visionary, communicator, administrator, consoler, leader, financier, diplomat, perfect example, counselor, and peacemaker.

6. The pastor is expected to produce riveting and life-changing messages at least twice weekly, fifty-two Sundays a year.

7. The pastor's work brigade is usually a volunteer force, not paid help.

8. The pastor and his family seem to live in a fishbowl where everyone can watch.

9. The pastor is often underpaid, underappreciated, underrefreshed, and overworked.

---

3. Marshall Shelly, *Well-Intentioned Dragons* (Waco: Word, 1985), describes in detail the major stresses that most pastors face at some time in their ministry.

10. As a public figure, the pastor can receive the harshest criticism from both the community and the congregation.

No thinking person can deny that the ministry is potentially hazardous to a pastor's marriage and family. But should it be that way? Better yet, must it be that way? Most importantly, does God intend for it to be this way?

THE BIBLICAL BENCHMARK

Two key Scriptures furnish God's imperative that a man have a strong family commitment as a prerequisite to being considered for pastoral ministry:[4] "He must be one who manages his own household well, keeping his children under control with all dignity (but if a man does not know how to manage his own household, how will he take care of the church of God?)" (1 Tim. 3:4–5); "Namely, if any man be above reproach, the husband of one wife, having children who believe, not accused of dissipation or rebellion" (Titus 1:6).[5]

At least three features of a pastor's marriage and family stand out:

1. He must be the husband of one wife—i.e., wholly devoted to his present wife with no roving eyes or affections for other women (1 Tim. 3:2; Titus 1:6).[6] He must demonstrate Christ's level of love for His bride, the church, by his own undistracted and uncompromised love for his own bride.

2. He is to lead his household (1 Tim. 3:4). He cannot delegate or deprioritize the duty of ultimate responsibility for the direction of his

---

4. The following two volumes contain excellent discussions concerning God's plan for marriage and the family: John Murray, *Principles of Conduct* (Grand Rapids: Eerdmans, 1957), 45–81; John Piper and Wayne Grudem, eds. *Recovering Biblical Manhood and Womanhood* (Westchester, Ill.: Crossway, 1991).

5. For an in-depth exposition of 1 Tim. 3:4–5, see John F. MacArthur, Jr. *The Master's Plan for the Church* (Chicago: Moody, 1991), 215–33. See also chapter 5, "The Character of a Pastor," earlier in this volume for an exposition of Titus 1:6. Also consult Alexander Strauch, *Biblical Eldership*, 2d ed. (Littleton, Colo.: Lewis and Roth, 1988), 166–206.

6. For the range of conservative views on divorce and remarriage in general and particularly for the pastor, consult William A. Heth and Gordon J. Wenham, *Jesus and Divorce* (Nashville: Thomas Nelson, 1984); J. Carl Laney, *The Divorce Myth* (Minneapolis: Bethany House, 1981); John MacArthur, Jr., *The Family* (Chicago: Moody, 1982), 105–28; and John Murray, *Divorce* (Philadelphia: Presbyterian and Reformed, 1975).

home. Thus, it is not enough merely to lead, but the quality of his leadership in the home should be excellent.

3. Children in the parsonage should be living in harmony with their father's example and instruction (1 Tim. 3:4; Titus 1:6). This does not mean that the pastor's children will not have their moments. However, it does demand that the overall pattern of their behavior not be an embarrassment to the church, a stumbling block for their father's ministry, or a pattern of contradiction regarding the Christian faith.

God's logic for these high standards moves from the lesser to the greater. If a man cannot lead the little flock of his own family effectively, he certainly cannot fruitfully undertake leadership of the larger flock—the church: "But if a man does not know how to manage his own household, how will he take care of the church of God?" (1 Tim. 3:5).

It is important to emphasize that these standards absolutely define one aspect of the prerequisites for the ministry. They are not culturally outdated; they are not optional or open for redefinition. These biblical imperatives are just as relevant today as they were when written by Paul two thousand years ago.

In this writer's judgment, neglect of these factors in qualifying men for ministry has significantly contributed to the crises that pastors face with their families after entering the ministry. The New Testament certainly does not ignore the potentially severe pressures of the ministry. However, it does demand the kinds of men and the kinds of families for ministry that can successfully avoid the potential damage to the pastor's marriage and/or family if he or they do not have a strong commitment to comply with the biblical standards.

It is true that biblical standards for the home are no different for a pastor's home than for any other Christian home. The difference lies in the responsibility that the pastor's home has to be an example of a mature Christian marriage and family as an encouragement to the other homes in the flock.

THE PARSONAGE UNDER SIEGE

Unfortunately, the age-old maxim, "As goes the culture, so goes the church," remains valid today. Little about the Corinthian syndrome has changed over the last two millennia. Although the church in general has not gained ground on the culture, both continue to move away from the biblical reference point at about the same speed. The church might not get any closer to current secular characteristics, but it always seems to move further away from God's absolutes.

For several decades some of the media have been alerting society regarding the decline of the nuclear family.[7] Books galore chronicle the slow demise of family strength and values in America.[8] Yet no Christian is too surprised in light of the culture's abandonment of its Judeo-Christian heritage.[9]

The amazing development is the difficulty that Christian homes in general and pastor's homes in particular have experienced by not avoiding the way of the world. Spiritual catastrophes ranging from adulterous pastors to divorce in the parsonage have become unacceptably too frequent.[10]

If the world, or the church for that matter, could look to any place or anyone for a model of the family, it should be to the pastor and the parsonage. That is too often not the case, however. Sad but true, some non-evangelicals have sensed the ultimate importance of the family—both in society and for the church—more clearly than some evangelicals.

Take Michael Novak, for instance.[11] He asked the elementary question, "Why the family?" His affirming response consisted of three assertions:

1.   Without it there is no future.

2.   It is the only department of health, education, and welfare that works.

3.   There is a learning of moral virtue produced under the conditions of normal family life that cannot be duplicated in any other way.

---

7. Representative periodical articles range from Lester Velie, "The War on the American Family," *Reader's Digest* 102 (January 1973): 106–10, to Barbara Dafoe Whitehead, "Dan Quayle Was Right," *The Atlantic Monthly* 271, no. 4 (April 1993): 47–84.

8. See Tim LaHaye, *The Battle for the Family* (Old Tappan, N.J.: Revell, 1982); George Barna, *The Future of the American Family* (Chicago: Moody, 1993). Barna's analysis on pp. 22–23 fairly represents the current state of families in America in general.

9. Consult Francis Schaeffer, *The Great Evangelical Disaster* (Westchester, Ill.: Crossway, 1984); Harold Lindsell, *The New Paganism* (San Francisco: Harper and Row, 1987); Thomas Oden, "On Not Whoring after the Spirit of the Age," in *No God But God*, ed. Os Guinness and John Seel (Chicago: Moody, 1992), 189–203.

10. Background for this assertion occurs in Goetz, "Pastor's Family," 38–43; London and Wiseman, *Pastors At Risk*; Dean Merrill, *Clergy Couples in Crisis* (Dallas: Word, 1985).

11. Michael Novak, "The American Family: An Embattled Institution," *Human Life Review* 6, no. 1 (winter 1980): 40–53.

What will it take to get the pastor, the pastor's wife, and the pastor's children back on track? What can be done to restore the parsonage to exemplary family living? How can we purge cultural decline from the church?

This writer's approach is, "Get back to basics! Get back to Scripture!" I like Novak's answers to "Why the Family?" but another answer is much better. It is that the family is God's only plan, so do not add to it nor take away from it. Do not go the way of culture! Do not go the way of psychology! Continually return to Scripture as the benchmark of God's will for the home.

Who could imagine living under worse conditions or more pressure than the early Puritan settlers of America? Yet their marriages and families thrived.[12] Why? Because they worked hard at mastering the fundamentals of Scripture regarding the family. Today's pastors must take seriously scriptural standards for men in ministry as they attend to their marriage and family.

Being strong in this regard at the start of a ministry does not automatically make one immune to the pressures later on. Rather, it demands that if a pastor is to *stay strong* by working hard on his marriage and family, then he must *start strong*. The challenge is twofold. First, seriously embrace the biblical standards for the Christian home and, second, deal realistically with the potential home wreckers of the contemporary culture. All such efforts require continual dependence upon the Lord in prayer for His strength and grace.

FIGHTING BACK

A strong home begins with the pastor. He must take the biblical qualifications for ministry seriously, even if no one else does. A weak home means a weak ministry—that's the pastor's bottom line. Regardless of the circumstances,[13] the pastor must lead—first at home as a biblical priority.

---

12. Leland Ryken, *Worldly Saints: The Puritans as They Really Were* (Grand Rapids: Zondervan, 1986), summarizes the Puritan approach to marriage (pp. 39–55) and the family (pp. 73–89).

13. London and Wiseman, *Pastors At Risk*, 32–51, list fifteen hazards in the ministry: (1) walk-on-the-water syndrome, (2) dealing with disasters in people's lives, (3) church member migration, (4) electronic media, (5) fast-paced living, (6) consumer mentality, (7) unrealistic expectations, (8) cultural abandonment of absolutes, (9) money struggles, (10) dwindling public confidence in pastors, (11) dysfunctional people, (12) pastoral defection, (13) pastoral infidelity, (14) lack of leadership strength, and (15) loneliness.

In the 1992 *Leadership* survey of pastors, 57 percent indicated that being a pastor benefitted their family, 28 percent said it posed a hazard, and 16 percent were neutral.[14] In a broad sense, the survey did not turn out as bleak as one might have expected. The good news is that the ministry might not be as hazardous to the family as some have conjectured.

> Overall, however, most pastors feel their home relationships are batting above average. To the question, "How satisfied are you in your marriage?" 86 percent of those surveyed felt positive. In a related question, "How satisfied are you with your family life?" 76 percent of the pastors indicated their home life was positive or very positive.[15]

In addition to the pastor taking this priority seriously, his wife must take the ministry just as seriously.[16] She must be unreservedly supportive, or pressures of the ministry will eventually impact the home.

Nowhere does Scripture give a list of qualities for pastors' wives. However, the standards for a deaconess in 1 Tim. 3:11 are probably a good starting place.[17] The verse lists only four qualities, but let me suggest that the standard for women is not less than that for men. Paul just decided to be a little briefer and condense his words about deacons in verses 8, 9, 12. He writes, "Women must likewise be dignified (semnays*emnas)," using the same word he used in 3:8 to describe deacons. Like deacons, women must earn the respect of others through their maturity.

Second, Paul deals with the woman's tongue, just as he made the tongue second on the agenda with deacons. He says women are "not to be malicious gossips" by employing the Greek substantive diabolou" (*diabolous*), the word translated "devil" elsewhere in the New Testament. He says they are not to be "devil-like" in their conversations—slandering,

---

14. Goetz, "Pastor's Family," 39.

15. Ibid., 43.

16. Helpful writings for the pastor's wife include Robert C. Anderson, *The Effective Pastor* (Chicago: Moody, 1985), 68–85; Joann J. Cairns, *Welcome Stranger: Welcome Friend*, (Springfield, Mo.: Gospel, 1988); Linda Dillow, *Creative Counterpart* (Nashville: Thomas Nelson, 1977); Elizabeth George, *Loving God With All Your Mind* (Eugene, Oreg.: Harvest Home, 1994); London and Wiseman, *Pastors At Risk*, 135–55; Bonnie Shipely Rice, "Married to the Man and the Ministry," *Leadership* 12, no. 1 (winter 1991): 68–73; Edith Schaeffer, *Hidden Art* (Wheaton, Ill.: Tyndale, 1971); Edith Schaeffer, *What Is A Family?* (Old Tappan, N.J.: Revell, 1975); Ruth Senter, *So You're the Pastor's Wife* (Grand Rapids: Zondervan, 1979); Pat Valeriano, "A Survey of Ministers' Wives," *Leadership* 2, no. 4 (fall 1981): 64–73.

17. Proverbs 31:10–31 and Titus 2:4–5 also profile the qualities of a mature godly woman.

starting rumors, and with their tongues setting fires that righteousness cannot put out.

Third, they are to be "temperate" (nhfalivon*ephalious*). This word does not describe deacons, but it is one of an elder's qualifications (1 Tim. 3:2). An elder is also to be temperate or sober, that is, moderate, balanced, and clear-headed. The term encompasses all that Paul has already said about wine and money in relation to the deacon (3:8).

Fourth, women must be "faithful in all things" (1 Tim. 3:11). Faithfulness is necessary with regard to the home and to her relationship with her husband and children. It is safe to say that her marriage and family are a top biblical priority for a pastor's wife.

When a pastor and his wife embrace God's mandates for the home and the ministry with the same seriousness and high priority level, they can achieve real strength. This strength then serves as the first line of defense and protects the pastor's family when the inevitable pressures and stresses arrive.

Without the strength of my home, I would never have made it through twenty years of ministry. My marriage and my family provide me a home where I can:

- retreat—get away from the pressures
- relax—enjoy a different environment
- recharge—gain a new supply of energy
- relate—enjoy my wife and children
- rehabilitate—heal the wounds
- reach out—to neighbors, friends, and flock
- research—uninterrupted study/writing
- raise a family—children and grandchildren
- ripen—grow in God's grace
- rejoice—praise the Lord
- reflect—quiet moments to contemplate
- reinvest—in my grandchildren
- regain perspective—in prayer and Scripture

When I leave the fair haven of my home for ministry, I depart in strength, not weakness. When I leave those I love most at home, I do not leave them unprotected and vulnerable to the temptations that will try to seduce them. [18]

> This seems to be the testimony of those whose home life has flourished even though it's planted in the soil of ministry. Overwhelmingly, the pastors with healthy marriages and children, I discovered, had made a concerted effort to protect their spouse and children from the various pressures that accompany ministry. [19]

A Place to Start

The purpose of the following eleven-question quiz is to detect problems and increase the communication of a couple in regard to the most common problems in an ailing marriage.[20] The recommendation is that you stop reading at this point and sit down with your spouse and talk through these questions.

1. Does your spouse regularly receive more "strokes" than "knocks" from you?   ( ) Yes   ( ) No

2. Is the majority of your pleasant, leisure time shared?
   ( ) Yes   ( ) No

3. Do you have at least one three-hour block of togetherness time every two weeks, or at least one getaway weekend every three months?
   ( ) Yes   ( ) No

4. Do you usually settle disagreements with mutual satisfaction and no bitterness?   ( ) Yes   ( ) No

5. Do you have a satisfying balance of at-home, away-from-home work load?   ( ) Yes   ( ) No

---

18. For the sake of space, this chapter will not deal with parenting. I recommend Wayne Mack, *Your Family—God's Way* (Phillipsburg, N.J.: Presbyterian and Reformed, 1991) as a starting point for reading.

19. Goetz, "Pastor's Family," 43.

20. Taken from Roger C. Smith, "Put Marriage On Your Checkup List," *Ministry* 52, no. 11 (November 1979): 18. Whether you have a great marriage or one that falters, this little quiz will test the validity of your previous self-assessment. Also see Wayne Mack, *Strengthening Your Marriage* (Phillipsburg, N.J.: Presbyterian and Reformed, 1977.)

6. In your relationship is there any game playing with money, sex, employment, etc.?   ( ) Yes   ( ) No

7. Is your physical expression of sex mutually satisfying?
    ( ) Yes   ( ) No

8. Is either of you dallying dangerously with someone?
    ( ) Yes   ( ) No

9. Do you feel wanted, loved, and appreciated? Even more important, does your spouse feel wanted, loved, and appreciated?
    ( ) Yes   ( ) No

10. Is anything missing in your relationship that you feel is necessary?
    ( ) Yes   ( ) No

11. Are you still trying your best to have a happy marriage?
    ( ) Yes   ( ) No

Where an answer indicates a problem, talk it out. Then follow these steps: (1) ask what Scriptures apply; (2) pray for God's enabling grace; (3) patiently obey God's will in the matter.

Taking the Initiative

Whether you are anticipating marriage, are a newlywed, or have been married for many years, the following material can serve either to prevent a problem or to correct a deficiency. I assert that the fruit of the Spirit and the love of Christ form the core strength for any Christian marriage and family.

The Fruit of the Spirit

What do you think would result from a husband and a wife being totally yielded to the Spirit of God in living out the will of God? It would be a relationship characterized by the fruit of the Spirit (Gal. 5:22–23). It would produce a marriage made in heaven. The following describe varying aspects of that fruit:

1. *Love*—a sacrificial commitment to the welfare of another person regardless of that person's response or what he or she might give to me in return.

2. *Joy*—a deep, abiding inner thankfulness to God for His goodness that is uninterrupted when less desirable circumstances of life intrude.

3. *Peace*—during the storms of life, heartfelt tranquility and trust anchored in the overwhelming consciousness that I am in the hand of God.

4. *Patience*—a quality of self-restraint that does not retaliate in the face of provoking situations.

5. *Kindness*—a sensitive awareness and willingness to seek out ways in which to serve others.

6. *Goodness*—an unswerving capacity to deal with people rightly in the best interest of God even when they need correction.

7. *Faithfulness*—an inner loyalty that results in remaining true to my spiritual convictions and commitments.

8. *Gentleness*—controlled strength dispensed from a humble heart.

9. *Self-control*—an inward personal mastery that submits my desires to the greater cause of God's will.[21]

The Love of Christ

If we add the love of Christ to the fruit of the Spirit, we have a marriage that will not fail (1 Cor. 13:8). How does your love match up with Christ's love as outlined in 1 Cor. 13:4–7?

1. "Love is patient." Therefore, I will bear with my spouse's worst behavior, without retaliation, regardless of the circumstances.

2. "Love is kind." Therefore, I will diligently seek ways to be actively useful in my spouse's life.

3. "Love is not jealous." Therefore, I will delight in the esteem and honor given to my spouse.

4. "Love does not brag." Therefore, I will not draw attention to myself exclusive of my spouse.

5. "Love is not arrogant." Therefore, I know I am not more important than my spouse.

---

21. Taken from Richard Mayhue, *Spiritual Intimacy* (Wheaton: Victor, 1990), 102.

6.   "Love does not act unbecomingly." Therefore, I will not engage my spouse in ungodly activity.

7.   "Love does not seek its own." Therefore, I will be marriage-spouse oriented.

8.   "Love is not provoked." Therefore, I will not resort to anger as a solution to difficulties between myself and my spouse.

9.   "Love does not take into account a wrong suffered." Therefore, I will never keep an account due on my spouse.

10. "Love does not rejoice in unrighteousness." Therefore, I will never delight in my spouse's unrighteous behavior, nor will I join in its expression.

11. "Love rejoices with the truth." Therefore, I will find great joy when truth prevails in my spouse's life.

12. "Love bears all things." Therefore, I will be publicly silent about my spouse's faults.

13. "Love believes all things." Therefore, I will express unshakable confidence and trust in my spouse.

14. "Love hopes all things." Therefore, I will confidently expect future victory in my spouse's life, regardless of the present imperfections.

15. "Love endures all things." Therefore, I will outlast every assault of Satan to break up our marriage.[22]

Every marriage needs continual refreshment through frequent reaffirmations of these biblical truths. Good marriages will become better. Weak marriages can gain strength.

A Scriptural Approach

Listed below are the most significant biblical attitudes and activities that produce healthy marriages. They provide checks for the most common causes of marital trouble. Husbands and wives, rate yourselves for each element on a scale of 1 (low) to 10 (high). Place your numerical evaluation in the space provided. Take your time, and do it together.

---

22. These personalized actions come from the writer's own expanded translation of 1 Cor. 13:4–7 from the Greek text.

1. Do I give myself unselfishly in our marriage relationship?
   H_____   W_____

2. Do we mutually agree on our biblically defined marital roles?
   H_____   W_____

3. Do I always put my love into action?
   H_____   W_____

4. Is my communication designed to build up my spouse?
   H_____   W_____

5. Does my response to conflict strengthen rather than weaken our marriage?   H_____   W_____

6. Do I always forgive my marriage partner when I am wronged?
   H_____   W_____

7. Do we have a common parenting strategy?
   H_____   W_____

8. Do I patiently accept my marriage partner as one who is still under construction?
   H_____   W_____

9. Do we practice joint financial planning and spending?
   H_____   W_____

10. Do we periodically sit down to evaluate our marriage and then set realistic goals for improvement?
    H_____   W_____

11. Do we nurture loving relationships with our in-laws?
    H_____   W_____

12. Am I able to control my temper?
    H_____   W_____

13. Do we share times of spiritual refreshment together (worship, Bible study, prayer)?
    H_____   W_____

14. Do I work hard to be an attractive and interesting marriage partner?
    H_____   W_____

15. Do I understand that my primary role in the physical side of marriage is to gratify my partner?
    H_____   W_____

Be encouraged by your high scores and let the low elements stimulate you to change. To get started, write out what you plan to do to improve your three lowest scores.

ONE LAST WORD

The only way to reverse the generally declining quality of the pastor's home is through a wholesale return to spiritual principles for a man's marriage and his family. It is this writer's estimate that whatever pressures are real today have had their relative equivalents in the past and will have their future equals.

God anticipated the unusual demands on the pastor's home by requiring that a potential pastor already have a strong commitment in these areas before he qualifies for ministry. The commitment will grow stronger through the progress of ministry, thus protecting and defending the pastor, his wife, and children from family catastrophes that seem to be on the increase in contemporary ministry. The pastor's home must be a top priority in his ministry.

10

The Pastor's Prayer Life—the Personal Side

James E. Rosscup

The focus is on two passages related to prayer and their teaching regarding the impact of prayer on pastoral ministry. The topic of John 15:7–8 is a life of prayer and the gaining of answers to that prayer. That kind of life results in glorification of God, multiplication of fruit, and authentication of the one praying. Eph. 6:10–20 emphasizes the power of the armor of God, details the various parts of that armor, and climaxes by referring to the prayer that must accompany that armor. A pastor dare not neglect these essential truths regarding the armor, particularly prayer, as he ministers to people.

God has given His Word as the pastor's main tool. God's Word makes clear that a proper blending of the Word with prayer is the most strategic approach to ministry. Two main passages underscore this, one from Jesus—the greatest leader—and the other from Paul—one of the finest examples of ministry for Jesus's sake.[1] The two agree that God-centered ministry profoundly shaped by the Word and prayer is ministry that produces God-approved fruit. A discussion of Jesus' words in John 15:7–8 and Paul's words in Eph. 6:10–20 verifies the importance of merging the Word and prayer in pastoral ministry.

Praying as in John 15:7–8

Abiding is at the heart of the Christian life according to the greatest of all shepherds, Jesus. In John 15:4 "abide in Me" expressed His passion for His own. In the same verse and the following one He continued, "and I in you. . . . He who abides in Me . . . bears much fruit. . . ." He finished verse 5 by adding, "apart from me you can do nothing." "Fruit" is anything that Christ the vine produces through one of His branches. The possibility of bearing what God would call "fruit" is nil without this abiding.

In this context of a branch (a believer) in a vine (Christ) one probably practices abiding or continuing in three ways:

1. A person who is in Christ (i.e., "in Me," in true union with Him) needs to *relate* to Christ the vine as a physical branch relates to its vine. A human, however, differs from a physical branch in his ability to think, exercise his will, and feel his emotions. He, therefore, can relate to Christ's person and His values and priorities. This is to think, speak, and do what is in harmony with Christ and His will as expressed in His Word. The believer can achieve this to some degree and yet have room for further growth.

2. The abiding person *rejects* what is opposed to Christ's person and purpose as clarified in the principles of Scripture.

3. The one who abides *receives* as a physical branch draws from its vine. He benefits from the adequacy of Christ and His Word. Christians begin their life in the Lord by receiving the eternal life He gives (John 1:12). They receive by faith (1:12; 3:16; 6:54). After they begin receiving, they continue in the Christian life by the same principle, walking by faith (7:37–38). "Abiding" is the name given to this continuance (6:56; cf. v. 54).

---

1. See the survey of the place of prayer in Jesus, Paul, and others in Scripture in James E. Rosscup, "The Priority of Prayer and Expository Preaching," in *Rediscovering Expository Preaching*, John MacArthur, Jr. (Dallas: Word, 1992), 63–84.

In John 15 Jesus goes on, "If you abide in Me, and My words abide in you, ask whatever you wish, and it shall be done for you" (v. 7). In other words, "If you are people who do abide in Me"—and all who in faith eat and drink of Him do abide in Him (John 6:54, 56)—"here is a boon that will be yours, the privilege of praying and experiencing God-given answers, which are the fruit of your life as a branch."

In the same discourse Jesus explains that both He (14:14) and the Father (15:16; 16:23) will give the answers. They will supply whatever His abiding people ask, praying in His name (15:16).[2] To ask in Jesus's name is to ask what is in harmony with His will as indicated in His Word. "My words" (v. 7) reflect loyalty to God that influences and infuses fruitful prayer. Jesus indicates a close relationship between abiding in Him and having His words abide in you. The words belong to Him, the perfect articulator and author of God's Word. The values and priorities in all of God's Word are what He exemplifies and stands for. In His person and in His words He unites with the Father and the Spirit. The person who abides in Him gladly allows His words to abide in him.

Jesus wants His people to pray in ways God's Word prescribes. He has just said, "He who has My commandments and keeps them, he it is who loves Me; and he who loves Me shall be loved by My Father, and I will love him, and will disclose Myself to him" (14:21). In what way does Christ disclose Himself to the person who prays in accord with His Word (14:21; 15:7)? He does so in the central essence of the fruit borne, which is Himself. The fruit comes from Christ the vine and manifests Him, His quality of life, and what He is like. It is the life of Christ at work, exhibited through His branches (Gal. 2:20; Phil. 1:21).

Jesus spoke these words about abiding, prayer, and fruit to His eleven disciples. Judas, the twelfth man, had left earlier (13:30). He was not a genuine believer and had never been spiritually cleansed as had the other eleven (13:10–11; cf. 15:2–3). God had drawn the eleven who remained (6:44, 65), and Jesus had trained them for ministry during much of His earthly ministry. A pastoral worker can learn much by paying attention to what Jesus here expressed as vital for anyone in ministry. The listeners were budding leaders who would eventually represent Christ in ministry to others. Christ's passion was that they be *praying* servants. In turn, they would teach others the importance of prayer.

---

2. See the discussion of praying in Jesus' name in W. Bingham Hunter, *The God Who Hears* (Downers Grove, Ill.: InterVarsity, 1986), 191–99.

John 15:8 defines how the life of abiding in Christ and having His Word abiding in them (i.e., the life of praying and gaining answers) relates to three great accomplishments. It shows that the praying life is a life of *glorification*, *multiplication*, and *authentication*.

Glorification

The link in thought between verses 7 and 8 is clear. "In this" that begins verse 8 points forward to "much fruit" later in the same verse. This fruit consists of answers to prayer promised in verse 7. Verse 8 indicates that in God's positive response to the prayer of one who abides in Christ (i.e., "in this," the "much fruit" resulting from abiding) the Father is glorified. The fruit glorifies God by making conspicuous His virtues, values, and purposes, the beauties found in His Christ and in His words.

The nature of the fruit is evident in the surrounding context: peace (14:27), love (15:8–12), and joy (15:11). It also consists of the outworking of allegiance to Christ in facing the world's hostility to Him (15:18–25), of a life that the Spirit of truth teaches (15:26; cf. 15:7), and of doing greater works than Christ did on earth (14:12). For He as the vine will continue His ministry by doing works through His branches (see Gal. 2:20; Phil. 1:21). These greater works by them and Him are answers to prayer shaped by His Word (John 14:13; 15:7–8).

What a message on values to guide those who lead in pastoral ministry! All the fruit resulting from the Christ-life—yes, all of it!—relates to what *God* accomplishes (John 15:7, 16). He does it through Christians in response to their prayer in harmony with the Word. Prayer is obviously of momentous consequence!

This speaks volumes to the Christian worker. It summons him to devote a much greater priority to prayer, in other words, to give prayer the place Jesus gave it. If he does *not* do so, he should rethink his value system. Otherwise, he will be ministering according to his own agenda rather than by Christ's expression of values here. This observation refines the oft-cited aphorism:

> "Only one life, 'twill soon be past.
> Only what's done for Christ will last."

The last line could well read, "Only what's done through prayer will last," according to John 15.

John 15:16 confirms this when it says that only when a person abides in Christ, allowing Christ to live His "vine-life" through him, will his fruit "remain" (the same word as is translated "abide" earlier in the chapter). This is the work of God done to you (vv. 7, 16) in answer to biblically oriented prayer, the "much fruit" of verse 8. This is what will glorify the Father.

Multiplication

"Much fruit" (v. 8) depicts the multiplication Jesus had in mind. Why did He think of fruit in such great quantity? Why not just "fruit"? We may gain some insight on this by relating the fruit to what He said about the fourth soil in the parable of Matt. 13:1–9 and its explanation in Matt. 13:18–23. This soil, representing a believer's heart, receives the seed of God's Word. Among four categories into which the seed falls, this kind of heart alone bears fruit—some a hundredfold, some sixtyfold, and some thirtyfold. All three quantities of fruit are relatively large. This could indicate that Jesus, teller of the parable, thinks big. He is confident of what He can do through His seed in people with whom the Word works (see John 15:7). The Word is powerful and can do great things. A great Savior can make *much* fruit possible. Laying hold of Him for more fruit comes *through the avenue of prayer*.

When a believer bears *some* fruit, the Father uses His Word to cleanse the believer so that he may bear even "more fruit" (John 15:2–3). Eventually believers can bear "much fruit" (vv. 4, 8).

The amount of fruit borne by believers varies, partly because of the problem of sin with which they must contend (Rom. 7:14–25). Failure may occur, but eventual victory can come with resulting fruit and even "much fruit." Pastor George W. Truett liked to say from his pulpit in the First Baptist Church of Dallas, "God can strike a mighty lick with a crooked stick." It is like a piece of ground covered with wild trees with which a farmer must contend. He begins to clear his land. He eliminates some trees, bushes with poisonous fruit, and wild grass. He cultivates the ground and plants his seed. The fruit he gets at first is not as much as he will see later. But compared to no fruit at all, the amount of fruit is a considerable change. Later, as he clears the land more, the fruit increases. Then the contrast with when the land was completely unproductive is even greater (John 15:5).

This example illustrates God's progressive sanctification of Christians' lives (Rom. 6–8) after He has justified them (Rom. 3:21–5:21). Those whom God has declared righteous have fruit with relation to holiness (Rom. 6:22). Paul writes with the understanding that *all* the justified ones have this fruit. It may vary in amounts (see Matt. 13:23), but justification eventually leads to holiness of life. Paul phrases it differently in Eph. 2:8–10: salvation by grace through faith leads on to God's purposed good works. Along with

God's purpose, the Christian has his role, too (Phil. 2:12), in cooperating with God, who is at work to will and to energize within him (Phil. 2:13). Fruitfulness may differ vastly from Christian to Christian, moment by moment or throughout a lifetime. Yet all will show a marked change from the nothingness in fruit that characterized their unsaved days.

The Father receives glory through the fruit multiplied in the activity of the Word and prayer. A pastoral worker, of all people, should be one of whose life multiplication of this type is characteristic.

Authentication

Leaders and all other true believers who follow Christ are His authentic disciples, according to the end of John 15:8. This is evident in the Great Commission (Matt. 28:19–20) and often in Acts (6:1–2; 11:26; etc.). Being disciples means that they are His learners, pupils, or followers. All true sheep follow Him in a real sense (John 10:27). These have the gift of eternal life and are kept by God (John 10:27–29).[3]

John 15:8 says that fruit borne through prayer is a confirmation or authentication of being a disciple: "So shall ye be ["prove to be," NASB] my disciples" (KJV) .[4] Since abiding is the life of those who believe (6:54, 56) and since fruit manifests abiding, fruit quite reasonably is an attestation of genuineness, a character witness for believers.[5] "By this shall all men know that ye are my disciples, if ye have love one to another" (13:35 KJV). Believers also see authenticating fruit (1 John 2:35). Other confirmations that bring assurance are the promises of God's Word and the inner witness of the Spirit of truth.

Jesus has cast prayer in a role of profound significance. Whoever serves Him can demonstrate he is His true follower in doing the same. A Christian's fruit reflects his discipleship in John 15:8, the secret of the fruit being prayer (v. 7). This is true for those in pastoral leadership as it was for

---

3. This conclusion makes sense for several reasons: (1) present tenses in John 10:27 point to a continuing action as in 6:56 and 14:21; (2) following is not just in an initial act of coming to salvation, but in a daily commitment as in Luke 9:23; (3) Jesus' sheep illustration in the context (10:1–9, etc.) refers to sheep following the shepherd all day, not just part of the day.

4. Obedience reflected by continuing in God's Word is one indicator of the genuineness of a person's profession as a believer (John 8:31; 1 John 2:3–5, 19).

5. Cf. Michael Horton, ed., *Christ the Lord, The Reformation and Lordship Salvation* (Grand Rapids: Baker, 1992), 53. The authors of this symposium believe with Calvin that the ground of assurance must finally be in God's work through the cross, in "a righteousness so steadfast that it can support our soul in the judgment of God . . ." (52).

the eleven disciples who made up Jesus' original audience for these words. They must proclaim the importance of prayer to others, but they must preach it first to themselves. As an exemplary follower of Christ (1 Cor. 11:1), each must apply the lesson to himself.

PRAYING AS IN EPHESIANS 6:10–20

Paul follows the lead of Jesus in emphasizing the importance of prayer. Before he exhorts the Ephesian readers to pray, Paul exemplifies prayer for them. Two spontaneous outbursts of intercession in the midst of descriptions of believers' wealth in Christ mark Ephesians 1–3. The bounty of grace, amounting to "all spiritual blessings" (1:3 KJV), leads him to pray that his readers will realize in their daily practice the style of life that such amazing wealth makes possible (1:15–23; 3:14–21).

Each of the intercessions reveals facets of paramount import in Christian living and in grasping how to pray relevantly for oneself and others.[6] Each shows deep concern for the readers' spiritual fruitfulness in pleasing God "in all respects" as the apostle prays in another epistle (Col. 1:10). His concern demonstrates itself as he asks God to fill them with the knowledge of His will, His power, His steadfastness, His joy, and thanksgiving to Him (Col. 1:9–12). The primary focus is on these vital concerns, not on physical relief for a broken arm, a new job, or sleep to resolve insomnia. The latter burdens are very important too, in that they relate to things Paul includes in his prayers. We are to cast *all* our care upon God (1 Pet. 5:7). Yet the life-shaping issues that Paul emphasizes ought to have a pervasive place in our prayers. Sadly, they are all too often absent from a prayer bulletin or show up only here and there. Pastoral leaders are responsible to correct this through their teaching, example, and emphasis.

After his focus on wealth and his modeling of prayer, Paul devotes his last three chapters in Ephesians to a lifestyle that matches this wealth by expressing it in practical relationships. He shows how believers can translate what he has prayed for them into a daily "walk," a term he has used in 2:2, 10 and now uses frequently in the rest of the epistle (4:1, 17; 5:2, 8, 15). They should conduct themselves in a manner consistent with the high, God-given privileges afforded them. They can do so through their unity (4:1–16),

---

6. See Donald A. Carson, *A Call to Spiritual Reformation* (Grand Rapids: Baker, 1991) for an excellent exposition of Paul's main prayer passages.

holiness (4:17–32), love (5:1–7), light (5:8–14), and Spirit-filled lives (5:15–6:9), all qualities that blend simultaneously in each life.

Certainly a walk of that nature is "worthy" (4:1)[7] of the wonderful calling in chapters 1–3. The benefits Paul prayed about so urgently for them in 1:15–23 and 3:14–21 mark such conduct.

Following his extended section on the filling of the Spirit, Paul arrives at his last crucial words of the letter. He relates the walk he has discussed to the real world that believers face, a world in which all the decent things God upholds are the opposite of all the evils of those who march under the black banner of the prince of darkness. Those possessing God's wealth and walking as He prescribes are fighting a deadly war (6:10–20).

Power in the Armor

To be victorious in the war, believers need the power of being "strong in the Lord and in the strength of His might" (Eph. 6:10). They need "the weapons of righteousness for the right hand and the left" (2 Cor. 6:7). "The weapons of our warfare are not carnal, but mighty through God . . ." (2 Cor. 10:4). Nothing less than God's power can conquer the enemy—a theme related to prayer and found frequently in the Scripture.[8] Christians are up against the ranks of devilish legions in the heavenlies and across international boundaries who wield influence and search out believers to attack (Eph. 6:12). The devil uses any opening to oppose those in Christ's church (Eph. 4:27). Divine strength (v. 10) is a must to combat the enemy's stratagems (v. 11).

Christians secure that power by appropriating weaponry God has made available. By faith they "put on" or "take" it as a gift, for God has given it in grace. "I take; He undertakes" has been the winning refrain for Christians in conflict. Made strong in the Lord and in the strength of His might, they stand

---

7. The root idea of ἀξιόω (*axioō*) in Eph. 4:1 is that of ancient scales with two arms and hence of "having equal weight with." It developed into the concept of one thing being a match to the other, and therefore means "appropriate, fitting, or consistent." So it is a term for a Christian life displaying a resemblance to or appropriate reflection of blessings God has given (Col. 2:10; 1 Thess. 2:12).

8. Scripture emphasizes His strength in various ways: believers need it (2 Cor. 12:9–10); God is the believer's strength and shield (Ps. 28:7; cf. Ps. 46:1; Isa. 40:29; Zech. 4:6); we are to pray for strength (Ps. 31:2) realizing He is our strength (Ps. 31:4); He girds us with strength for battle (2 Sam. 22:40; Pss. 18:39; 61:3); He guides men in His strength (Exod. 15:13; Deut. 8:18); we can celebrate His giving of strength (Ps. 138:3; Phil. 4:13; 2 Tim. 4:17). Strength relates to the main aspects of prayer: praise/thanks (Pss. 59:16, 17; 81:1), petition (Pss. 31:2; 86:16; 105:4; 119:28), intercession (Isa. 33:2; Eph. 3:16), affirmation of love or trust (Exod. 15:2; Pss. 18:1; 73:26); and confession (Psalm 51).

their ground as spiritual soldiers whatever the attack may be. They can stop the forces of evil individually and corporately as a church. They are to "stand, therefore" (v. 14 KJV). This is the main exhortation of the section on warfare.

The themes of Eph. 6:10–20 find frequent repetition elsewhere.[9] Much of the essence of Jesus' upper room discourse, of which John 15:7–8 is a part, is strikingly similar. Paul, a good disciple of Christ, reflects his saturation with Jesus' teachings as indicated in the following:

Key Words	*John 13–17*	*Ephesians 6:10–20*
Power from God (ability)	15:4–5	v. 10
Prayer related to the Word	15:7, 16	vv. 18–20 cf. 6:17
Presence of evil one	13:2; 17:15	vv. 11, 13, 16; cf. 2:2; 4:26
Protection from evil one	17:15	vv. 10–17, esp. 11–13, 16
Truth	14:6, 17; 16:13	v. 14
Righteousness	17:15, 19	v. 14
Peace	14:27; 16:33	v. 15
Faith	14:1, 10–12; 16:9, 27, 30	v. 16
Salvation	14:6; 17:3	v. 17
Word of God	14:21; 15:3, 7	v. 17
Spirit of God	14:26; 15:26; 16:9–11, 13–15	vv. 17, 18

FIG. 1

---

9. Comparable themes are frequent in Psalm 18; Jesus' teaching in Matt. 4:1–11 and its parallels resembles the Ephesians passage; and 2 Cor. 6:2, 6–7 does the same. In the last passage, for example, Paul draws together salvation, the Spirit, truth, the Word, God's power, weapons, and righteousness. He relates these to the ministry (2 Cor. 6:7) just as he wanted Pastor Timothy to do in "fight[ing] the good fight" (1 Tim. 1:18; 6:12).

Parts of the Armor

Six pieces[10] make up the list of armor,[11] drawn from Paul's knowledge of Roman military dress and the Scriptures. The few pieces he specifies represent all aspects of the Christian life. The list implies other qualities mentioned elsewhere in the epistle—e.g., grace, love, joy, goodness. God's grace is abundant in all His provisions (1:3–14; 2:8–10). So is love (1:4–5; 2:4–6; 4:14–16; 5:2). Paul also refers earlier to humility, gentleness, and patience (4:2), holiness (4:24), and kindness (4:32).

Truth. Paul begins this list with two elements that characterize fruit in the sphere of light. These are the belt of truth and the breastplate of righteousness (6:14). He groups a third quality of goodness with these two in 5:9. Goodness is prominent in the context (4:28–29; 6:8). Truth precedes righteousness as it sometimes does elsewhere (Isa. 48:1; Zech. 8:8), though righteousness sometimes comes first (Eph. 5:9; 1 Tim. 6:11). The sequence is flexible, but it is quite appropriate for truth to be first here. The Christian has come into the realm of God's truth and is pitted with Him against all outworkings of the devil's lie. So truth is as fitting as anything to begin the armor. God's truth against the tempter's falsehood was the issue in the original creation (Gen. 3:5). Truth was the crux again in the conflict Jesus waged against the tempter before launching His public ministry (Matt. 4:1–11). And truth was the issue when the deceitful one made Ananias and Sapphira fall in the infant church (Acts 5:3). Truth is ever the point that the unsaved face when they listen to the father of lies (John 8:44).[12] The Christian's struggle against the devil is also in the realm of truth (1 John 4:1–6).

The armor passage also comes in a context that has made truth crucial (4:15, 21, 24). Truth works in the battle not only defensively against what is false, but offensively in ministering positively to help others and foster growth (4:3, 15, 25, 28). It is a fragrance "pleasing to the Lord" (5:9–10).

---

10. Prayer in Eph. 6:18–20 is not a *seventh* piece of armor, but a *saturating* environment for all the pieces of armor, because (1) Paul uses no figurative language about armor after v. 17; (2) "and" is used before four of the six pieces but absent with the introduction of prayer, and the fourth piece, though having no "and," has three figures before it and two after it; (3) there is no genitival form following mention of a figure such as appears with *prayer* in five of the six (the first figure being the other exception); (4) no part of the body is used with prayer as with the others.

11. The armor is "the armor of light" (Rom. 13:12), as fruit is "the fruit of light" (Eph. 5:9) and "the fruit of the Spirit" (Gal. 5:22). Light emphasizes the *nature* of the fruit, and the Spirit the *source* of it. We might well refer to the armor as the "armor of the Spirit," who is prominent close by in Eph. 6:17–18.

12. Various forms of the word "true" are frequent in the Gospel of John.

Paul names the girded loins first, because securing the armor here allows freedom of movement for the feet and legs. Since this assures good balance, agility, and speed in fighting, the upper part of the body will keep upright. For an effective effort against the enemy, everything depends on basic commitment to God's truth (4:21, 24).

Righteousness. We often see righteousness linked with truth in God's Word.[13] It is the area regarding which the Spirit of truth (John 16:13)—the same Spirit who is so crucial in the armor passage (Eph. 6:17–8)—convicts the unsaved (John 16:8–11). God imputes righteousness to believers (Rom. 3:21–5:21). Righteousness is an absolute necessity as He continually imparts it in practical, everyday life (Rom. 6:1–22; 8:1–39).

Peace. It is fitting that the third piece of armor is "the preparation of the gospel of peace." People first close with the truth of the gospel and with righteousness, and peace ensues. By the gospel, God reconciles those who receive it (2 Cor. 5:18–21), thereby conferring peace *with* Himself (Rom. 5:1)—amity in place of enmity—as well as the peace *of* Himself for the recipient (Phil. 4:7). The center of that gospel, Christ, *is* our peace (Eph. 2:14), He *established* peace (Eph. 2:15), and He *preached* peace (Eph. 2:17). Those who receive His message are to be peacemakers (Matt. 5:9), bearing witness about how God gives peace with Himself and then a daily peaceful composure that can cope with any circumstance (Phil. 4:6–7). One of the craftiest tricks of the devil is to get his foot in the door (Eph 4:27) by replacing that peace with agitation in a believer's heart or with discord among believers.

The "preparation" of the gospel of peace for the feet may refer to the firm foundation (see Ps. 18:36) that enables one to remain immovable (Pss. 18:33; 37:31; Hab. 3:19) or to a skill in displaying a God-given composure based on the gospel. Four verses later (Eph. 6:19) Paul bears down on his consuming passion to impart the gospel and focuses on the important role of prayer in the successful preaching of it. He wanted more people to enjoy the peace of God and peace with God through receiving "the gospel of peace."

Faith. How fitting it is for "the shield of faith" to follow truth, righteousness, and the preparation of the gospel of peace (Eph. 6:16). Faith is the instrument by which the unsaved came to salvation (see Eph. 2:8) and continues to be of paramount importance in the life of a saved person. Paul says, "We walk by faith, not by sight" (2 Cor. 5:7). Though unspecified in this passage, he believes that this faith works "through love" (Gal. 5:6). To him, love and faith go together (Eph. 6:23). He would agree with John that faith is the victory that overcomes the world (1 John 5:4), because here he

---

13. E.g., Ps. 119:142; Isa. 48:1; Zech. 8:8; Eph. 5:9.

depicts faith as a defensive shield to ward off fiery-tipped arrows the devil's emissaries aim at Christians. Arrows of all kinds seek to penetrate God's people—arrows of disunity (Eph. 4:2–3); unholy anger expressed or unexpressed (4:25–32); sexually permissive thoughts, words, or acts (5:3–7); temptations to indulge in drunkenness (5:18); attitudes that threaten joy, thanksgiving, and submission (5:19–21); unloving attitudes and acts instead of Christlike love (5:22–33); and more.

Pastors as well as their flocks need faith, because all face the same jeopardy. God offers the same weaponry to leaders as He does to their followers. They need to set an example for the flock as did the faithful in Hebrews 11 who made victorious offensive advances as well as defensive stands for God's cause. In Ephesians, most references to faith deal with positive advances.[14]

Salvation. Fifth on the list of armor comes the piece called "the helmet of salvation." This may mean the helmet of protection that salvation is—the wealth is unlimited (see Ephesians 1–3, esp. 1:3)—or the protective helmet that salvation supplies. In the final analysis, either nuance points to salvation as being protective. Salvation means the threefold deliverance that God gives in Christ: in the *past* sense, eternally clearing us from sin's penalty; in the *present* process of struggles against sin's power (Rom. 7:14–25; 8:39); and *prospective* anticipation of His promises to set us free from sin's *presence*. Some day we shall no longer have a sin principle within but will be redeemed most completely, glorified, and totally monopolized by God's holiness (Rom. 8:30; Phil. 3:21; 1 John 3:2).

The Word of God. Paul urges believers to take up a final weapon that is "the sword of the Spirit, which is the word of God" (Eph. 6:17). In many senses the Word is the Spirit's sword. He gave it in inspiration, uses it to penetrate hearts with conviction at the new birth, uses it to encourage growth, and employs it to minister through believers in their witness to the lost and instruction to other believers. Through faith the Word wards off enemy arrows and also makes its swordly thrusts. With the Word believers not only stop the enemy, inflicting damage to the devil's cause, but also open the way to forge ahead positively in Christ's cause.

As in John 15:7–8, this passage makes a close tie between God's Word and prayer. The Word is the sword *of the Spirit* (Eph. 6:17), and Christians are to pray *in the Spirit* (v. 18). The Spirit teaches the Word together with

---

14. Faith in offensive advances is evident in Eph. 1:13, 15; 2:8; 3:12, 17; 6:23, and in most of the cases in Hebrews 11.

God's will (John 14:26; 1 Cor. 2:12–13) and helps Christians respond to God's will in their praying (cf. Rom. 8:26–27).

Christ Himself is every aspect of the armor. He is the *truth* (John 14:6; Rev. 19:11)—the Son—that sets us free (John 8:32, 36). He is our *righteousness* imputed and imparted (1 Cor. 1:30); He has "put on righteousness like a breastplate" (Isa. 59:17). He is our *peace* (Eph. 2:14) and the subject of the Good News, the gospel. He is the *Faithful One* in whom faith rests (Rev. 19:11).[15] He is our *salvation* (Ps. 27:1) and has worn "a helmet of salvation on His head" (Isa. 59:17). So He has covered the believer's head in the day of battle, evidently with a helmet (Ps. 140:7). He is the *Word of God* (John 1:1; Rev. 19:13) that the Spirit ministers. His mouth as the ideal Servant speaking His Word is "like a sharp sword" (Isa. 49:2). Christ is the armor, and when Paul personalizes this armor in a composite sweep, he says, "But put on the Lord Jesus Christ, and make no provision for the flesh in regard to its lusts" (Rom. 13:14). We put on Christ in putting on the new man, which is created in righteousness and holiness of the truth (Eph. 4:24).

Above all others, the all-important mandate to today's pastor is to show forth Christ as his "full armor" to the glory of God.

Prayer with the Armor

Christ represents the essence of each aspect of the armor, which is closely associated with prayer. Prayer lays hold of *Him*: "be strong in the *Lord*" (Eph. 6:10). Prayer derives its purpose, commitment, passion, values, and priority from the Word.[16]

Paul and other writers bring out the importance of prayer in a number of ways:

1. Paul underscores how vital prayer is by his own modeling of it in intercession for others (1:15–23; 3:14–21).

---

15. Hudson Taylor celebrated a new joy when John McCarthy shared this concept with him in a letter: "How then to have our faith increased? Only by thinking of all that Jesus is and all He is for us; His life, His death, His work, He Himself as revealed to us in the Word, to be the subject of our constant thoughts. Not a striving to have faith . . . but a looking off to the Faithful One seems all we need" (Dr. and Mrs. Howard Taylor, *Hudson Taylor's Spiritual Secret* [Chicago: Moody, n.d.], 156).

16. See James E. Rosscup, "Prayer Relating to Prophecy in Daniel 9," *The Master's Seminary Journal* 3, no. 1 (spring 1992): 47–71. God has a plan, will fulfill it, and "allows men the privilege of laboring together with Him by yearning and praying for the same wonderful ends (Jer. 29:12)" (71).

2. His words about the armor flow without a break into the cruciality of praying (6:17–18). Praying is vital for every part of the armor. This is evident in his fourfold use of the word *all* in v. 18 (e.g., in "praying at all times in the Spirit").

3. Scripture often shows believers praying that God will strengthen them or celebrating His power that came through prayer (Ps. 138:3; Acts 4:29–31).

4. Although Eph. 6:10–17 does not mention prayer, Scripture sees it as a saturating element in the armor (see figure 2). "Put on the gospel armor, each piece put on with prayer" is the call of the famous old song, "Stand Up, Stand Up for Jesus." How apt!

5. Many personal examples in the Word of God emphasize the close relationship of victories to prayer. Jehoshaphat and his subjects prepared by prayer and won overwhelmingly against their invaders (2 Chronicles 20). Daniel and his friends responded to a death threat by a night vigil in prayer (Dan. 2:17–23). Jesus faced various trials, steeping His life in prayer (Mark 1:35; Luke 5:16; 6:12; Heb. 5:7).[17]

Key Words in Warfare	Ephesians 6	Biblical Relation to Prayer
power	v. 10	Pss. 119:28; 138:3; Acts 4:24–31
deliverance from evil	vv. 11, 13, 16, 17	Ps. 119:41; Matt. 6:13; Rom. 10:13
truth	v. 14	Pss. 25:5; 69:13; 119:43; John 17:17
righteousness	v. 15	Ps. 5:8; 71:2; Phil. 1:11
gospel	v. 16	Rom. 10:1; Col. 4:2–4
witness	vv. 19–20	Acts 4:24–31; Col. 4:2–4

---

17. Luke's Gospel, in sensitivity to Jesus' humanity, shows that Jesus prayed before several major critical points: before the Spirit's descent (3:21–22), the naming of the twelve (6:12), the transfiguration (9:18), Peter's testing (22:31–32), His arrest, trial, and crucifixion (22:41–45).

peace	v. 15	Ps. 4:6–8; Phil. 4:6–7; 1 Thess.5:23; 2 Thess. 3:16
faith; victory	v. 16	Pss. 55:23; 119:42; 143:8; James 5:15; 1 John 5:4–5
Word of God	v. 17	Pss. 119:17–18, 26, 32, 33–40
Spirit of God	vv. 17–18	Eph. 6:18; Jude 20

Fig. 2

And ourselves? When we make prayer a lower priority, do we fancy that we will somehow win battles where these could not? Do we dare depend on the personal power of some driving energy, polished skills, and trusted methods? Are we able on our own where the people of prayer saw urgent need to throw themselves on God? How much more candid could our Lord be than in John 15:7–8 or Paul than in Eph. 6:10–20? We show that we are fools, setting ourselves up for mediocrity, emptiness, and disaster unless we devote ourselves wholeheartedly to prayer.

The prayer to which Paul summons Christians is marked in verse 18 by the repetition of *all*, so it is all-out prayer.

Prayer is for all situations ("in every prayer"). It is for every form prayer can take, be it praise, thanks, confession, petition, intercession, or affirmation. In the last of these we say something like "I love Thee, O Lord, my strength" (Ps. 18:1).

Prayer is for all seasons ("at all times"). Scripture puts prayer at every conceivable time.[18] Spurgeon commented on praying seven times a day (Ps. 119:164), "at every touch and turn."[19] *Seven* denotes completeness in prayer and its habitual recurrence.

Prayer is all in the Spirit. Proper prayer is in His power (Eph. 6:10) and faithful to the Word, which is His sword (v. 17; cf. John 15:7). Correctly patterned prayer draws from the Word its motives, which the Spirit produces in us. It gains its guidance and in every way learns commitment to the Spirit's purposes.

---

18. Various times, e.g., morning, noon, and night (Ps. 55:17), seven times a day (Ps. 119:164), midnight (Ps. 119:62), before dawn (Ps. 119:147), day and night (Neh. 1:6; Ps. 22:1–5; 1 Thess. 3:10), three weeks (Dan. 10:2–3), and others.

19. C. H. Spurgeon, *The Treasury of David*, 6 vols. (reprint, London: Marshall, Morgan and Scott, 1950), 5:429.

Prayer is in all steadfastness. Paul uses two words to express steadfastness. One means "being on the alert" (from ἀγρυπνέω, *agrypneō*). It refers to staying awake or maintaining a watchful sensitivity. This is strategic in prayer to enable one to know what to pray at the right time and not be asleep at the switch. The person praying is to keep this alert vigil "with all perseverance" (προσκαρτέρησις, *proskarterēsis*), a quality of steadfast endurance, literally "a holding fast to." Early cowboys guarding a herd at night sometimes took drastic measures to keep alert and hold fast to their work. They rubbed tobacco juice in their eyes to keep at their vigil and to stay awake when weary. They did it in the interests of their boss and for the safety of the cattle. Can we keep effectively steadfast in prayer for the sake of our Lord and for the benefit of others?

Prayer is for all saints. Christians in various collective ways can pray for many and conceivably for all saints. Paul's letter has all saints of the church in view as Christ's building (Eph. 2:11–21), body (3:1–13), and bride (5:29–30). No single believer can ever know all the saints or all the needs of those even in a local fellowship. However, Paul probably intended both the corporate coverage and each individual in encouraging sensitive prayer about as many Christians as he can be responsibly aware of and mention in his prayers.

Paul also emphasizes his own need of prayer by others (6:19–20). Every pastor ought to have many praying on his behalf. Paul requests prayer for boldness and clarity in proclaiming the gospel.[20] It is crucial for any who impart God's Word to do so with God's help obtained by prayer, whether they speak to many or to one. The Word can pierce as "the sword of the Spirit" (v. 17; cf. Heb. 4:12).

A FINAL WORD

Jesus in John 15:7–8 and Paul in Eph. 6:10–20 put forth the role of prayer in ministry. God has moved to entrust to us this priority. He would say to us, as common parlance has it, "It's your move." Let us make the right move, following the lead of Jesus' and Paul's teachings and examples.

---

20. Paul asks prayer not only for boldness, but for clarity (Col. 4:2–4), rapid spread of the gospel and its being glorified (2 Thess. 3:1), and protection from evil men (2 Thess. 3:2).

11

The Pastor's Prayer Life—the Ministry Side

Donald G. McDougall

A pastor can utilize various practical means for implementing scriptural calls to prayer into the life of a local church. It is of highest importance to emulate good models of prayer, both from Scripture and from everyday experience. As their motivation to pray, God's people need to appreciate the importance of prayer. Prayer by individual Christians, by Christian leaders, by the corporate body of the church, by small groups, and by men are all necessary. The content of prayers should focus predominantly on ultimate spiritual battles with the forces of evil rather than on the mundane affairs of everyday life. A right purpose and a proper attitude should determine the manner of prayers. The outworking of prayer needs to show in one's personal life, family life, daily meetings, prayer meetings, small group meetings, staff meetings, Sunday services, and leadership meetings. Ultimately, members of the congregation must have as examples leaders who model the importance of prayer in their lives.

Discipling is receiving a lot of attention lately. A major part of discipling is modeling, a fact that is evident from Scripture and from everyday life. A conference speaker recently observed that a church, in time, tends to mirror its pastor. Since children in a home tend to mirror their parents, it should not be a surprise that imitation takes place in ministry as well. Paul said to the church at Thessalonica, "You also became imitators of us and of the Lord" (1 Thess. 1:6). That is why it is challenging for a pastor to consider discipling people to pray. We talk about prayer, but are we willing to model it, even though we know that no matter how much we pray, we will still be far from perfect?

One of the rare privileges of the disciples was watching the Lord model prayer. Our Savior found it necessary to spend extended periods of time in prayer, so much so that He did not have to remind His close followers to pray. He modeled prayer and did so without making a public display of His prayer life. He certainly did not hide it, however. The influence of His prayer life is evident in the attention given it by the gospel writers. He not only modeled prayer, but He also responded to His disciples' request for instruction in how to pray (Luke 11:1–4).

Scripture provides many other models of praying people. One of the best ways to learn about prayer is to study the prayer life of people like Moses, Nehemiah, David, Paul, and numerous other biblical characters. They talked and wrote about their prayer life. What kind of letter could we write were we to share our prayer life with others as they did? We are reticent to discuss our prayer life, because it is not what we wish it were.

In addition to profiting from models of prayer in Scripture, some of us have been blessed by other models God has brought into our lives. Two men have taught me much about prayer. One of them was my father, who brought me the greatest joy as I listened to him pray. As a child, I would find my father either reading his Bible or praying very early every morning. A fellow missionary told me of an occasion when my father was not well, and yet each morning his office light was on at 4:00 A.M. One day she asked him, "Why don't you sleep later in the morning and try to get better?" He replied, "Because I have too many things to pray for, and I can't afford to sleep in." The other example was my father-in-law, with whom I had some of my greatest experiences in prayer. I have never known anybody who prayed the way he did, during the day or through the night. Prayer was his response to any problem he faced. I spent countless nights of prayer with him, praying principally for revival, which he loved to do. What a heritage!

Although many of us can in no way measure up to the examples in Scripture or in life, we do have some patterns to follow. The contents of this chapter are the result of a quest to learn some of the principles Scripture sets forth for prayer. The purpose is not to give an exhaustive statement on prayer. In fact, even the topics addressed cannot receive exhaustive treatment in a work this size. The principles included here stem from the reflections of a fellow-servant and a fellow-shepherd regarding truths that have emerged in his heart over many years. The following principles are not mere theory, but have proven their practical effectiveness time and time again.

THE IMPORTANCE OF PRAYER

God's people need to learn to pray. We miss so many things necessary for the spiritual victory that God would gladly provide if we would come to Him in prayer. James 3 ends with a reminder of the need for peace to reign in relationships among Christians. James 4 begins with a description of the cause of the conflict that all too often replaces that peace. James 4:2 then provides a most interesting remedy for problems of conflict, a remedy called prayer: "You do not have because you do not ask." Yet we fail to use the remedy by not going to God in prayer. Joseph Scriven stated it well in the first stanza of "What a Friend We Have in Jesus":

> O what peace we often forfeit,
>
> O what needless pain we bear,
>
> All because we do not carry
>
> Everything to God in prayer.

Why do we seek solutions to our problems so many other ways besides through prayer? Often the first response to a problematic situation in the church is to call a meeting to decide how to overcome it. In contrast, when on one occasion Jesus identified a major challenge facing Him and His disciples, "The harvest is plentiful, but the laborers are few" (Luke 10:2), His first action was to instruct the twelve, "pray therefore . . ." (RSV). In response to this philosophy, Hull writes, "

> Prayer is the most effective recruiting tool that leaders possess. . . . Leaders can employ various recruiting tools: entertainment followed by an appeal; guilt stimulation followed by an appeal; calling favors followed by an appeal; arm twisting followed by an appeal; and old reliable, the tear-jerker film or story followed by a tear-jerker appeal. These are common, but not commanded recruiting techniques. The various appeals mentioned above are prefaced or followed by the obligatory prayer. But how common is the organization that uses prayer as their primary recruiting method? . . . I do not argue against the use of other methods in addition to prayer, but against the use of other methods as primary means of recruiting.[1]

---

1. Bill Hull, *The Disciple Making Pastor* (Grand Rapids: Revell, 1993), 143–44.

At the very root of it all is the need for each believer to realize that prayer is foundational; prayer is not supplemental. Believers need to pray more, to pray more often and to pray over many more issues. The reminder to Israel in 2 Chron. 7:13–14 is just as applicable today as it ever was. If we are to experience the blessings that only God can give, we as God's people must humble ourselves and pray.

The Need for People to Pray

A major problem—perhaps *the* major problem—facing many evangelical churches today is the failure to appreciate the need for prayer. The ultimate challenge is not to convince people to pray. It is rather to help them realize *why* they need to pray.

In times of crisis very few need convincing that they should pray. Let a major illness or financial catastrophe come into the life of an individual or community, and even those not normally inclined to pray will commit themselves to prayer. It does not always take something major. It can be just something that is important to the individual, something that triggers a sense of the need of prayer.

If Christians understood what kind of crises they face, they would not need constant reminders to pray. They would be continually on their faces before God. Believers usually focus their prayer on physical or financial needs, the types of things that are solvable from a merely physical or financial perspective. They could arrange more planning meetings, more work days, or whatever else would resolve the issues. On the other hand, if they were convinced that their problems are spiritual, they would spend more time in prayer meetings than in planning meetings.

An average day in the life of a pastor reflects this faulty mentality. He gets up in the morning and faces a full schedule of responsibilities. He has many meetings to attend and many crises to tend to. Not to be forgotten among other duties are two sermons to prepare for Sunday. He sets out to meet the many demands on his time through applying himself diligently to the extent that his physical strength will allow. He later realizes that, aside from a few token prayers throughout the day, he has not had time alone with the Lord. If he really believed that the real issues facing him in each of those situations were ultimately spiritual rather than physical, he would spend a great deal more time in concentrated prayer to God for His intervention in them.

We pastors tend to address surface problems without looking beyond them to the real problems facing the church. We often forget that "our struggle is not against flesh and blood, but against the rulers, against the powers, against the world forces of this darkness, against the spiritual forces of wickedness in the heavenly places" (Eph. 6:12). If human effort is the means of victory over spiritual forces, then the more believers exert themselves physically, the greater the chance of victory. On the other hand, if the only recourse is to depend fully upon the Lord, then they would spend more time on their faces in His presence, seeking His help.

Many passages in Scripture address this issue. In Neh. 1:3, Nehemiah's brother described Israel's problem as follows: "The remnant there in the province who survived the captivity are in great distress and reproach, and the wall of Jerusalem is broken down and its gates are burned with fire." On the surface, the problem seemed to be simply physical, but Nehemiah realized that such was not the case, as Neh. 1:4–11 reflects. The problems were primarily spiritual, not physical, so the only answer was to seek God's intervention. Therefore, he went to God in prayer, and God answered by intervening in the way described in Nehemiah 2.

Nehemiah's situation and prayer recalls Israel's earlier history when they had been without rain for three years, and "David sought the presence of the LORD" (2 Sam. 21:1). God revealed to him that the real problem was not physical but spiritual.

Another very important passage points out the believer's dependence on the Lord's strength and empowerment even in areas that are very physical. In Zechariah 4, Zerubbabel was leading the people of Israel in rebuilding the temple after their return from exile. In this case, God came to a man, not man to God. He encouraged Zerubbabel, the leader of the people, in directing the people to rebuild the temple in Jerusalem. The key statement reminded Zerubbabel that it is "'not by might nor by power, but by My Spirit,' says the LORD of hosts" (Zech. 4:6). Dr. Charles Feinberg's rendering of this statement to our class one day is unforgettable: "'Not by human strength, nor by human ingenuity, but by My Spirit,' says the LORD of hosts."

The Need for Leaders to Pray

If the church wants to succeed in its God-given mission, its leadership must realize that one of its greatest needs is more prayer meetings, not more planning meetings. If the monthly leadership meetings would give more time to praying than to planning, leaders would soon find changes in attitude, in perspective on ministry, and in results.

The bottom-line objective is for the leadership to face the fact that the church of which they are a part is not their church; it is God's church.

And the people they lead are not their flock but very distinctly God's flock. The purpose of their meetings is not to come to a consensus about running the church but to wait upon God to find out how He wishes His church to run.

Leaders in the early church brought in other individuals to plan and program so that they might "devote" themselves "to prayer, and to the ministry of the word" (Acts 6:4). By their example they evidenced that the two best ways of knowing and yielding to the mind of God are prayer and a commitment to reading, obeying, and teaching God's Word without rationalization or reservation. Prayer was and is a major key. To our shame, many of us who are committed to the importance of the ministry of the Word do not have an equal commitment to the importance of prayer.

The Need for the Corporate Body to Pray

Prayer by individuals and by the leadership is not sufficient, however. The church needs to spend more time in corporate prayer. A contemporary perspective is that the midweek prayer service is outmoded and does not belong in the church of the 90s. The broader and more important issue is why so many do not consider corporate prayer meetings an essential part of the church schedule. One suggestion has been that small groups now exist in order to provide for more meaningful prayer. Yet can smaller, more meaningful prayer groups ever replace what the larger body accomplishes when it gathers for periods of prayer?

Actually, this move away from midweek congregational prayer meetings is not a recent innovation. It has been coming for years, but believers have found it difficult to dismiss such an established part of the church life. Part of the problem is that what has been called a prayer meeting has not been that at all. It has rather been a midweek Bible study with a little prayer thrown in. Bible study is important and appeals to a larger number of people than does prayer. The idea of a midweek Bible study is very commendable, but it should not crowd out the important role that prayer plays just because prayer is less attractive. If it does, the unspoken message of such action is that prayer is not that important.

Churches often decide to eliminate corporate prayer meetings (whether midweek or at some other time) simply for pragmatic reasons. One of the major problems with extended corporate prayer services has not been the services themselves, but the way of conducting them. Some mishandled services should have seen their end a long time ago. Another pragmatic reason is that some who are responsible for terminating corporate prayer services have never attended corporate prayer services where meaningful prayer continued for an extended time, because relatively few services of this type are still available for them to attend. Having never seen God move powerfully through a purposeful prayer service, they have not understood the need to continue with the meaningless and merely perfunctory exercises that they have witnessed.

A standard question I ask whenever anyone initiates a new idea for the church is, "Why?" What is our purpose? What are we trying to accomplish? How does it fit into the purpose statement of the church (if in fact such a statement exists)? With that criterion in mind, a question might be, "Why did the church set apart a night for corporate prayer in the past?" What was its purpose? The issue does not relate just to the midweek prayer meeting. It is whether or not the need still exists for extended periods of corporate prayer. If it does, how is that need being met?

The Need for Small Groups to Pray

Small-group prayer definitely has a place. It is not an either/or proposition in comparison with corporate prayer; it is both/and. Small groups are a setting where people often feel a greater sense of security and confidentiality. They feel free to share things they would not otherwise share. Sharing in a smaller group can lead participants to do so more freely in a larger setting. An atmosphere of openness is a worthy objective to be developed by the church. It is a part of the church's functioning as a body.

The Need for Men to Pray

An additional part of discussing the importance of prayer is to note the part that men play. When it comes to prayer, men have a God-given responsibility to provide leadership for the entire congregation. First Timothy 2 begins with an emphatic statement of the need for prayer. Verses 2–7 are somewhat of a digression. With the conjunction "therefore" in verse 8, Paul resumes the general subject of prayer initiated in verse 1. In returning to the theme of prayer, it is the men whom he addresses. Verses 9–15 address women with respect to their demeanor, but verse 8 addresses men with reference to prayer. The Greek word for *men* clearly indicates that it is males who are in view. The location of their prayer is "in every place." The preparation made before coming to prayer is to have "holy hands, without wrath and dissension" (1 Tim. 2:8). How exciting it is when men take the leadership in prayer both at home and in the church!

THE CONTENT OF PRAYER

God gives a significant warning in James 4:3 as He points to the danger of asking for the wrong kinds of things and for the wrong reasons: "You ask and do not receive, because you ask with wrong motives, so that you may spend it on your pleasures." Many areas of our prayer life certainly need examining in that regard. A comparison of our prayer lives with many examples in Scripture—especially that of the apostle Paul—reveals glaring weaknesses in our prayer life. The weaknesses lie in the kinds of things for which we pray and what they indicate about our understanding of prayer and its ultimate purpose.

Have we reflected that much on the kinds of things we pray for? Are the real challenges of the Christian life primarily physical, financial, or interpersonal? If not, why are they so prominent in our prayers? What is our purpose in coming to Him and what do we seek from Him?

It is interesting to see what the Bible identifies as the root cause of problems. The problem of family strife receives treatment in Eph. 5:22–6:9, but the next section (Eph. 6:10–20) identifies the devil as the ultimate source of that problem. The problem of self-control over such things as the tongue (James 3:1–5) has its ultimate source in hell itself (James 3:6). The problem of internal tensions is ultimately traceable to demonic forces (James 3:13–18). The ultimate solution to interpersonal strife (James 4:1–6) is to "submit . . . to God" and "draw near to God" and to "resist the devil" (James 4:7–8). Problems between the leadership of the church and those being led have their source largely in the onslaught of the devil (1 Pet. 5:1–11).

What is the bottom-line problem? Peter identifies it very clearly in 1 Pet. 5:8 when he commands members of the church to "be of sober spirit, be on the alert," or as one has put it, "Pay Attention! Wake Up!"[2] The tenses of the imperatives make it clear that he is not saying, "Stay awake," but rather, "Become awake."[3] Immediately afterward he reminds

2. J. Ramsey Michaels, *Word Biblical Commentary, I Peter* (Waco: Word, 1988), 49:297.
3. Ibid., 297.

his readers of their need to be aware that their singular and very real adversary is the devil. The words recall Paul's statement that "our struggle is not against flesh and blood, but against the rulers, against the powers, against the world forces of this darkness, against the spiritual forces of wickedness in the heavenly places" (Eph. 6:12). A clear understanding of this can and will transform the prayer life of individuals and local churches.

I personally struggled for years with the first three chapters of Ephesians. As difficult as the grammatical and lexical problems were, they were not the major problem. The real issue was how the subjects discussed fit practically into my life or into the life of the church. What was difficult for me to understand were the things for which Paul prayed. They were in another world. They did not fit into the kind of prayers I regularly prayed and certainly not into the kind of prayers I heard others pray. One time when concluding a series of messages on Ephesians, I came to Ephesians 6:10–20, and finally the light dawned. Paul's prayers related to another sphere, because he understood that our real struggles are in that other sphere.

That was life-changing. I then reflected on my own personal prayers and on the majority of prayer requests regularly given by people at prayer meeting and on cards submitted by members. Almost everything mentioned as an item for prayer was either physical or financial. This may reflect a worldly mind-set that is totally absorbed with things in the material sphere. Such thinking fails to consider that the real issues of life find their roots in the sphere of the heavenlies. Failure to take into account that our problems do not have roots in the physical sphere but in the spiritual will show up in the nature of our prayer. The reason we do not see answers to prayer often is that our eyes are not on the sphere where true warfare takes place. Is that not partly why we find ourselves in the dilemma described by James: "You ask and do not receive, because you ask with wrong motives, so that you may spend it on your pleasures" (James 4:3)?

THE MANNER OF PRAYER

In addition to the importance and the content of prayer is the need for care in praying in the right manner. Two matters pertaining to the manner of prayer are the purpose and the attitude of the one approaching God's throne in prayer.

The Purpose of Prayer

Prayers often seem to reflect an attitude of attempting to use prayer to accomplish the purpose of the one praying, and that in his own way. This is wrong, because prayer is a God-ordained way for man to ask God to accomplish His purpose in His way. One of the most important aspects of praying is to come to see what God desires and then to pray that He will accomplish it.

Many passages reflect God's desire to fulfill His will in response to prayer. One clear one is Zechariah 3. Development of the entire passage is not possible, but a summary of the message is as follows: Zechariah is in the midst of recording the night visions he had received from God. In his account, Joshua the high priest was standing before God in filthy garments. Then in a beautiful picture of God's gracious work for sinners, He says to the angelic beings standing by, "Remove the filthy garments from him" (3:4). He then says to Joshua, "See, I have taken your iniquity away from you and will clothe you with festal robes" (3:4). In all his night visions, only one time does Zechariah attempt to interject something into God's stated plan and purpose. This is when he asks, "Let them put a clean turban on his head" (3:5), which is exactly what they do.

Why does Zechariah interfere with the proceedings to request this of God? The answer is a helpful reminder for us in our prayer life. The robes which the Angel of the LORD (the preincarnate Christ) was going to put on Joshua were "festal robes" (3:4). Zechariah sensed something lacking in the attire of this high priest and therefore asked for the placing of a clean turban. The turban worn by the high priest was of fine linen and "bore upon the front of it, 'Holiness to the LORD' (Exod. 28:36) and indicated that Joshua was morally and spiritually cleansed."[4] Zechariah realized that after the removal of the filthy garments and before the putting on of the festal robes, the turban, which spoke of holiness and purity, had to be in place. The beauty is that God concurred and granted Zechariah's desire.

What a beautiful picture! We need to be in such a close relationship with the Lord and have such an understanding of His will that we are sensitive to what He desires. We are not to take God's desires for granted but should rather make our request according to what we know His wishes are. He is then ready to respond to our request.

---

4. Merrill F. Unger, *Zechariah* (Grand Rapids: Zondervan, 1963), 62.

We often try to use prayer to change difficult circumstances that God purposes to use to change us. Joshua wanted victory; God wanted a change in the lives of His people (Joshua 7). David wanted rain; God wanted a change in the lives of His people (2 Samuel 21). Ultimately, both Joshua and David received what they wanted, because God ultimately wanted the same thing, but He did not want it until they had done something tangible to evidence a change of behavior.

Attitude in Prayer

What kind of attitude do we portray when we pray? Several Scriptures address this need, but one that stands out is 1 Pet. 4:7. Drawing on verse 5, which says God is "ready to judge the living and the dead," Peter concludes in verse 7 that "the end of all things is at hand." Since the end will be very soon, he reminds the readers that "there is an increased need for watchfulness and prayer. . . . Men are not to neglect their duties, or fall into panic."[5] The first verb telling those praying to "keep your heads . . . connotes the cool head and balanced mind which is the opposite of all μανία or undue excitement."[6] This fits with Peter's subsequent command about "casting all your anxiety upon Him" (5:7).

In approaching God in prayer, one needs to be careful to enter His presence with the right purpose and the right attitude. He must desire His will to be done (not the will of the one praying) and must exhibit the right attitude. Christ's return is near, and when He comes, He will manifest His sovereign control over all things and all people. Such a God presently controls every circumstance we face. It is because of this that our Lord Jesus Christ "kept entrusting Himself to Him who judges righteously" (1 Pet. 2:23). Peter reminds his readers, "Let those also who suffer according to the will of God entrust their souls to a faithful Creator in doing what is right" (1 Pet. 4:19). As we approach God in prayer, we must not become unduly excited but must maintain a cool head and balanced mind for the purpose of prayer. We must exhibit confidence in Him, cast all anxiety upon Him (1 Pet. 5:7), and "be anxious for nothing, but in everything by prayer and supplication with thanksgiving let your requests be made known to God" (Phil. 4:6).

---

5. Charles Bigg, *A Critical and Exegetical Commentary on St. Peter and St. Jude*, ICC, ed. S. R. Driver, A. Plummer, and C. A. Briggs (Edinburgh: T. and T. Clark, 1924), 172.

6. Edward Gordon Selwyn, *The First Epistle of St. Peter* (London: Macmillan, 1964), 216.

The Outworking of Prayer

It is important to apply the above principles to the life of the church and not merely theorize regarding what ought to be. We have many books on prayer and soul-winning, and yet we seem to do so little of both. What follows is not an attempt to tell others what they ought to do or to provide guidelines by which to measure one's prayer life or ministry. The suggestions are merely steps the author has tried or is trying to implement or has learned from the lives of others in attempting to apply biblical concepts about prayer to both life and ministry.

In Personal Life

The most basic test of what we believe is whether or not we apply the truths to our own personal lives and ministries. The question is not, "Should we pray?" "Should prayer be foundational?" or "Should prayer play a pivotal role in our daily or weekly life?" It is rather, "Do I pray?" "Is prayer foundational in my life and not just supplemental?" and "Does prayer play a pivotal role in my daily or weekly life?"

I recently heard a speaker who referred to a covenant group of which he is a part and with whom he meets about five times a year. In those meetings he is asked whether he has been praying for an hour a day, and if not, why not. Maybe you and I do not want to covenant with someone else to whom we are accountable that we will pray for an hour a day. We should not necessarily do so, but if I am not willing to covenant to pray for an hour a day, why not? An hour a day in prayer is minimal at best if I really see prayer as foundational. Am I ready to make that kind of commitment?

In Family Life

Prayer in the life of a family needs constant reexamination and adjustment. As our personal and married lives and the lives of our children change in circumstances, we need to readjust those times we spend together before the Lord. Sad to say, many families have not made those adjustments as well as they should have. Do I pray with my wife as often as I should? How often would that be? That last question has no specific answer, but whatever the answer may be and in spite of how great the overall relationship has been, the times of prayer together have not been as often as they could or should have been. Do I pray with family members as much as I ought? Do

I pray as much as I should with our youngest son, who as our only teenager is still in that significant developing stage of his life? Is the time we spend together by his bed or mine enough?

In Daily Meetings

Many times when someone drops by or has an appointment to come into the office, the conversation begins and ends without any time spent in prayer. It happens all too often. More tragically, in some of those meetings we make decisions affecting the life of God's local body of which we are a part. It is very easy for a casual conversation to turn into a business matter, and we simply neglect, though not purposefully, to stop to acknowledge God's presence and concern for what we are doing.

We could make it a practice to remind each other when we fail to include prayer in our times of discussion. We should feel free to stop a conversation for the purpose of pausing to recognize the presence of the Lord. Prayer can come at the beginning, in the middle, or at the end of our meetings. Doing all three is not a bad idea either.

Why pray in times like that? Is it simply some type of perfunctory thing we do just because we should? No, it is much more than that. It is recognition of His presence with us. It is recognition that our total dependence is upon Him for everything we do and discuss doing. It is because we realize that without Him we can do absolutely nothing (John 15:5).

In Leadership Meetings

In our church, we are concentrating our efforts on making prayer a focal part of all our leadership meetings. This is worthy of a more extended discussion than is possible here. We can only suggest some basic principles by which we attempt to operate, which when applied cause the focus to be on prayer. We continually attempt to move the decision-making process down, not up. That is not a statement about authority, but it does have a lot to do with the matter of power. This also has nothing to do with what is commonly termed "congregational rule." It is rather a planned step away from centers of power at the board level, staff level, or anywhere else in the church. According to Peter, "to Him be power for ever and ever" (1 Pet. 5:11 NRSV). God is the only one to whom power belongs in the church. The board members do not abdicate their place of leadership but allow others to be involved with the decision-making process in areas that do not pertain to policy or matters of spiritual direction. Instead of letting a variety of housekeeping issues dictate the nature and length of meetings, as they often have done in the past, the spiritual leaders (i.e., board members) devote their time to spiritual ministry—in large part, to prayer.

This emphasis does not just happen; the leadership must plan it and work it out. Five important principles facilitate the achievement of this goal. Some of them may not seem immediately to relate to prayer, but all of them, when seen together, lead to a greater emphasis on prayer.

Church leadership is about overseeing God's church, not our church. For prayer to become a priority, it is essential to remember that the church we serve is God's church. Paul addresses one of his letters "to the church of God which is at Corinth" (1 Cor. 1:2). It is God's church, and the flock to which we have received a call to minister is God's flock, as Peter so aptly indicates in 1 Pet. 5:2. God's ownership of His flock is not a concept that originated in the New Testament. Through Ezekiel, God reminds his people,

> "As I live," declares the Lord GOD, "surely because My flock has become a prey, My flock has even become food for all the beasts of the field for lack of a shepherd, and My shepherds did not search for My flock, but rather the shepherds fed themselves and did not feed My flock. Thus says the Lord GOD, "Behold, I am against the shepherds, and I shall demand My sheep from them and make them cease from feeding sheep" (Ezek. 34:8, 10).

It is God's church. God's flock and God's sheep fill God's church. That is an important reminder to those of us who refer to our/my church, our/my people, our/my board, or our/my leaders. They do not belong to us; they belong to Him and to Him alone. Reportedly, over 80 percent of all church problems center around power struggle or control. That stems from viewing the local church as our church, because we have been there for so long or have sacrificed to bring it to the point where it is. No matter what price we have paid, it will never compare with the price He paid to bring His church into being.

Church leadership is about authority, not power. A major problem facing contemporary society is authority. Disrespect for secular authority has grown and has spread into Christian homes and churches in an alarming fashion. Christians do not respect the authority of the Word of God, the authority of church leaders, or the authority of parents as they should. In many cases, those who are supposed to be in authority have caused the problem. They have abdicated their role of leadership and often blame the problem on those whom they are supposed to lead.

In addition to the matter of authority, the church must address the issue of power. Authority is one thing; power is another. We need a greater sense of authority and a lesser sense of power. We must continue emphasizing the need for authority; we must rid ourselves of the many instances of power abuse. Church leadership is not about having or wielding power. We need to dispense with all centers of power within the church, especially those among the leadership.

Centers of power or power bases in the church follow the pattern of secular corporate structure, not the pattern or teaching of Christ and the apostles. Power bases lead to politics within the church, which in turn leads to manipulation. Neither belongs in the body of Christ. Scripture upholds the need for servant leadership in the church.

Church leadership is about servant leadership, not lordship leadership. Peter tells church leaders not to lord it over the flock, but rather to put on the apron of a slave and provide a servant leadership that is an example to the rest of the flock (1 Pet. 5:1–5). Is this not what Jesus continually used many means to remind His disciples about? So important was this matter that all three Synoptic Gospels refer to it (Matt. 20:25–28; Mark 10:35–45; Luke 22:24–27). Matthew records,

> But Jesus called them to Himself, and said, "You know that the rulers of the Gentiles lord it over them, and their great men exercise authority over them. It is not so among you, but whoever wishes to become great among you shall be your servant, and whoever wishes to be first among you shall be your slave; just as the Son of Man did not come to be served, but to serve, and to give His life a ransom for many" (Matt. 20:25–28).

Church leadership is about releasing and confronting, not controlling. The typical leadership meeting spends much time making sure that the leaders do not lose control. If doctrinal issues are at stake, this is proper and necessary, but excessive control of opportunities for ministry is detrimental. First Corinthians 12:11 teaches that God sovereignly bestows gifts on all Christians, and 1 Cor. 14:26 describes individual members coming to a time of worship with a song or a teaching. The fourteenth chapter then establishes the guideline by which the church works together in love to allow the expression of worship by appropriately gifted people while maintaining orderliness in their worship (14:27–33). Much of the giftedness of God's people, whether in worship or in ministry, is not currently evident because the leadership has stifled the exercise of many of the gifts, being unwilling to release people to use their God-given gifts, (within the guidelines of

Scripture and orderliness, of course) preferring instead to control the ministry of people in a categorical fashion.

It is this felt need to control everything that consumes so much time and energy of those in spiritual leadership of God's church. Because of this obsession, relatively unimportant household issues consume an inordinate amount of time, while important issues that deserve prayer suffer from neglect.

The ongoing debate over elder rule versus congregational rule has ignored an important fact. God has never abdicated His leadership over His people. Both the Old Testament and the New Testament have many examples where God puts people in places of leadership but then indicates clearly that He has not thereby relinquished His own leadership. Moses received a leadership role from God, but God continued to lead by directing the actions of Moses and the people. When Saul became king, he could not do as he wished— much to his dismay. When Saul failed to follow God's directive, God replaced him with David. When David numbered the people, God reminded David of His ultimate leadership over His people. In the New Testament, an appropriate title for the fifth book is "The Book of the Acts of the Holy Spirit," since it is very clearly an account of the Holy Spirit's guidance in the life of His church. Human beings are only instruments that He used to provide leadership.

Most would probably agree that God leads today, but He is leading in a more direct way than some recognize. How can we as leaders in local churches see God leading the day-by-day operation of His church in a tangible way? The first way is through His Word. To allow God His rightful place of leadership through His Word means accepting without qualification or reservation the directives of God in Scripture.

The second way God provides direct guidance to each local church is through the giftedness of people He has sovereignly given to each church. God has given gifts to all believers and then has given those gifted people to churches. As each individual is unique, so each local church is equally unique. It is easy for pastors or leaders to adopt their own agendas for a church, and consequently to place people in positions that will best accomplish their purposes. They do this instead of directing people into areas of service that best enable them to use their unique gifts in the greatest possible way.

We would do well to set aside our own agendas and wait upon God for His agenda in each church situation. The constant in each church will be His Word. That which makes the ministry of each church unique will be the mix of gifted people whom God gives to the church. The gifted people whom He has sent will be the basis for determining God's plan for the church and the pattern for the leadership to follow. Building the church's programs around the gifted people will result in the outworking of God's specific design for that church. When we design our own, merely human programs and then find people to fill the holes in accomplishing our agenda, it is very easy to miss God's direct design for His church.

Finding God's design for each local church forces the leadership to do three things: (1) spend more time studying Scripture to determine God's will for His church, (2) spend a lot of time in prayer, seeking God's will and preparing their hearts to receive whatever God should reveal, (3) take the time necessary to become closely acquainted with God's sheep.

Church leadership is about handing much of the decision-making process over to other members of the body. Many seem to have a tendency to want to control everything. Whether it is a desire to protect their own domain or whatever it is, they deal with too many things at the leadership level that should be released to others. One of the first lessons from the early church is that the leaders of God's church in Jerusalem assigned the important matter of caring for widows to other spiritual individuals so that they could devote themselves to what was of primary importance: prayer and the ministry of the Word (Acts 6:3–4).

This principle relates to prayer and the ministry of the Word, because a failure to understand the nature of true biblical leadership is at the root of so much of the prayerlessness in conducting leadership meetings. We should understand clearly that church leaders are not obligated to decide everything or manage everything. Instead, they are to oversee a church and a flock that belong solely to God and not to them. This awareness will cause us to take ourselves less seriously but to take our responsibility more seriously. It will free us up to spend more time doing the more important things in life and ministry rather than spending the endless and often senseless hours merely managing a business.

In Prayer Meetings

As noted above, "prayer meeting" has often been a misnomer, because prayer does not occupy much of the meeting time. Prayer requests take up a good part of the time, but actual prayer for any extended period is often lacking. This writer has attempted over the years to make prayer meeting a time of actual prayer. The results have usually resembled what is happening in our present ministry.

When I entered my present ministry, the church had a prayer meeting. The hour-long meeting each Wednesday night included almost equal parts of Bible study and prayer. Now we have no Bible study, although we do start with the reading of Scripture to prepare our hearts for praise and prayer. The format each week begins with praise. This recognizes our dependence on the Lord and our thanksgiving to Him for all He means to us and has done for us. We try to focus on praise for Who He is and not what He has given to us. Praying for missionaries is the next part of the format. Then we pray for the needs of the ministry of the church, and last of all, for individual needs. This sequence is an attempt to keep prayer from focusing primarily on personal or selfish things and to assure that the focus is on needs foremost in God's sight (outreach). We then give attention to praying for others before praying for ourselves. We often do the last two parts—praying for the church and for individual needs—together for the sake of time. With this format, the prayer meeting now lasts two hours and not just a single hour as it once did. Also, attendance (which is not an issue or a matter of emphasis) has increased to such an extent that we had to change to a larger room to accommodate everyone.

Something else we have done over the years is to have a "night of prayer." Most recently, it concluded a prayer-emphasis week. Prayer groups met early in the morning or in the evening. The night of prayer was on Friday night after this extended prayer emphasis. Instead of beginning at 9:00 P.M. and praying until 5:00 A.M., we planned it from 7:00 P.M. until 2:00 A.M. This enabled the senior citizens to attend in the early hours and get home before it was too late. Some people remained the entire night, while others came for portions of it. An exciting development was that the older people started us off with a tremendous burst, and the college and career young people arrived around midnight to help us finish the night in a resounding fashion. What a blessing it was!

Another feature that worked well was to divide the time into segments, each of which centered around a special ministry in the church. For example, the children's ministry was the topic in one portion, and the choir in another. During their allotted time periods, people involved with the respective areas of ministry came to share their needs and spend time in prayer.

In Small Groups

Before going further, let me introduce a backdrop. As stated earlier, the *why* question is very important. Why do any of our ministries exist? To answer that, we must first understand why we as a local church exist. Many churches have understood their purpose or biblical mandate to include four things: worship, outreach, shepherding care, and spiritual development.[7] If these are valid (whatever titles are used), aside from the administrative needs of a church—its buildings and financial records—all other aspects of the church's life should exist only if they fulfil one or more of these purposes. This principle provides a standard for measuring the validity of any ministry. A ministry must fit under one of the four purposes adopted in the church's philosophy of ministry.

To minister personally to each individual in a growing church without leaving anyone out—if humanly possible with God's help—we concentrate on two basic smaller care-group concepts. Others exist, but the goal of these two is to provide a connection with everyone in the church. The first centers around such things as age and marital status. The geographical area in which people live is the focus of the other.

The first of these small groups is what has been known traditionally as a Sunday school class. In the overall scheme of things, we view the purpose of these as not primarily for outreach or worship but for shepherding care and spiritual development. That does not say that outreach and worship cannot occur in that setting, but they are not the primary purpose of the classes. Some churches emphasize spiritual development and, therefore, use Sunday school classes for teaching primarily or exclusively with little attention to shepherding care. Our church uses these classes for both teaching and shepherding care. It is a smaller setting than the worship service and allows more opportunity for sharing and prayer. That is one of the small-group settings where prayer takes place.

The other small group, which we continue to develop as the church grows, is our area-care groups. For us, the purpose of these groups is also twofold. They do not exist primarily for worship or teaching, although both may occasionally happen there; their purpose is for shepherding care and outreach. It is our goal for these groups to provide another level of shepherding care and prayer. This type of group has a different dynamic since age, marital status, or personal interest does not determine its members. Such a group may have people all the way from newborns to grandparents. A different type of prayer request usually surfaces here, and a different type of interaction and discipling than in the Sunday School setting. The fact that the area-care groups usually meet in homes influences the degree of freedom people feel to share as well.

---

7. See the three purposes of the church in chapter 4: worshiping, witnessing, and working. The last of these covers "shepherding" and "spiritual development."

Other types of small groups exist, from personal discipling groups to men's or women's groups. Prayer should be a major focus of each small group. A different type of atmosphere prevails in a small group than in a larger setting, but not necessarily one that is more beneficial. That is why both must exist.

In Staff Meetings

Prayer should be a major part of our staff meetings. It is important to pray for the ministry and needs of each staff member and of the church. In our present ministry, we distribute the praise and prayer items submitted by the congregation the previous Sunday among members of the ministry team, and then we have a time of prayer for each need. One morning each month, the entire staff—secretarial staff, receptionist, bookkeeper, librarian, ministry team—meets for a time of personal sharing and prayer. That has become one of the highlights of the month.

In Sunday Services

For the family and body of Christ to function most effectively, it is essential to manifest care for each other through prayer on a regular basis. Most members of the body have no way of knowing about or participating in the needs of others. One way of rectifying this is by praying for special needs in the morning worship service. The offering of such prayers can come in a variety of ways. In one service, following the death of a family member, church leaders and their wives gathered around a young family while we prayed for their need. In our evening services, we conclude with the sharing of praise and prayer needs, often leading into a time of praise or prayer for those needs. Though it is often difficult to hear each other in an auditorium, the ministry to the hearts of everyone is most effective.

MODELING PRAYER

If it is true that people tend to imitate the life of someone who ministers to them (see chapter 16, "Modeling"), what kind of prayer example are we as leaders providing for those we lead? Do they see the importance of prayer reflected in the program of the church, in the worship life of the church, and in the meetings held in the church? If people imitate what they see in our lives, what will the content of their prayers be like? Will the requests evidence an awareness of the spiritual warfare that is going on, or will they be mired in the mundane matters of this life? Will the manner of prayer portray an attitude of confidence in the power and sovereign control of our mighty God? Will the purpose be to see God's will, not ours, done? Will the model be one of prayer that permeates every relationship we have, whether in the home, in the church, or even in society? May God help us to model the kind of prayer life evident in the life of our Lord and in the lives of the apostles who followed Him, so that if others imitate us, they will be people of prayer.

12

The Pastor's Study

John MacArthur, Jr., and Robert L. Thomas

This dialogue between John MacArthur, Jr., a seminarian of the 1960s, and his former seminary professor, Robert Thomas, emphasizes the crucial place of the pastor's study in the total pastoral ministry responsibility. The impact of seminary training on how a pastor uses his study and the importance of diligence, discipline, and other qualities also receive special attention. Finally, the discussion turns to the relationship of the pastor's study to other pastoral duties.

We have had the privilege of a long relationship dating back to 1961 when John MacArthur, Jr., initiated his seminary training at the institution where I, Robert Thomas, was chairman of the New Testament Department. It was our privilege to learn together, one as a student and the other as a relatively new seminary instructor. This chapter, in the form of a dialogue, will probe how well we filled our roles at that time, how beneficial the training for pastoral ministry in the study has proven to be, and what improvements experience has dictated in the current emphases of the program at The Master's Seminary.

As initiator of this dialogue, I will pose questions along with a few observations to which my former student, Dr. MacArthur, will respond with elaborations regarding the pastor and his study.

The Role of the Pastor's Study
in Pastoral Ministry

THOMAS (hereafter RT):   John, on one occasion years ago I remember a chapel speaker—a rather well-known evangelical pastor of a prominent church—who emphasized the importance of the Sunday morning sermon for the total life of a local church. His opinion was that this message delivered to the largest number of the church family was the major factor in establishing the atmosphere that pervades every phase of life and service by a body of believers. Would you concur with this assessment of the importance of that one weekly message?

MACARTHUR (hereafter JM):   Absolutely! The Sunday morning sermon is the crucial point of contact for the whole church. It is the one place where everyone hears the same thing. It is the driving force for a local body of believers. It is also the place where you teach your people uniformly. The rest of the week, they are fragmented in Bible studies, discipleship groups, Sunday school classes, and other smaller settings, but the worship service on Sunday morning is the greatest common ground that you have with your people. I have said that very thing through the years, that the Sunday morning teaching and preaching that I do is the driving force and the strongest influencing factor in the life of our church. Sunday night comes a close second behind that because we have always had such a large response to our Sunday night services. That figures in the picture, too. But the Lord's Day morning service tends to be the number-one driving force.

RT: The pastor cited in the last question was one noted more for his attention to relational issues in Christian ministry. For that reason, his public acknowledgment of the importance of the Sunday morning message surprised me. Given the strategic importance of the Sunday message or messages in setting the tone for local church ministry, what responsibility does this put on a pastor's shoulders regarding his attention to study?

JM: The answer to your question is obvious. If the Sunday morning message is the driving force in the life of the church and right behind it the Sunday evening message, if this is where people are taught, if it is the time and place for teaching the great truths around which the church builds and grows, then it demands the most rigorous kind of study. It also demands Bible exposition because you must give people the Word of God. You can talk about relational issues and whatever else at other times in the church's schedule, but when it comes to that time on the Lord's Day when you build the foundation for living, it has to come from the Word of God. To do this demands the greatest amount of effort in preparation and study and the greatest attention and devotion to the Scriptures so that you are, on Sunday morning and evening, propounding the Word of God, that is, letting God speak through His Word. Here you develop those principles that are absolutely foundational doctrines for the life of the church.

Through the years I have spent equal amounts of time on the Sunday morning and Sunday evening messages. I suppose that is because if you are going to deal with the Word at all, you must deal with it with the same level of intensity—an intensity that will yield the correct meaning of the truth. This has required the utmost in diligence.

The Influence of Seminary Training on the Pastor's Study

RT: John, in helping you choose a seminary to attend, your father had as his primary desire that you become a Bible expositor, did he not? I know you had him as an excellent example to follow in many ways, but I am sure that one of those ways was his diligence in study as he prepared his sermons. How much influence did his hard work in the study have on your habits? How did seminary training add to or change your method of study compared to what you learned from your father?

JM: Yes, my father's desire was for me to become a Bible expositor. His diligence in study has been a great influence on me. In fact, beyond his eightieth birthday he continues to read and read and read. He used to hammer into me, "Don't ever go into a pulpit unprepared. Be prepared." And he has always been totally and comprehensively prepared whenever he has preached.

My study methods are generally the same as my father's. The major difference that my seminary training made lies more in the types of resources we use in our study. My father tended to study the more popular type of commentaries and to look at more of the apologetic task of defending the text against attack. My style is different in that I am concerned to explain what the Bible means—probably a result of my training—so I use commentaries and other tools that are of a more technical nature. In spite of this difference, however, I learned so much from him that I want to continue to follow the pattern of diligent study that he demonstrates even to this day.

RT: You have often spoken of your training in seminary as being one of the richest and most formative periods of your Christian life. Could you single out two or three areas in particular that you found to be particularly enriching?

JM: Obviously the intensity of biblical study in seminary enriched me. During college experience I had been involved in a myriad of extracurricular activities such as athletics, work, and student government. Those consumed a lot of time. Beyond this, many of my general education classes were not too appealing to me. My minors were in history and Greek, but my major was in religion; the courses in Bible and theology really grabbed my heart. I did well in these, much better than in the other courses.

When I entered seminary, however, everything taught in every class seemed crucial to me. I moved to a completely new level in terms of my commitment as a student. Even though I took between seventeen and twenty units per semester, I loved it because I was learning God's Word and being equipped for ministry. My whole motivation changed dramatically. The higher level of expectation in seminary stretched me. I was learning so much more than in my undergraduate biblical and theological courses. Even though I had had four years of Greek in college, I found the Greek exegesis classes more exciting since I knew I was gaining proficiency needed to do the work of ministry.

Another area of enrichment would have to be personal relationships I formed with the seminary faculty. I came to know these men personally and to love them. They made me a part of their life. Many of them spent hours with me privately, challenging me, answering my questions, and building real friendships. The value of knowing them is beyond estimation when you see their lives, their integrity, their virtue, and the zeal they have for spiritual things and for biblical truth.

Another aspect of seminary I appreciated was the discipline of completing the program in three years. This caused everything to be interwoven and overlapping. The educational process was not a long strung-out process that seemed to last forever. It was all bunched up in a condensed amount of time, with everything interrelated and one kind of information interacting with another kind. For me it was the most dynamic learning format to take the program in as brief a period as I could.

A further value of seminary has been the friendships I made with fellow students. The sharpening that went on as we bantered about doctrine, theology, and ministry strategies and styles as well as the shaping that accompanies the interchange have been invaluable. My fellow students challenged me to read books that the faculty had not mentioned. All those relationships were part of the shaping process. All in all, I could not do what I do apart from my seminary experience.

RT: I can sense your deep appreciation for your seminary training in general, but more specifically our dialogue pertains to how your training has benefitted your ministry in the study. Your program of study devoted a major portion of its curriculum to what some have called the cognitive or substantive areas of study. These are areas of concentration on Bible content, the biblical languages of Hebrew and Greek, systematic theology, and church history. What has been the relative contribution of each of these to your ministry of study during your twenty-six years in the pastorate?

JM: The specific areas you mentioned are all vital. In fact, as I have already stated, there is no way I could do what I do without them. It is crucial to have a basic working knowledge of the Hebrew language. Even though we are ministers of the new covenant and I spend most of my time in the New Testament, it is still important to have enough of a grasp of Hebrew to be able to evaluate commentaries and to make critical judgments on what others say about a given text or doctrinal issue.

The same is true about Greek. It is impossible to be sure whether what you are reading is accurate unless you know the language. Without such knowledge you are stuck with what the commentators say and cannot go beyond that because you do not know the language. You cannot be certain whether or not they are accurate. So if you are going to be a serious student and an expositor of Scripture, the original languages are a tremendous enrichment. Furthermore, much of the literature written about Scripture refers to and builds on those original-language texts. To be able to deal with that material requires you to have facility with the Hebrew and Greek.

Systematic theology is absolutely crucial as a framework. To think systematically and analytically, to see a framework on which you can hang various teachings and see them come together, and to grasp the uniformity of that framework from the perspective of each faculty member is most fulfilling. I cannot imagine what it would be like to attend a seminary where each instructor had a different theology. The seminary I attended had no such problem. The systematic theology taught was the conviction of the whole faculty, so each class reinforced the others. The framework was there, a framework erected on a foundation of an exegetical understanding of the biblical text. I have always said a person has no right to be a theologian until he has been an exegete. As I have systematically exegeted Scripture through the years, I have found my exegesis has sharpened, enriched, modified, and clarified, but never violated the system of theology that I learned in seminary. That is because it arose from an exegetical understanding in the first place.

An understanding of church history is critical to seeing the flow of doctrinal development and the progress of dogma through the centuries. An awareness of the ecclesiastical battles over doctrine is beneficial in knowing how to respond to similar challenges in the present. Knowing how church-related issues resolved themselves in the past is a lesson that helps us keep from repeating the mistakes made earlier. I think the best part of church history is studying conflicts and conflict resolution—doctrinal discussions and debates and their settlement. It is helpful to view how various elements of the church deviated into this or that kind of error, how the rest addressed the problem and the deviators were brought back into the mainstream again. This kind of study of the past has continued to shape my ministry. I also love biographies of historical leaders in the church.

RT: Your study of Scripture in seminary was from two perspectives, one more of an overview approach and the other more a scrutiny of small details of the original languages. As you review your experience since seminary, has the bird's-eye or the worm's-eye emphasis proven more valuable, or does each have an equal contribution? Is either of the two dispensable in preparation for ministry?

JM: I would have to say that the worm's-eye view is more valuable to me, because it allows me to scrutinize the details, to get right down into the original text and really search it out and dig deeply. I do think the bird's-eye view is helpful. It is important to understand an overarching flow, including a bird's-eye view of a whole book, of the New Testament and of the Old Testament, and of general redemptive themes running throughout Scripture—in other words, theological themes. Those are important, but most important to me—since I have spent all the years of my ministry digging into the text—has been the ability to handle the details of the language and dissecting the text to discover what God intended. I think you need both, but if you had to choose between the two, you would want the ability to handle the details of the text. On that basis you can conclude what the bird's-eye view should be, but the opposite would not be true.

RT: My observation of your preaching and teaching ministry has convinced me that you have a proclivity toward systematic theology. Could you furnish a couple of examples of how you responded to this field of study while in seminary and what benefit it has brought to your study in pastoral service?

JM: It is true, my teaching and preaching does tend to be theological. I want to principlize the text so that it comes across as clear, theological truth. In other words, I believe that truth is simply a series of principles. The process of exegesis should yield those principles. Some of those principles you may find in a variety of texts. For instance, a given theological principle may appear in fifty different passages. It is our job in expositing a passage to find that principle and then to demonstrate how it fits into the larger context. If it is a principle about the ministry of the Holy Spirit, the question is, how does that principle fit into the larger context of the Holy Spirit's ministry, and how does His ministry fit into the larger redemptive context? I always try to trace categories of meaning as far back as possible and eventually fit a teaching into the big picture.

With this kind of inclination, it is easy to tell why, as a student in seminary, I did enjoy systematic theology. Yet I never want to say that I preach systematic theology. I prefer to say that I preach one aspect of biblical theology—theology that a study of the text yields. This theology does, however, fit into a sweeping understanding of all of Scripture. Understanding the categories of systematic theology provides a framework into which you can fit various teachings. This framework that I received in seminary has stood the test of years of study and proven to be, with minor adjustments from my own study, quite accurate.

RT: If I may return to the subject of church history once again, for me the benefit of this field of study was not apparent while I was pursuing seminary training, but since seminary days my appreciation for the value of the field has grown immensely each year I have been in a teaching ministry. How has it been for you? Did you appreciate it while in school, or has your appreciation for lessons from the history of the church been a late bloomer?

JM: My appreciation for church history has been slow in coming too. When I was in seminary studying church history, it just seemed like an endless string of dates and events that had some significance at the time but did not have much significance to my situation. However, as I have continued to preach and teach the Word of God, church history has become more and more of a great benefit. This is true because as I live out my ministry in this contemporary setting, I increasingly see that the battles and controversies that face the church today have historic precedent. So I continually refer back to church history to see how the controversy arose, what the components of that controversy were, and how it was ultimately resolved. Reading the literature about past generations and how they handled similar issues is important in providing guidance for my present ministry. These are days when issues facing the church seem to be escalating at a dramatic rate. This makes church history that much more valuable, because none of these controversies is new. They may wear new clothing, but they are basically the same old animal.

Specific lessons from Seminary for the Pastor's Study

Diligence

RT: Your earlier comment about diligence leads me to note that you probably agree with me that study is *hard* work. Did you learn this lesson during your theological training or later?

JM: I do agree. Study is hard work. I have been doing it for over twenty-five years now, and it is still hard work. Did I learn this during my theological training? I began to learn it then, but I really see the relentlessness of it now. When I was in seminary, it was hard work, very hard work, but I always had the sense that it was going to end. After the first year I said, "Oh, just two more years." After the second it was "one more," and after the third, "I'm done. All that hard work is behind me." As soon as I started in ministry, however, I realized the hard work was still there, only this time I was never going to graduate. Twenty-five years later, it is still hard work, and twenty-five from now, Lord willing, it will still be hard work.

RT: Your seminary program was a demanding one. Have you ever thought that an easier program would have prepared you for the study phase of pastoring just as well as the harder one did?

JM: No, because there are certain things you have to learn, and there is only one way to learn them—that is by diligent study. You cannot learn a language, you cannot learn theology, church history, apologetics, and all that goes along with them without the discipline of study. An easier program would not help at all because one would not learn the same amount of material. A student would not be forced to think deeply about issues and learn the very, very helpful rigid discipline that it is going to take to be effective when you get into the ministry. I mean, if a student is allowed to float his way through seminary, he is programming himself for doing the same thing in his ministry. I think doing hard work in seminary prepares you to do hard work when you get out.

Discipline

RT: Dr. Charles Feinberg was dean while you were a student in seminary. I know that as I served with him on the faculty, the disciplined character of his life had a strong impact on me. Did it rub off on you as a student?

JM: It certainly did. I think more than anyone else in my seminary experience, Dr. Feinberg influenced me in the matter of discipline. He pounded into me the necessity of being on time, of being prepared, of diligently dealing with Scripture and making sure I got the point that Scripture was trying to make consistent with what the writer intended. His disciplined reading schedule, his disciplined study schedule, his reading through the Bible four times a year, his tremendous commitment to putting the Word of God into his heart and being accurate—all of that rubbed off on me. Even his polemical nature made a great impression on me—he was a battler and a fighter for truth. Then, of course, I just loved him as a man because of his devotion. He had so much devotion. I mean, he was so one dimensional—totally consumed by the Word of God. It was one great driving force of his whole life. I certainly loved and appreciated that level of devotion.

RT: You mentioned Dr. Feinberg's practice of reading through his English Bible four times a year. He did this by setting aside one hour each afternoon to do his reading. Have you followed any such practice in your reading and study of the Bible?

JM: Well, the truth of the matter is, off and on. In recent years, I just have not done that. I have not really taken the time to maintain such a consistent pattern of reading. I wish I could sustain that kind of ongoing reading pattern, and I did it for a time, after Dr. Feinberg's example. I also got into the habit of reading the New Testament over and over, one portion every day for thirty days. I did that for a number of years early in my ministry. I continue to do a tremendous amount of reading, but I read many books and many manuscripts that I am involved in writing. In the midst of all this, I do long to have time just to sit down and go repeatedly through the Scripture.

One of the things that challenges me, though, is that I have a hard time doing that because as soon as I hit something I do not understand, I stop and reach for a book or resources and tools to help me understand what I just read. So, it is not easy for me to sit down and read continuously. I need to grasp everything I am reading. I am driven to understand as I read and that bogs down the process a little bit.

RT: John, did the example of your professors have an impact on the way you approach your studies as a pastor? Were there any lessons you learned from their diligence, intellectual and academic integrity, honesty about areas of ignorance, and the like?

JM: No question about it! What shocks every first-year seminary student, of course, is the depth of knowledge possessed by his professors. They have read widely and are expert in the areas of their respective disciplines. They are conversant in areas the new student has not even thought about. So he is just overwhelmed by the intellectual and academic ability and the deep knowledge of these men. This makes them models of what a student needs to do, not for the sake of earning a doctorate necessarily, but for the sake of having a ministry of integrity. I think one of the most important lessons that seminary professors teach is this: To be profound, you must give your whole life to the discipline of study. You have to keep it up; you can never quit. That is obviously an important lesson.

Integrity

RT: Is there such a thing as pastoral intellectual integrity when standing before a congregation to preach? If a pastor has not had time to prepare Sunday's text, should he confess this to his audience, or should he pretend that he has put in the proper study time?

JM: You never pretend anything. Pastoral integrity is crucial. The issue here is not your sermon. God's Word is at stake here. If you have not had time to prepare, then preach something you have had time to prepare. Just tell the folks that next Sunday you will come back to the text you had planned to preach on, that you need more time to work it through. There is never any virtue in preaching for the sake of preaching. The only virtue is in proclaiming truth—truth that you cannot preach until you know what it is.

Obviously times will come when you will study and find it impossible to reach a dogmatic conclusion on an issue. At that point you must make a decision, the decision you believe is consistent with what you believe the Word of God teaches elsewhere. Teach it and then just move on. Maybe years down the road someone will write a journal article and give you more light on the passage. But right now, you need to do the best you can with the time you have by making sure that what you say represents a true understanding of the text as reflected by the most careful study possible. Yet observe this caution once again: If you cannot come to an understanding of a text, do not preach it until you do. This is a good reason to start your preparation early in the week or even weeks before, so that you have time.

RT: Were there any cases of doctrinal stability or instability among your instructors that may have tended to influence you? Some of those men are present with the Lord now, but of the remaining ones, are there any who have changed their positions on any key issues?

JM: I do not think so. And that, again, is very encouraging. I think as I look back on my seminary professors, I do not know of any who have changed their views, though they may have refined them. I can't think of any who have deviated from what they taught me. That says so much for the integrity of their scholarship and their devotion to the Word of God. They were immovable. Even though the tide may have changed and people may have written with the hope of changing them with their new ideas here and there, they have remained consistent. I believe that is because their foundation was so strong.

Accuracy

RT: We have touched on Hebrew and Greek and the importance of accuracy a couple of times already, but please permit me one other observation and question related to them. Individual Christians have differing abilities and differing spiritual gifts. I attest, however, that in thirty-five years of teaching, I have never encountered a student who could not learn the original languages of Scripture if he had a strong desire to do so. I have come to the conclusion that if God calls a man to preach His Word, He also provides him with the capability to learn the Hebrew and Greek languages in which that Word was inspired. Do you feel that a facility in these languages is important in study for a preaching ministry?

JM: I think they are essential. As I have already observed, obviously someone could preach without them. He can be mentored and can read good source material. But to have confidence and boldness and to really know what he is reading when he reads commentators and other reference tools, it is really indispensable to have a knowledge, particularly of the Greek language. It is good to know the Hebrew language, but the New Testament is where all the Old Testament doctrine finds its culmination and refinement. To be able to grip the text of the New Testament in its original language is really crucial for accuracy and boldness in preaching. Effective preaching does demand a high level of intelligence, an ability to think clearly, relate data, analyze, synthesize, and present logically. That kind of ability certainly equips one to learn biblical languages.

Efficient Use of Time

RT: You were very active in ministry as a staff member in a local church while you were in seminary. You had to scratch to find time for studies. Did this experience help you learn how to use your study time more efficiently once you finished school? Have you ever wished that you had more time for preparation while in school?

JM: Yes, it did help, and no, I would not change it. I am glad for the way circumstances worked out. I am glad I was involved in ministry because it expedited the learning time. By the time I graduated from seminary, I had already had three years of ministry in a local church, so I was just that much further along. I had also begun to preach quite extensively during my seminary days. That gave me a running start. I felt like I was able to give to the study what it needed and at the same time be involved in using what I learned in ministry. I really recommend that as the way to do it.

RT: John, since your student days were very busy, I am sure you must have had many a night that you did not get much sleep. Did you ever doze off in class while you were in seminary? What would be your advice to students who periodically experience all-nighters because of an upcoming exam or a paper that is due?

JM: Well, I rarely dozed in class. One of the things I always did to avoid sleeping in class was to sit in the front of the room so that I would be conspicuous. This motivated me to stay awake. Then, too, I have always been a quizzical kind of guy, and the teacher could pull me into a discussion easily. I could always think of questions to ask, so any time I could ask a question or engage in a dialogue and get stimulated that way, I would try to do it. And I always took careful notes.

I know there were times when I kind of blanked out. Mentally I might have been tired, having studied all night. My daily habit was to get up about 3:30 or 4:00 every morning, and sometimes if I did not get to bed until late, getting up that early to study before driving out to seminary would make me tired. But once I arrived at the classroom, I was able to make it through class.

My advice to students who periodically experience those all-nighters is to sit up in the front of the room where they are conspicuous. That makes it a little tougher to fall asleep. Also you could ask the guy next to you to keep you awake.

THE PASTOR'S STUDY AND OTHER PASTORAL DUTIES

RT: If you have to work so long and hard on study—which seems to be the message coming through loud and clear—what does this do to the important responsibility of getting along with people and meeting their personal needs through social interaction? Must you fit your study around relational-type ministries, or must you fit relational matters around your study needs? Which comes first?

JM: Well, there's no question about it. Study comes first. What meaning is there to my relationship with people if I am not helping them understand the Word of God? As one who has been in the same pastorate for twenty-five years and lived my life with many of the same people throughout those years, I have not been able to be a part of every backyard barbecue and socialize with people by going here and there with them and doing this and that with them. But I know this: I have devoted myself to teaching them the life-changing truths of the Bible. This has built between them and me the deepest kind of relationship. It is a relationship in which their debt to me is great and my responsibility to them is great. I discharge my responsibility by giving the Word to them, and they repay their indebtedness to me with love, devotion, and faithfulness. That is the kind of relationship that I think really matters and satisfies.

RT: Would you say that your seminary training provided the proper balance between cognitive study and developing practical skills such as how to preach, how to counsel, how to administer, how to visit, how to perform marriages, etc.? If not, what received too much attention and what did not receive enough?

JM: I think my seminary training was pretty well balanced. Yet as I reflect, most of the practical courses that I took were relatively useless, to be honest, with the possible exception of the homiletics or preaching class. I took a course on counseling that was sort of meaningless. The same was true of some courses on administration, in which I received a little book on performing marriages and that kind of thing. All of that material is available without taking courses, so those were not too helpful. Most of these techniques are learned through practice, through the struggle of working with people's lives, and through being mentored by an older, experienced pastor.

When I came to Grace Church, I was not very skilled in any of those administrative or practical processes. But through the years, experience has refined those skills. The world does not take a college graduate in business administration and make him the president of a corporation immediately. They bring him in on the lowest level and he learns, even though he has had courses in management. He develops management skills through applying what he has learned and works his way up the ladder. The same is true in the ministry. The best use of the seminary years is to load them heavily on the cognitive side and learn from a mentoring pastor, then sprinkle in a few practical courses to give some direction. The practical courses can be helpful, but the process of ministry after seminary will develop these skills to the greatest degree. Through this developmental process, it is extremely advantageous to have someone available to serve as a model.

RT: You formed your biblical and theological study habits while attending classes on a traditional seminary campus. Does it matter one way or the other that students of The Master's Seminary are forming their habits of study in a local-church environment? Why?

JM: It matters tremendously! It matters because it centralizes the local church in the life of the student. Obviously one can learn on a seminary campus that is not a church campus. One can learn the truths and be involved in church ministry, and the two can dovetail wonderfully as has happened in my case. But when the seminary is right on the church campus, the focal point of life there is the church. I think this sends out great signals. It also allows the pastoral staff to interface with students so that what they are learning has application, not several years down the road, but now! It also gives students opportunity to have immediate involvement in the life of the church and to put into immediate practice the things they are learning.

RT: Of course, you have had opportunity as president of The Master's Seminary to implement some of the changes you would make in a preparatory program. Are there any differences in particular that distinguish this program of study from the one you experienced in your preparation?

JM: I think there is a group of differences. One would be that here we have fewer of the pragmatic kinds of courses. I do not think those had any lasting value. In those days we had emphasis on how to counsel alcoholics, how to speak correctly, educational administration, and various things like that. Our program at The Master's Seminary has replaced those with more profound and more theological courses that are very important and that have lasting value.

Second, I think that the approach to the preaching process here is more integrated than it was in my seminary program. Our current faculty places a great amount of stress on the whole exegetical process that lies behind expositional preaching. Throughout the curriculum the approach is uniform, with everything funneling right down to the preaching. I believe the way it is laid out produces a much more effective end product. The proclamation that results at the end of the training hooks up with all that goes before it. In my preparation there was a gap between the exegetical method, the theological study, and the homiletics that I learned. In sermon preparation the emphasis was on the sermon outline, preaching without notes, the big idea in the text, and such mechanics as these. Exegetical methodology received very little attention in those classes. The training was not antiexegetical; it just was not emphasized nearly as much as it is in our seminary now. Our homiletics faculty has achieved the necessary empha-sis on exegesis by making a close connection between sermon delivery and what is done in other classes preparatory for it. This kind of preparation results in expositors who are more concerned with accuracy than with the form, outline, and cleverness of the message they preach.

THE PASTOR'S STUDY IN PERSPECTIVE

RT: In reflecting on our dialogue, John, I am more impressed than ever with the crucial function of the pastor's study in the life of a local church. This is where the generative force in church life originates. What happens in the study determines what happens in the lives of people as they attend the Sunday services, particularly the Sunday morning service, which is so strategic. A fruitful study will eventually become a fruitful body of be-lievers as the Spirit uses the Word transmitted to mold people into the image of Christ.

In your experience, as in the experience of so many others, one can-not overestimate the importance of the right kind of training to make the pastor's study what it needs to be. This is the rationale for the existence of seminaries such as The Master's Seminary. Seminary training is a life-shaping experience. It was for me; it has been for you. Besides affecting our broad outlook on life and ministry, it teaches many specific lessons. Among these are the importance of diligence in study, discipline in estab-lishing priorities, integrity in preaching the Scriptures, accuracy in inter-preting the text, and the efficient use of the precious time given us to serve the Lord.

Contrary to what others may claim, adequate time spent in the pastor's study will enhance the performance of other responsibilities that fall on the shoulders of a local church leader. Through learning the meaning of the text so that he can communicate it to others, the Bible expositor will find his relationships to others greatly enhanced. His ability to help them under-stand the Word of God will deepen his personal relationships with those whom he serves, even though it may mean he does not have as much time to spend with them individually.

Thus, vigorous application in his study will play an indispensable role in the pastor's overall ministry, a role that cannot be filled by anyone else or by any other way he may chose to apply himself.

13

The Pastor's
Compassion for People

David C. Deuel

*The title "pastor" suggests two functions of church leaders so desig-
nated: nurturing and guidance. The nurturing aspect includes the
general Christian responsibility of showing compassion for others,
but this responsibility is accentuated because a pastor must set the
example for others. A consideration of relevant Scriptures shows that
he must at the same time delegate acts of compassion to other leaders
who are motivated by his compassionate example so that he may concentrate on what is his main function of guidance through teaching
the Word to his people and guarding them from error. He must balance exemplary compassion with his teaching ministry.*

It is by no means easy for a young man to become a shepherd, and he
ought not to be discouraged if he cannot become one in a day, or a
year. An orator he can be without difficulty. A reformer he can become at once. In criticism of politics and society he can do a flourishing
business the first Sunday. *But a shepherd he can become only slowly, and
by patiently traveling the way of the cross.*[1]

---

1. Charles Jefferson, *The Minister As Shepherd* (Fincastle, Va: Scripture Truth, n.d.),
32, emphasis added.

Upon leaving seminary, many a young man discovers that his love for the Chief Shepherd does not extend to a love for God's sheep. Without dispute, difficulties in dealing with people is the number one cause for ministry dropouts (85 percent according to one denomination).

For the undershepherd who by God's grace weathers the personal storms, predator attacks, and sundry challenges against the sheepfold, bitterness often prevails over the joy with which he began his pastorate. Such finds himself saying with others, "The ministry would be great if you didn't have to work with people." Words like these reflect a very disheartening but all too common perspective on pastoral ministry.

Not surprisingly, some pastors react by selecting and focusing on an aspect of ministry responsibilities that does not bring them into contact with people too often. Others champion a philosophy of ministry that bolsters their aversion for people. In fact, some argue that a pastor's only two responsibilities are to preach the Word and to offer intercessory prayer on behalf of God's people. Biblical *guidance* and little personal contact, they say, is what their people need—nothing more. They never had a heart for people, or else they lost it along the way.

On the other side are those who insist that the pastor meet every kind of need for every person—a servant of servants, a consummate deacon. Their focus is almost exclusively on the *nurture* aspect of shepherding that seeks to meet human needs in a broad way. In this case, compassion lacks biblical control and, left unbridled, may overlook serious spiritual needs.

How does the Bible profile the pastor's heart for people? Or, put slightly differently—How is Jesus' proxy and exemplar to love His people best? How much scriptural guidance and how much personal nurture are most beneficial? An elaboration on the title "shepherd" may help supply the answer.

THE SHEPHERD'S TITLE AND ROLE

A major part of the issue of nurture versus guidance arises from the ambiguity of the term *shepherd* or *pastor*. Various biblical pictures describe aspects of the believer's relationship to God. *Master-servant* highlights the believer's submission to and ownership by God; *father-son* looks at the tender but sometimes disciplinary parental role; *potter-clay* depicts the creative shaping of form and character; *husband-wife* denotes the companionship and intimacy; *perfect shepherd-sheep* speaks of God's guidance and nurturing of His sheeplike follower. Herein lies the issue: what transfer or contact point of this last metaphor relates to the pastor and his people?[2] The manner in which people use the term *shepherd* indicates two possible understandings of the pastor's function. They focus primarily either on the nurturing aspect or on the guidance aspect, either on the tenderness of a pastor toward those whom God has entrusted to him or on his specific guidance of them through the proclamation of God's Word and exemplary implementation of the Word in his life (see chapter 16 of this book).

Several hundred years ago this double role found expression in the title *pastor*, another word for shepherd. The similar spellings of *pastor* and *pasture*, the place of a shepherd's activity, illustrates the connection between the two words. The Hebrew terms for *shepherd* and *pasture* also convey this relationship. Yet, much like other pictorial terms employed to depict the believer's relationship to God, this term does not include all that God's servant is and should do. Other terminology such as *bishop* (*episkopos*) and *elder* (*presbyteros*) enlarge the job description by conveying other primary aspects of his task, much like *shepherd, bishop,* and *elder* do not convey the respective roles of a church leader as well as they once did when first translated into English.[3] What is more, other comparisons, many of them secondary, describe the church leader and his function in other ways, according to the objective of the biblical writer.[4] The down side of relying on the meaning of a single word is that one tends to inject the term with all kinds of meanings that may not have been the intention

---

2. It would be easy to carry over all of the import of God's shepherdly relationship with His sheep to the pastor's relationship with and responsibilities to his people. But the same shepherd image could be used to convey any one of a number of points. Only by studying a specific biblical context can an interpreter discover the metaphor's specific transfer in that particular passage. What makes the present discussion even more challenging is that metaphorical application of the term *shepherd* to the pastor recurs in many passages by many writers. It is tempting to form a generalization from them all and to apply that generalization in each of the passages (i.e., illegitimate totality transfer). This would obscure the distinctive contribution of each passage, however.

3. The import of the metaphors is extended by some beyond the title and role of the pastor to entire systems of local church polity. E.g., J. T. Burtchaell, *From Synagogue to Church: Public Services and Offices in the Earliest Christian Communities* (Cambridge, England: Cambridge University, 1992).

4. E.g., Paul uses the similes of *farmer, soldier, athlete* in 2 Timothy 2. The primary difference between a simile and a metaphor is that similes are indirect comparisons and metaphors are direct comparisons. Aristotle disputed this distinction between the two figures (cf. M. H. McCall, *Ancient Rhetorical Theories of Simile and Comparison* [Cambridge: Harvard, 1969], 24)

of the biblical writer.[5] It is necessary to limit these titles within the broad scope of their many meanings, according to individual contexts.[6] In addition, aspects of the shepherd's office not indicated in the titles *shepherd*, *bishop*, and *overseer* appear elsewhere in Scripture.[7]

If the titles assigned to the pastor tell anything certain, it is that the pastor's role *is* diverse in nature. To deal with the topic of this chapter, it is better to sidestep the *title* and ask, "What do specific passages of Scripture reveal clearly with respect to the pastor's heart for people as expressed in his biblically defined functions?"

THE SHEPHERD'S HEART FOR HIS PEOPLE

A fundamental misunderstanding of the pastor's role arises from the function the Bible assigns to all Christians.[8] Scripture admonishes every believer to show compassion toward others. The "one another" passages demonstrate some of the ways they are to do this. Confusion arises, however, when comparing pastoral responsibilities to those of all Christians. When it comes to his responsibilities, is a pastor 100 percent Christian and 100 percent pastor? A closer look at each side of his responsibilities should help resolve this issue, although the lines are unclear and the functions overlap considerably, and added to this is the pastor's responsibility to be an example to the flock (1 Pet. 5:3) in the area of compassion.

---

5. Charles Jefferson, in his excellent devotional work *The Minister As Shepherd*, gives many good thoughts regarding the shepherd's character and role. However, not only does he downplay the titles *bishop* and *elder* (9), but he also forces the shepherd metaphor into a conceptual grid from which he infers the pastor's character and role. This method of interpretation risks misunderstanding the true character and role of a pastor, because it confuses the clear teaching of Scripture on these matters. At best, it misreads the clear teaching about the pastor's role and character taught in passages about bishops and overseers.

6. Logician Max Black warned that "recognition and interpretation of a metaphor may require attention to the *particular circumstances* of its utterance" ("Metaphor," in *Models and Metaphors* [Ithaca, NY: Cornell University, 1962], 29).

7. Add to this the fact that popular usage has taken the term *pastor* and applied it to all kinds of care. For some, pastoral care applies exclusively to the attention given to hospital patients that is not medical in nature. For them it is compassionate care, but often has very little to do with admonition from Scripture.

8. This continues as an ongoing source of confusion. In a recent article, J. N. Collins surveys the history of the debate as to whether or not all Christians are called to ministry ("Ministry as a Distinct Category among Charismata [1 Corinthians 12:4–7]," *Neotestamentica* 27, no. 1 [1993]: 79–91).

The General Responsibility of Compassion

The biblical expectation is that all Christians will love. Paul devotes an entire chapter to the love responsibility in 1 Corinthians 13. Elsewhere he expresses his statement of purpose in teaching: "But the goal of our instruction is love from a pure heart and a good conscience and a sincere faith" (1 Tim. 1:5).

The same apostle who lists the qualifications for overseers and elders in 1 Timothy 3 and Titus 1 presents the fruit of the Spirit in Galatians 5 as a challenge for every Spirit-led Christian. In short, an assumption of the Timothy and Titus passages is that the fruit of the Spirit that requires interaction with people will characterize the shepherd. "But the fruit of the Spirit is love, joy, peace, patience, kindness, goodness, faithfulness, gentleness, self control" (Gal. 5:22–23).

One would be hard-pressed to bear any part of this fruit (or to resist their counterparts in the deeds of the flesh, vv. 19–21) in isolation from people. By nature they require involvement with others. Christianity has a relationship-oriented theology and ethic. In his basic character as a Christian, the pastor cannot avoid involvement with people.

The Leadership Responsibility of Compassion

Five categories summarize his special responsibility in the area of developing compassion.

1. **Leading by example.** It is easy to confuse the pastor's general responsibility of showing compassion with his leadership responsibility of providing an example of compassion for his flock to follow. First Peter 5:3 stresses the importance of leading by example rather than by "lording it over" the sheep. First Timothy 4:12 lists love as a specific virtue to be modeled by the pastor. Scripture teaches that a pastor must be compassionate and that he must model compassion.

Being compassionate precedes the modeling aspect both in time and in importance. In the story of the good Samaritan, Jesus noted that the Samaritan "felt compassion" first, then he "took care" of the wounded traveler (see. Luke 10:30–37). Like the Lord Jesus, the shepherd must be a man with deep compassion for those in need. Only then can he set the right example.

The Old Testament is full of passages that make compassion a prominent (and communicable) attribute of God. Outstanding among these is the Lord's own statement in Exod. 34:6: "The LORD, the LORD God, compassionate and gracious, slow to anger, and abounding in loving-kindness and truth." Jonah quotes this passage in objecting to God's compassionate demonstration of forgiveness toward Ninevah (Jon. 4:2). The Servant, Messiah, in Isaiah has similar character: "A bruised reed He will not break, and a dimly burning wick He will not extinguish" (Isa. 42:3). In fact, throughout the Old Testament God reveals His deep concern for the downtrodden—particularly the widow, the orphan, and the poor. Society denied full privileges to these, leaving them vulnerable to exploitation of all sorts. God's legislative provisions woven into the fabric of Old Testament social prescriptions demonstrate His compassion for them. The New Testament assigns the church the same responsibility toward the downtrodden. The obligation stands side by side with that of personal purity: "This is pure and undefiled religion in the sight of our God and Father, to visit orphans and widows in their distress and to keep oneself unstained by the world" (James 1:27).

Long before government and secular public agencies assumed responsibility for hospitals, orphanages, facilities for the poor, and other such social services, the church and its pastors blazed a trail of compassion. In both America and England, the earliest Sunday schools focused upon educating children, particularly in reading. They wanted to provide instruction to poor working children on their only free day of the week. Naturally, teachers used the Bible as their textbook, because evangelism and indoctrination were in many instances the primary objectives.[9]

A pastor with a heart for people will show special compassion for the lost. The Bible teaches two eternal destinies. Failure to have compassion for the unregenerate is either to disbelieve the eternal existence of a person or to be uncaring. Over a century ago Murray referred to "the missionary problem," by which he referred to a lack of compassion for those without Christ.[10] In the mind of Christ was a clear picture of what the world is and needs, so He felt compassion for the lost and gave His life a ransom for many. A congregation cannot respond adequately to the Great Commission if its pastor is cold or indifferent toward the needs of a lost world.

A reawakening of one expression of compassion has come only recently. That is interest in meeting the needs of the disabled. The renewal of this avenue of concern has come with the trend to provide services at

---

9. Anne M. Boylan, *Sunday School: The Formation of an American Institution, 1790–1880* (New Haven: Yale University, 1988), 6.

10. Andrew Murray, *Key to the Missionary Problem*, rev. Leona Choy (Fort Washington, Pa: Christian Literature Crusade, 1979), 13.

home or through outpatient services to this group of the population. Before this, many who had more serious physical and developmental disabilities remained in institutions away from the public eye. Their current visibility has aroused the church's interest in serving this deserving segment of society. This is good, for churches of all places should provide services to people who for one reason or another have handicaps. (Pastor, build that ramp!) John MacArthur, Jr., a pastor much concerned for this group, stresses the shepherd's exemplary role in ministering to this largely ignored group: "If a pastor is not completely committed, and if he isn't modeling his concern, it is going to be very difficult to get the people to minister to this population. . . . The pastor has to care about special populations because it is right to care."[11]

In his exposé of modern faith healers, Mayhue reminds the pastor that compassion is a quality originating in the heart of God: "Compassion cannot remain optional for Christians if we are to be like God. Someone once defined compassion as 'your pain in my heart, which moves me to deeds of comfort and mercy on your behalf.' That's healing ministry at the core—when we serve the suffering with God's compassion."[12]

Being an example of compassion is not optional for the undershepherd. He must care for the lambs entrusted to him and watch them grow, especially the weaker ones. Simply being an example just for the sake of being an example is not enough. Jefferson underscores the importance of the pastor following another example whose motivation was true, heartfelt compassion:

> Would you know, then, the work of a shepherd? Look at Jesus of Nazareth, that great Shepherd of the sheep, who stands before us forever the perfect pattern of shepherdhood, the flawless example for all who are entrusted with the care of souls. "I am the Good Pastor", he says, "I watch, I guard, I guide, I heal, I rescue, I feed. I love from the beginning, and I love to the end. Follow me!"[13]

2. **Leading by administration.** In many respects, the office of deacon originated to meet certain human needs. The frequent question is, "What portion of a pastor's time should he devote to meeting physical needs?" The

---

11. Gene Newman and Joni Eareckson Tada, *All God's Children: Ministry to the Disabled* (Grand Rapids: Zondervan, 1987), 33.

12. Richard L. Mayhue, *The Healing Promise* (Eugene, Oreg.: Harvest House Publishers, 1994), 262.

13. Jefferson, *Minister As Shepherd*, 66.

question Scripture addresses throughout is, "What kinds of needs is a pastor to address?" That depends. The person Paul has in mind in 1 Timothy 3 and Titus 1 models a sort of care based on example and instruction, particularly the latter. Titus 1:9 gives the most qualified character trait: "Holding fast the faithful word . . . that he may be able both to exhort in sound doctrine and to refute those who contradict."

The books of 1 and 2 Timothy focus on this instructive aspect of the pastor's role. This focus does not absolve the pastor from caring for people's physical needs. It merely prioritizes his focus. It also speaks clearly to the mentality that argues that the pastor is primarily a caretaker of people's physical needs. Mind you, he is not above this, but his time and energy will limit what he can do in light of his primary focus, as illustrated in Acts 6:1–7.[14] In this passage, seven men of good reputation, full of the Spirit and wisdom, were put in charge of the task of compassionate care. The contemporary church, much like the early church, has erroneously taken the responsibility of nurturing care for the people of God from under the leadership of deacons and has reassigned it to the pastor.[15] Historically, people have professionalized the expression of the Christian love commanded of all Christians by expecting the pastor do it all. In turn, they have delegated the pastor's primary role of teaching and administering the Word to others. Pastors must be caring people, but all the saints should do the work of the ministry. This is the lesson of Acts 6 for today's church.

Pastors who prefer to spend time caring for people's physical needs may be depriving the deacons of assuming their God-given function. If they feel led to focus on such needs instead of teaching the Word, perhaps they unapologetically should step out of their role as pastors-teachers and live out their goals as helpers, people of deep compassion for physical needs. This would open up pastoral slots for others to preach and teach the Word. Christians need the teaching of God's Word at all costs. This must not be neglected.

---

14. Perhaps the passage most cited in defense of the "preach and pray only" philosophy of ministry is Acts 6. One must remember, however, that even though Acts 6 contains an accurate account of the division of labor within the church, it is a narrative section and must be studied in conjunction with more clearly didactic passages. The church of today does not imitate indiscriminately all that Acts attributes to the early church. It follows, then, that the church of today must not draw its church leadership practices from Acts without considering the rest of Scripture.

15. Church history is replete with abuses of this sort. In the Middle Ages large houses were built for communities exercising pastoral duties who were called "ministers" (John Blair, ed., *Ministers and Parish Churches: The Local Church in Transition 950–1200* [Oxford: Oxford University Committees for Archaeology, 1988], 1).

Churches who prefer having a pastor spend most of his time doing visitation and counseling should consider finding a person specifically for these tasks. Churches with greater needs in such areas cannot afford to neglect the needs, but neither churches nor pastors should tolerate a situation where the pastor selected to minister the Word of God exchanges his functions with the deacons or the church membership. By biblical definition, *the pastor-teacher is not a deacon;* he should not "neglect the Word of God and prayer in order to serve tables" (Acts 6:2). He can through proper administration see that his deacons serve the tables, however.

Pastors and churches who subscribe to the biblical pattern can expect the same outcome as that of the Acts experience: "And the Word of God kept on spreading; and the number of disciples continued to increase greatly" (Acts 6:7).

3. **Leading by nurture of the flock.** The passages that list the qualifications of an elder also focus upon the interactive and relational character of his role in the church. In the 1 Timothy 3 passage, "gentle" and "uncontentious" (v. 3) are two such qualities, but the rhetorical question, "How will he take care of the church of God?" is perhaps the most specific quality. The words "take care of" (v. 5) have strong pastoral and nurturing overtones, and the larger analogy to the care of his own family is an even more revealing characteristic.

These qualities point to an obvious trait of pastoral ministry: without implying that the pastor must be what is popularly termed "a people person," they do suggest that a pastor must have "a heart for people," properly defined.

A shepherd's heart for people is not always clearly visible, particularly if identified and measured by standards other than those of Scripture. Those who watch a pastor who has difficulty interacting with people might conclude that he is not a people person or does not have a heart for people. From this they may extrapolate that this individual is not called to the gospel ministry. Hasty generalizations of this sort are unfortunate. Some pastors naturally have gregarious and likeable personalities. Others have come from very communicative families where they learned the skill of interacting with people early on. However, some need time to develop in this area, and still others will always express their affection for their sheep in a reserved manner. These communicative skills must not be the criteria for measuring a pastor's heart for people.

When attempting to measure the heart of a pastor, one should guard against quick judgments based on only superficial evidence. Many a pastor with a deep heart may not do well at demonstrating his compassion, but within him is a full commitment to give his life for the sheep. On the other side, many who make great displays in words lack the heartfelt realities of compassion. Talk is cheap. One cannot always judge a book by its cover. What is inside is what counts.

What about the shepherd's heart for those outside God's church? Paul prioritizes, first to the household of God, then to unbelievers around him who do not know Christ: "Let us do good to all men, and especially to those who are of the household of the faith" (Gal. 6:10). When asked by a lawyer, "Who is my neighbor?" (Luke 10:29), Jesus answered the lawyer's real question, "Whom should I love enough to show compassion and care for?" Jesus' answer indicted the religious leaders (priests and Levites, the pastors of the day), those who should have been exemplary shepherds (recall Zechariah). Even a Samaritan would take care of a beaten and robbed man! When Jesus inquired of the lawyer, "Which of these three do you think proved to be a neighbor?" the lawyer correctly (perhaps reluctantly) responded, "The one who showed mercy toward him." Jesus then pressed beyond the issue and responded, "go and do the same" (Luke 10:36–37). To deny compassion to a needy neighbor is to contradict the very significance of the term. Then again, to redefine the gospel in the face of overwhelming social need is to distort and diminish man's *greatest* need.

4. **Leading by cultivating maturity**. Paul and his fellow missionaries had a heart for people, yet their priority was the people's need for the ministry of the Word. Put slightly differently, they practiced love for their people best by giving them what they needed most—biblical teaching. It does not mean that they did no deaconly work. It does mean that the deaconly needs did not override the primary need. One of the passages that best captures the essence of a shepherd's nurture for his flock is 1 Thess. 2:1–12. After a prolonged discussion of the motives with which Paul did *not* come to the Thessalonian church, the beloved apostle selected more intimate terms characterized by parental metaphors: "But we proved to be gentle among you, as a nursing *mother* tenderly cares for her own children" (1 Thess. 2:7). And again after several more expressions of their pastoral interest: ". . . just as you know how we were exhorting and encouraging and imploring each one of you as a *father* would his own children" (1 Thess. 2:11, emphasis added).[16]

Paul reminds the believers that he could have approached them with grand displays of his apostolic authority, but this would not have befitted

---

16. Compare the family emphasis in 1 Tim. 3:5.

the love that he had for them. Individual attention as well as gentle coaxing and nurturing are evident in this passage. To be sure, this posture varied, but who can dispute the fact that this is the ideal. The ideal for what? Paul lays bare his intent in verse 12: "so that you may walk in a manner worthy of the God who calls you into His own kingdom and glory" (1 Thess. 2:12).

He follows with his ultimate goal, which is to give direction to a worthy walk through "the word of God, which also performs its work in you who believe" (v. 13). The pastor's instrument of nurture is God's Word reinforced by personal example. This and this alone is adequate food for the sheep's growth. Paul is consistent on this point.

Once again, this does not mean that the pastor can be insensitive to physical needs. In fact, the pastor should model a concern (albeit spiritually prioritized) for the needy (e.g., people with disabilities, both physical and mental). In so doing, he will be following the example of his Creator as well as explicit biblical commands. Yet even here he must see their *spiritual* needs as the end of his endeavors. These are everyone's greatest needs.

5. **Leading by guarding from harm.** In Acts 20, a context that builds on the shepherd image, the apostle Paul adds another dimension to the shepherding task. Not only does a loving, caring pastor feed Christ's sheep the Word of God, he also guards them (but himself first!) against spiritual predators. These will enter both from outside the fold and, sadly, from within. These wolves will consume the flock rather than feed them. The analogy is telling. The shepherd does not nurture the flock for what he can get from them in the same way that wolves do—this is the essence of the true shepherd's heart. Paul's reasoning is a challenge: The Ephesian elders were to be watchful shepherds, because Paul did not sleep on his shepherd's watch for three solid years. He demonstrated that his ministry was sincere by the tears he shed for them. Paul then gave back his post to God, the Chief Shepherd, who will complete the shepherding. Paul knew where his responsibility began and ended. He could shepherd compassionately, but he could let go when it was time to.

Nurture and Guidance

Returning to the original question—does the shepherd's role focus on the *nurture* or on the *guidance?*—one sees that the answer is certainly *both*. The shepherd who does not slight His teaching of the Word of God "in order to serve tables" can expect the same outcome as from the Acts strategy. "And the Word of God kept on spreading; and the number of the disciples continued to increase greatly" (Acts 6:7). If the shepherd does not give up on people but expresses his compassion in nurturing them through exhortation, encouragement, and appeals that they respond to the Word of God, he will have the joy of seeing his sheep "walk in a manner worthy of God" (1 Thess. 2:12). But his heart for people must be big enough to nurture (*noutheteō*) with tears (Acts 20:31).

He must also be prepared to face a challenging reality for all sheep including himself: People are looking for someone (like a pastor?) to meet their needs *as they define and prioritize them.* A response to the consumer-driven philosophy of church growth and mission comes from *Time* magazine in an article titled "The Church Search." The author pictures baby boomers as a segment of church goers who once dropped out of the church. They have returned and are now shopping for a church that will meet their needs, but needs as they define and prioritize them. The author says, "Many of those who have rediscovered churchgoing may ultimately be short-changed, however, if the focus of their faith seems subtly to shift from the glorification of God to the gratification of man."[17]

A pastor must prepare to redirect the interests of his flock beyond the green pastures and still waters of their own personal gratification to the glorification of Christ and the seeking first of His kingdom—heaven comes later. In short, sheep need to be nurtured, but good shepherds understand that spiritual guidance and protection are the essence of nurture.

What about the pastor who has lost his own spiritual passion? In the routine of ministry, it is far too easy to get so concerned about the spiritual growth of others that the shepherd neglects his own or his own family's. In an attempt to lean on his own resources or on a steady diet of self-help publications, he allows the people portion of his role to become overwhelmingly difficult. It will, at times, be difficult regardless, but in reality, his fatigue has far more to do with spiritual than physical exhaustion. The apostle Paul wrote to a spiritually haggard Timothy who had lapsed into such a weakened state. His advice? You have all the power resources you need; be strengthened (2 Tim. 2:1). Paul does not need to mention who actually does the strengthening. Timothy knew, but like the rest of us he needed a brief reminder.

A fifth-century letter from one pastor to his "challenged" pastor friend who is considering leaving the ministry to "live in quietness and ease" rather than "continue in the office committed to" him is as encouraging as it is timeless.

---

17. "The Church Search," *Time,* 5 April 1993, 49.

But I am surprised, beloved, that you are so disturbed by opposition in consequence of offenses, from whatever cause arising, as to say you would rather be relieved of the labors of your bishopric, and live in quietness and ease than continue in the office committed to you. But since the Lord says, "Blessed is he who shall persevere unto the end," whence shall come this blessed perseverance, except from the strength of patience? For as the Apostle proclaims, "All who would live godly in Christ shall suffer persecution." And it is not only to be reckoned persecution, when sword or fire or other active means are used against the Christian religion, for the direct persecution is often inflicted by nonconformity of practice and persistent disobedience and the barbs of ill-natured tongues, and since all the members of the church are always liable to these attacks, and no portion of the faithful are free from temptation, so that a life neither of ease nor of labor is devoid of danger, who shall guide the ship amidst the waves of the sea if the helmsman quit his post? Who shall guard the sheep from the treachery of wolves if the shepherd be not on the watch? Who, lastly, shall resist the thieves and robbers if love of quietude draw away the guard that's set to keep the outlook from the strictness of the watch? One must abide, therefore, in the office committed to him and in the task undertaken. Justice must be steadfastly upheld and mercy lovingly extended. Not individuals, but their sins must be hated. The proud must be rebuked, the weak must be borne with; and those sins which require severer chastisement must be dealt with in the spirit not of vindictiveness but of desire to heal. And if a fiercer storm of tribulation fall upon us, let us not be terror stricken as if we had to overcome the disaster in our own strength, since both our counsel and our strength is Christ, and through him we can do all things, without him nothing, who, to confirm the preachers of the gospel and the ministers of the mysteries, says, "Lo, I am with you all the days even to the consummation of the age." And again he says, "These things I have spoken unto you that in me you may have peace. In this world you shall have tribulation, but be of good cheer because I have overcome the world." The promises, which are as plain as they can be, we ought not to let any causes of offense to weaken, lest we should seem ungrateful to God for making us his chosen vessels, since God's assistance is powerful as his promises are true.[18]

---

18. Leo, the Bishop, to Rusticus, Bishop of Gallia Narbonensis (Letter 167.1-3, par. 2), cited by Philip L. Culbertson and Arthur Bradford Shippee, eds., *The Pastor: Readings from the Patristic Period* (Minneapolis: Fortress, 1990), 192–93.

Because every pastor (and pastor's wife!) faces interpersonal challenges in God's work, his heart must be energized from without. God gives us a means in our relationship with Him. When shepherds' hearts would melt like wax within them, God supplies the strength to endure, and His Spirit to comfort. To echo Leo's word's, "Both our counsel and our strength is Christ, and through him we can do all things."

The pastor running on his own resources soon will be tempted to leave the ministry. But the pastor who maintains his relationship with the Chief Shepherd will have resources to love God's people sacrificially because "God's assistance *is* powerful as His promises are true."[19]

---

19. Ibid., 15 [emphasis added].

Part IV

Pastoral Perspectives

14

Worshiping

John MacArthur, Jr.

*Much that transpires in the church today under the name "worship"
is unacceptable to God. Scripture has at least four categories of false
worship. God has designed worship to be honor and adoration directed to Himself. It has outward, inward, and upward dimensions
and touches every area of a Christian's life in doing good, sharing
with others, and praising God. It is the basis for his behavior and
his ministry. The church needs to return to the basic essence of true
worship and not be distracted by activities that are void of honor
and adoration of God.* [1]

The word *worship* often evokes images of holy hardware and sacred
rites. Most of the world's religions reflect this. Many see beads, prayer
wheels, sacred art, and such things as essential to the worship experience.
In some systems the *place* of worship is paramount. In these religions, worship is not acceptable unless it involves a prescribed ceremony at some
established holy site. *Worship* has thus come to mean *ritual*. Even in some
Christian traditions candles, incense, holy vestments, and liturgy have become virtually synonymous with worship.

These elements and practices have sometimes lulled evangelicals into
careless thinking about worship. Over the past decade or so, a number of
new books from evangelical authors on the subject of worship have appeared. Some of these contain much excellent material, but many of them
fall into the trap of equating worship with liturgy. Thus when they call for a

---

1. Portions of this chapter are adapted from *The Ultimate Priority* (Chicago: Moody,
1983) and are used by permission.

deepening of the evangelical worship experience, quite often what they actually have in mind is more formal liturgy. One otherwise very fine book on worship repeatedly stated that evangelical worship is not as rich as that of the Catholic and Eastern Orthodox traditions. The author seemed to imply that without a formal liturgy having ceremonial solemnity, worship is lame.

The number of people who share this perspective is astonishing. I heard a man on the radio recently say that he attends "an evangelical church for the preaching, and an Anglican high church for the worship." This is a poor understanding of what Scripture teaches about worship.

Jesus himself addressed this error. Remember His conversation with the Samaritan woman? She was keen to know whether the most acceptable place to worship God was in the temple at Jerusalem or at the Samaritan holy place on Mount Gerizim (John 4:20). Jesus told her,

> Woman, believe Me, an hour is coming when neither in this mountain, nor in Jerusalem, shall you worship the Father. You worship that which you do not know; we worship that which we know, for salvation is from the Jews. But an hour is coming, and now is, when the true worshipers shall worship the Father in spirit and truth; for such people the Father seeks to be His worshipers. God is spirit, and those who worship Him must worship in spirit and truth (John 4:21-24).

In other words, it is not the location or the external forms of worship that really matter, but the attitude of the worshiper's heart toward God. Deepening our worship is not accomplished by more formal liturgy; indeed, that may actually be counterproductive. A deepening of true worship occurs when the heart of the worshiper becomes more earnest and when the truth consumes the mind of the worshiper. All worship not offered in spirit and in truth is utterly unacceptable to God—no matter how beautiful the external forms.

Deviant Worship

Scripture is very clear about this. Approximately half of everything the Bible says about worship condemns false worship. The first two of the Ten Commandments are prohibitions against false worship:

> I am the LORD your God, who brought you out of the land of Egypt, out of the house of slavery. You shall have no other Gods before Me. You shall not make for yourself an idol, or any likeness of what is in

heaven above or on the earth beneath or in the water under the earth. You shall not worship them or serve them; for I, the LORD Your God, am a jealous God (Exod. 20:2–5).

Consider how much of the Old Testament describes the evil consequences of false worship. Cain and Abel, the Israelites and golden calf at Sinai, Nadab and Abihu's offering of strange fire, King Saul's intrusion into the priest's office, Eli's wicked sons who pilfered what was offered to God, Elijah's confrontations with Jezebel and the priests of Baal, and Nebuchadnezzar's golden image are all variations on this same theme: God does not accept worship not offered in spirit and in truth.

Many people foolishly believe God will accept anything offered by well-meaning worshipers. It is clear, however, that sincerity is not the test of true worship. All self-styled or aberrant worship is utterly unacceptable to God. Consider how often these things are reiterated in the Old Testament law. And notice the severity of God's threats against those who worship falsely:

> You shall not make for yourself an idol, or any likeness of what is in heaven above or on the earth beneath or in the water under the earth. You shall not worship them or serve them; for I, the LORD your God, am a jealous God, visiting the iniquity of the fathers on the children, on the third and the fourth generations of those who hate Me, but showing loving-kindness to thousands, to those who love Me and keep My commandments (Exod. 20:4–6).

> Watch yourself that you make no covenant with the inhabitants of the land into which you are going, lest it become a snare in your midst. But rather, you are to tear down their altars and smash their sacred pillars and cut down their Asherim—for you shall not worship any other god, for the LORD, whose name is Jealous, is a jealous God—lest you make a covenant with the inhabitants of the land and they play the harlot with their gods, and sacrifice to their gods, and someone invite you to eat of his sacrifice (Exod. 34:12–15).

> You shall fear only the LORD your God; and you shall worship Him, and swear by His name. You shall not follow other gods, any of the gods of the peoples who surround you, for the LORD your God in the midst of you is a jealous God; otherwise the anger of the LORD your God will be kindled against you, and He will wipe you off the face of the earth (Deut. 6:13–15).

> And it shall come about if you ever forget the LORD your God, and go after other gods and serve them and worship them, I testify against you today that you shall surely perish (Deut. 8:19).

Beware, lest your hearts be deceived and you turn away and serve other gods and worship them. Or the anger of the LORD will be kindled against you, and He will shut up the heavens so that there will be no rain and the ground will not yield its fruit; and you will perish quickly from the good land which the LORD is giving you (Deut. 11:16–17).

Beware that you are not ensnared to follow [the nations], after they are destroyed before you, and that you do not inquire after their gods, saying, "How do these nations serve their gods, that I also may do likewise?" You shall not behave thus toward the LORD your God, for every abominable act which the LORD hates they have done for their gods; for they even burn their sons and daughters in the fire to their gods. Whatever I command you, you shall be careful to do; you shall not add to nor take away from it (Deut. 12:30–32).

I command you today to love the LORD your God, to walk in His ways and to keep His commandments and His statutes and His judgments, that you may live and multiply, and that the LORD your God may bless you in the land where you are entering to possess it. But if your heart turns away and you will not obey, but are drawn away and worship other gods and serve them, I declare to you today that you shall surely perish. You shall not prolong your days in the land where you are crossing the Jordan to enter and possess it (Deut. 30:16–18).

Worship of False Gods

Scripture outlines at least four categories of unacceptable worship: worship of false gods, worship of the true God in a wrong form, worship of the true God in a self-styled manner, and worship of the true God with a wrong attitude. The God of the Bible is the only God, and He is a jealous God who will not tolerate the worship of another. In Isa. 48:11, God says, "My glory will I not give to another." Exodus 34:14 says, "You shall not worship any other god, for the LORD, whose name is Jealous, is a jealous God."

The lure of false gods seems irresistible to those who turn away from the true God. Indeed, it is the natural tendency of sinful humanity to pursue false worship. Romans 1:21 indicts the entire human race for this very sin. "Even though they knew God," the apostle Paul writes, "they did not honor Him as God, or give thanks." In fact, when they refused to worship God, they began to make images. They "exchanged the glory of the incorruptible God for an image in the form of corruptible man and of birds and four-footed animals and crawling creatures" (v. 23).

They refused to worship God, turning instead to false gods. That is unacceptable. Verse 24 tells the consequences of worshiping a false god:

"God gave them over in the lusts of their hearts to impurity." Verse 26 says, "God gave them over to degrading passions." Verse 28 adds, "God gave them over to a depraved mind."

The result of their improper worship was that God simply gave them over to their sin and its consequences. Can you think of anything worse? Their sin grew to be the dominating factor in their lives. Ultimately, they faced judgment, with no excuse for their actions (Rom. 1:32–2:1).

Everyone worships—even atheists. Atheists worship themselves. When people reject God, they always worship false gods of their own choice. Those gods are not necessarily personalities. People may worship money, material things, popularity, or power. All those things are as idolatrous as worshiping a stone god—idolatry which is precisely what God forbade in the first and second commandments.

Most people who worship material things do so without the consciousness that they are worshiping deities. Is that still idolatry? Absolutely. Job 31:24–28 says,

> If I have put my confidence in gold,
> And called fine gold my trust,
> If I have gloated because my wealth was great,
> And because my hand had secured so much;
> If I have looked at the sun when it shone,
> Or the moon going in splendor,
> And my heart became secretly enticed,
> And my hand threw a kiss from my mouth,
> That too would have been an iniquity calling for judgment,
> For I would have denied God above.

Job was a righteous man who refused to worship his material wealth. To do so, he said, would be to deny God. That is a sobering thought—one that many Christians in this materialistic age would do well to ponder carefully. Professing Christians abhor the superstition and compromise of the Israelites when reading in the Old Testament about their constant turning to pagan worship, but they forget their own habit of putting their trust in material things and setting their hearts on houses, cars, and temporal goods. They are in fact guilty of the same sin of idolatry.

Idolatry has other forms as well. Habakkuk 1:15–16 describes the false worship of the Chaldeans: "The Chaldeans bring all of them [the righteous] up with a hook, drag them away with their net, and gather them together in their fishing net. Therefore, they rejoice and are glad. Therefore, they offer a sacrifice to their net, and burn incense to their fishing net." "Their net" was their military might, and the god they worshiped was armed power—also a false god.

Even today, people formulate supernatural gods, supposed deities. The rise of the New Age movement has produced a revival of pagan religions. People today are worshiping earth goddesses, animals, spirit beings, and even mythological deities on a scale unknown since before the Middle Ages. That is nothing more than demon worship. First Corinthians 10:20 says that things sacrificed to idols are really sacrificed to demons. Therefore, if people worship false beings, they are actually worshiping the demons that impersonate those false gods.

What folly it is to worship creation rather than the Creator! In Acts 17:29 Paul made this observation: "Being then the offspring of God, we ought not to think that the Divine Nature is like gold or silver or stone, an image formed by the art and thought of man." Those created in God's image dare not attempt to remake God into another image (see Rom. 1:21, 25).

Worship of the True God in a Wrong Form

Exodus 32:7–9 records God's response when the Israelites made a golden calf to worship:

> Then the LORD spoke to Moses, "Go down at once, for your people, whom you brought up from the land of Egypt, have corrupted themselves. They have quickly turned aside from the way which I commanded them. They have made for themselves a molten calf, and have worshiped it, and have sacrificed unto it, and said, "This is your god, O Israel, who brought you up from the land of Egypt!"

When the Israelites constructed the golden calf, they thought they were worshiping the true God, but by reducing Him to an image, they corrupted both their worship and their concept of God. This is why God forbids such idolatry. It is impossible to reduce God to a form represented by a statue or a painting. Those who worship such things may believe they worship the true God, but their worship denigrates God and is therefore unacceptable.

Years after the Sinai incident, Moses said to the assembled Israelites,

> And the LORD commanded me at that time to teach you statutes and judgments, that you might perform them in the land where you are going over to possess it. So watch yourselves carefully, since you did not

see any form on the day the Lord spoke to you at Horeb from the midst
of the fire, lest you act corruptly and make a graven image for yourselves in the form of any figure, the likeness of male or female, the
likeness of any animal that is on the earth, the likeness of any winged
bird that flies in the sky, the likeness of anything that creeps on the
ground, the likeness of any fish that is in the water below the earth.
And beware, lest you lift up your eyes to heaven and see the sun and the
moon and the stars, all the host of heaven, and be drawn away and
worship them and serve them, those which the Lord your God has allotted to all the peoples under the whole heaven (Deut. 4:14–19).

When God revealed Himself to the Israelites, he was unrepresented
in any visible form. There was purposely no tangible representation of God.
Why? Because God does not wish to be reduced to an image. That is true
of God throughout the Scriptures.

Only the Incarnation of Christ was adequate to reveal God in a tangible form. "No man has seen God at any time; the only begotten God, who
is in the bosom of the Father, He has explained Him" (John 1:18). There is,
therefore, a tone of wonder in John's words when he writes,

What was from the beginning, what we have *heard*, what we have
seen with our eyes, what we *beheld and our hands handled*, concerning
the Word of Life—and the life was *manifested*, and we have *seen* and
bear witness and proclaim to you the eternal life, which was with the
Father and was *manifested* to us—what we have *seen and heard* we proclaim to you also (1 John 1:1–3, emphasis added).

Only the living Person of Christ can reveal God in any visible or tangible form. To attempt to express God in any lesser image is to commit
idolatry.

In fact, one must guard even his thoughts about God. To envision
God as an old man with a beard sitting on a throne is unacceptable.
Idolatry does not begin with a sculptor's hammer; it begins in the mind.
How should one visualize God? He should not! No visual conception of
God can properly and adequately represent His eternal glory. That may
be why the Bible describes God as light. It is impossible to make a statue
of light.

Worship of the True God in a Self-Styled Manner

This is false worship just as surely as worshiping a stone idol is false
worship. God does not accept it.

The Pharisees tried to worship the true God with a self-styled system, and Jesus told them, "You yourselves transgress the commandment of God for the sake of your tradition" (Matt. 15:3). Their worship was an abomination.

The basis of the biblical rule for worship is the principle of *sola Scriptura*—Scripture alone. When it comes to worship, whatever the Scripture does not expressly command is forbidden. "You shall not add to the word which I am commanding you, nor take away from it, that you may keep the commandments of the LORD your God which I command you" (Deut. 4:2). "Whatever I command you, you shall be careful to do; you shall not add to nor take away from it" (Deut. 12:32). Both of those commandments appear in the context of laws given to regulate worship—and they limit all forms of worship to what the law expressly commanded.

Worship of the True God with a Wrong Attitude

By far the most subtle kind of false worship—more difficult to measure from outward appearances than any of the first three already mentioned—is the worship of the true God in the right way, with a wrong attitude. Even with the elimination of all false gods, all images of the true God, and all self-styled modes of worship, worship will still be unacceptable if the heart attitude is not right. True worship requires devotion of the whole heart, soul, mind, and strength (Luke 10:27). When it is time to give, one must give the best of all he has, not the leftovers (Prov. 3:9). Awe and reverence and a focus on the truth must fill his mind (Ps. 138:2). That is what it means to worship in spirit and in truth. How much present-day worship qualifies as acceptable under those guidelines?

In Malachi 1 God denounced the people of Israel for the inadequacy of their worship. "You are presenting defiled food upon my altar," He said (v. 7). They were treating worship with disdain, with flippancy. By offering blind, lame, and sick animals (v. 8) instead of bringing the best they had, they were demonstrating contempt for the seriousness of worship. In v. 10, God says, "I am not pleased with you . . . nor will I accept an offering from you." He declined to accept their worship, because their attitude was not right.

Amos also gives insight into the intensity of God's hatred of worship with the wrong attitude. In Amos 5:21–24, God says,

> I hate, I reject your festivals,
> Nor do I delight in your solemn assemblies.
> Even though you offer up to Me burnt offerings
>   and your grain offerings,
> I will not accept them;

And I will not even look at the
      peace offerings of your fatlings.
Take away from Me
      the noise of your songs;
I will not even listen to the sound of your harps.
But let justice roll down like waters
And righteousness like an ever-flowing stream.

Hosea saw the same truth. Hosea 6:4–6 gives God's words:

What shall I do with you, O Ephraim?
What shall I do with you, O Judah?
For your loyalty is like a morning cloud,
And like the dew which goes away early.
Therefore I have hewn them in pieces by the prophets;
I have slain them by the words of My mouth;
And the judgments on you
      Are like the light that goes forth.
For I delight in loyalty rather than sacrifice,
And in the knowledge of God
      rather than burnt offerings.

It was hypocrisy, not worship. The offerings were empty—like many today, they were guilty of giving God the symbol, but not the reality.
      Isaiah 1 has the same indictment:

What are your multiplied sacrifices to Me?" says the Lord.
"I have had enough of burnt offerings of rams,
      and the fat of fed cattle.
And I take no pleasure in the blood of bulls,
      lambs, or goats.
When you come to appear before Me,
Who requires of you this trampling of My courts?
Bring your worthless offerings no longer,
Incense is an abomination to Me.
New moon and Sabbath, the calling of assemblies—
I cannot endure iniquity and the solemn assembly.
I hate your new moon festivals
      and your appointed feasts,
They have become a burden to Me.
I am weary of bearing them.

So when you spread out your hands in prayer,
I will hide My eyes from you,
Yes, even though you multiply your prayers,
I will not listen (Isa. 1:11–15).

Read carefully the minor prophets. The prophecies of Israel's and Judah's destruction result from their failure to worship God with the proper attitude.

Perhaps the greatest need in all of Christendom is for a clear understanding of the biblical teaching about worship. When the church fails to worship properly, it fails in every other area.

A fresh understanding of worship is a necessity. God has commanded it. Pastoral ministry depends on it. It is crucial to a personal relationship with Him and a testimony in this world. No one can afford to ignore it; too much is at stake.

WORSHIP AS GOD DESIGNED IT TO BE

Where do people go astray in their understanding of worship? Surely it is in a lack of understanding of what real worship is. As noted early in this chapter, most people think of worship as an external thing—ritual, performance, activity that takes place at a prescribed time and place, following predetermined forms. But that is not at all the spirit of true worship.

It is impossible to isolate or relegate worship to just one place, time, or segment of life. Verbally thanking and praising God while living a life of selfishness and carnality is a perversion. Appropriate acts of worship must be the overflow of a worshiping life.

In Ps. 45:1, David wrote, "My heart overflows with a good theme." The Hebrew word for *overflow* means "to boil over," and in a sense that is what praise actually is. Righteousness and love so warm the heart that, figuratively, it reaches the boiling point. Praise is the boiling over of a hot heart. It is reminiscent of what the disciples experienced on the road to Emmaus: "Were not our hearts burning within us?" (Luke 24:32). As God warms the heart with truth, righteousness, and love, the resulting life of praise that boils over is the truest expression of worship.

Here is a simple definition of worship: *worship is honor and adoration directed to God.* That definition is sufficiently detailed. A study of the concept of worship in the Word of God will fill that definition with richness.

The New Testament uses several words for worship. Two of them are particularly noteworthy. The first is *proskuneo*, a commonly used term whose literal meaning is "to kiss toward," "to kiss the hand," or "to bow down." It is the word for worship used to signify humble adoration. The second word is *latreuo*, which suggests rendering honor or paying homage. *Latreuo* speaks of the kind of reverent veneration reserved solely for God.

Both terms carry the idea of giving, because worship *is* giving something to God. The Anglo-Saxon source of the English word is *weorthscipe*, which relates to the concept of worthiness. Worship is ascribing to God His worth, or stating and affirming His supreme value.

So to talk about worship is to talk about something *we* give to God. Modern Christianity seems committed, instead, to the idea that God should be giving to us. God *does* give to us abundantly, but we need to understand the balance of that truth—we are to render ceaseless honor and adoration to God. That consuming, selfless desire to give to God is the essence and the heart of worship. It begins with the giving first of ourselves, and then of our attitudes, and then of our possessions—until worship is a way of life.

Worship in Three Dimensions

A key adjective, used often in the New Testament to describe proper acts of worship, is the word *acceptable*. Every worshiper seeks to offer what is acceptable. Scripture specifies at least three categories of acceptable worship.

The outward dimension. First, how we behave toward others can reflect worship. Romans 14:18 says, "For he who in this way serves [*latreuo*] Christ is acceptable to God." What is this acceptable offering given to God? The context reveals that it is being sensitive to a weaker brother. Verse 13 says, "Therefore let us not judge one another anymore, but rather determine this—not to put an obstacle or a stumbling block in a brother's way." In other words, treating fellow Christians with the proper kind of sensitivity is an acceptable act of worship. It honors God, who created and loves that person, and it reflects God's compassion and care.

Romans 15:16 implies that evangelism is a form of acceptable worship. Paul writes that he received special grace "to be a minister of Christ Jesus to the Gentiles, ministering as a priest the gospel of God, that my offering of the Gentiles might become acceptable." The Gentiles won to Jesus Christ by his ministry became an offering of worship to God. In addition, those who were won became worshipers themselves.

In Phil. 4:18, Paul thanks the Philippians for their monetary gift to help him in his ministry: "I have received everything in full, and have an abundance; I am amply supplied, having received from Epaphroditus what you have sent, a fragrant aroma, an acceptable sacrifice, well-pleasing to

God." Here, acceptable worship consists of giving to those in need. That glorifies God by demonstrating His love.

So it is possible to express worship by sharing love with fellow believers, sharing the gospel with unbelievers, and meeting the needs of people on a very physical level. A single word sums it up: acceptable worship is *giving*. It is a love that shares.

The inward dimension. A second category of worship involves personal behavior. Ephesians 5:8–10 says, "Walk as children of light (for the fruit of the light consists in all goodness and righteousness and truth), trying to learn what is pleasing to the Lord." The word *pleasing* is from a Greek word that means "acceptable." In this context, Paul refers to goodness, righteousness, and truth, saying clearly that to do good is an acceptable act of worship toward God.

He begins 1 Timothy 2 by urging Christians to pray for those in authority in order that believers may live tranquil lives in godliness and dignity. Note carefully that the final words in verse 2 are "godliness and dignity." Verse 3 goes on to say, "This is good and acceptable in the sight of God our Savior."

So in addition to sharing with others as an act of worship (i.e., the effect of worship on others), doing good is also an act of worship (i.e., its effect in our own lives).

The upward dimension. Worship affects one other relationship—the relationship with God. Hebrews 13:15–16 marvelously sums up worship. Verse 15 says, "Through Him then, let us continually offer up a sacrifice of praise to God, that is, the fruit of lips that give thanks to His name." Worship in its Godward focus is thanksgiving and praise. With verse 16, the passage brings together all three categories of worship: "And do not neglect doing good and sharing; for with such sacrifices God is pleased."

Praising God, doing good, and sharing with others—all are legitimate, scriptural acts of worship. That includes in the concept of worship every activity and relationship of human living. The implication is that just as the Scriptures from cover to cover center on the subject of worship, so the believer should dedicate himself to the activity of worship, consumed with a desire to use every moment of his life to devote himself to doing good, sharing, and praising God.

Whole-Life Worship

The understanding that true worship touches each area of life enriches our original definition. We are to honor and adore God in everything.

Paul makes a powerful statement in Rom. 12:1–2 about the concept of whole-life worship. His words there follow what is possibly the greatest exposition of theology in all of Scripture. Those first eleven chapters of Romans are a monumental treatise, moving from the wrath of God through the redemption of man, to the plan of God for Israel and the church. They include all the great themes of redemptive theology, and Rom. 12:1–2 are in response to them:

> I urge you therefore, brethren, by the mercies of God, to present your bodies a living and holy sacrifice, acceptable to God, which is your spiritual service of worship. And do not be conformed to this world, but be transformed by the renewing of your mind, that you may prove what the will of God is, that which is good and acceptable and perfect.

"The mercies of God" are what Paul has described in the first eleven chapters. The theme of those chapters is God's merciful work on behalf of mankind. Through eleven chapters of doctrine, Paul defines the Christian life and all its benefits. Now he says that the only adequate response to what God has done and the starting point for acceptable spiritual worship, is to present oneself as a living sacrifice.

First Peter 1 reiterates the same basic truth. Peter gives there a full and rich statement of what Christ has done for us:

> May grace and peace be yours in fullest measure. Blessed be the God and Father of our Lord Jesus Christ, who according to His great mercy has caused us to be born again to a living hope through the resurrection of Jesus Christ from the dead, to obtain an inheritance which is imperishable and undefiled and will not fade away, reserved in heaven for you, who are protected by the power of God through faith for a salvation ready to be revealed in the last time (1 Pet. 1:2–5).

Note the Christian response to that in 1 Pet. 2:5: "You also, as living stones, are being built up as a spiritual house for a holy priesthood, to offer up spiritual sacrifices acceptable to God through Jesus Christ." Peter's argument is identical with Paul's: Because of what God has done for us, we should be offering up acceptable spiritual sacrifices of worship.

Another New Testament passage that parallels Rom. 12:1–2 is Heb. 12:28–29. Verse 28 says, "Therefore, since we receive a kingdom which cannot be shaken [again he is dealing with what God has done for us], let us show gratitude, by which we may offer [the word is a form of *latreuo*] to God an acceptable service with reverence and awe." Our all-inclusive response to God—our chief priority and the only activity that matters—is pure, acceptable worship.

The Order of Priorities

God's Word repeatedly confirms the absolute priority of worship. Hebrews 11 contains a list of Old Testament heroes of faith. The first is Abel. His life echoes one word: *worship*. The single dominant issue in Abel's story is that he was a true worshiper; he worshiped according to God's will, and God accepted his offering. That is really all we know about his life.

The second person in Hebrews 11 is Enoch, whose single word of identification is *walk*. Enoch walked with God; he lived a godly, faithful, dedicated life. One day he walked from earth to heaven!

Third on the list is Noah. The word suggested by Noah is *work*. He spent 120 years building the ark. That is work—the work of faith.

Hebrews 11 has an order that goes beyond the chronological. It is an order of priorities: first comes worship, then walk, then work. The order is the same as in the layout of the camp of Israel around the tabernacle. The priests, those whose function was to lead the people in worship, camped immediately around the tabernacle. Beyond them were the Levites, whose function was service. The positions illustrated that worship was the central activity, and service was secondary.

The law displayed the same order. Moses established specific age requirements for different ministries. According to Num. 1:3, a young Israelite could serve as a soldier when he was twenty. Numbers 8:24 says that a Levite could begin to work in the tabernacle when he was twenty-five. But Num. 4:3 says that to be a priest and lead the people in worship, a man had to be thirty. The reason is simple: Leading in worship demands the highest level of maturity, because as the first priority in the divine order, worship holds the greatest significance.

Activities of the angels shows the same order of priority. In Isaiah 6, the prophet described his vision:

> In the year of king Uzziah's death, I saw the Lord sitting on a throne, lofty and exalted, with the train of his robe filling the temple. Seraphim stood above Him, each having six wings; with two he covered his face, and with two he covered his feet, and with two he flew. And one called out to another and said, "Holy, Holy, Holy, is the Lord of Hosts, the whole earth is full of His glory" (vv. 1–3).

The seraphim are a class of angelic beings associated with the presence of God. It is particularly interesting to note that of their six wings, four related to worship and only two related to service. They cover their feet to protect the holiness of God. They cover their faces because they cannot look upon His glory. With the two remaining wings, they fly and take care of whatever tasks their service requires.

It is necessary to keep ministry in perspective. Gibbs correctly observed that ministry is that which comes down from the Father by the Son in the power of the Spirit through the human instrument. Worship starts in the human instrument and goes up by the power of the Holy Spirit through the Son to the Father.[2]

In the Old Testament, the prophet was a minister of God's Word and spoke from God to the people. The priest, who led the worship, spoke from the people to God. Worship is the perfect element to balance with ministry, but the order of priority begins with worship, not ministry.

Luke 10 has the familiar account of Jesus' visit to Mary and Martha:

> Now as they were traveling along, He entered a certain village; and a woman named Martha welcomed Him into her home. And she had a sister called Mary, who moreover was listening to the Lord's word, seated at His feet. But Martha was distracted with all her preparations; and she came up to Him, and said, "Lord, do You not care that my sister has left me to do all the serving alone? Then tell her to help me." But the Lord answered and said to her, "Martha, Martha, you are worried and bothered about so many things; but only a few things are necessary, really only one, for Mary has chosen the good part, which shall not be taken away from her" (vv. 38–42).

Worship is the primary essential, and service is a wonderful and necessary corollary to it. Worship is central in the will of God—the great *sine qua non* of all Christian experience.

Later Jesus taught a similar lesson, again at the home of Mary and Martha while Lazarus their brother, whom Jesus had raised from the dead, was there:

> So they made Him a supper there, and Martha was serving; but Lazarus was one of those reclining at the table with Him. Mary therefore took a pound of very costly perfume of pure nard, and anointed

---

2. A. P. Gibbs, *Worship* (Kansas City: Walterick, n.d.), 13.

the feet of Jesus, and wiped His feet with her hair; and the house was filled with the fragrance of the perfume. But Judas Iscariot, one of His disciples, who was intending to betray Him, said, "Why was this perfume not sold for three hundred denarii, and given to poor people?" Now he said this, not because he was concerned about the poor, but because he was a thief, and as he had the money box, he used to pilfer what was put into it. Jesus therefore said, "Let her alone, in order that she may keep it for the day of my burial. For the poor you always have with you, but you do not always have Me" (John 12:2–8).

What Mary did was very humiliating. A woman's hair is her glory; and a man's feet, dirty with the dust or mud of the roads, are nobody's glory. To use such costly ointment (worth a year's wages) seemed incredibly wasteful to the pragmatists. Notice that Judas Iscariot represented a pragmatic outlook. Jesus rebuked him for such an attitude. Mary's act was sincere worship, and Jesus commended her for understanding the priority.

How Are We Doing?

Tragically, the element of worship is largely absent from the church amid all its activity! A number of years ago I read a newspaper account of a christening party in a wealthy Boston suburb. The parents had opened their palatial home to friends and relatives, who had come to celebrate the wonderful event. As the party was progressing and the people were having a wonderful time eating, drinking, celebrating, and enjoying one another, someone said, "By the way, where is the baby?"

The heart of that mother jumped, and she instantly left the room and rushed into the master bedroom, where she had left the baby asleep in the middle of the massive bed. The baby was dead, smothered by the coats of the guests.

I have often thought about that in reference to the treatment the Lord Jesus Christ receives from His own church. We are busy supposedly celebrating Him, while He is smothering under the coats of the guests.

We have many activities and little worship. We are big on ministry and small on adoration. We are disastrously pragmatic. All we want to know about is what works. We want formulas and gimmicks, and somehow in the process, we leave out that to which God has called us.

We are too many Marthas and too few Marys. We are so deeply entrenched in the doing that we miss the being. We are programmed and informed and planned and busy—and we slight worship! We have our functions, our promotions, our objectives, our success-driven, numbers-conscious, traditionalistic, even faddish efforts. But too often acceptable, true, spiritual worship eludes us.

Years ago, A. W. Tozer called worship "the missing jewel of the church." If he were still with us, I am sure he would reiterate that statement. In America 350,000 churches own 80 billion dollars worth of facilities dedicated to worshiping God. But how much true worship takes place?

A distinguished explorer was making a trek in the Amazon jungle. Native tribesmen were bearing his great burdens, and he was driving them with great force to cover a lot of ground rapidly. At the end of the third day they rested, and when morning came and it was time to embark again, the natives sat on the ground by their burdens. The explorer did everything he could to get them up and moving, but they would not budge. Finally, the chief said to him, "My friend, they are resting until their souls catch up to their bodies."

Here's hoping that will happen in the church.

15

Preaching

John MacArthur, Jr.

Among the varied responsibilities assigned to a pastor, that of preaching stands head and shoulders above the rest in importance. Paul repeatedly emphasized the importance of preaching to Timothy, sounding a note that echoes continually throughout the New Testament. High points in church history have verified the importance of biblical preaching. The proper foundation for preaching is the Word of God, a foundation that is missing in much contemporary preaching. The content of preaching should include teaching matter as well as exhortations to behavior based on that teaching. Only preaching by one whose commitment is intense can be persuasive with listeners. Among other ways, that commitment exhibits itself in the hard work the preacher is willing to put into the preparation of his sermons.[1]

The God-ordained means to save, sanctify, and strengthen His church is preaching. The proclamation of the gospel is what elicits saving faith in those whom God has chosen (Rom. 10:14). Through the preaching of the Word comes the knowledge of the truth that results in godliness (John 17:17; Rom. 16:25; Eph. 5:26). Preaching also encourages believers to live in the hope of eternal life, enabling them to endure suffering (Acts 14:21–22). The faithful preaching of the Word is the most important element of pastoral ministry.

---

1. For a comprehensive discussion of the key elements in expository preaching, see John MacArthur, Jr., et al., *Rediscovering Expository Preaching* (Dallas: Word, 1992).

Preaching Must Have
the Proper Priority

As he neared the end of his life, the veteran pastor Paul addressed this exhortation to his young protégé Timothy:

> I solemnly charge you in the presence of God and of Christ Jesus, who is to judge the living and the dead, and by His appearing and His kingdom: preach the word; be ready in season and out of season; reprove, rebuke, exhort, with great patience and instruction. For the time will come when they will not endure sound doctrine; but wanting to have their ears tickled, they will accumulate for themselves teachers in accordance to their own desires; and will turn away their ears from the truth, and will turn aside to myths (2 Tim. 4:1–4).

In those words, which may be the last Timothy ever received from his beloved mentor, Paul set forth the pastor's highest priority. While the duties of the pastorate are many and varied, as the other chapters in this section on "Pastoral Perspectives" indicate, none is more important than preaching. Charles Jefferson perceptively notes:

> Pastoral work is not simply making social calls; pastoral work is also preaching. The minister does not cease to be a pastor when he goes into the pulpit; he then takes up one of the minister's most exacting and serious tasks. We sometimes hear it said of a minister: "He is a good pastor, but he cannot preach." The sentence is self-contradictory. No man can be a good pastor who cannot preach, any more than a man can be a good shepherd and still fail to feed his flock. A part of shepherding is feeding, and an indispensable part. Some of the finest and most effective of all a minister's pastoral work is done in his sermon. In a sermon he can warn, protect, guide, heal, rescue, and nourish. The shepherd in him comes to lofty stature in the pulpit. . . . A shepherd who is skilled in his work never fails to feed his flock.[2]

Paul did not wait until the end of his life to stress the importance of preaching to Timothy; it had been a constant theme in his letters to the young pastor. In 1 Tim. 4:11 he instructed Timothy to "prescribe and teach these things." He further commanded Timothy,

---

2. Charles Jefferson, *The Minister As Shepherd* (Hong Kong: Living Books For All, 1980), 63–64.

Until I come, give attention to the public reading of Scripture, to exhortation and teaching. Do not neglect the spiritual gift within you, which was bestowed upon you through prophetic utterance with the laying on of hands by the presbytery. Pay close attention to yourself and to your teaching; persevere in these things; for as you do this you will insure salvation both for yourself and for those who hear you (1 Tim. 4:13–14, 16).

In 1 Tim. 5:17 he ordered that "the elders who rule well be considered worthy of double honor, especially those who work hard at preaching and teaching." After giving him instructions about relations between Christian masters and slaves, Paul told Timothy to "teach and preach these principles" (1 Tim. 6:2). What Timothy had "heard from [Paul] in the presence of many witnesses," he was to "entrust to faithful men, who will be able to teach others also" (2 Tim. 2:2). So important is preaching and teaching that the only qualification for an elder relating to a skill or function is that he be "able to teach" (1 Tim. 3:2).

Nor was this emphasis on preaching unique to Paul; it runs throughout the New Testament. In Luke 4:43 the Lord Jesus Christ revealed the important place preaching held in His earthly ministry when He said, "I must preach the kingdom of God to the other cities also, for I was sent for this purpose." Indeed, His earthly ministry was largely one of preaching and teaching (e.g., Matt. 4:17; 11:1; Mark 1:14, 38–39; Luke 8:1; 20:1). He left His church with the charge, "Go into all the world and preach" (Mark 16:15).

Preaching was also central to the early church's ministry, as even a cursory reading of Acts indicates. Immediately after the church came into being on the Day of Pentecost, Peter preached and three thousand were converted (Acts 2:14–41). Shortly afterward, Peter preached another major sermon from Solomon's portico in the Temple (Acts 3:11–26). The preaching of Philip (8:5, 12, 35, 40), Paul (9:20; 13:5, 16–41; 14:7, 15, 21; 15:35; 16:10; 17:13; 20:25; 28:31), the apostles (4:2; 5:42), and others in the church (8:4; 11:20) is also a prominent feature in Acts.

The true church throughout its history has strongly emphasized biblical preaching. Preaching held a central place in the Reformation of the sixteenth century, the Puritan revival of seventeenth-century England, and the Great Awakening of the eighteenth century. The nineteenth-century church countered the rising tide of apostasy and modernity with the powerful preaching of men such as Charles Spurgeon, Joseph Parker, Alexander Maclaren, and Alexander Whyte.

The words of Paul in 1 Cor. 1:17–25 best sum up the priority of preaching:

For Christ did not send me to baptize, but to preach the gospel, not in cleverness of speech, that the cross of Christ should not be made void. For the word of the cross is to those who are perishing foolishness, but to us who are being saved it is the power of God. For it is written, "I will destroy the wisdom of the wise, and the cleverness of the clever I will set aside." Where is the wise man? Where is the scribe? Where is the debater of this age? Has not God made foolish the wisdom of the world? For since in the wisdom of God the world through its wisdom did not come to know God, God was well-pleased through the foolishness of the message preached to save those who believe. For indeed Jews ask for signs, and Greeks search for wisdom; but we preach Christ crucified, to Jews a stumbling block, and to Gentiles foolishness, but to those who are the called, both Jews and Greeks, Christ the power of God and the wisdom of God. Because the foolishness of God is wiser than men, and the weakness of God is stronger than men.

No man's pastoral ministry will be successful in God's sight who does not give preaching its proper place.

Preaching Must Have
the Proper Foundation

If preaching is to play its God-designed role in the church, it must be built upon the Word of God. In years past such a statement would have been obvious, even axiomatic. Stitzinger writes, "A study of the history of expository preaching makes it clear that such preaching is deeply rooted in the soil of Scripture."[3] Unfortunately, that is no longer true, even in evangelical churches. Much preaching today emphasizes psychology, social commentary, and political rhetoric. Bible exposition takes a back seat to a misguided craving for "relevance." Mayhue observes, "As the '90s dawn, an irresistible urge for a focus in the pulpit on the *relevant* seemingly exists, with a resultant inattention to God's *revelation*."[4] Lamentably, "there is a discernable trend in contemporary evangelicalism *away* from biblical

---

3. James F. Stitzinger, "The History of Expository Preaching," in *Rediscovering Expository Preaching*, John MacArthur, Jr. et al. (Dallas: Word, 1992), 60.

4. Richard L. Mayhue, "Rediscovering Expository Preaching," *The Master's Seminary Journal* 1, no. 2 (fall 1990): 112.

preaching and a drift *toward* an experience-centered, pragmatic, topical approach in the pulpit."[5]

The problem with such an approach to preaching is that

> preachers today have no authority for preaching their own notions and opinions; they must "preach the word"—the apostolic Word recorded in the Scriptures. Whenever preachers depart from the purpose and intent of a biblical portion, to that extent they lose their authority to preach. In short, the purpose of reading, explaining, and applying a portion of Scripture is to obey the command to "preach the Word." In no other way may we expect to experience the presence and power of the Holy Spirit in our preaching. He did not spend thousands of years producing the Old and New Testaments (in a sense, the Bible is peculiarly *His* Book) only to ignore it! What He "moved" men to write He now motivates us to preach. He has not promised to bless our word; that promise extends only to His own (Isa. 55:10, 11). Since . . . there is no genuine preaching where the Spirit of God is not at work, . . . we may say that the fundamental purpose behind preaching from the Bible is simply that, in any genuine sense of the word, we may preach at all![6]

The loss of its biblical foundation is the primary reason for the decline of preaching in the contemporary church.[7] And the decline of preaching is a major factor contributing to the church's weakness and worldliness. If the church is to regain its spiritual health, preaching must return to its proper biblical foundation.

The apostles based their ministry on the Word. In Acts 6:4 they declared, "We will devote ourselves to prayer, and to the ministry of the word." They knew quite well that it is the Word of God, not human wisdom, that causes spiritual growth, exposes sin, and reveals the will of God.

Paul stressed not only the priority of preaching, but also its proper foundation. To another of his young protégés, Titus, he wrote that a preacher must be noted for "holding fast the faithful word which is in accordance with the teaching, that he may be able both to exhort in sound doctrine and to refute those who contradict" (Titus 1:9). "Holding fast" is from *antecho*, which means

---

5. John F. MacArthur, Jr., "The Mandate of Biblical Inerrancy: Expository Preaching," *The Master's Seminary Journal* 1, no. 1 (spring 1990): 4 .

6. Jay E. Adams, *Preaching With Purpose* (Grand Rapids: Zondervan, 1982), 19–20.

7. For a discussion of some of the other factors involved see D. Martyn Lloyd-Jones, *Preaching and Preachers* (Grand Rapids: Zondervan, 1972), 13–25.

"I cling to" or "I hold tightly." A comparison with its opposite elucidates its meaning. In Luke 16:13 Jesus said, "No servant can serve two masters; for either he will hate the one, and love the other, or else he will hold to one, and despise the other. You cannot serve God and mammon." To "hold to" (*antecho*) is the opposite of "to despise." To hold fast to the Word, then, is to have a strong affection for and devotion to it. It is to love it, adhere to it, and believe it. Beyond a commitment to its inspiration and inerrancy, it also entails a commitment to its absolute authority and sufficiency.

Scripture alone is the foundation for preaching. In it alone lies the life-giving message of salvation and edification God wants proclaimed from the pulpit. Scripture is the faithful Word, the trustworthy, reliable, dependable Word, in contrast to the untrustworthy, unreliable words of human wisdom. Only in the Scriptures are the mind of God, the will of God, the purpose of God, and the plan of God revealed. The psalmist wrote,

> The law of the LORD is perfect,
>   restoring the soul;
> The testimony of the LORD is sure,
>   making wise the simple.
> The precepts of the LORD are right,
>   rejoicing the heart;
> The commandment of the LORD is pure,
>   enlightening the eyes.
> The fear of the LORD is clean,
>   enduring forever;
> The judgments of the LORD are true;
>   they are righteous altogether.
> They are more desirable than gold,
>   yes, than much fine gold;
> Sweeter also than honey
>   and the drippings of the honeycomb.
> Moreover, by them Thy servant is warned;
> In keeping them there is great reward (Ps. 19:7–11).

Scripture alone is the source of spiritual food. Peter urged believers to "long for the pure milk of the word, that by it you may grow in respect to salvation" (1 Pet. 2:2). Scripture alone is "able to build [believers] up and to give [them] the inheritance among all those who are sanctified" (Acts 20:32). In Scripture alone is found "the wisdom that leads to salvation through faith which is in Christ Jesus" (2 Tim. 3:15). Scripture alone "is inspired by God and profitable for teaching, for reproof, for correction, for training in righteousness" (2 Tim. 3:16).

Preachers must return to their calling as expositors of Scripture. Like Ezra they must "set [their hearts] to study the law of the Lord, and to practice it, and to teach His statutes and ordinances" (Ezra 7:10). Like Apollos, they must strive to be "mighty in the Scriptures" (Acts 18:24). And like Paul, they must realize that they were made ministers "according to the stewardship from God," that they "might fully carry out the preaching of the word of God" (Col. 1:25). Only then will they recover the proper foundation of preaching.

PREACHING MUST HAVE
THE PROPER CONTENT

"Sermons," wrote Spurgeon, "should have real teaching in them, and their doctrine should be solid, substantial, and abundant."[8] He underscores an important point: Preaching must not only have the proper foundation, the proper edifice must also be built on that foundation. Preaching based on Scripture will naturally seek to communicate the teachings of Scripture. Spurgeon went on to advise,

> Rousing appeals to the affections are excellent, but if they are not backed up by instruction they are a mere flash in the pan, powder consumed and no shot sent home. . . . The divine method is to put the law in the mind, and then write it on the heart. . . .
>
> Sound information upon scriptural subjects your hearers crave for, and must have. Accurate explanations of Holy Scripture they are entitled to, and if you are "an interpreter, one of a thousand," a real messenger of heaven, you will yield them plenteously. Whatever else may be present, the absence of edifying, instructive truth, like the absence of flour from bread, will be fatal.[9]

In the same vein, Paul wrote to Titus that a pastor must be able "to exhort in sound doctrine" (Titus 1:9). *Exhort* is from *parakaleo*, and means "to come alongside" someone, to call and strengthen that person. The con-

---

8. C. H. Spurgeon, *Lectures to My Students: First Series* (reprint, Grand Rapids: Baker, 1972), 72.

9. Ibid., 73, 74.

cept expressed here is a tender, passionate, and powerful pleading for obe-dience to the truths of Scripture. That presupposes, however, that the people have been taught those truths. It is pointless to urge them to obey truths they do not understand. *Sound* is from *hugiaino*, from which our English word *hygiene* is derived. It means "healthy," "life-giving," or "life-preserving," in contrast to the devastating, murderous error of false teaching. Pastors are to come alongside their flocks and strengthen them by bringing them healthy, divine teaching.

The flip side of exhorting in sound doctrine is found in the second part of Titus 1:9. To be able to protect his flock from the "savage wolves" (Acts 20:29) who seek to destroy it, a pastor must be able "to refute those who contradict." False teachers have plagued the church from its inception, and will continue to do so. They are a deadly peril against which a pastor must constantly be on guard. Jefferson warns,

> Many a minister fails as a pastor because he is not vigilant. He allows his church to be torn to pieces because he is half asleep. He took it for granted that there were no wolves, no birds of prey, no robbers, and while he was drowsing the enemy arrived. False ideas, destructive in-terpretations, demoralizing teachings came into his group, and he never knew it. . . . There are errors which are as fierce as wolves and pitiless as hyenas; they tear faith and hope and love to pieces and leave churches, once prosperous, mangled and half dead.[10]

The best antidote to false teaching is sound doctrine. Spurgeon wisely counsels that "sound teaching is the best protection from the heresies which ravage right and left among us."[11] A well-instructed congregation is much less susceptible to false teaching. Therefore, the pastor's primary emphasis in his preaching is to be on teaching his people the truth. There are times, however, when he must refute false teaching publicly from the pulpit. The contradictors, the gainsayers, those who like Elymas, the magician, do not "cease to make crooked the straight ways of the Lord" (Acts 13:10), must have their errors pointed out before the church.

To accomplish its purpose, true biblical preaching must contain both proclamation and instruction, both *kerugma* and *didache*. *Didache* forms the content of *kerugma* for, as noted above, Scripture is the foundation of preach-ing. Yet the preacher must urge people to apply the biblical truths they learn.

---

10. Jefferson, *Minister As Shepherd*, 43–44.

11. Spurgeon, *Lectures*, 73.

That is the function of *kerugma*—the public proclamation intended to move the will. The Puritan Thomas Cartwright vividly expressed that truth when he said, "As the fire stirred giveth more heat, so the Word, as it were, blown by preaching, flameth more in the hearers than when it is read."[12]

Only when preaching has the proper content can it fulfill its God-ordained function in the church. Preaching is not an exercise in oratory for the preacher but an essential element in the spiritual growth of Christ's body. No passage in Scripture states that more clearly than Eph. 4:11–16:

> He gave some as . . . pastors and teachers, for the equipping of the saints for the work of service, to the building up of the body of Christ; until we all attain to the unity of the faith, and of the knowledge of the Son of God, to a mature man, to the measure of the stature which belongs to the fulness of Christ. As a result, we are no longer to be children, tossed here and there by waves, and carried about by every wind of doctrine, by the trickery of men, by craftiness in deceitful scheming; but speaking the truth in love, we are to grow up in all aspects into Him, who is the head, even Christ, from whom the whole body, being fitted and held together by that which every joint supplies, according to the proper working of each individual part, causes the growth of the body for the building up of itself in love.

PREACHING MUST HAVE
THE PROPER COMMITMENT

It was not Paul's desire to become a preacher of the gospel of Jesus Christ. In fact, he had dedicated his life to destroying the Christian church, thinking that he "had to do many things hostile to the name of Jesus of Nazareth" (Acts 26:9). On his way to Damascus to persecute the church there, he met the Lord Jesus Christ instead. That dramatic encounter forever changed his life, turning him from Christianity's most terrifying persecutor to its most zealous advocate. From that time, on Paul proclaimed the gospel of Christ with a commitment unmatched by any other preacher in history.

Many desire to preach with Paul's persuasive power but without his intense commitment—an impossibility. Those called to preach God's Word must realize that a stewardship has been entrusted to them, and they must be

---

12. Thomas Cartwright, cited by D. Martyn Lloyd-Jones, *The Puritans: Their Origins and Successors* (Edinburgh: Banner of Truth, 1987), 376.

committed to it. Paul understood that clearly (Titus 1:3). He did not volunteer for the ministry but was "appointed a preacher" (1 Tim. 2:7; cf. Col. 1:25; 2 Tim. 1:11). To the Corinthians he admitted, "If I preach the gospel, I have nothing to boast of, for I am under compulsion; for woe is me if I do not preach the gospel. For if I do this voluntarily, I have a reward; but if against my will, I have a stewardship entrusted to me" (1 Cor. 9:16–17).

As a stewardship from God, preaching demands diligence, discipline, and hard work. It is "those who work hard at preaching and teaching," Paul writes, who are especially "worthy of double honor" (1 Tim. 5:17). John Stott writes,

> Expository preaching is a most exacting discipline. Perhaps that is why it is so rare. Only those will undertake it who are prepared to follow the example of the apostles and say, "It is not right that we should give up preaching the Word of God to serve tables. . . . We will devote ourselves to prayer and to the ministry of the Word" (Acts 6:2, 4). The systematic *preaching* of the Word is impossible without the systematic *study* of it. It will not be enough to skim through a few verses in daily Bible reading, nor to study a passage only when we have to preach from it. No. We must daily soak ourselves in the Scriptures. We must not just study, as through a microscope, the linguistic minutiae of a few verses, but take our telescope and scan the wide expanses of God's Word, assimilating its grand theme of divine sovereignty in the redemption of mankind. "It is blessed," wrote C. H. Spurgeon, "to eat into the very soul of the Bible until, at last, you come to talk in scriptural language, and your spirit is flavoured with the words of the Lord, so that your blood is *Bibline* and the very essence of the Bible flows from you."[13]

Jay Adams is convinced that "good preaching demands hard work. . . . I am convinced that the basic reason for poor preaching is the failure to spend adequate time and energy in preparation."[14] The noble seventeenth-century Puritan pastor Richard Baxter agreed with that truth:

> If we were duly devoted to our work, we should not be so negligent in our studies. Few men are at the pains that are necessary for

13. John R. W. Stott, *The Preacher's Portrait* (Grand Rapids: Eerdmans, 1979), 30–31.

14. Jay E. Adams, "Editorial: Good Preaching is Hard Work," *The Journal of Pastoral Practice* 4, no. 2 (1980): 1.

the right informing of their understanding, and fitting them for their further work. Some men have no delight in their studies, but take only now and then an hour, as an unwelcome task which they are forced to undergo, and are glad when they are from under the yoke. Will neither the natural desire of knowledge, nor the spiritual desire of knowing God and things Divine, nor the consciousness of our great ignorance and weakness, nor the sense of the weight of our ministerial work—will none of all these things keep us closer to our studies, and make us more painful in seeking after truth? O what abundance of things are there that a minister should understand! and what a great defect it is to be ignorant of them! and how much shall we miss such knowledge in our work! Many ministers study only to compose their sermons, and very little more, when there are so many books to be read, and so many matters that we should not be unacquainted with. Nay, in the study of our sermons we are too negligent, gathering only a few naked truths, and not considering of the most forcible expressions by which we may set them home to men's consciences and hearts. We must study how to convince and get within men, and how to bring each truth to the quick, and not leave all this to our extemporary promptitude, unless in cases of necessity. Certainly, brethren, experience will teach you that men are not made learned or wise without hard study and unwearied labour and experience.[15]

Preachers are to commit themselves to proclaiming the truth at all times and under all conditions, when it is fashionable and when it is not. In his farewell letter to Timothy, his beloved son in the faith, Paul commanded him to

preach the word; be ready in season and out of season; reprove, rebuke, exhort, with great patience and instruction. For the time will come when they will not endure sound doctrine; but wanting to have their ears tickled, they will accumulate for themselves teachers in accordance to their own desires; and will turn away their ears from the truth, and will turn aside to myths (2 Tim. 4:2–4).

The seasons come and go, the trends arrive and depart, the popular mood shifts and changes, but the preacher's task remains the same: to proclaim God's Word faithfully. In an age like ours, where many cannot "endure sound doctrine," but want to "have their ears tickled," Paul's words are especially compelling.

---

15. Richard Baxter, *The Reformed Pastor* (reprint, Edinburgh: Banner of Truth, 1979), 146–47.

There is no place for laziness in the ministry, above all in the preaching of the Word. All preachers should remember the sobering words of James, "Let not many of you become teachers, my brethren, knowing that as such we shall incur a stricter judgment" (James 3:1; cf. Heb. 13:17). Those not committed to putting in the effort that preaching demands should stay out of the pulpit.

The Highest Calling

The failure to preach expositionally and doctrinally is inexcusable. It can only be attributed to ignorance of, or indifference to, the implications of an inerrant, God-breathed Scripture. God gave His Word to His people, and He expects His undershepherds to feed it to them. And the need is great. Kaiser observes,

> It is no secret that Christ's Church is not at all in good health in many places of the world. She has been languishing because she has been fed, as the current line has it, "junk food"; all kinds of artificial preservatives and all sorts of unnatural substitutes have been served up to her. As a result, theological and Biblical malnutrition has afflicted the very generation that has taken such giant steps to make sure its physical health is not damaged by using foods or products that are carcinogenic or otherwise harmful to their physical bodies. Simultaneously a worldwide spiritual famine resulting from the absence of any genuine publication of the Word of God (Amos 8:11) continues to run wild and almost unabated in most quarters of the Church.[16]

Only when truly biblical preaching resumes its rightful place in the church will the church regain its spiritual strength and power. It is the preacher's privilege and awesome responsibility to be a part of that process. There is no higher calling.

---

16. Walter C. Kaiser, Jr., *Toward An Exegetical Theology* (Grand Rapids: Baker, 1985), 7–8.

16

Modeling

George J. Zemek

An often neglected part of leading a local church is the element of providing an exemplary lifestyle for the flock to follow. Modeling has its origin in the creation of man in God's image, but through the fall and new creation of man in Christ, it has assumed a renewed importance. New Testament usage of the τύπος *(tupos, "type") and* μιμητής *(mimētēs, "imitator") word-groups provides a good idea of the responsibility of church leaders to live as good moral examples before those whom they lead. Only when they do so can pastoral ministry fulfill the biblical standards of that office.*

Reportedly, a pastor once said, "Do as I say; not as I do." This frank adage has unfortunately characterized numerous past and present preachers, many of whom have reputations as great teachers of God's Word. However, when measured by the Bible's qualifications for communication and character, such ministers come up woefully short.

Saying but not doing in its multiplied forms and settings has always been particularly detestable in the eyes of the Lord. Jesus spoke to the crowd about the scribes and Pharisees, telling them to follow their instructions from Moses but not to follow their personal example, because "they keep on saying and yet are not doing" (Matt. 23:3, author's translation, note Greek present tenses). His indictment ultimately embraced a whole lineage of dark examples of hypocrisy throughout fallen mankind's history.

All men are accountable to God for profession without practice (James 1:22–27); yet certain ones by virtue of their office are responsible at the highest level of divine accountability for *prescription* without practice (James 3:1). Therefore, it is no wonder Paul emphasized to Timothy and to Titus God's mandate not only for exhortation but also for exemplification (1 Tim. 4:12-16;

Titus 2:7). Similarly, Peter, in his directives to elders, spotlights the *show-ing* dimension of shepherding (1 Pet. 5:1–4).

What the Scriptures say on spiritual leadership is intimidating to con-temporary ministers of the gospel. How can we who are not yet perfect hold ourselves up as ethical examples? How can we whose practice does not yet match our position say, "Do as I do"? A consideration of the macro- and micro-theological contexts on modeling will bring some relief from intimi-dation, but God designs all theological tensions to be constructive. As in the cases of other equally powerful biblical magnets, the poles of this one—i.e., the revealed reality that we are not yet glorified and the inescapably clear mandate for modeling—should first develop in us genuine humility and then a renewed dependence upon God and His resources.

THE MACRO-THEOLOGICAL CONTEXT OF MODELING

This context of modeling is exceedingly broad. It entails some of the most panoramic issues of theology: Christ *as* the image of God, man's *cre-ation* in the image of God, commensurate issues of Adam Theology, salvation history with a special emphasis upon moral re-creation in the image and like-ness of God, and the ethical significance of the Lord's operations of sovereign grace primarily through His efficient means of the Word and the Spirit.

The Importance of Image

A theological priority rather than a logical one is the best starting point. When viewed from a historical perspective, traditional theologies usually begin with the creation of mankind/humanity (originally Adam, or from a theological vantage point, the first Adam) "in"/"according to" the "image"/"likeness" of God.[1] However, the theological archetype, Christ Himself, furnishes the better beginning place. Since He is uniquely the effulgence of God's glory and the exact impress of His being or essence (Heb. 1:3), and since He alone perfectly displays the Godhead (John 1:18,

---

1. Both the Hebrew terms for *image* and *likeness* and the two prepositions used with them, function essentially in a synonymous fashion within the context of the early chapters of Genesis. Cf. John F. A. Sawyer, "The Meaning of בְּצֶלֶם אֱלֹהִים (*bĕselem ʾelōhim*, 'In the Image of God') in Genesis I–XI," *Journal of Theological Studies* 25 n.s. (October 1974): 418–26 on a technical level; John J. Davis, *Paradise to Prison: Studies in Genesis* (Winona Lake, Ind.: BMH, 1975), 81 on a popular level.

cf. 14:9), the Lord is the image of the invisible God (Col. 1:15). Consequently, He fully manifests and represents God and concretely stands ethically as the ultimate and perfect Exemplar (1 Cor. 11:1).

Christ is uniquely the image of God, but in a derived sense God "made" or "created"[2] mankind in His own image and likeness. Although "the Bible does not define for us the precise content of the original *imago*,"[3] generally it appears to be "cohesive unity of interrelated components that interact with and condition each other."[4] This vague conclusion is exegetically credible but does not consider some of the major extrapolations about the *imago Dei*. In the history of systematic theology, three basic views relating to the image of God in man have surfaced: the substantive, the relational, and the functional.[5] Historically, these views relate to (1) analogy of being, (2) analogy of relation, and (3) dominion, respectively.[6] Erickson describes the general characteristic(s) of each camp:

[1] The substantive view has been dominant during most of the history of Christian theology. The common element in the several varieties of this view is that the image is identified as some definite characteristic or quality within the makeup of the human. . . .

[2] Many modern theologians do not conceive of the image of God as something resident within man's nature. Indeed, they do not ordinarily ask what man is, or what sort of a nature he may have. Rather, they think of the image of God as the experience of a relationship. Man is said to be in the image or to display the image when he stands in a particular relationship. In fact, that relationship is the image. . . .

[3] We come now to a third type of view of the image, which has had quite a long history and has recently enjoyed an increase in popularity. This is the idea that the image is not something present in the makeup of man, nor is it the experiencing of relationship with God or with fellow man. Rather, the image consists in something man does. It is a function which man performs, the most frequently mentioned being the exercise of dominion over the creation.[7]

2. The Hebrew is עָשָׂה (*ʿāśâ*, "made") in Gen. 1:26 and בָּרָא (*bārā'*, "create") in 1:27. Both verbs speak of the creation of humanity in Gen. 5:1–2.

3. Carl F. H. Henry, *God, Revelation and Authority* (Waco: Word, 1976), 2:125. Chap. 10 of his work is particularly worthy of study.

4. Ibid.

5. Millard J. Erickson, *Christian Theology* (Grand Rapids: Baker, 1984), 495–517.

6. G. C. Berkouwer, *Man: The Image of God* (Grand Rapids: Eerdmans, 1962), 67–118.

7. Erickson, *Christian Theology*, 498, 502, 508.

The basic shortcoming of both the second and third views is that they are the consequences of the *imago Dei*. They are valid functions, but do not answer the apparently ontological implications of key scriptural texts.[8] It is difficult to eliminate some sort of analogy in man's image-bearing. Yet, as historically expressed, problems have plagued the first view, especially in light of the catastrophic effects of the fall of man. Erickson seems to be on the right analogical track when he suggests "the attributes of God sometimes referred to as communicable attributes constitute the image of God."[9] Indeed, the moral attributes of God constitute a significantly large dimension of His image in man—a fact that is acutely relevant in a consideration of the issue of modeling.

The Retention of the Image: Devastated but Not Destroyed

After deciding for the analogy-of-being view, the haunting question remains: What about the effects of the fall? Once again, the biblicist must endure the poles of another scriptural tension. On the one hand,

> the fall of man was a catastrophic personality shock; it fractured human existence with a devastating fault. Ever since, man's worship and contemplation of the living God have been broken, his devotion to the divine will shattered. Man's revolt against God therefore affects his entire being. . . . His revolt against God is at the same time a revolt against truth and the good.[10]

On the other hand, however, "there is some sense in which the image of God must persist even in fallen man."[11] The *potential* for the communication and sovereign application of the Word of grace, a restored relationship, and moral renovation remains. Avoiding endless pursuits through logical labyrinths, Kidner wisely makes the soteriological transition with his brief synopsis: "After the Fall, man is still said to be in God's image (Gen. 9:6)

---

8. Ibid., 510–12.

9. Ibid., 514. He is also right in making a Christological connection: "The character and actions of Jesus will be a particularly helpful guide . . . since he was the perfect example of what human nature is intended to be."

10. Henry, *God, Revelation and Authority*, 2:134–35.

11. Charles M. Horne, "A Biblical Apologetic Methodology" (unpublished Th.D. dissertation; Grace Theological Seminary, Winona Lake, Ind., 1963), 84.

and likeness (James 3:9); nonetheless he requires to be 'renewed . . . after the image of him that created him' (Col. 3:10; cf. Eph. 4:24)."[12]

The Re-Creation of Image

By original creation man bore the image of God, including its significantly moral dimension. His fall[13] radically perverted the whole image, so much so that no hope for any kind of self-reformation remained. Yet the Word of God says that the image and likeness continue even with man in this horrible condition. By God's grace, men redeemed in Christ have embarked on an upward and onward journey of moral restoration (2 Pet. 3:18). Their destination is moral perfection—Christlikeness. Consequently, the overarching challenge to all genuine disciples is still, "Be ye holy; for I am holy" (see Lev. 11:44–45, 19:2; 1 Pet. 1:16 KJV).

The primary means of grace in moving the saved along that highway of sanctification is the Word of God attested by the Spirit of God, and a vital constituent of this divine testimony is the incarnate example of Christ. Indeed, He abides as God's perfect moral manifestation.

THE MICRO-THEOLOGICAL
CONTEXT OF MODELING

Because of Christ's pattern, the attitude and actions of His people should mature in integrity and consistency of Christlikeness (Phil. 1:27–30; 2:5–18; 1 John 2:6). As they mature morally, some more rapidly than others, they themselves are to become reflections of His moral model (1 Thess. 1:7). Growth should characterize all His "saints,"[14] but the New Testament holds

---

12. Derek Kidner, *Genesis: An Introduction and Commentary* (Downers Grove, Ill.: InterVarsity, 1967) 51; cf. O. Flender, "εἰκών," *NIDNTT*, 2:287–88.

13. For discussions of Adam Theology, i.e., the "First Adam" as representative of and in solidarity with the whole race and the "Last Adam" as representative of and in solidarity with God's elect, see John Murray's *The Imputation of Adam's Sin* (Grand Rapids: Eerdmans, 1959); *Principles of Conduct: Aspects of Biblical Ethics* (Grand Rapids: Eerdmans, 1957); S. Lewis Johnson, Jr., "Romans 5:12—an Exercise in Exegesis and Theology," in *New Dimensions in NT Study*, ed. Richard N. Longenecker and Merrill C. Tenney (Grand Rapids: Zondervan, 1974).

14. A profession without practice constitutes a highly culpable state of pretense. For a discussion of progressive sanctification, see O. Procksch, "ἁγιασμός," *TDNT*, 1:113; George Eldon Ladd, *A Theology of the New Testament* (Grand Rapids: Eerdmans, 1974), 519–20.

those recognized as church leaders especially responsible to be examples. They are visible and derived moral models for the Exemplar's ἐκκλησία (*ekklesia*, "church"). This awesome responsibility is the focus of the rest of this study.

The Vocabulary of Modeling

The Old Testament is replete with commands and implicit obligations concerning the holiness of God's people, but it contains no transparent teaching about following the example of God or His chosen leaders.[15] However, the New Testament abounds with this concept. As a matter of fact, a whole arsenal of modeling terms surfaces.[16] Of these, the τύπος (*typos*, "example") and μιμητής (*mimētēs*, "imitator") word-groups are the most important.

In ancient secular Greek, *typos* exhibits the following usage categories: "a. 'what is stamped,' 'mark,' . . . 'impress'. . . 'stamp,' " (e.g., of letters engraved in stone, images, or painted images); "b. 'Mould,' 'hollow form' which leaves an impress," . . . and in a transferred sense "ethical 'example' " . . . ; and "c. . . . 'outline,' 'figure,' " (i.e. of the stamp or impress).[17] "In the LXX *typos* occurs in only four places":[18] for the model or pattern for the tabernacle and its furnishings in Exod 25:40; for idols or images in Amos 5:26; for the " 'wording', 'text,' of a decree" in 3 Macc. 3:30; and for "(determinative) 'example'" in 4 Macc. 6:19.[19]

---

15. Michaelis concludes that "on the whole the idea of imitation is foreign to the OT. In particular, there is no thought that we must imitate God" (W. Michaelis, "μιμέομαι, μιμητής, κ. τ. λ.," *TDNT*, 4:663. In the LXX this word-group appears only in the Apocrypha, where it does not refer to divine emulation. Yet in the pseudepigraphical writings, some occurrences urge the imitation of Old Testament men of renown and even God Himself. Philo exhibits this same pattern of usage. (Ibid., 664–66). Michaelis's controlling presupposition distorts his interpretation of these data, however.

16. For a general discussion of the most significant of these terms see W. Mundle, O. Flender, J. Gess, R. P. Martin, and F. F. Bruce, "Image, Idol, Imprint, Example," *NIDNTT*, 2:284–91. Their opening paragraph on essential synonymity is important, and subsequent discussions of the Christological model are worthy of special attention.

17. L. Goppelt, "τύπος, ἀντίτυπος, κ. τ. λ.," *TDNT*, 8:247. Regarding etymology, Müller states, "The etymology of τύπος is disputed. It may be derived from τύπτω, strike, beat, . . ." (H. Müller, "Type, Pattern," *NIDNTT*, 3:903); cf. Goppelt, who is more impressed with this etymological connection. He suggests the development goes from a blow "to the impress made by the below," then "from these basic senses τύπος develops an astonishing no. [number] of further meanings which are often hard to define. In virtue of its expressiveness it has made its way as a loan word [i.e., "type"] into almost all European languages." (Goppelt, "τύπος", 8:246–47).

18. Müller, "Type," 3:904.

19. Goppelt, "tpow," 8:248.

In the New Testament its full range of semantical usages include:[20]

1. *visible impressions* of a stroke or pressure, *mark, trace* (e.g., John 20:25)

2. *that which is formed, an image or statue* (e.g., Acts 7:43)

3. *form, figure, pattern* (e.g., Rom. 6:17)

4. historically as *(arche)type, pattern, model* (e.g., Acts 7:44, Heb. 8:5); and ethically as *example, pattern* (e.g., 1 Tim. 4:12)

5. in reference to divinely ordained *types*, whether things, events, or persons (e.g., Rom. 5:14)

Of the fourteen occurrences of the noun *typos* in the New Testament, half relate to modeling, either implicitly as a negative illustration (e.g., the adverb τυπικῶς [*tupikōs*, "typically,"], 1 Cor. 10:6) or explicitly as positive patterns (Phil. 3:17; 1 Thess. 1:7; 2 Thess. 3:9; 1 Tim. 4:12; Titus 2:7; 1 Pet. 5:3). Further, one other occurrence has a tangential theological relation: "In Rom. 6:17 [τύπος refers to] the context, the expressions of the doctrine. . . . However, the original meaning of the form which stamps can still be strongly felt. As previously sin, so now the new teaching, i.e. the message of Christ, is the factor which stamps and determines the life of the Christian."[21] The efficient means of the Word of God is seen here as a press and die that leaves an amazing mark on the people of God.

Though the data relating to modeling are quite conspicuous, contemporary scholarship is reluctant to attribute to the concept a fully ethical significance. For example, Goppelt refuses to allow that a disciple's life is "an example which can be imitated."[22] His emphases on the primacy of the

---

20. This follows the classifications of BAGD, 829–30. The subcategory *"copy, image,"* has not been cited because it furnishes no New Testament examples; however, two of the extrabiblical references that are cited—i.e., a reference to a master being the image of God to a slave and children as copies of their parents—bear illustratively upon the moral references of category 4. This fourth category encompasses the doctrine of modeling in the New Testament. On the history of the hermeneutical significance of subcategory 5, see Goppelt, "τύπος," 8:251–59, and Müller, "Type," 3:905–6.

21. Müller, "Type," 3:904–5; cf. Goppelt: "τύπος is . . . the impress which makes an impress, so that in context the teaching can be described as the mould or norm which shapes the whole personal conduct of the one who is delivered up to it and has become obedient thereto" ("τύπος," 8:250).

22. Goppelt, "τύπος," 8:249–50. Interestingly, two sentences later he comments on 1 Pet. 5:3 and 1 Tim. 4:12 wherein he apparently concedes a more direct association with ethical emulation. It would seem that a good share of Goppelt's reluctance is due to Michaelis's quite dogmatic conclusions about the μιμητής word-group; cf. Michaelis, "μιμητής," 4:659 ff.

Word of God and the priority of an ultimate reference to faith are commendable, but as subsequent treatments of the key texts will reveal, the inescapable overtones are patterns from people. In his discussion of this issue, Müller is not quite as one-sided. For example, he asserts that the crucial texts "are not simply admonitions to a morally exemplary life. . . . The shaping power of a life lived under the Word has in turn an effect on the community (1 Thess. 1:6), causing it to become a formative example."[23] He carefully interrelates the effectual means of the Word with a derived means consisting of ethical examples.

The *mimētēs* word-group, the source of the English word *mime*,[24] furnishes a rich semantical heritage also. Generally speaking, "the word group μιμητής etc., . . . arose in the 6th cent. [B.C.], and came into common use in both prose and poetry. Μιμέομαι has the sense 'to imitate,' 'to mimic,' i.e. to do what is seen to be done by someone else."[25]

Bauder subclassifies the classical Greek usages as follows:

(a) imitate, mimic . . .

(b) emulate with joy, follow

(c) in the arts (plays, paintings, sculpture and poetry), represent reality by imitation, imitate is a artistic way. . . . An actor is therefore a *mimos*, a mimer. . . . A *symmimētēs* (Lat. imitator) is an imitator, especially a performer or an artist who imitates. When used in a derogatory sense, the words refer to quasi-dramatic "aping" or feeble copying with lack of originality.[26]

Significantly, from the earliest stages of this group's history in classical Greek, "the words were used to express ethical demands made on men. One should take as one's model the boldness of a hero, or one should imitate the good example of one's teacher or parents."[27] Such imitations are without a revelational norm, but they nevertheless illustrate a *linguistic* background for usage in the New Testament.

---

23. Müller, "Type," 3:905.

24. E.g., W. E. Vine, *An Expository Dictionary of New Testament Words* (New York: Charles Scribner's Sons, 1908), 2:248.

25. Michaelis, "μιμητής," 4:659.

26. W. Bauder, "μιμέομαι," *NIDNTT*, 1:490.

27. Ibid.

One particular nuance in classical usage deserves special attention. It is this word-group's place within the typically dualistic cosmology of the ancient Greeks. Of course, Plato is especially fond of its employment in this sense. Bauder captures the gist of it: "The whole of the lower world of appearances is only the corresponding, imperfect, visible copy or likeness (*mimēna*) of the invisible archetype in the higher world of the Ideas."[28] Such thinking is antibiblical, but in the process of its development among pagan philosophers, discussions arose about "divine" imitation.[29] Though Michaelis concludes "that in such statements the *imitatio dei* is not too closely bound to the cosmological mimesis concept," this study concludes that such ancient references "have quite plainly an ethical thrust,"[30] albeit without revelational norms.

Since "The Vocabulary of Modeling" earlier in this chapter alluded to the Jewish usage of this word-group, it will suffice to add that two of the four occurrences in the Apocrypha speak of emulating heroes of the faith in martyrdom[31] and that in subsequent history

> the Rabbis were the first to speak of imitation of God in the sense of developing the image of God in men. In the Pseudepigrapha in addition to the exhortation to imitate men of outstanding character . . . one can also find the thought of the imitation of God (i.e. keeping his commands . . .) and of particular characteristics of God.[32]

Again, apart from any accretions, eccentricities, perversions, etc., in these materials, such usages are a linguistic link in the conceptual chain culminated in the corpus of the New Testament teachings.

Bauder's breakdown of the word-group is succinct and accurate: "In the NT *mimeomai* is found only 4 times (2 Thess. 3:7, 9; Heb. 13:7; 3 Jn. 11); *mimētēs* 6 times (1 Cor. 4:16; 11:1; Eph. 5:1; 1 Thess. 1:6; 2:14; Heb. 6:12); and *symmimētēs* only once in Phil. 3:17."[33] The deponent middle verb meaning "imitate, emulate, follow" occurs with accusatives of person, and the uncompounded noun form *mimētēs* ("imitator") occurs either with a personal referent or with an impersonal genitive.[34] Also, "it is noteworthy that in

---

28. Ibid., 491.

29. Michaelis, "μιμητής," 4:661–62.

30. Ibid., 663.

31. Ibid., 4:663.

32. Bauder, "μιμέομαι," 1:491.

33. Ibid.

34. BAGD, 522.

all its NT occurrences μιμητής is joined with γίνεσθαι, denoting moral effort."[35] Indeed, a safe assertion is that "all [words in the group] are used with an ethical-imperative aim and are linked with obligation to a specific kind of conduct."[36]

Michaelis opposes this ethical-emulation thrust of the words and reinterprets according to his chosen viewpoint. He bolsters his contention with a few textual observations, especially pertaining to contextual emphases on faith, suffering, persecution, death, industriousness, obedience, etc.[37] All these contextual colorings have some credibility, but specific applications do not negate the all-embracing ethical perspective of total character and consistent lifestyle. Much more subjective is his discussion built upon a presuppositional foundation of apostolic authority, though nearly all interpreters will empathize with its apparent motivational tension—i.e., how can any finite and fallible person, including Paul, say, "Follow my ethical example"? Despite this tension, no exegete should forge a few implicit references into a hermeneutical hammer for driving many round texts into square contexts.[38] The ensuing treatment of key passages will document the fact that the New Testament evidence "cannot be reduced to a demand for personal obedience."[39]

The Vocation of Modeling

The best way to organize key New Testament texts dealing with modeling is by an essentially theological development.[40] Whether historically noted or ethically urged, the New Testament data present God's model

---

35. James Hope Moulton and George Milligan, *The Vocabulary of the Greek Testament* (Grand Rapids: Eerdmans, 1930), 412.

36. Bauder, "μιμέομαι," 1:491.

37. Michaelis, "μιμητής," 4:666–68, passim.

38. Ibid., 667–74, contains eccentric applications and overstated conclusions based on some glaring examples of totality transfers, which are always hermeneutically counterproductive. Bauder supports the essential thrust of Michaelis' thesis but is usually much more careful in his expressions of it (cf. "μιμέομαι," 1:491–92).

39. Bauder, "μιμέομαι," 1:491.

40. Another approach would be to follow canonical order. Still another is a biblical theological approach, i.e., modeling in the Pauline corpus, in the Epistle to the Hebrews, in Peter, in 3 John, etc. Though this method has inductive advantages, it does not lend itself to viewing the total New Testament picture through a common lens. Another way of organizing the data is the grammatical, i.e., noting the passages that historically exemplify modeling and then examining others that command it. Yet it seems better to employ another organizational category, at the same time calling attention to the indicatives and imperatives.

to His people, show the moral example of the apostolic circle to all the churches, emphasize the particular area of responsibility in reference to church leaders, and advocate that all Christians be maturing moral models for the spiritual well-being of the whole body. This plan is basically consistent with both the early church's historical development and special gradations of judgment or reward pertaining to church leaders. It does not dictate some sort of ethical apostolic succession, however. Essentially an unbreakable chain, it comes full circle, creating a theological necklace that begins and ends with the sovereign grace of God and Christ's moral model.

God: The Ultimate Model for His Church. Ephesians 5:1 instructs the church to "keep on becoming (or being) imitators of God" (author's translation). Michaelis argues that this passage along with similar ones "does not speak of true imitation of Christ or God."[41] Yet it is in a setting that begins with an identical imperative (4:32) urging reciprocal kindness, tenderness, and forgiveness based on Christ's example. Furthermore, the καθώς (*kathōs*, "just as") clause, which bridges to the Lord's perfect pattern, assumes analogy and infers emulation. Immediately after 5:1 comes another continuously binding imperative to "keep on walking in love," followed by another indication of Christ as the Exemplar (περιπατεῖτε . . . καθώς [*peripateite . . . kathōs*], 5:2, author's translation). Additionally, the simple adverb of comparison ὡς (*hōs*, 5:1b), "*as* beloved children," points to the propriety of ethical emulation by believers.

On a larger scale, this command to imitate God and Christ is part of a larger section about holy living (Eph. 4:25–6:20). This in turn is a subset of the practical half of the epistle (i.e., the "do" section) beginning at 4:1. All these exhortations are appropriate responses to the sovereign grace of God, expounded in the theologically indicative section (i.e., the "done" section) of this great epistle (Ephesians 1–3).[42] On yet a grander scale of inclusion is the comprehensive scriptural challenge to be holy because God is holy. From the reversed perspective, the obligation to "be holy for God is holy" receives definitive resolution through the prevalent indicative/imperative presentation of ethical obligation, with a variety of explicit exhortations as elaborations. This is the natural theological setting of moral modeling (e.g. "be imitators of God, as beloved children," Eph. 5:1).

---

41. Michaelis, "μιμητής," 4:673; Michaelis' presupposition of utter moral transcendence causes him to reject the implications of the thrust of Paul's argument in Eph. 4:25–5:2. (4:671–73).

42. See Ladd, *Theology of the NT*, 493–94, 524–25, for a discussion of the indicative/imperative motif related to sanctification.

The Derived Apostolic Model in the Church. The designation "apostolic" pertains to the apostolic circle and allows for God's use of both apostles and transition men such as Timothy and Titus in establishing churches during the first century. The latter group were not apostles, but they were in a special sense apostles of an apostle. They supervised the planting and the solidification of local New Testament churches. When doing this, they were not technically one of the pastors-teachers-elders-overseers of a given local church or group of regional churches, so this section treats them as mediate models. However, apparently in their day-to-day ministries they worked alongside and functioned similarly to pastoral leaders. Therefore, it is also appropriate to apply what is said here about 1 Tim. 4:12 and Titus 2:7 to the next major division, "The Third Generation Model of Church Leadership."

1. *Modeling Directly.* Paul did not shy away from offering himself as an ethical model for believers he had personal contact with (e.g., 1 Cor. 4:16; 11:1; Phil. 3:17; 2 Thess. 3:7, 9).[43] Maintaining an accurate theological perspective must begin with a treatment of 1 Cor. 11:1 and Phil. 3.

First Corinthians 11:1, "be imitators of me, just as I also am of Christ," is basic to all modeling on the horizontal plane. Paul was not *the* Exemplar; only Christ can be that. However, that did not exempt him from the divine responsibility of being a derived moral example. The contextual application of his statement has to do with not becoming an offense because of one's personal freedom in Christ (10:23–33). He closes his discussion with a command to comply (10:32), and then holds himself up as an example (10:33), then picking up that same thread but repeating it with the vocabulary of moral modeling (11:1). He is careful to add, however, that when they follow his example, they are following the ultimate pattern of Christ's treatment of others (11:1).[44]

Philippians 3 has raised significant questions about the propriety of human moral example. After Paul urges the following of his own example (3:17), does he not confess his own finiteness and moral fallibility (3:3–16)?[45] Or, in the words of Bauder, "Prior to the demand to imitate him, he deliberately places a confession of his own imperfection (Phil. 3:12)."[46]

---

43. This treatment will discuss only passages explicitly employing "model" or "type" terminology, omitting the many conceptual allusions to Paul's own example.

44. Bauder concludes, "Paul never intends to bind the demand for imitation to his own person. It is always ultimately to the One whom he himself follows" ("μιμέομαι," 1:491).

45. Michaelis is quite dogmatic ("μιμητής," 4:667–68), and Bauder more subdued ("μιμέομαι," 1:491).

46. Bauder, "μιμέομαι," 1:491.

He does indeed assert he has not arrived at moral perfection. "He does not think of himself as the personal embodiment of an ideal which must be imitated,"[47] but this saint in process *does* urge the Philippian church to keep on becoming (or being) fellow-imitators of (or with) him (3:17a).[48] In addition to Paul, others are consistently living (3:17b) according to the pattern (i.e., *typon*) of the apostolic circle.[49] It is wrong to ignore one facet of biblical revelation because of another equally important truth that raises an apparent logical contradiction.

Is it possible to resolve this scriptural tension? Like most other biblical paradoxes, not fully. Nevertheless, several observations will ease the difficulty it causes our limited logic. For example, the major portion of this epistle has to do with ethical exhortation (Phil. 1:27–4:9). From the beginnings of this section, the theme of unity through humility, including the preferring of others over self, dominates. But the supremely important example of Christ (2:5–8) undergirds all subsequent moral responsibilities. The Lord is the primary pattern for attitude and actions. Based directly on that perfect example, Paul challenged the Philippians to progress in their sanctification (2:12), reminding them that the resources for such a holy calling reside with God (2:13). The Philippian disciples were fully responsible but not adequate in themselves. Interestingly, following this general challenge to holy living, Paul refers to Timothy and Epaphroditus (2:19–30) as others-oriented examples.

To begin chapter 3, Paul rehearses his pre- and postconversion experiences (vv. 3–16). These not only compare and contrast the preconversion Paul (especially vv. 4–6) and other genuine Christians (3:7–21) with some externalists in Philippi (e.g., 3:1–2, 18–19), but they also compare the postconversion experience of Paul with that of all true disciples. Although both Paul and true believers at Philippi were positionally "perfect" in Christ, neither he nor they were perfect experientially. Consequently, his quest like theirs should be one of an intensifying pursuit of moral purity. Such a focus, by the grace of God, qualified one to be a reflected model of ethical development. However, the perfect moral mold remains the one who said, "You are to be perfect, as your heavenly Father is perfect" (Matt. 5:48).

---

47. Ibid.

48. This is the only New Testament occurrence of the compounded plural form συμμιμητής. Here it stands as the predicate nominative of the now familiar present plural imperative γίνεσθε (cf. Eph. 5:1). The personal pronoun in the genitive refers to Paul.

49. In the context ἡμᾶς of 3:17 probably includes Timothy and possibly Epaphroditus with Paul (cf. Phil. 2:19, 25).

This theological perspective sheds light on other Pauline statements. For example, when he writes earlier in 1 Corinthians, "Therefore I urge you to imitate me" (4:16 NIV), he does not disregard Christ as the ultimate example (1 Cor. 11:1), nor does he intend to leave the impression that he had arrived. He has already negated any claims to self-sufficiency, especially in his exposé of all human wisdom (1 Cor. 1–3). In addition, he has built a solid bridge to genuine ministry (1 Cor. 3–4), largely with prominent personalities as illustrations. That sets the stage in chapter 4 to challenge Corinthian arrogance. By weaving in positive examples, he exposes the heinousness of their pride (4:6–13.). He also mixes in several testimonials to God's ultimacy and sufficiency to His servants (e.g., 3:5–7; 4:1–4). This is hardly the context for a Pauline ego trip. His personal example in 1 Cor. 4:16 once again reflects the pattern of Christ and His grace.

Paul wrote to the Thessalonian church to encourage them to follow the apostolic example (2 Thess. 3:7, 9). Paul, Silvanus, and Timothy (2 Thess. 1:1) supplied positive examples as a corrective for any who were out of line among the Thessalonians (i.e., ἀτάκτως [ataktōs, "disorderly"], 3:6, 11; cf. the verb form in v. 7), especially in matters of freeloading and meddling. The disciples at Thessalonica recognized "how it was necessary [for them] to imitate (μιμεῖσθαι [mimeisthai]) us [the apostolic circle]" (2 Thess. 3:7, author's translation). Paul and his associates offered themselves as a "model" (τύπον, typon) for the members of body there to emulate (2 Thess. 3:9).[50]

2. **Mediately Modeling.** First Timothy 4:12–16 is an exceedingly important passage regarding moral exemplification. It equals 2 Tim. 4:2 in importance as a qualification for Christian ministry. In fact, it stresses that in importance, patterning the Word is a necessary corollary to preaching it, with the former usually preceding the latter.

Furthermore, the whole epistle places a very high priority on character and conduct. The man of God is always accountable in areas of personal and professional responsibility. He cannot just be faithful in teaching the truth; he must live the truth. Heralding God's gospel is a highly motivating and worthy call, yet the human instrument must possess certain qualities of integrity (e.g., 1 Tim. 3:1–7). As with Paul (e.g., 1 Tim. 1:12–17), he must accept both responsibilities with a profound sense of humility and in utter dependence upon the one who commissions. Indeed, by the time 1 Timothy closes (6:11–16), the young man of God certainly understood the two primary obligations of spiritual leadership.

---

50. In this context the industry of the apostolic circle (2 Thess. 3:8) is what provides the example for the Thessalonians to follow (2 Thess. 3:9).

First Timothy 4 is especially cogent. Verses 7–8 set the tone for verses 12–16 with Paul's command to Timothy to "work out" strenuously (γυμνάζω, *gymnazō*, "I train, exercise") to develop spiritual muscle for godliness (v. 7). For all intents and purposes, the many imperatives in verses 12–16 supply the *whys* and the *wherefores* of the exhortation to holiness. In 1 Tim. 4:12–16, three waves of commands pound Timothy with his two general responsibilities. The first wave crashes with an overwhelming reminder of his personal responsibility (v. 12). As it begins to ebb, commands relating to his professional accountability drench him (vv. 13–14). For most conservative evangelicals, the professional requirements (v. 13) are an authoritative given. The same applies concerning personal requirements; however, the application of these is far more sensitive personally. The intimidation factor at times seems to be overwhelming. For that reason, this discussion will concentrate on the modeling requirements.

The first command of 1 Tim. 4:12 does not directly address the man of God; it addresses those he leads. Indirectly it implies that he himself must be irreproachable (cf. the first and general qualification of 3:2). The implication of the first part of verse 12 finds confirmation in the conclusion of that verse. His obligation is one of exemplifying before members of the flock: He was to "be (or become) a type (or pattern or model) (*typos*) for the believers."[51] Paul typifies the moral example in five areas:

1. in the language (communications) of the man of God

2. in his general lifestyle,[52]

3. in his ἀγάπη (*agapē*, "love," i.e., that unselfish, extending, all-give variety that exudes tenderness, compassion, tolerance, etc.)

4. in his "faith" (or better, "faithfulness, trustworthiness, reliability," the passive meaning of πίστις [*pistis*])

5. in his personal purity

Without integrity of life, his pronouncements, preachings, proclamations, and indoctrinations (vv. 11, 13) are severely limited.

---

51. Moulton and Milligan (*Vocabulary*, 645) cite an ethical parallel to 1 Tim. 4:12 in an inscription from the first century B.C. It speaks of being a model for *godliness* (εὐσέβεια [*eusebeia*]), a noun used in 1 Tim. 4:7).

52. The word ἀναστροφή (*anastrophe*, "way of life, behavior") relates to cognates in Heb. 13:7 (discussed below); 1 Pet. 1:15, 17, 18; 3:1–2; 2 Pet 3:11. Here it connects with εὐσέβεια ("godliness"), i.e., holiness of lifestyle. This word-group was also ethically significant in Hellenistic Judaism (cf. Tobit 4:14; 2 Macc. 5:8; 6:23).

A second wave of commands comes in verse 15 to remind the man of God to concentrate on both his personal and professional responsibilities[53] so that his advancement might be clearly visible to all. The concluding purpose clause of verse 15 stresses the importance of Timothy's modeling.[54] His life was to exhibit significant "progress."[55] Therefore, verse 15 not only reiterates his patterning responsibility, but it also confirms that it is not necessary for ethical models to be absolutely perfect; however, they must be growing in holiness.

Two imperatives in verse 16, Paul's third crashing wave, emphasize the same two areas, "yourself" and "your teaching" (cf. vv. 12–14; see also Acts 20:28), but in a slightly different way. Putting person before ministry, Paul writes, "Pay close attention" to yourself and to your teaching (v. 16). Calvin summarizes, "Teaching will be of little worth if there is not a corresponding uprightness and holiness of life."[56] Guthrie expresses it, "Moral and spiritual rectitude is an indispensable preliminary to doctrinal orthodoxy."[57] Paul emphasizes even further Timothy's personal and ministerial responsibilities with his closing injunction to "persist (or continue or persevere) in them."

The rationale for these commands is overwhelming: "because as you go on doing *this* [singular pronoun referring to both duties], you will save both yourself and the ones who hear you." Almost unbelievably, personal example is side-by-side with the ministry of God's Word in a salvific context.[58]

---

53. Two present imperatives, μελέτα and ἴσθι, point to a continuing responsibility: "keep on caring for" these things and "be" in them. Robertson suggests that the force of the latter is "give yourself wholly to them," and adds, "It is like our 'up to his ears' in work . . . and sticking to his task" (A. T. Robertson, *Word Pictures in the NT* [Nashville: Broadman, 1931], 4:582).

54. As Stahlin urges, Timothy's moral and ministerial advancement "is to be visible, for he is to show himself hereby to be a τύπος for believers (v. 12). . ." (G. Stahlin, "προκοπή, προκόπτω," *TDNT*, 6:714).

55. In secular Greek προκοπή (*prokopē*, "progress") was a nautical term for "making headway in spite of blows," and was employed in an extended ethical way, especially among the Stoics. Philo picked up the ethical sense and tried to give it a theocentric orientation (cf. Stahlin, "προκοπή, προκόπτω," 6:704, 706–7, 709–11). The verb form is used of Jesus' "progress" (Luke 2:52).

56. John Calvin, *The Second Epistle of Paul to the Corinthians and the Epistles to Timothy, Titus and Philemon*, trans. by T. A. Small, in *Calvin's Commentaries*, ed. D. W. and T. F. Torrance (Grand Rapids: Eerdmans, 1964), 248.

57. Donald Guthrie, *The Pastoral Epistles, The Tyndale NT Commentaries*, ed. R. V. G. Tasker (Grand Rapids: Eerdmans, 1957), 99.

58. Calvin's theological comments are helpful here (*Timothy*, 248–49).

Titus 2 has the same message more briefly stated. Along with instructions about appointing elders (1:5–9) and combatting false teaching (1:10–16; 3:9–11) with healthy doctrine (2:1, 15; 3:1, 8), come directions for how Titus is to handle various groups: older men (2:2), older and then younger women (2:3–5), younger men (2:6), slaves (2:9-10), and the whole flock (3:1-8). A major message was the priority of good deeds (1:16; 2:7, 14; 3:1, 8, 14).

Among the instructions to young men, probably Titus' age group, Paul reminds Titus of his obligation to be a moral model. Preaching alone was not enough (2:6); he must also live before them (2:7). In other words, he must both exhort *and* exemplify. For the man of God, a pattern (*typon*) of good works is never optional (see Eph. 2:10). It is essential to preaching and teaching.

The "Third Generation"[59] Model of Church Leadership

The same thread permeates the epistle to the Hebrews, from the superior model of Jesus Christ, through the faith's hall of fame (chap. 11), into important statements about church leaders (chap. 13). Accountability of church leaders is the subject of 13:17, but 13:7 deals specifically with their modeling responsibility. The writer instructs the recipients, "Remember your leaders, who spoke the word of God to you. Consider[60] the outcome of their way of life and imitate their faith" (NIV). Examining the result of their lifestyle (from *anastrophe*) and emulating (present imperative of *mimeomai*) their persevering faith are parallel efforts. Such concrete examples dovetail with the total thrust of the epistle, which is to keep on keeping on.

Peter's corresponding message addresses the leaders of the church directly. He commands the elders, "Shepherd [tend or feed] the flock of God among you" (1 Pet. 5:2; cf. John 21:15–17; Acts 20:28). This is the only imperative in the passage, but its obligatory force permeates all the qualifiers to follow (vv. 2–3). Three contrasts highlight motives for spiritual leadership:

1.   Spiritual leaders must not serve because of human constraints *but* because of divine commitments.

---

59. "Third generation" applies to the passing of the precedent from the "second generation" of Timothy and Titus to the permanent local church leaders (cf. 2 Tim. 2:2).

60. The participle ἀναθεωροῦντες (*anatheorountes*, "consider") is best taken as imperatival in force in light of its subordination to μιμεῖσθε (*mimeisthe*).

2. Spiritual leaders must not minister for unjust profit *but* with spiritual zeal.

3. Spiritual leaders must not lead as prideful dictators *but* as humble models.[61]

New Testament shepherds have the binding obligation of being an ethical model for the flock of God. The sheep in turn are to emulate their leaders' lives (Heb. 13:7). This requires genuine humility (1 Pet. 5:5–6).

The Model of the Church to the Church

All believers are to be examples for other believers to follow. For example, Paul mentions two instances of this. Paul asserts that when the Thessalonians received God's gospel, they did so in a societal setting analogous to that of the Judean churches, i.e., while being persecuted (2 Thess. 2:14–16). Paul's words, "For you, brethren, became imitators μιμηταὶ ἐγενήθητε (*mimētai egenēthēte*) of the churches of God in Christ Jesus that are in Judea" (v. 14), provided an incentive to the church to keep on persevering.

Besides being a reflection of the Judean churches (2:14), the Thessalonians in their persecution modeled both the apostolic circle and the Lord Himself, and in turn became a pattern for believers throughout the regions of Macedonia and Achaia (1:6–7). Michaelis objects to any form of "conscious imitation,"[62] but the subsequent verses not only document their persecution, but also mention continuing evidence of their faithfulness (1:8–10). These vivid exhibitions were a vital element in the pattern displayed before other believers.

Hebrew 6:12 speaks of modeling also. The exemplars here are all "who are inheriting the promises through faith and longsuffering." The writer urges the recipients of this epistle to join their ranks by mimicking conduct.

---

61. Cf. v. 3b with 1 Tim. 4:12b. Cf. the discussion above, especially in reference to the vocabulary of 1 Tim. 4:12b. Goppelt aptly synthesizes the key passages as follows: "Along the same lines as in Paul, the exhortation in 1 Pt 5:3 admonishes those who represent the word to become τύποι . . . τοῦ ποιμνίου, 'examples to the flock.' The word cannot just be recited; it can be attested only as one's own word which shapes one's own conduct. The office-bearer is thus admonished: 'Be thou an example of the believers, in word (i.e., preaching), in conversation,' 1 Tim 4:12; cf. Tt 2:7: 'In all things shewing thyself a pattern (in the doing) of good works'" (Goppelt, "τύπος," 8:250).

62. Michaelis, "μιμητής," 4:670. Some of his contextual comments are credible, but his controlling assumption that modeling relates only to authority limits his conclusion about the verses by his presuppositional mold.

Michaelis is correct when he says,

> The admonition of 3 Jn. 11: μὴ μιμοῦ τὸ κακὸν ἀλλὰ τὸ ἀγαθόν [*mē mimou to kakon alla to agathon*, "do not emulate what is bad but what is good"] is general, but it stands in close relation to what precedes and follows. Gaius must not be ensnared by the Diotrephes who is denounced in v. 9f. He should follow the Demetrius who is praised in v. 12.[63]

The Scripture never tells believers to imitate an abstraction. As here, the example is always concrete. This passage furnishes both negative and positive patterns.

God's people should emulate not only other mature disciples but also the men whom God has given to them as spiritual leaders (Eph. 4:11–13). They in turn, in accord with testimonies of the apostolic circle, should strive to model Christ, who alone displays the perfect moral image of God. In the New Testament the vital link of ethical emulation represented in church leaders is particularly conspicuous. Consequently, rediscovering pastoral ministry according to God's Word requires that today's church leaders not only recognize and teach the priority of moral modeling but accept its overwhelming challenge personally and, by His grace, live as examples before His sheep and a scrutinizing world ready to level the accusation of hypocrisy.

---

63. Michaelis, "μιμητης," 4:666 (transliteration and translation added).

17

Leading

Alex D. Montoya

*Leadership in a local church is indispensable if the church is to have di-
rection and purpose. The ultimate leader—normally the pastor—leads others
to the accomplishment of a common goal. The Bible contains numerous examples of how God has been pleased to use leaders to accomplish His purposes.
The Christian leader must be careful to observe biblical guidelines in leading the church, principally in assuming the role of a servant-leader. Seven
traits of a good leader are self-management, good decision making, effective communication, appropriate leadership style, compatibility with people,
ability to inspire, and a willingness to pay a high price. The act of leading
requires vision, enlistment, delegation, and motivation.*

Leadership is essential to the life and mission of the church. Without
it the church flounders and staggers on a haphazard course in its pilgrimage to the better place. Without leadership the church is unable to fulfill its
purposes of ministering effectively to those within and reaching those on the
outside, nor can it render the glory to God that He deserves.

According to Means, the church is undergoing a leadership crisis that
is evident from five symptoms:[1]

1.   the absence of meaningful growth in the churches

2.   the amount of discord and disharmony among congregations

3.   the number of brief pastorates and ministerial burnout

4.   the rise of a spectator religion that caters to the fallout from churches
     with leadership problems

---

1. James E. Means, *Leadership in Christian Ministry* (Grand Rapids: Baker, 1989),
18–22.

5.   the high percentage of nonministering churches.

Lack of leadership seems to be the plague of modern society. Bennis, a foremost authority on secular leadership, sizes up today's world in this way: "Where have all the leaders gone? The leaders who remain are the struggling corporate chieftains, the university presidents, the city managers, the state governors. Leaders today sometimes appear to be an endangered species, caught in the whisk of events and circumstances beyond rational control."[2] Effective leadership is the need of the hour, and for the church under mandate to evangelize the world, it is an indispensable requirement—indeed an urgent agenda.

The pastor is the one called to provide ultimate leadership for the church regardless of church polity. The success of the church depends heavily on his ability to lead. This chapter purposes to help the pastor in his leading of God's flock by outlining the biblical perspectives on pastoral leadership and the essential concerns that comprise this leadership—namely vision, enlistment, delegation, and motivation.

DEFINITION OF LEADERSHIP

Before considering the biblical perspectives, we shall attempt to define leadership. The variety among proposed definitions of leadership makes the task of defining it somewhat difficult. "Leadership," one says, "is the process of motivating people."[3] Another states, "Leadership is that which moves persons and organizations toward the fulfillment of their goals."[4] George places emphasis on the effect of leaders on others: "By increasingly focusing on *leading others* into ministry a pastor increases church growth potential, because the entire church becomes capable of working in ministry."[5]

The secular arena defines leadership in terms that may help pastors comprehend their leadership roles. "The chief object of leadership is the

---

2. Warren Bennis, *On Becoming a Leader* (Menlo Park, Calif.: Addison-Wesley, 1989), 14.

3. Harold Myra, ed., *Leaders* (Waco: Word, 1987), 158.

4. Harris W. Lee, *Effective Church Leadership* (Minneapolis: Augsburg Fortress, 1989), 27.

5. Carl F. George and Robert E. Logan, *Leading and Managing Your Church* (Old Tappen, N.J.: Revell, 1987), 15.

creation of a human community held together by the work bond for a common purpose," according to Bennis.[6] Burns states:

> I define leadership as leaders inducing followers to act for certain goals that represent the value and the motivations—the wants and needs, the aspirations and applications—both of leaders and followers. And the genius of leadership lies in the manner in which leaders see and act on their own and their followers' values and motivations.[7]

For the Christian leader, however, we offer two definitions as being closest to the mark. The first is from Means:

> Spiritual leadership is the development of relationships with the people of a Christian institution or body in such a way that individuals and the group are enabled to formulate and achieve biblically compatible goals that meet real needs. By their ethical influence, spiritual leaders serve to motivate and enable others to achieve what otherwise would never be achieved.[8]

Gangel's equally concise and excellent definition describes leadership as "the exercise of one's spiritual gifts under the call of God to serve a certain group of people in achieving the goals God has given them toward the end of glorifying Christ."[9] Hence, "the pastor or administrator or executive, therefore, works with and through people to get things done. He takes the proper leadership in following up each objective to the end that God might be glorified."[10]

All these definitions of leading have one thing in common: the leader is one who leads others to the accomplishment of a common goal. If no one follows, he is obviously not a leader, regardless of what titles and degrees may precede or follow his name. Or it has been said, "A church can call you to be a pastor because *pastor* is a title. The call does not make you a leader. *Leader* is not a title but a role. You only become a leader by functioning as one."[11]

---

6. Bennis, *Becoming a Leader*, 163.

7. Lee, *Church Leadership*, 153.

8. Means, *Leadership in Christian Ministry*, 59.

9. Kenneth O. Gangel, *Feeding and Leading* (Wheaton: Victor, 1989), 31.

10. Charles V. Wagner, *The Pastor: His Life and Work* (Shaumburg, Ill.: Regular Baptist Press, 1976), 137.

11. Fred Smith, *Learning to Lead* (Waco: Word, 1986), 22.

THE BIBLICAL PERSPECTIVE ON LEADING

Leadership is biblical. The idea of someone leading others is rooted in the Scriptures. For someone to assume the role of leader in God's church and to expect others to follow his example is not egotistical, authoritarian, condescending, or sinful. We are assured of this because the Scriptures lay down a basis and guidelines for Christian leadership.

The Biblical Basis

In this area of leading, some may question whether one should even assume that he has the right to tell others what to do. Yet the Scriptures are everywhere quite clear about this calling to leadership.

1. **The entire history of God's dealings with His people is actually God's involvement with a particular person whom He used to accomplish His will.** God always worked through one person who led the people in the execution of God's will. Whether it was Abraham in Ur and then Canaan, Joseph in Egypt, Jacob, Moses in the wilderness, Joshua in the conquests, the judges in the interim, the kings, or even in the prophets and apostles, God led through human leadership. When God purposes to accomplish an objective, He looks for a person who in turn becomes His leader of His people. It is not surprising that He continues the practice in the Christian church.

2. **The New Testament spells out in clear terms that God had a designated leadership for His church.** The apostles were the first designated leaders appointed by Christ and ordained with the authority to lead and make judgments among the people (Matt. 10:1–42; 18:18–20) as well as to serve as the very foundation of His blessed church (Eph. 2:20).

In the establishment of the church, the office of elder and deacon surfaced as spiritual leadership to lead the congregations. The eldership by its very nature is leadership. *Elder* implies age and experience–essential ingredients for those assigned to lead the congregations (Acts 14:23; 20:17; Titus 1:5). The elder was also an "overseer," one assigned the task of watching over the congregation (Phil. 1:1; 1 Tim. 3:1; Titus 1:5–6).

Acts 20 is pivotal in understanding the leadership qualities of New Testament leaders. Acts 20 called the recipients of Paul's words "elders of the church" (v. 17). Then it identified them as "overseers" and told them to "be on guard for yourselves and for all the flock, among which the Holy Spirit has made you overseers" (Acts 20:28). Then their assignment was "to shepherd the church of God which He purchased with His own blood"

(v. 28). The Ephesian elders thus illustrated the functions of a pastor–one who guards, leads, and feeds the sheep.

The Bible also uses specific terms to identify the existence of leaders in the church. Leading is listed among the gifts given to the church: "*He who leads*, with diligence" (Rom. 12:8);[12] "*administrations*" (1 Cor. 12:28).[13] Leading is listed among the requirements for church elders: "But if a man does not know how to manage his own household, how will he *take care of the church of God*" (1 Tim. 3:5).[14] In other words, if you cannot lead your own family, what makes you think you can lead the entire church?

3. **Certain charges addressed to individuals in the New Testament indicate that these men were to exercise leadership in the church.** Consider Paul's advice to Timothy and Titus about the treatment of elders (1 Tim. 5:17–25; Titus 1:5–9). Peter also gives an extended and clear exhortation to elders (1 Pet. 5:1–5). Here the references to leading are conclusive.

4. **The church has received special exhortations regarding treatment of church leaders.** The church was to "be in subjection to such men" (1 Cor. 16:16) and to acknowledge them (1 Cor. 16:18). Paul told the Thessalonians to "appreciate those who diligently labor among you, and have charge over you in the Lord and give you instruction, and that you esteem them very highly in love because of their work" (1 Thess. 5:12–13). The writer of Hebrews tells believers, "Obey your leaders, and submit to them; for they keep watch over your souls, as those who will give an account" (Heb. 13:17). He also instructs, "Greet all of your leaders" (Heb. 13:24). Indeed the readers were to remember "those who led you, who spoke the Word of God to you" (Heb. 13:7).[15] "Clearly, leaders were over the church and the church was under authority. No one had the right to disregard or disrespect the spiritual leaders."[16]

Both pastors and people must realize that God prescribes leadership for His church, and both must be careful to perform their respective tasks

---

12. The word is προϊστάμενος (*proistamenos*), which is from προϊστημι (*proistēmi*, "I preside, rule, govern" (G. Abbott-Smith, *A Manual Greek Lexicon of the New Testament* [Edinburgh: T. and T. Clark, 1973], 381).

13. The word is κυβερνήσεις (*kybernēseis*) which is from κυβέρνησις (*kybernēsis*, "steering, pilotage," then metaphorically "government") Ibid., 260.

14. The word is ἐπιμελήσεται (*epimelēsetai*) from ἐπιμελέομαι (*epimeleomai*, "I take care of" Ibid., 171–72).

15. The word in Heb. 13:7, 17, 24 is from ἡγέομαι (*hēgeomai*, "I lead, guide, to go before," hence "a ruler, leader") Ibid., 198.

16. Means, *Leadership in Christian Ministry*, 96.

dutifully. The pastor must lead and do so effectively and scripturally; the people must respect, obey, and uphold in prayer those who have received the oversight of their souls. There is, then, a biblical basis for such a relationship, as Lee so aptly summarizes:

> Leadership in the church is rooted in what we believe about God and the church, the body of the Son, Jesus Christ. The church may have much in common with organizations of various kinds, and it may operate in similar ways, but its beliefs about leadership are rooted deeply in the faith. In the church, we believe leadership is one of God's gifts given for the sake and welfare of the church's life and mission. We believe also that leadership is a calling from God and a ministry through which we serve God.[17]

Biblical Guidelines for Leadership

A brief word is in order to reiterate the importance of leaders understanding the biblical guidelines given them by God. The Christian ministry has suffered greatly from the violation of these guidelines. Indeed, ministerial reputation is at an all-time low during this last decade of the twentieth century, all because some pastors have rejected God's standards and have tarnished and stained the good name of those who also wear the title of pastor.

Not all the ill will expressed toward Christian leaders is self-caused. Contempt for leaders comes also from a contemporary attitude of rejecting authority, people's increased educational level, media publicity, secularization of the church, a lack of shepherding, and humanistic attacks upon religion.[18] Yet Christian leaders have earned their fair share of the criticism. So their actions must be in line with biblical principles if the problem is to find resolution.

A pastor is a spiritual leader, a man of God charged with a mandate and required to embody in his person the ideals of the faith he proclaims. He is to practice what he preaches. In an age of pragmatism in the secular world, where the end justifies the means, the temptation is for leadership to prostitute Christian character for the sake of success. Moreover, in a culture that increasingly extols success at any cost and puts down virtues as a worthy goal, leaders may unwittingly pursue the glitter of success and lose

---

17. Lee, *Church Leadership*, 25.

18. Means, *Leadership in Christian Ministry*, 37–40. See also Michael Medved, *Hollywood vs. America* (New York: HarperCollins, 1992), 37–70.

the joy of serving Christ. Means recalls that "God measures achievement in terms of integrity, faithfulness, devotion, and righteousness, qualities that do not always produce statistical impressiveness."[19] Paul himself, a failure by today's standards, tells the true test of successful ministry: "It is required of stewards that one be found trustworthy" (1 Cor. 4:2).

The New Testament tells the Christian leader what kind of man he ought to be (1 Tim. 3:1–7; Titus 1:5–8). To be a leader, one needs to be aware that he must first *measure up* to these traits as a qualification to *enter* into the office of pastor, and then he must *maintain* these qualities in his life if he is to *stay* in the pastoral ministry. (See chapter 5, "The Character of a Pastor," for further explanation and application of these traits.) The same applies to the office of deacon (Acts 6:1–7; 1 Tim. 3:8–13).

The Scriptures also tell the leader how he is to perform his pastoral duties (Acts 20:17–35; 2 Tim. 4:1–5; 1 Pet. 5:1–4). The pastoral leadership is to guard and shepherd the flock of God, which includes all that it takes to bring the church to maturity. Peter portrays the manner of oversight beautifully in his first epistle, telling how to implement the charge he himself received from the Chief Shepherd (1 Pet. 5:1–4; cf. John 21:15–22). Pastors have their work clearly defined for them so that they ought not to have confusion as to what they are to do or how they are to perform their work.

The pastor, then, is by his calling a *spiritual leader*. His calling comes from God. His allotment is the spiritual oversight of a Spirit-led body of believers (1 Pet. 5:3; cf. 2:5–10). His qualifications for holding office are spiritual (1 Tim. 3:1–8). His methods for ministering are spiritual (Acts 6:4; 2 Cor. 10:4; 2 Tim. 4:1–4). His accountability (Heb. 13:17) and rewards are spiritual (2 Tim. 4:8; 1 Pet. 5:4). Though we may learn much from the study of the leadership practices of the world, we must always keep in mind that "leadership in the church is different from leadership in the world."[20]

The warning offered by the mentor of spiritual leaders, J. Oswald Sanders, is important: "Choosing men for office in the church or any of its auxiliaries without reference to spiritual qualifications must of necessity result in an unspiritual administration. . . . Appointment of men with a secular or materialistic outlook prevents the Holy Spirit from carrying out His program for the church in the world."[21] God uses spiritual leaders to accomplish spiritual purposes. He does not violate this axiom.

---

19. James E. Means, *Effective Pastors for a New Century* (Grand Rapids: Baker, 1993), 123.

20. Gangel, *Feeding and Leading*, 35.

21. J. Oswald Sanders, *Spiritual Leadership* (Chicago: Moody, 1980), 113–14.

As a spiritual leader, the pastor then becomes a *servant leader*. Here is the great paradox of Christian leadership: He leads in serving and by serving. His greatness lies in his status as the servant of all. The Lord Jesus introduced and modeled this concept of leadership when He said,

> You know that the rulers of the Gentiles lord it over them, and their great men exercise authority over them. It is not so among you, but whoever wishes to become great among you shall be your servant, and whoever wishes to be first among you shall be your slave; just as the Son of Man did not come to be served, but to serve, and to give His life a ransom for many (Matt. 20:25–28).

Our Lord also said, "The greatest among you shall be your servant" (Matt. 23:11).

The Lord Jesus was a model servant leader. Every aspect of His life and ministry illustrated the type of spiritual leader He expected His disciples to be. At the Last Supper he dramatically portrayed what he meant by servant leadership. There He humbled Himself and washed the feet of the disciples, and then drove home the lesson with these words: "Do you know what I have done to you? You call Me Teacher and Lord; and you are right, for so I am. If I then, the Lord and the Teacher, washed your feet, you also ought to wash one another's feet. For I gave you an example that you also should do as I did to you" (John 13:12–15).

Leadership as portrayed by the world or even as practiced in some Christian churches and organizations runs contrary to the leadership principle commanded by the Lord. Gangel asserts that servant leadership, an attitude that should govern managerial functions, "runs in direct opposition to the thinking of the world."[22]

When people think of *leadership*, they see it as synonymous with *lordship*. Quite the opposite is true of biblical leadership. Ponder this poignant statement:

> Never are church leaders to think of their status as lordship, but as servanthood. Leaders are not selected so that they might have dominion over the body of believers, but that there might be guidance in spiritual matters by qualified, godly individuals under the lordship of Christ. Therefore, however we interpret the words rule, direct, obey and submit, they cannot be interpreted in a way that gives leaders the

---

22. Gangel, *Feeding and Leading*, 50.

kind of authority that the rulers of the Gentiles had, or that officials exercise in the secular world.[23]

Two clarifications are necessary here. The first is that servant leadership is not enslavement to every whim of the church. We must keep in mind that "the Christian leader is primarily a servant of God, not a servant of the sheep."[24] His ultimate accountability is to God. Hence, he does what God commands him to do for the sheep and obviously only what is for the ultimate good of the sheep. A servant-leader is not the church's errand boy.

The other clarification is that servant leadership *is* successful. The idea that such a view of pastoral leadership will weaken the leader's authority and credibility is wrong. Rush concurs: "Many leaders have the mistaken idea that if they serve their followers, they will be viewed as weak and unfit for leadership. . . . Servant leaders are *more* effective leaders than traditional leaders."[25] Even secular leaders are discovering the importance and effectiveness of this approach.[26]

The indispensable quality of any Christian leader is that he be *Spirit-led* or Spirit-filled. Since the Holy Spirit is the author and power in the church, it is only logical and natural that to be an effective leader of His church, a man must be filled and led by the same Spirit. Sanders writes,

> To be filled with the Spirit, then, is to be controlled by the Spirit. Intellect and emotions and volition as well as physical powers all become available to Him for achieving the purposes of God. Under His control, natural gifts of leadership are sanctified and lifted to their highest power. The not-grieved and unhindered Spirit is able to produce the fruit of the Spirit in the life of the leader, with added winsomeness and attractiveness in his service and with the power in his witness to Christ. All real service is but the effluence of the Holy Spirit through yielded and filled lives (John 7:37–39).[27]

Christian leaders must ponder this statement before attempting to find some secret or new ingredient for more effective ministry. If no celestial breeze is blowing, no matter how large the sails, the vessel goes nowhere!

---

23. Means, *Leadership in Christian Ministry*, 97.
24. Smith, *Learning to Lead*, 24.
25. Myron Rush, *The New Leader* (Wheaton: Victor, 1987), 85.
26. See Stephen R. Covey, *Principle-centered Leadership* (New York: Summit, 1990), 34.
27. Sanders, *Spiritual Leadership*, 117–18.

Practical Requirements for Leading

Almost every notable work on leadership has its list of leadership traits essential for effective service. In studies and surveys of effective leaders, certain ones stand out as being more essential than others, however. The following seven traits appear to be the ones that characterize good leaders.

1. **A good leader manages himself.** Self-mastery is what every aspiring leader needs to achieve. The Lord Jesus required it of all His disciples; they could not help others until they had conquered issues in their own lives. He also accused the Jewish leaders of being unfit for leadership, calling them "blind guides" (Matt. 15:14; 23:16, 24). If a person sets about to do what he must do in life and disciplines himself so as to accomplish those goals and desires, he will soon see that he has outdistanced the pack and even has a following trying to get what he has obtained. Bennis puts it this way: "No leader sets out to be a leader. People set out to live their lives, expressing themselves fully. When that expression is of value, they become leaders."[28] This is obviously an expression of self-management and discipline in pursuing the priorities of life. Consider these lines:

> If you want to
> manage somebody,
> manage yourself.
> Do that well
> and you'll
> be ready to
> stop managing.
> And start leading.[29]

A leader, then, must be one who has his life under control, which includes his personal habits and activities. A leader is self-managed; he is his own boss. He is one who knows how to manage his time, his money, his energies, and even his desires.

2. **A good leader knows how to make good decisions.** "Leaders are decision makers."[30] The buck stops with him, meaning that he is usually the one who needs to make the decision that affects the outcome of the organization. Decision making is a difficult and lonely business. The ability to

---

28. Bennis, *Becoming a Leader*, 111.

29. Calvin Miller, *Leadership* (Colorado Springs: Navpress, 1987), 23.

30. Ibid., 50.

make quick and knowledgeable decisions separates the leaders from the followers. "When all the facts are in," states Sanders, "swift and clear decision is the mark of a true leader."[31] A leader spends most of his time in dealing with or solving problems.[32] Hence, all leaders have one thing in common: "They are continually required to make decisions affecting others as well as themselves."[33]

Decision making is the lot of leaders, and indecision or poor decisions can become their undoing. The inability to make decisions is one of the major reasons administrators fail, and this "inability-to-make-decision syndrome is a much more common reason for administrative failure than lack of specific knowledge or technical know-how."[34] Leaders need to heed these words:

> Procrastination and vacillation are fatal to leadership. A sincere though faulty decision is better than no decision. Indeed the latter is really a decision, and often a wrong one. It is a decision that the status quo is acceptable. In most decisions the root problem is not so much in knowing what to do as in being prepared to live with the consequences.[35]

So how do leaders learn to make decisions? By making decisions, even bad ones. Rush offers a five-step process for making effective decisions:

Step one: Correctly diagnose the issue or problem.

Step two: Gather and analyze the facts.

Step three: Develop alternatives.

Step four: Evaluate alternatives pro and con.

Step five: Select from among the positive alternatives.[36]

3. **A good leader communicates effectively.** Skill in communicating ideas, concepts, and directives to the organization is essential for leadership. The Lord Jesus demonstrated His ability to communicate by the literature

---

31. Sanders, *Spiritual Leadership*, 83.

32. Myron Rush, *Management: A Biblical Approach* (Wheaton: Victor, 1983), 112.

33. Ibid., 98.

34. Ted W. Engstrom and Robert C. Larson, *Seizing the Torch* (Ventura, Calif.: Regal, 1988), 140.

35. Sanders, *Spiritual Leadership*, 88.

36. Rush, *Management*, 102–6.

He inspired, the church He created, and by the death He suffered. His enemies also understood well the message of His Lordship.

If we cannot communicate, we cannot lead. Even evil men have risen to lead great movements because of their superb abilities to articulate their beliefs and communicate them passionately to their followers—Hitler and Marx are prime examples.

An effective pastor is more than a theologian. He must also be an effective preacher, a communicator of the divine message. There is never a leader with a sizable following who does not communicate effectively. Each one of the megachurches today has a great communicator as its leader. In fact, in our age of communication, articulation and communication are necessary for survival in any organization.

Just the fact that one speaks or writes does not mean he communicates. Communication is "the process we go through to convey understanding from one person or group to another."[37] The key to being a good communicator is, first of all, to understand people. Next one needs to know his subject thoroughly. Then he must perceive or create the right climate, and finally, he must listen for feedback to see if he is getting through.

A pastor or preacher should always be looking for ways to improve his ability to communicate. The message never changes but the audience does, and so does the messenger. It is expedient for the messenger to keep his skill honed, and for most pastors, the preaching skills are not fully mature until long after graduating from seminary. It is unfortunate that some preachers cease to improve their preaching abilities. It is a trade and skill we *must* master at all cost.[38]

4. **A good leader is one who manages his leadership style.** Leaders are unique. They have differing personalities and different ways of leading people. This is why it is often said that leaders are born, not made. Leadership classes and seminars do not produce leaders. Life and its experiences mingled with a distinct personality and the unction of God produces a Christian leader.

It is impossible to discuss the various styles of leadership here, but certain other works do describe them.[39] In relation to style, we need to keep these observations in mind:

---

37. Ibid., 115.

38. As a tool for improvement in the communication of God's Word, I recommend to the reader John MacArthur, Jr., et al., *Rediscovering Expository Preaching* (Dallas: Word, 1992).

39. For leadership styles see Gangel, *Feeding and Leading*, 48–61; Rush; *Management*, 217–32; Ted W. Engstrom, *The Making of a Christian Leader* (Grand Rapids: Zondervan, 1976), 67–94.

1.   Be at least casually acquainted with the differing styles of leadership and know which best suits your personality and the circumstance that calls for the exercise of leadership.

2.   Understand that the circumstances may dictate a style of leadership to which you are *not* accustomed but that needs to be utilized for the sake of the organization.[40]

3.   Settle into your particular leadership style and be consistent with it.

Listen to what this leader says: "Since there are different ways to lead, it's important to make a very clear selection. . . . Followers have an amazing ability to accommodate themselves to leadership styles. . . . If you will select your style, implement it, and stay consistent, you can use almost any style you want."[41]

Leaders of growing churches and organizations agree that the growth of these organizations had much to do with their ability to change their style of leadership. Miller testifies to this:

> What great deterrent keeps churches from growing? I believe lack of growth can be attributed to a failure on the part of individual pastors or leaders to adjust their management styles. . . . I began as pastor in the parish I serve some twenty years ago. The management of the church from a very small one to a very large one means that I have had to change my management style continually.[42]

Good leaders, then, know styles of management and are able to adjust their styles to the need of the organization.

5. **A good leader gets along with people**. Someone has said in jest, "The ministry would be a wonderful occupation if it weren't for people." That puts the finger on the problem with some want-to-be-leaders: They cannot get along with people. Effective leaders have learned the fine art of getting along with the people they lead and expect to lead. People are led, not driven. If a leader cannot win them over to himself, they simply walk away. It is amazing how many Christian leaders destroy their churches because they are not tactful, loving, compassionate, patient, and shrewd in their care of the flock. The proverbial back door is sometimes held open by

---

40. "The research indicates that there is not a style that is best under all circumstances" (Lee, *Church Leadership*, 45).

41. Smith, *Learning to Lead*, 40.

42. Miller, *Leadership*, 113.

the pastor himself. He then has some other excuse for the loss of members. Church members rarely leave churches over issues; it is usually over person-alities and conflicts over personal issues.

Means makes this observation: "In pastoral ministry the most basic cause of ineffectiveness and failure is an inability to build and sustain mean-ingful collegial relationships with the church's lay leaders."[43] Scripture states that "a brother offended is harder to be won than a strong city" (Prov. 18:19). A wise leader seeks to avoid giving offense, keeps from creating needless discord, and chooses well the hills upon which he is willing to die. Unfor-tunately, too many pastoral carcasses are found upon molehills.

A man may be a scholar and an expert in the Scriptures. He may be articulate in his delivery and knowledgeable in the basic skills of management, yet if he does not truly love people and cannot be at peace with them, he can never lead them. He may have the title of pastor, but he will never be viewed as the pastor. We need to take to heart Paul's advice, "Never pay back evil for evil to anyone. Respect what is right in the sight of all men. If possible, so far as it depends on you, be at peace with all men" (Rom. 12:17–18).

6. **A good leader is one who inspires.** An indispensable trait of effec-tive leaders is their ability to inspire others in an almost unconscious manner. Good leaders inspire discouraged and demoralized people; they add new life to a dying organization. Sanders says, "The power of inspir-ing others to service and sacrifice will mark God's leader. His incandescence sets those around him alight."[44] It is not enough to be at the front of the pack; the leader must also inspire the pack to pick up the pace and do it with a willing and an enthusiastic attitude.

People are not generally enthusiastic but are subject to the ebb and flow of life, affected by circumstances and even by poor leadership who dis-courage activity. The twelve spies sent into Canaan brought back good news and bad news: The land was indeed fertile, but there were also giants there. The punishment of the nation Israel is traceable to ten leaders who did not inspire the people but instead gave "a bad report of the land which they had spied out" (Num. 13:32). Poor leadership doomed the people to waste their years wandering in circles in a wasteland. The same can be true of churches and organizations led by people who cannot inspire others to look beyond the obstacles to the opportunities God provides. Spiritual leaders "inspire people to recognize their own spiritual needs, values, and objectives, and

---

43. Means, *Effective Pastors*, 220.
44. Sanders, *Spiritual Leadership*, 105.

then facilitate growth in their vital areas. Good effective spiritual leaders infuse others with an animating, quickening, and exalting spirit of enthusiasm for the person of Christ, growth in Christ, and the mission of the church."[45]

Inspiration begins and ends with attitude. Inspiration is a spiritual artificial respiration where the one who is inspired gives inspiration to those who have none. Good leaders are consistently optimistic and full of faith. They do not have an attitude problem. They have long since realized the importance of a good attitude. Rush reminds us that "the Christian leader's attitude plays a major role in determining what he or she does and achieves. If a person thinks something is impossible, he usually doesn't bother to try doing it. Thus the thoughts frequently become a self-fulfilling prophecy."[46] Inspirational leaders also attract inspirational people, and this snowballing effect has a major impact upon the rest of the followers.

How does a leader develop inspiration, and how does he maintain it? What separates leaders from nonleaders is that a leader knows how to inspire himself. He has learned the secret of keeping his own furnace hot and ablaze. Here are some suggestions for developing inspiration:

1. Maintain a vibrant and fresh devotional life, because God is the source of all life (John 15:5; Phil. 4:13).

2. Be a realist. Gather all the facts. Do not fear the truth. Inspiration is not built on fantasy.

3. Be an optimist. Believe that all things do work for good (Rom. 8:28). Obstacles become opportunities. Stumbling blocks become steppingstones.

4. Be a man of faith. Attempt big things for God, and expect big things from God.

5. Avoid negative people, and surround yourself with positive people.

6. Cultivate a happy home life. The hot embers for our lives come from heaven and the home.

7. Keep a healthy and refreshed body. Body chemistry and inspiration are related.

8. Dwell on your successes, not on your failures. Consider failures

---

45. Means, *Leadership in Christian Ministry*, 65.
46. Rush, *Management*, 171.

simply as gaining experience for future success. You cannot win if you do not try, and if you try, you will sometimes fail.

9.   Read inspirational literature.

10.   Think positively of others. Look for the good in people. They are made in the image of God!

7. **A good leader is one who is willing to pay the price**. Leaders pay a hefty price to be in leadership. Spiritual leadership entails discipline, self-sacrifice, great patience, and a host of hardships. Leadership is a lonely place and calls for critical and difficult decisions, which runs the danger of alienating even one's closest friends. "A cross stands in the way of spiritual leadership," confesses Dr. Sanders, "a cross upon which the leader must consent to be impaled."[47] No one can enjoy the fruit of leadership without paying the price.

The pastorate is not an easy task; it is not for the fainthearted, for the weak, for those who want to avoid hardship. It is an extremely "hot kitchen," and if one cannot stand the heat or does not want to endure it, then he needs to get out. Criticism, low pay, loneliness, frustration, long hours, rejection, and even burnout are all the hazards of ministry. As in war, there will be casualties. But as in war, the battle must be won, and the troops will be led by leaders who understand the risks and are willing to pay the price.

Developing these traits of effective leadership takes time and experience, along with some serious personal study and research. Spiritual leadership evolves out of the daily ministry and struggles of God's people. Difficult times call for good leadership that sometimes is nowhere to be found, but we must remember the best of leaders always arise in times of great distress. We await the new generation of leaders that God will raise up from this intense spiritual struggle the church is enduring.

THE ACT OF LEADING

Leaders lead! The tasks of leaders is to have a vision of what needs to be, enlist others in owning this vision, delegate the task to others, and then keep the whole group motivated to bring the completion or fulfillment of the vision. Spiritual leaders derive their vision or purpose from

---

47.   Sanders, *Spiritual Leadership*, 170.

God. Then they enlist the church to help in the achievement of the purpose, which logically demands that leaders must keep the church motivated until the goal is reached. The act of leading, then, comprises four things: vision, enlistment, delegation, and motivation. If a pastor or spiritual leader can succeed in accomplishing these four activities, he will succeed in his leadership.

Vision

Pastors must be men of vision. They must possess a deep sense of what they are to do, where they ought to go, and how they are to do it. Vision supplies these directions. Vision is critical to the life of the church as it is for any organization. "A vision gives life," writes Lee, "and if there is no vision, the seeds of death are being sown and it is just a matter of time until death will prevail."[48]

Here is where the main difference exists between leadership and management. Leadership provides the vision, and management executes the vision. Stephen Covey captures the distinction in this pithy statement: "Management is efficiency in climbing the ladder of success; leadership determines whether the ladder is leaning on the right wall."[49] In other words, "Management is doing things right; leadership is doing the right things."[50]

Regarding leadership and vision, Bennis observes that "all leaders have the capacity to create compelling vision, one that takes people to a new place, and then to translate the vision into reality."[51] Sanders attests that "those who have most powerfully and permanently influenced their generation have been the 'seers'—men who have seen more and farther than others—men of faith, for faith is vision."[52]

What then is vision? We found this definition in Mean's fine work: "A vision is an attempt to articulate, as clearly and vividly as possible, the desired future state of the organization. The vision is the goal that provides direction, aligns key players, and energizes people to achieve a common

---

48. Lee, *Church Leadership*, 131.

49. Stephen R. Covey, *The Seven Habits of Highly Effective People* (New York: Simon and Schuster, 1989), 101.

50. Ibid.

51. Bennis, *Becoming a Leader*, 192.

52. Sanders, *Spiritual Leadership*, 77.

purpose."[53] Peters and Austin are helpful when they add, "You have to know where you're going, to be able to state it clearly and concisely—and you have to care about it passionately. That all adds up to vision, the concise statement/picture of where the company and its people are heading, and why they should be proud of it."[54]

Lee observes, "When the organization has a clear sense of its purpose, direction and desired future state and when that image is widely shared, individuals are able to find their roles both in the organization and in the larger society of which they are a part."[55] Hence, vision is first knowing what the church should do and then sharing the vision with the people in such a way that they too "see" the "unseen." We feel that vision for the pastor is primarily to see what God wants the church to be and to do, and more specifically, what God wants that particular church to be. The matter is not necessarily mystical or revelatory. It is, rather, having an acute sense of what is possible and drawing others into the similar vision.[56]

A leader develops vision from a number of sources. First and foremost, it comes from God through the Holy Scriptures, which are the blueprint for God's people. We can say in some sense that all pastors share the same vision about the church: to glorify God, to make disciples, and to build up His body, the church. Yet the application of the overall vision will be personalized in each leader and congregation.

Vision also proceeds from past experience—the more experience the greater the vision. The greater the contemplation of the past, the clearer the focus on the future: "It appears that when we first gaze into our past, we elongate our future. We also enrich the future and give it detail as we recall the richness of our past experiences."[57] Involvement also adds to creating vision. The act of doing—of applying the knowledge of the past to the present—enhances vision. We need to be seizing the present doors of opportunity, which in turn give birth to vision.

We also need to keep vision alive, because like dreams, it has a tendency to fade away. Calvin Miller offers two suggestions in keeping vision alive:

---

53. Means, *Effective Pastors*, 143.

54. Tom Peters and Nancy Austen, *A Passion for Excellence* (New York: Random House, 1985), 284.

55. Lee, *Church Leadership*, 132.

56. James M. Kouzes and Barry Z. Posner, *The Leadership Challenge* (San Francisco, Calif.: Jossey-Bass, 1987), 85.

57. Ibid., 95.

Number one is an adequate quiet time. When you are quiet at the altar of your own trust, your vision will hold its place in your life. Visions rebuild themselves in quietness, not in the hurry and noise of life. A second ingredient of vision-keeping is rehearsal. Constantly, you must rehearse your dreams. It is not enough to have rehearsed them in the past. They must be a part of every day, or soon they will not keep faith with any day.[58]

Pastors cannot tread water. They cannot simply maintain the work, "holding the fort" until Christ returns. They must be in the act of leading, of instilling vision in their people. The church must realize it is there to do something, and the pastor must tell it what that something is and lead in accomplishing it.

Enlistment

Imparting the vision is the first act of leading; the second is enlisting others to buy into the vision. We may also call this *recruitment*. Effective leaders know how to recruit people to bring about the vision for the organization. Leaders must follow the example of Christ, whose call was "follow Me" (Matt. 4:19). Our Lord recruited or enlisted people and made them His disciples, people who shared His vision and set about to bring it to pass.

Churches today suffer from the lack of workers. Rush observes,

The lack of volunteers is one of the greatest tragedies in the church today. In fact, there are so few true volunteers in the modern church that we probably need to remind ourselves of what a volunteer is: a person who by his own initiative and free will steps forward to perform a task. Such persons are so rare in Christendom today that most Christian leaders go into temporary shock when approached by one.[59]

Our world is becoming a spectator society produced by addiction to entertainment and by the increasing role of professionals in our churches. The pew-warmer demands excellence that only a professional can deliver. The end result is that we have fewer and fewer volunteers, and eventually less and less being done for the kingdom of God. The cycle must be broken if we are to survive into the next century.

---

58. Miller, *Leadership*, 42.

59. Rush, *New Leader*, 119.

Leaders must enlist followers in the cause of Christ, not only in believing the message of the cross, but also in the exercise of their gifts for the perfecting of the body of Christ. In thinking of enlisting others for ministry, let leaders keep these principles in mind:

1. People do want to serve: "We need to understand that people will stand in line to volunteer for a job if they are aware of its importance and know they are needed and appreciated when they offer to perform the tasks."[60]

2. People will serve if we "ask specific people for a specific ministry for a specific length of time."[61]

Leaders must recruit and recruit effectively to bring about the goals to which they aspire. We must learn the art of recruitment. After all, it is part of the job description of the leader.[62] Enlistment of volunteers is an act of leading.

Delegation

Following the act of enlistment is the act of delegation, for the whole purpose of enlistment is to delegate to everyone a task and thus get everyone busy in achieving the vision of the body. Delegation is one of the essential tasks of leadership, spiritual or secular. "He who is successful in getting things done through others," states Sanders, "is exercising the highest type of leadership."[63] According to some, "delegation may be the most important single skill of an executive."[64]

What does *delegation* mean? Delegation is the art of assigning part of your job to someone else, entrusting responsibility and authority as well as a task to other people who are in the ministry with you, or simply put "getting rid of everything you can and doing only what remains."[65] Rush gives this comprehensive definition:

---

60. Ibid., 125.

61. Gangel, *Feeding and Leading*, 144.

62. See Gangel's chapter, "Recruiting Effective Volunteers" in *Feeding and Leading*, 133–47.

63. Sanders, *Spiritual Leadership*, 202.

64. E.g., Gangel, *Feeding and Leading*, 175.

65. Ibid.

Delegation consists of transferring authority, responsibility, and accountability from one person or group to another. In most cases, it involves moving authority to a higher level in an organization to a lower one. Delegation is the process by which decentralization of organizational power occurs. Decentralization involves the dispersion of authority and responsibility from the top downward through the organization, allowing more people to become involved in the decision making process.[66]

Delegation is *not* the abandonment of leadership, but rather the exercising of the most profound act of leadership. Great leaders are effective delegators. They realize that personally they are not able to do or attend to all they want accomplished. As an organization grows, it will reach a point where if it is to continue growing and if its leader is to survive the work load, he must delegate. Exodus 18 is a classic biblical example of the need for organization. A close scrutiny of the chapter will reward leaders caught in the same predicament as Moses.

The personal and corporate benefits of delegation are incalculable. Delegation serves the following purposes:[67]

1.   it relieves the leaders of some work

2.   it assures that the work will be done properly

3.   it helps expedite decision making

4.   it improves the skills of people

5.   it increases productivity

6.   it turns the leader into a participant in a group

7.   it prepares future leaders

8.   it makes people increase in skills for their own sake.

With so many benefits to delegation, we may wonder why more leaders do not practice effective delegation. The answer probably lies in the fact that some occupy the office of leader who do not possess the traits of leadership. They simply do not want to delegate and never intend to do so. The main reason is fear of losing power or control. These leaders also never

---

66. Rush, *Management*, 132.

67. Donald H. Weiss, *How to Delegate Effectively* (New York: American Management Association, 1988), 15–21.

intend to share the glory with their followers. Miller points out this fallacy: "You can never arrive at a real plateau of leadership by insisting that others do your work while you take the glory."[68]

Improper delegation will also frustrate the people led. There are proper ways to delegate, and the ingredients of proper delegation must all be there. They are responsibility, authority, and accountability. Responsibility is knowing full well what needs to be done; authority is having the decision-making power to perform the task; and accountability is knowing the limitations under which the task is being carried out. If one of these is missing, the delegation process will not succeed.

Perhaps this acrostic[69] will help recall the proper steps to take in delegation:

D	Determine the ministry
E	Examine the duties
L	Lay out the leadership selection
E	Educate the leader
G	Guide the leader
A	Authorize the leader
T	Trust the leader
E	Evaluate the leader.

We cannot overestimate the importance of this act of leadership, and we concur with this statement: "The degree to which a leader is able to delegate work is a measure of his success."[70]

Motivation

A leader may instill vision, enlist workers, and delegate responsibilities, but what is to make sure that the people stay at the assigned tasks with the enthusiasm required to bring it to pass or to sustain the effort over a prolonged period of time? The answer is *motivation*. Leaders must perform the act of

---

68. Miller, *Leadership*, 79.

69. I received this acrostic from Professor Jim George of The Master's Seminary.

70. Sanders, *Spiritual Leadership*, 203.

motivation, of inspiring followers to stay to the task. Rush affirms that "a leader will never be successful unless his followers are motivated to succeed."[71]

By *motivation* we mean the unleashing of the inner drive in people that launches them into action.[72] Someone has said, "Motivation is the act of creating circumstances that get things done through other people."[73]

Of all the duties that leaders perform, the act of getting people to move on something has been open to much abuse. Spiritual leaders have been guilty of the worst kinds of manipulations and outright deceptions in their efforts to get their churches to perform. They have used flattery, threats, favoritism, begging, cajolery, proof-texting, bribery, and even claims to direct revelation to manipulate their followers.[74]

How does a leader motivate? The leader himself is the key to motivation—his integrity, his skill, his knowledge of what is to be done, and his example are all basic to motivation. All motivational tactics are ineffective if the leader lacks these personal qualities.

Leaders who possess these qualities can improve their motivational skill by understanding people and what makes people do their best. Lee provides the following list to help in motivating people to do their best:[75]

- People need to know what is going to happen to them as persons, what will be expected of them, and how their contributions will fit into the group.

- People need a sense of belonging, a feeling that no one objects to their presence, a feeling that they are sincerely welcomed, a feeling that they are wanted for their total self.

- People need to share in planning the group goals and the confidence that the goals are within reach.

- People need to have responsibilities that challenge and yet are within range of their abilities and that contribute to the achievement of the group goals.

- People need to see that progress is being made toward the goals of the organization.

---

71. Rush, *Management*, 109.

72. Ibid., 108.

73. Engstrom and Larson, *Seizing the Torch*, 62.

74. Means, *Leadership in Christian Ministry*, 182.

75. Lee, *Church Leadership*, 152–53.

- People need to have confidence in the leadership of the group, with assurance that the leaders will be fair as well as competent, trustworthy, and loyal.
- People need at any given time to conclude: "This situation makes sense to me."

Of course, nothing ultimately motivates like a motivated leader. If leaders can somehow keep themselves motivated, their enthusiasm for a task will become contagious. The secret, then, to motivation is keeping oneself motivated.

The pastoral ministry is a wonderful privilege. It is leadership in God's church, a stewardship entrusted by God, a service to be performed for the Great Shepherd and to His sheep. We count ourselves deeply blessed of God to be called pastors. It is easy to lose sight of our most fundamental responsibility: to lead! Therefore, let us be about our God-given task of leading!

18

Outreaching

Alex D. Montoya

Since evangelism constitutes one of the church's main purposes, the pastor must play a key role in leading his church to fulfil this responsibility. The New Testament mandates for evangelism specifically command the church to reach out. Among them, Matt. 28:18–20 indicates that evangelism entails going out to the lost, gospel preaching, teaching obedience, and an ongoing discipleship. Various ways to accomplish the task of outreach include personal evangelism, public evangelism, and the planting of churches. The main motivations for a pastor to do evangelism come from obedience to Christ, love for Christ, and love for mankind. The pastor can pass on this motivation to his people through his example, expectations, exhortations, excitement, and promotion of special evangelistic efforts. Specific methods for doing evangelism should not obscure the pure message of the gospel. These include personal evangelism, prospect evangelism, evangelistic home Bible studies, evangelism in depth, and inquirer ministries through the local church. In addition, media evangelism, crusade evangelism, and specialty evangelism are additional possible methods.

Why should evangelism be the concern of the church, and why should involvement in evangelism be the ambition of the pastor? The answer is simple: Our Lord Jesus told us to evangelize (Matt. 28:19–20; Mark 16:15–16; Luke 24:46–49; John 20:21; Acts 1:8). We are under obligation to fulfill the Great Commission to make disciples of all the nations, beginning with our own. The Lord's purpose, aim, and ambition is the salvation of mankind: "For even the Son of Man did not come to be served, but to serve, and to give His life a ransom for many" (Mark 10:45). "For the Son of Man has come to seek and to save that which was lost" (Luke 19:10). Winning the lost was for Christ the highest desire and was the express purpose for which He came into the world (John 4:32–33).

Christ called the disciples to follow Him and learn from Him to become "fishers of men" (Matt. 4:19). He schooled the disciples to become messengers of the kingdom news and witnesses of His sufferings. He ultimately commissioned them to evangelize the world, which they began doing as soon as they received power from the Holy Spirit (Acts 1:8; 2:1–4). The record in Acts describes the church's obedience to the Great Commission, the same commission entrusted to the church today.

The Mandate for Outreaching

The mandate, then, is to evangelize the world. But what does *evangelize* mean? Some key definitions will clarify the meaning of evangelism. Packer defines evangelism as

> just preach[ing] the gospel, the evangel. . . . It is a work of communicating in which Christians make themselves mouthpieces for God's message of mercy to sinners. Anyone who faithfully delivers that message, under whatever circumstances, in a large meeting, in a small meeting, from a pulpit, or in private conversation, is evangelizing.[1]

A well-known American evangelist gives this definition:

> Winning souls means that we can take the Bible and show people that they are sinners, show people that according to the Scriptures God loves them, that Christ has died on the cross to pay for their sins, and that now all who honestly turn in their hearts to Christ for mercy and forgiveness may have everlasting life. And we can encourage them to make that heart decision that they run from sin and trust Christ to save them. So winning souls means getting the Gospel to people in such power of the Holy Spirit that they will be led to turn to Christ and be born again, be made children of God by the renewing of the Holy Ghost.[2]

Any definition of evangelism or outreaching takes into consideration Matt. 28:18–20, which includes more than just a proclamation

---

1. J. I. Packer, *Evangelism and the Sovereignty of God* (Downers Grove, Ill.: InterVarsity, 1961), 41.

2. John R. Rice, *Personal Soul Winning* (Murfreesboro, Tenn.: Sword of the Lord, 1971), 11–12.

of a simple evangel. The command to "make disciples" includes at least four features:

1. going, that is, taking the initiative to reach out to unreached people—we go to them, and do not expect them to come to us

2. presenting the gospel, the message of the cross with all its implications of Christ's Lordship, atonement, grace, repentance, and faith

3. baptizing, i.e., calling sinners into a public declaration of their faith in Christ and repentance from sin

4. teaching them; forming converts into an assembly where the ongoing process of teaching is possible.

Biblical outreaching is more than dropping gospel leaflets over a city or inviting someone to a church concert. These four elements deserve a closer examination.

1. **Evangelism is proactive**. English translations of the original Greek text of Matt. 28:19 begin with "Go," which is the translation of an aorist participle conveying the sense "having gone." The main verb of the verse is "make disciples," or literally "disciple" all the nations. Hence, what the command assumes is that Christians will go out for the express purpose of making the nations disciples of Christ.

Biblical evangelism is outreaching, that is, going out to the lost souls of this world. Many pastors have fallen into the error of thinking that if sinners among the nations want to be saved, they need to come to the church. The greatest single reason why the church is declining is that it has ceased to go out to the lost. For some reason, evangelism has become something to do in church—within the walls of the church building. The church today expects unbelievers to come to it, when in fact the church should go out to them. Effective outreach will take place when Christians realize that the starting point of the Great Commission is to move out from the comfort zones of ecclesiastical structures into the lives of the lost around them. From the pulpit to the pew—from the pastor to the parishioner—the perspective of evangelism must be that of a proactive, aggressive endeavor.

2. **Evangelism is gospel preaching**. The command to make disciples entails calling men and women to faith, obedience, and submission to Jesus Christ. Some equate evangelism with preaching social change, human rights, political liberation, economic equality, and many more causes. These issues, though they are righteous endeavors, are not biblical evangelism.

Evangelism is the preaching of the cross of Christ, that He died for the sins of the world, that He arose from the dead, that He is Lord of the universe and of His church, and that people must believe the truth of the message before it can have any effect on their souls (Rom. 3:1–31; 10:9–10; 1 Cor. 15:1–4; Gal. 2;16–21). It must include the deity of Christ, His incarnation, His sinless nature, His vicarious substitutionary death for sinful humanity, His bodily resurrection, repentance and faith on the part of sinners, and the coming judgment of the world.

In recent times, it has been a tendency of pastors and churches to water down the gospel of Christ. In an effort to make more converts, preachers have resorted to a diluted gospel void of the saving features. They have resorted to "another gospel," and inferior results are evident. An effective presentation of the true gospel will take careful preparation, time, thought, prayer, and patience. Evangelistic preaching is a call for souls to become disciples of Christ. Anything short of that is not biblical evangelism. Pleadings for professions of faith, decisions, or other outward manifestations just to elicit a response, if they do not result in making true disciples of the Lord Jesus, are not effective evangelism.

3. **Evangelism is transformed lives.** Christ commanded that the disciples baptize the nations into the triune name of God as a symbol of their turning from their sins to the Savior. The gospel call is always "be saved from this perverse generation" (Acts 2:40) and "turn from these vain things to a living God" (Acts 14:15). The gospel is to let the nations know that God "is now declaring to men that all everywhere should repent" (Acts 17:30). It always involves "repentance toward God and faith in our Lord Jesus Christ" (Acts 20:21). Paul summed up his proclamation when he told King Agrippa that Christ called him to open the eyes of the Gentiles, "that they may turn from darkness to light, and from the domain of darkness to God, in order that they may receive forgiveness of sins and an inheritance among those who have been sanctified by faith in Me" (Acts 26:18). Hence effective biblical evangelism always results in changed lives, souls yielded to Christ, believers submitted to the Lordship of Christ.

4. **Evangelism is an ongoing discipleship.** The Lord included in the Great Commission the additional task of perfecting and maturing disciples by "teaching them to observe all that I commanded you" (Matt. 28:20). Effective evangelism has as its goal the incorporation of the disciple into the context of a local church or assembly of believers, where under the ministry and influence of gifted believers, the new disciple can grow into the fullness of the image of Christ (Eph. 4:11–16). New Testament evangelism issued from the local church and resulted in converts added to the local

church. The measure of results was not the number of professions but the numbers added to the church, and later the number of churches formed through the churches' evangelistic outreach.

The lethargy, lukewarmness, and compromising attitude within the church is responsible for the anemic and stagnant condition of the modern church. The church needs to renew its commitment to obey the mandate of our Lord Jesus Christ: Go! Rice speaks to this generation with a heart-stirring exhortation:

> The first great essential in soul winning is to go after sinners! This is the simplest part of soul winning, but one on where most people fail. They do not go after sinners. One may cry, and pray, and read his Bible, and go to church, and have family altar, and give his tithes, and pay his honest debts, and yet his own family may go to hell and all his friends around him, because he simply does not go after them, does not take the Gospel to them, does not urgently try to win them to Jesus Christ. No one ever becomes a soul winner who is not willing to work at it. Aggressive efforts are blessed of God in soul winning. One who does not make the effort will not get people saved.[3]

THE MANNER OF OUTREACHING

With the mandates in mind, the next step is to draw some broad strokes to describe various ways of outreaching, reserving until later in the chapter specific, reproducible methods for local church evangelism. The New Testament church used at least three main avenues in its efforts to fulfill the Great Commission: (1) personal evangelism, (2) public evangelism, and (3) the planting of churches. A brief glance at these three is enlightening.

Personal Evangelism

All evangelism is ultimately personal, with the heralder appealing to a lost soul either face-to-face or in a crowd. A person responds to the gospel in the privacy of his or her soul and in the uniqueness of the moment when the Holy Spirit lifts the veil, allowing that person to see the glory of the gospel. In that sense, all evangelism is personal.

---

3   Ibid., 89–90.

In the stricter sense, however, personal evangelism is the effort of one person toward leading another individual to Christ. It is Andrew finding Simon Peter (John 1:40–42). It is Philip finding Nathaniel (John 1:45). It is Jesus finding Nicodemus (John 3:1–5) and then the woman at the well (John 4:7–15). Personal evangelism was the first work of the disciples and the ministry that the Lord Jesus perfected superbly. Personal evangelism was the ongoing work of the early church, where daily from house to house they kept on preaching Jesus (Acts 5:42). The early witnesses to Christ were renowned for their ability to engage in a personal wrestling to bring a soul to believe in Christ (Acts 8:26–39; 20:20).

Emphasis on personal evangelism is a great need because of the vast number of Christians and even of pastors who do not engage themselves in the work of personal evangelism. The greatest success at evangelism will be through personal evangelism, and the greater the number who are doing it, the better the results will be. Concerning personal evangelism Macaulay and Belton say,

> In the long run, every other form we have mentioned reduces itself to this. Whatever the characteristic of the group with whom we are working, our aim is to win the individual. We are not after the crowd but the persons who make up the crowd. We are not interested in the students as such, the railway man as such, the youth as such, the derelict as such, but we are seeking the person who happens to be a student, a railway man, a youth, or a derelict. They are all lost. They are all precious. Christ died for them all. We see them all as souls, as persons. As such we must seek them.[4]

Are we pastors personally leading souls to Christ? Have we equipped the laity to lead their family, friends, and neighbors to Christ? These are obviously the priority of our evangelistic efforts.

Public Evangelism

The Lord Jesus, the Twelve, and the early church made great use of public presentations of the gospel to large gatherings and crowds of all sorts. Peter's first two recorded evangelistic efforts after Pentecost were to unusually large gatherings that yielded bountiful results—3,000 and 5,000 souls,

---

4   J. C. Macaulay and Robert H. Benton, *Personal Evangelism* (Chicago: Moody, 1965), 33–34.

respectively (Acts 2:14–41; 3:12–4:4). The disciples purposely sought a crowd that they might proclaim the cross of Christ more efficiently (Acts 5:42).

The early preachers designed their homilies not just to instruct believers but also to convert unbelievers. Preachers today are sadly deficient in addressing publicly the needs of the unconverted. The pastor must seek training in the public presentation of the gospel to the lost and then make liberal use of such training in the numerous opportunities to preach evangelistically.

Mass evangelism is not just for the mass evangelist. Every preacher of the Word must be ready to use public proclamation to do the work of an evangelist (2 Tim. 4:5). In every public forum exists a splendid opportunity to do public evangelism. Every generation has a certain group of unconverted people who frequent the halls of churches and will remain dead unless the preacher quickens them with the gospel. Dare to preach the gospel in church services for the sake of those who may need it.

Planting Churches

As soon as the early disciples reached out to their Jerusalem, Judea, and Samaria, they set about the task of reaching the remotest parts of the earth and evangelizing all the nations. These converts great distances away were obviously not going to belong to the church in Jerusalem. The only logical step was to plant churches in every city where they lived alongside lost men and women. Church planting was not a special pet project or an experimental endeavor; it was in direct fulfillment of the Great Commission. The apostles and disciples literally scattered themselves throughout the then-known world, evangelizing and planting churches in their wake.

The church today fails to see the correlation between evangelism and church planting, but any casual reading of the New Testament will quickly reverse this failure. Church planting is evangelism. Though not in agreement with all the theological premises of Wagner, we do concur with this statement of his: "The single most effective evangelistic methodology under heaven is planting new churches. . . . Not to make an explicit connection between evangelism and the local church is a strategic blunder."[5] Church planting is evangelism. If we care about evangelizing communities, cities, and nations, we will be aggressively planting new churches. A church planting expert states, "The idea is that planted churches reproduce themselves

---

5   C. Peter Wagner, *Church Planting for a Greater Harvest* (Ventura, Calif.: Regal, 1990), 11–12.

and make disciples by planting other churches. This is a process that will continue until the Savior returns. In fact, this is the true meaning behind the Great Commission."[6] Hence, Great Commission churches are church-planting churches. How many has your church helped to plant?

MOTIVATIONS OF OUTREACHING

The vast majority of Christians in our churches do not evangelize, and during the course of their lives will not lead one soul to the Master. Some do not evangelize because they are ignorant of the mechanics and substance of evangelism. Most, however, do not evangelize because they lack the adequate motivation to reach out to the lost. The following motivations, first for the pastor and then for his people in general, should provoke Christians to be about the sacred and urgent task of bringing the gospel to the lost.

Motivations for the Pastor

Indeed all the motivations that follow apply readily to all believers, who should make every effort to place themselves on the highest plane in obedience to Christ. However, the need to motivate the shepherd is crucial because he can serve as a catalyst to prompt his people into a life of witnessing for the Savior. Pastor, consider the following particular motivations for being actively engaged in evangelism.

Obedience to Christ. As undershepherds, pastors are under appointment from the Chief Shepherd, and it is their duty to evangelize the lost. They are not only responsible to feed the flock, they are to add to the flock by doing the work of an evangelist as well. The apostle Paul's great motive for preaching the gospel to the lost was his duty of fulfilling the stewardship given to him by Christ (1 Cor. 9:16–17). Green, in his masterful book *Evangelism in the Early Church,* states that from the beginning obedience to Christ was a major motivational factor for fulfilling the Great Commission. Early Christians felt it was "their responsibility before God to live lives consistent with their profession. . . .The note of personal responsibility and accountability before God, the sovereign Judge, was a prominent spur to

---

6. Aubrey Malphurs, *Planting Growing Churches for the 21st Century* (Grand Rapids: Baker, 1992), 25.

evangelism in the early church."[7] Evangelism for the pastor is not a gift, nor is it an option. It is a command; one he should be careful to obey!

Love of Christ. Paul sets down the love of Christ as a motive for his ministry when he states, "For the love of Christ controls us" (2 Cor. 5:14). In the verses following, Paul gives several reasons for his persevering ministry of evangelizing. Christ loves us, and He loves the world for which He died and thus wants the world redeemed and reconciled to Himself. For that reason, Christ's ministers serve as ministers of reconciliation (2 Cor. 5:18–21). Of the early Christians it has been said,

> These men did not spread their message because it was advisable for them to do so, nor because it was the socially responsible thing to do. They did not do it primarily for humanitarian or agathistic utilitarian reasons. They did it because of the overwhelming experience of the love of God which they had received through Jesus Christ. The discovery that the ultimate force in the universe was love, and that this love had stooped to the very nadir of self-abasement for human good, had an effect on those who believed it which nothing could remove.[8]

Love for Christ will motivate us to reach out to people, just as it motivated the early church. If we dearly love Christ and if we know anything of the love of Christ, we will be about the supreme task of sharing the love of Christ with others. How can we—how dare we do less?

Love for mankind. A genuine love for lost sinners also prompts evangelism. Enlightened souls with uplifted veils, who have experienced regeneration, escaped eternal torment, and received the pledge of the Holy Spirit, will naturally consider the dreadful plight of their fellow citizens. Compassion for the lost will move the hearts of Christians to reach out with the same remedy that quickened their own souls. The great apostle loved his own countrymen with affection so profound that it stoked the fires of his soul to agonize for their salvation. Paul twice testifies of his great love in his epistle to the Romans: "I have great sorrow and unceasing grief in my heart. For I could wish that I myself were accursed, separated from Christ for the sake of my brethren, my kinsmen according to the flesh" (Rom. 9:2–3). "Brethren, my heart's desire and my prayer to God for them is for their salvation" (Rom. 10:1). What love! What zeal!

---

7. Michael Green, *Evangelism in the Early Church* (Grand Rapids: Eerdmans, 1975), 243, 248.

8. Ibid., 236.

Outreaching has roots in love for sinners. Love prompted God (John 3:16), love prompted Christ (Luke 19:10), and love prompted the early church. Green writes about the zeal of the early church for the lost:

> But these early Christians believed implicitly that Jesus was the only hope for the world, the only way to God for the human race. Now if you believe that outside of Christ there is no hope, it is impossible to possess an atom of human love and kindness without being gripped with a great desire to bring men to this one way of salvation. We are not surprised, therefore, to find that concern for the state of the unevangelized was one of the great driving forces behind Christian preaching of the gospel in the early church.[9]

It is a great contradiction to be called a child of God—even worse a Christian minister—without having love for lost souls. Packer says, "The wish to win the lost for Christ, should be . . . the natural, spontaneous out-flow of love in the heart of everyone who has been born again. . . . May I stress again: if we ourselves have known anything of the love of Christ for us, and if our hearts have felt any measure of gratitude for the grace that has saved us from death and hell, then this attitude of compassion and care for our spiritually needy fellow-men ought to come naturally and spontaneously to us."[10]

In such a book as this, it is expedient to ignite the fire for evangelism in those who ought to be the vanguard of the church in rescuing souls from the hell fire. Are we ministers with love for the lost? Are we burdened and grieving for our fellowmen? The following paragraph should stir up the minister to outreaching:

> A compassionate leadership in the Christian movements of the world is now our greatest need. Every niche of this lost world needs the ministry of a fired soul, burning and shining, blood-hot with the zeal and conviction of a conquering Gospel. Spiritual dry rot is worse than the plague of Egypt, the simooms of a thousand Saharas, to the churches of Jesus Christ throughout the world. Many a minister is in a treadmill, marking time, drying up, living a *professional life*, without power, not earning his salt because he has no passion for God or souls and no power for effective service. May our God kindle

---

9. Ibid., 249.

10. Packer, *Evangelism* 75, 76.

holy fires of evangelism in all our churches and pulpits where such are needed.[11]

Motivations for the People

Next to motivating the pastor for outreaching, the second greatest need is to motivate rank-and-file Christians to be about this vital work of soul winning. The average Christian needs to be on fire with a white-hot zeal for lost souls. "How enormous and wonderful and glorious would be the result," writes Torrey, "if all Christians should begin to be active personal workers to the extent of their ability!"[12] In fact, the greatest moments of outreaching in church history have come through efforts by the masses of average believers. Church historian Latourette states, "The chief agents in the expansion of Christianity appear not to have been those who made it a profession or made it a major part of their occupation, but men and women who carried on their livelihood in some purely secular manner and spoke of their faith to those they met in this natural fashion."[13] Church leaders need to mobilize, motivate, equip, and unleash their churches on the pagan communities where they stand. Evangelism never was nor can it be the work of only the professional, the pastor, or a select few. It is the prerogative and privilege of the masses in our churches. They need equipping and motivation to do the job, though.

Some believers do not evangelize because they have never received instruction in how to evangelize. Others do not evangelize because they have never seen the need to evangelize. Still others do not carry on an active part in evangelism because they do not have new opportunities to share their faith. Every pastor should urge evangelistic activity upon his parishioners, train them for it, and see that they do it.[14] What can the pastor do to motivate his people? Consider five suggestions for accomplishing this.

1. **The pastor motivates by his example.** The Lord said to His disciples, "Follow Me, and I will make you fishers of men" (Matt. 4:19). Jesus did the work of evangelism, and at the same time gave His disciples a demonstration in how to evangelize and a motivation for why to do it. Coleman

---

11. Rice, *Personal Soul Winning*, 117–18.

12. R. A. Torrey, *How to Work for Christ* (Old Tappan, N. J.: Revell, n.d.), 11.

13. K. S. Latourette, *The First Five Centuries* (Grand Rapids: Zondervan, 1970), 116–17.

14. Torrey, *How to Work*, 11. Torrey's volume is an excellent manual on equipping the saints for the work of evangelism.

asserts about the Lord's habits, "Through this manner of personal demonstration, every aspect of Jesus' personal discipline of life was bequeathed to His disciples, but what perhaps was most important in view of His ultimate purpose was that all the while He was teaching them how to win souls."[15]

If a pastor wins souls, he will in so doing encourage his people to win souls by his example. Spurgeon writes in his classic *The Soul Winner*, "We must *always set an earnest example ourselves*. A slow-coach minister will not have a lively zealous church, I am sure. A man who is indifferent, or who does his work as if he took it as easily as he could, ought not to expect to have a people around him who are in earnest about the salvation of souls."[16] Are we about the business of soul winning? Are we frustrated because our people are slack and apathetic in reaching out to others? Perhaps we need to stoke the embers by getting down to doing it ourselves. Then our people will follow suit.

2. **The pastor motivates by his expectations.** Most behavior is learned behavior. Hence, in evangelism people will eventually do what is expected of them. Evangelism is not prominent in the New Testament epistles. It is as if God expects His people to evangelize without constant reminders. We need to pick up on that expectation and communicate such an attitude to the congregation. Excessive references to all the obstacles in evangelizing and a continual haranguing on the difficulties of the task will only extinguish the flames of the most ardent soul winners; neither will it serve any purpose in motivating the most timid.

3. **The pastor motivates by his exhortations.** The pastor as the chief speaker is also the best motivator, and he ought to make use of his charisma in the pulpit to excite the people into soul winning. Sermons on personal evangelism ought to pepper the yearly preaching schedule. A series of sermons on evangelism does wonders in motivating hearts toward compassionate soul winning. The preacher ought not fear infringing on the sovereignty of God or laying a guilt trip on his people. If they do not care enough about others to tell them of the saving grace of Christ, they need to feel guilty because, in fact, they are guilty of disobedience to the Great Commission. As pastors and preachers, we need such exhortations to soul winning; how much more average Christians whose hearts are dulled by daily contact with a sinful world. Let's keep them focused with gentle but

---

15. Robert Coleman, *The Master Plan of Evangelism* (Grand Rapids: Revell, 1993), 73.

16. C. H. Spurgeon, *The Soul Winner* (reprint, Grand Rapids: Eerdmans, 1963), 134.

solemn reminders of the perils of unbelief and the transforming power of the gospel.

4. **The pastor motivates with the excitement of new converts.** The best way to prime the pump of evangelism is by means of new believers being added to the church. Just as a newborn baby adds excitement to a home, so does a new convert to a local church. The testimony of a changed life, the visible demonstration of the power of the gospel, the innocence and sincerity of a new Christian—all these can create a renewed vigor for lost souls. Often it is the new Christian himself or herself who leads the charge into a lost world. New believers bring new faces into the church by introducing old believers to friends and family who need the Savior. The pastor needs to use this zeal and excitement wisely to promote a renewal in evangelism.

5. **The pastor motivates by promoting special evangelistic efforts.** Even in the finest of circumstances, churches can reach a point where the number of lost people accessible to the church dwindles dramatically. Special efforts are necessary to provide Christians with new opportunities to share their faith. These can be in the form of evangelistic rallies held in the church or sites conducive to evangelism, citywide crusades, evangelistic home Bible studies, literature distribution campaigns, short-term missionary trips, evangelistic sport programs, and the like. The point here is that these events do not just happen. They need planning and promotion, and usually that begins with the pastor or the church leaders. Here is an excellent and exciting way to get a large portion of the church involved in evangelism, but the key again is the pastor. These events need his support and aggressive endorsement.

Undoubtedly, the evangelistic zeal of the church relates directly to the evangelistic fervor of the church's leadership. Our Lord was evangelistic. The first apostles were evangelistic. The first associates of the apostles were evangelistic (Acts 6:8; 8:5). The first missionaries were evangelistic. We can assume that all the leaders of the early church had a heart for souls. Shouldn't the church's leaders have the same today? Shouldn't they be the chief promoters of evangelism in the assembly of the saints?

METHODS FOR OUTREACHING

Each generation of Christians must find ways to reach the lost in its own generation. With the bulk of the world's people still unconverted after two thousand years of church history, the conclusion is inevitable that evangelizing the world is a formidable task. Along with motivation and energizing for evangelism must come a strategy by which to reach the world for Christ.

The subject of methodology can provoke debate among leadership, and sometimes it is possible to spend more energy and time in arguing over the merits or demerits of a specific method than in doing actual evangelism. Sometimes these debates may very well be a satanic smoke screen to keep believers from the main task. Christians need to keep in mind the following observations by Coleman in his masterpiece on evangelism:

> Objective and relevance—these are the crucial issues of our work. Both are interrelated, and the measure by which they are made compatible will largely determine the significance of all our activity. Merely because we are busy, or even skilled, doing something does not necessarily mean that we are getting anything accomplished. The question must always be asked: Is it worth doing? And does it get the job done?
>
> This is a question that should be posed continually in relation to the evangelistic activity of the church. Are our efforts to keep things going fulfilling the Great Commission of Christ? Do we see an ever-expanding company of dedicated people reaching the world with the Gospel as a result of our ministry? That we are busy in the church trying to work one program of evangelism after another cannot be denied. But are we accomplishing our objective?[17]

This is a sobering question and must serve to sift the thinking and plans in regard to the formulation of an evangelistic methodology. The danger of suggesting particular methods for evangelism is that methods become dated with use, and the methods do not apply to every situation. Methods also have a tendency to accumulate cultural baggage that makes them unsuitable for other cultures or settings.

Another issue deserving attention is the possibility of methodology distorting the purity of the message, the prominence of the gospel, and the power of the gospel to save apart from the human methods used. The nature of methods, especially if they are effective in producing visible results, gives them a tendency to appear to supplement the power of God. This has happened throughout history, from the days of ancient relics to contemporary Christian rock concerts. The keen insight of Packer helps in the formulation of methods for evangelism. He says,

---

17. Coleman, *Master Plan*, 11–12.

So, in the last analysis, there is only one *method* of evangelism: namely, the faithful explanation and application of the Gospel message. From which it follows—and this is the key principle which we are seeking—that the test for any proposed strategy, or technique, or style of evangelistic action must be this: will it in fact serve the Word? Is it calculated to be a means of explaining the Gospel truly and fully and applying it deeply and exactly? To the extent to which it is so calculated, it is lawful and right; to the extent to which it tends to overlay and obscure the realities of the message, and to blunt the edge of their application, it is ungodly and wrong.[18]

These words of caution must be before the church as it develops specific approaches to reaching a lost generation. Assuredly, some methods will be more effective than others; nonetheless, each must be beneath the microscope for scrutiny regarding its fidelity to the presentation of the pure and unadulterated Word of the cross. In light of these words of caution, the following are suggested methods.

Local Church Evangelism

By far the most effective tool for evangelism is the local church. No other agency comes close in effectiveness for bringing the community to Christ. Actually all the other agencies for evangelism are parachurch, meaning that they come alongside and depend upon the local church for effectiveness. Local church evangelism involves the equipping and motivation of the members of local churches to reach out effectively to their communities. In other words, the local church is the primary mover in evangelism and the primary recipient of the fruits of evangelism. Local church evangelism should include the following:

Personal evangelism. The individual believer should learn to share his or her faith and to go out into the community personally to draw men and women to Christ. Churches need to provide special training programs for laypeople to prepare them for personal evangelism. The program of Coral Ridge Presbyterian Church in Florida is an example of such a program, which effectively teaches its members the art of soul winning. By far the most effective means of evangelism is a person sharing with a friend or loved one the blessed news of the gospel. Most church growth takes place through personal

---

18. Packer, *Evangelism*, 87.

evangelism and personal invitation.[19] The finest effort a local church can muster, then, is to equip and mobilize its entire army to evangelize the lost.

Prospect evangelism. This is a takeoff from personal evangelism whereby a church sets about to visit and win to Christ every visitor who comes within a ministry or function of the church. Visitors to churches are usually persons with an interest or curiosity about the gospel of Christ and, therefore, will usually give the evangelist a good hearing. Local churches that do not take advantage of this opportunity are missing a highly effective means of outreach.

Evangelistic home Bible studies. Home Bible studies are another effective tool available for evangelizing through the local church. Designated homes in strategic neighborhoods are useful as vehicles to present Christ to people who otherwise would not go to church. By training a select team of teachers and hosts, a church can have a vibrant and effective witness to the community. Home Bible classes are a haven for an inquirer to have his questions answered.

Evangelism in depth. This is a program originating in Latin America to help churches reach their communities. It is a plan for presenting the gospel to every home in a city by mapping out the city and assigning a certain section to each group. In time, every home receives the gospel. This noble undertaking is sure to tax the resources of any church, but it is worth consideration.

Inquirer services. These are a new phenomenon whereby a local church designates a worship service of the church as a service designed to reach the lost for Christ. Although the idea lends itself to some rather bizarre innovations, the inquirer service can be useful in presenting Christ to a lost generation. Again, caution is in order not to dilute the message of the gospel or not to confuse the inquirer service with a truly Christian worship service. The biblical perception of it should be as an evangelistic service held in the church on a regular basis, but at a time separate from the usual Lord's Day worship services.[20]

Media Evangelism

Another group of methods that can find effective use in evangelizing the lost is the vast array of resources that are so appealing to the masses in

---

19. See George Barna, *Marketing the Church* (Colorado Springs: Navpress, 1988), 109.

20. See Packer's criticism of these services, *Evangelism*, 83–84.

the categories of radio, television, gospel films, and literature. Though expensive, when used strategically, these can be very effective means of reaching a segment of the population that may be unreachable by conventional methods. For instance, currently the film *Jesus* has been dubbed into many languages, and millions of viewers the world over are seeing it. Recently, the film has been shown in strong Muslim centers in North Africa, where other means had been futile.

Crusade Evangelism

The day of mass evangelism is not over. Though not among the most efficient in producing church growth, it is a very effective tool in promoting evangelism and in reaching a mass audience with the gospel. From citywide crusades to local rallies, these efforts at reaching large numbers at one time have their place. Let's not forget that the Jerusalem church originated as a result of mass evangelism (Acts 2). A number of gifted evangelists and revival preachers specialize in this method of evangelism, and they serve a special purpose in promoting evangelism in the Christian church.

Specialty Evangelism

In this age of specialization, the church has developed creative programs that target specific groups of lost people. The local church can capitalize upon these creative efforts by adopting and adapting these methods to reach out to select groups. Campus Crusade for Christ and the Navigators are organizations that started by targeting collegians and servicemen, respectively. They have both developed excellent materials for the local church to use in reaching collegians. For example, there are Christian businessmen's luncheons, sports evangelism, programs for mothers of preschoolers (MOPS), Good News Clubs for children by Child Evangelism Fellowship, AWANA for boys and girls through high school, and even outreaches into the public high schools. The church need not shy away from creating special ministries to target a special group of unreached people. It needs to continue to be creative in seeking to win this world to Christ.

19

Discipling

S. Lance Quinn

God has called pastors to the indispensable task of discipleship. Both the Old and New Testaments mark out discipleship as a requisite part of ministry—not an option. Jesus, the greatest disciple-maker, utilized four reproducible principles in His ministry, which remain equally relevant today. They are prayerful meditation, careful selection, purposeful association, and powerful proclamation. The Scripture never refers to a nondiscipling shepherd; it commends only reproducing pastors.

Biblical instruction about disciple-making dates as far back as Jethro's counsel to Moses to choose godly men to help him adjudicate the affairs of Israel. Jethro's own words are,

> Now listen to me: I shall give you counsel. . . . You shall select out of all the people able men who fear God, men of truth, those who hate dishonest gain; and you shall place these over them, as leaders of thousands, of hundreds, of fifties and of tens. And let them judge the people at all times; and let it be that every major dispute they will bring to you, but every minor dispute they themselves will judge. So it will be easier for you, and they will bear the burden with you. If you do this thing and God so commands you, then you will be able to endure, and all these people also will go to their place in peace (Exod. 18:19, 21–23).

The Mandate for Discipling

Discipling in the Old Testament

Moses learned well from his father-in-law and told the men of Israel in the wilderness, "How can I alone bear the load and burden of you and your strife? Choose wise and discerning and experienced men from your tribes, and I will appoint them as your heads" (Deut. 1:12–13). Also, what Moses commanded for the effective leadership in the daily affairs of Israel, he saw as the need also for future generations:

> And these words, which I am commanding you today, shall be on your heart; and you shall teach them diligently to your sons and shall talk of them when you sit in your house and when you walk by the way and when you lie down and when you rise up. And you shall bind them as a sign on your hand and they shall be as frontals on your forehead. And you shall write them on the doorposts of your house and on your gates" (Deut. 6:6–9; cf. 11:18–21; 16:18–20).

Moses instituted a discipling process between fathers and sons (and even grandsons) that would ensure godly leadership in the home and society for God's people, both then and in the future. Wherever a need exists to discern God's will in the affairs of men—in the world or home—the clearly prescribed principle is to develop leadership through making disciples.

As an example, Moses did not leave Israel without leadership. He discipled Joshua with the result that "the LORD exalted Joshua in the sight of all Israel; so that they revered him, just as they had revered Moses all the days of his life" (Josh. 4:14; cf. Exod. 24:13; 33:11; Num. 11:28). Moses handed down an administrative principle: Reproduce yourself in others so that the leadership of God's people will continue throughout your generations.

Through the rest of the Old Testament, the same principle was very obvious in the training relationship between Elisha and Elijah (1 Kings 19:19–21; 2 Kings 2:3; 3:11) and in that between Baruch and Jeremiah (Jer. 36:26; 43:3). Samuel seemed to have a group of prophets under his oversight too (1 Sam. 10:5–10; 19:20–24).

One suggestion has been that these "individual master-disciple relationships within the leadership of the nation enabled the leadership function to be passed from one leader to the next until God had accomplished his purposes through them to meet the need of his people."[1] The same author has summarized the Old Testament concept of discipleship as follows:

> Master-disciple relationships behind the perpetuation and dissemination of the wisdom tradition would be found in informal father-son relationships, in training of elders for making judicial decisions in the city gate, in the wisdom orientation of advisers in the court, and within certain groups who specialized in wisdom and were involved with the recording of wisdom sayings.[2]

Discipling, whether called that or not, is the heartbeat of wise counsel in the Old Testament: "Iron sharpens iron, so one man sharpens another" (Prov. 27:17).

Discipling in the New Testament

Following these examples from the Old Testament, pastors should keep endeavoring to build themselves into others. This is not just a worthwhile option; it is a mandate from the Word of God!

The mandate from Jesus. Jesus Christ Himself commanded that His disciples (and in turn all who follow in their lineage) make disciples[3] of others. Matt. 28:18–20 records that nonnegotiable imperative:[4]

> And Jesus came up and spoke to them, saying, "All authority has been given to Me in heaven and on earth. Go therefore and make disciples of all the nations, baptizing them in the name of the Father and the Son and the Holy Spirit, teaching them to observe all that I commanded you; and lo, I am with you always, even to the end of the age."

Because of the context, it is possible to say that *Christians* and *disciple-makers* are synonymous terms. If all Christians are disciple-makers, how much more should pastors/elders lead the way in doing the same in nurtur-

---

1. Michael Wilkins, *Following the Master: Discipleship in the Steps of Jesus* (Grand Rapids: Zondervan, 1992), 63.

2. Ibid., 65.

3. Wilkins helps in defining the term *disciple*. He speaks of general and specific senses of the term: the "specific sense is seen most clearly toward the end of Jesus' earthly ministry, in the Great Commission, and in the early church"; the general sense is "a committed follower of a great master"; the Christian sense is "one who has come to him for eternal life, has claimed him as Savior and God, and has embarked upon the life of following Him . . . grow[ing] as a Christian in every area of life" (ibid., 39–41).

4. Mark 16:15–16; Luke 24:44–48; Acts 1:8–11 give similar commands.

ing disciples toward Christlikeness.[5] This is where the relationship of the pastor to other men is crucial. Pastors are to set the example of what it means to disciple men for spiritual leadership. To borrow John's terminology, "fathers" have the responsibility to disciple "young men," as young men would "little children" (1 John 2:12–14).

Jesus spoke of the "yoke" of his discipleship: "Take my yoke upon you, and *learn from Me*, for I am gentle and humble in heart; and you shall find rest for your souls. For my yoke is easy, and my load is light" (Matt. 11:29–30, emphasis added). Elsewhere He said, "I gave you an example that you also should do as I did to you" (John 13:15). In exhorting believers in Ephesus to live in righteousness and not as they had lived before, Paul wrote, "You did not *learn Christ* in this way" (Eph. 4:20, emphasis added). Regarding humility, Paul reminded the Philippians, "Have this attitude in yourselves which was also in Christ Jesus" (Phil. 2:5).

The mandate from John and Peter. Likewise, Peter reminded his readers that they had "been called for this purpose, since Christ also suffered for you, leaving you *an example for you to follow in His steps*" (1 Pet. 2:21, emphasis added). The apostle John instructed that "the one who says he abides in Him ought himself to walk in the same manner as He walked" (1 John 2:6; cf. 3:24; 4:13–15; 2 John 9; 3 John 11).

The writer to the Hebrews tells his readers to be "imitators of those who through faith and patience inherit the promises" (Heb. 6:12; cf. 13:7, 9).

The mandate from Paul. Paul also exemplifies the pastor's mandate to disciple-making. He wrote the Corinthians, "I exhort you therefore, be imitators of me" (1 Cor. 4:16). It was not simply Paul they were to imitate, however, because he later wrote, "Be imitators of me, *just as I also am of Christ*" (1 Cor. 11:1, emphasis added). Further, he exhorted the Ephesians to "be imitators of God, as beloved children" (Eph. 5:1). He encouraged the brethren in Philippi to "join in following my example, and observe those who walk according to the pattern you have in us" (Phil. 3:17). He also told them, "The things you have learned and received and heard and seen in me, practice these things" (Phil. 4:9). That is why the Thessalonians were such an encouragement to Paul: "You also became imitators of us and of the Lord, having received the word in much tribulation with the joy of the Holy Spirit, so that you became an example to all the believers in Macedonia and in Achaia" (1 Thess. 1:6–7; cf. 2:14, 3:7).

---

5. Proper caution should be taken, however, not to overstate the disciple/discipler relationship because ultimately everyone is a disciple of Jesus, not of the individual who made him a disciple.

Of course, one of the best-known passages conveying the principle of making disciples, especially for pastors, is 2 Tim. 2:2: "And the things which you have heard from me in the presence of many witnesses, these entrust to faithful men, who will be able to teach others also."

Commenting on this verse, Adams has written,

> Men who qualify for the work of ministry are men who can keep the gospel torch burning brightly, *so that they are able to pass it on (undimmed) to those who follow.* . . . The people that Paul has in mind are men who "have what it takes" from God to do the work of the ministry. They are men with the gifts who have learned to use them skillfully in the work of shepherding.[6]

And they receive much of their skill by being discipled by other godly men. "Paul sees the whole Christian life as a recapitulation of the existence of Jesus and hence as an exercise of what other authors call discipleship."[7] Discipling as a mandate in the church is nowhere better summed up than in Rev. 14:4, where the 144,000 "follow the Lamb wherever He goes."

The evidence from the Old Testament and the New is clear: All believers, especially pastors/elders and other church leaders, are to make disciples of Jesus Christ. The question is, "What is the best way to implement this mandate?" The answer, of course, is to follow the method employed by Christ Himself!

CHRIST'S METHOD FOR DISCIPLING

The best method for discipling others is that of the Master discipler. Faithful pastors should look to Him to discover a methodology. When they do so, they will discover four key principles followed by Jesus; principles that when applied, will revolutionize their making of disciples. The most succinct expression of those principles is in Mark 3:13–15, "And he went up to the mountain and summoned those whom He Himself wanted, and they came to Him. And He appointed twelve, that they might be with Him, and that He might send them out to preach, and to have authority to cast out the demons."

---

6. Jay Adams, *Shepherding God's Flock* (Grand Rapids: Zondervan, 1975), 16, emphasis added.

7. Wilkins, *Following the Master*, 306.

Prayerful Meditation

The first principle Jesus used was that of prayerful meditation. Though Mark only says that Jesus "went up to the mountain" (v. 13), Luke 6:12–13 says plainly that "He went off to the mountain to pray, and He spent the whole night in prayer to God. And when day came, He called His disciples to Him." Somewhere on the west side of the Sea of Galilee, Jesus Christ was praying for the Father's guidance in choosing His disciples. This was no insignificant task in the life of our Lord. This decision would affect not only the coming age of the church, but also the entire course of history! The suggestion that Jesus—being God in human flesh—did not need to pray (as some have suggested) since He already knew the perfect will of God, questions the very integrity of Jesus Himself. Mark records explicitly that Jesus did pray! He is the God-Man, but He desired to commune with His heavenly Father in order to make a God-honoring choice. The choice was a monumental commitment, and the Lord faithfully bathed His decision in prayer. In his classic, *The Example of Jesus Christ*, Stalker has written,

> We find Him [Jesus] engaged in special prayer just before taking very important steps in life. One of the most important steps He ever took was the selection from among His disciples of the Twelve who were to be His apostles. It was an act on which the whole future of Christianity depended; and what was He doing before it took place? "It came to pass in those days that He went into a mountain to pray, and continued all night in prayer to God, and, when it was day He called unto Him His disciples, and of them He chose twelve, whom He also named apostles." It was after this night-long vigil, that He proceeded to the choice which was to be so momentous for Him, and for them, and for all the world. There was another day for which, we are told, He made similar preparation. It was that on which He first informed His disciples that He was to suffer and die. Thus it is evident, that, when Jesus had a day of crisis or difficult duty before Him, He gave Himself specially to prayer. Would it not simplify our difficulties if we attacked them in the same way? It would infinitely increase the intellectual insight with which we try to penetrate a problem and the power of the hand we lay upon duty. The wheels of existence would move far more smoothly and our purposes travel more surely to their aims, if every morning we reviewed beforehand the duties of the day with God."[8]

---

8. James Stalker, *The Example of Jesus Christ* (New Canaan, Conn.: Keats, 1980), 92.

The principle of Christ's prayerful meditation for the selection of His disciples is obvious. If a pastor is going to fulfill the mandate of the Great Commission, he must prayerfully meditate on choosing those whom he would devote his available time to nurture.[9] Whether it is someone whom he personally has led to the Master or a believer who needs further nurturing in the faith, his duty is to pray for them. And if Jesus Christ Himself spent all night in prayer for His disciples, how much more should church leaders? Paul commands us to pray without ceasing (1 Thess. 5: 17), and selecting those for discipleship certainly deserves this unceasing attitude of prayer.

Paul's encouragement to pray about everything (Phil. 4:6) no doubt must include the discipling of others (cf. Eph. 6:18). His prayers for his younger associates are numerous in the Pastoral Epistles (e.g., 1 Tim. 1:2; 2:8; 6:21; 2 Tim. 1:2–3; 4:1, 22; Titus 1:4; 3:15).

When Jesus Christ prayed for His own, He set a tremendous example, especially for pastors. He gave His disciples an example by choosing them prayerfully.

Careful Selection

The second principle from Jesus' example is careful selection, as Mark 3:13 indicates: "[He] summoned those whom He Himself wanted, and they came to Him."

Historically, Jesus Christ commanded men to follow Him. The pastor committed to discipling others can have three distinct assurances in implementing this process. First, he has the assurance that Christ has *commanded* those whom *He* wants for discipleship. In general, Matt. 28:18–20 guarantees the making of disciples, because Christ commanded it, and what He commands, His grace will accomplish. The book of Acts shows clearly that Christ promised the empowering of the Holy Spirit to those who were to make disciples (e.g., Acts 1:8; 4:7–8, 31–33; 6:8). It also shows the result (e.g., Acts 2:41, 47; Acts 6:7; 8:12). This is also a great promise to rest on in the process of making disciples.

Second, those whom Christ summons will be "those whom He Himself" wants (Mark 3:13). This attests to His real sovereignty in salvation and sanctification. Morgan has rightly observed,

---

9. It should also be mentioned that not only did Jesus pray for their selection, He prayed for His disciples throughout His earthly ministry (cf. John 17; Luke 22:31–32), and beyond (cf. Heb. 7:25).

This word suggests self-determining sovereignty, choice based upon reason within personality. . . . He was entirely uninfluenced by temporary appeals. No appeal that any man might have made to Him would have influenced Him in the least. No protests of inability that any man might have suggested would have changed His purpose. His choosing was choosing from within, the choosing of His own sovereignty; a choosing therefore in which He assumed all responsibility for what He did.[10]

It is only by the will of God that anyone becomes a disciple of Christ and that anyone receives discipleship training in Christ (John 1:12–13; 3:6; 6:44, 63, 65, 70; 8:36; 10:3–4, 16; 15:5, 16; 1 John 4: 19). Subject to that same sovereignty, spiritual leaders should carefully select and disciple those to whom God chooses to impart eternal life. Just as the apostles led the congregation in selecting servants in Acts 6:1–6, so leaders today must carefully select others to nurture and teach for service in the body of Christ (Eph. 4:11–16). In addition, as Paul instructed Timothy to entrust spiritual truth to faithful men, church leaders should select such men in whom to reproduce spiritual leadership.[11]

The third assurance a pastor can have in careful selection of prospective disciples is in Mark's phrase, "and they came to Him" (Mark 3:13). This shows that though discipling is a matter of Christ's command and sovereignty, obedience will be the result. Likewise, those who respond in obedience to the gospel summons will obviously be the most likely candidates. These will be willing to take up their cross daily (Luke 9:23)[12] and will evidence their readiness for discipleship. However, a word of caution is in order. Eims has warned, "Whoever is thinking about or is now involved in a ministry of making disciples . . . should think soberly about this matter of selection. It is much easier to ask a man to come with you than to ask him to leave if you learn, much to your chagrin and sorrow, that you

---

10. G. Campbell Morgan, *The Gospel According to Mark* (Tarrytown, N.Y.: Revell, 1927), 66.

11. For a discussion of the call to ministry, please refer to chapter 6 of this book and to John MacArthur's taped message, GC 55–23, "Marks of the Faithful Preacher, pt. 4," (Grace To You, P.O. Box 4000, Panorama City, CA 91412). See also John MacArthur, Jr., *Ephesians, The MacArthur New Testament Commentary* (Chicago: Moody, 1986), 94–95. See also C. H. Spurgeon's, *Lectures to My Students* (Grand Rapids: Zondervan, 1954), 22–41.

12. For an in-depth analysis of this and other crucial passages in these contexts, see John MacArthur, Jr., *The Gospel According to Jesus*, rev. ed. (Grand Rapids: Zondervan, 1994); also MacArthur, *Faith Works: The Gospel According to the Apostles* (Dallas: Word, 1993).

have chosen the wrong man."[13] The chooser must, therefore, be sober and vigilant in his choice. The principle of careful selection was Jesus' method of identifying men to propagate God's kingdom. Church leaders must not forget that men, not programs, are the method of Jesus. Eims has cautioned,

> I have watched men catch the vision of reaching the world for Christ. I have caught this vision, and have dedicated my life to this grand and glorious aim. But I have seen some men become so goal-oriented that to achieve their goals they roughly shoulder their way past people who need help and encouragement.
>
> But what is our objective? What are our goals? When we all get to heaven it will all be vividly and pointedly clear. We will find only people in heaven. There will be no committee notes, no scholarly papers on intriguing themes, no lengthy studies, memos, or surveys. People are the raw material of heaven. If we become enamored with projects, goals, and achievements, and never lend a hand to people along the way; and if we say, "Doing this will not help me accomplish my objective," what are we really thinking about? Self! Exactly opposite to the lifestyle of Jesus Christ.[14]

Similarly, Hull says,

> Most Christians believe that men are indeed the method of Jesus, but precious few are willing to invest their lives by putting all their eggs in that one basket. Believing this people-oriented philosophy and practicing it are entirely different matters. A large problem in Christendom is that we don't want to take the risk or the time to invest in the lives of people, even though this was a fundamental part of Jesus' ministry. We fear, that the basket is really a trap to ensnare us.[15]

In his classic work, *The Training of The Twelve*, Bruce summarizes this matter of careful selection:

> Why did Jesus choose such men? . . . If He chose rude, unlearned, humble men it was not because He was animated by any petty jealousy

---

13. Leroy Eims, *The Lost Art of Disciple Making* (Grand Rapids: Zondervan, Colorado Springs: Navpress, 1978), 29.

14. Leroy Eims, *Disciples in Action* (Colorado Springs: Navpress, and Wheaton: Victor, 1981), 40.

15. Bill Hull , *Jesus Christ: Disciple Maker* (Old Tappan, N.J.: Revell, 1984), 22. For two similar works by the same author and publisher, see his *The Disciple Making Church*, 1990 and *The Disciple Making Pastor*, 1988.

of knowledge, culture, or good birth. If any rabbi, rich man, or ruler had been willing to yield himself unreservedly to the service of the kingdom, no objection would have been taken to him on account of his acquirements, possessions, or titles. . . . The truth is, that Jesus was obliged to be content with fishermen, and publicans, and quondam zealots, for apostles. They were the best that could be had. Those who deemed themselves better were too proud to become disciples, and thereby they excluded themselves from what all the world now sees to be the high honor of being the chosen princes of the kingdom. . . . He preferred devoted men who had none of these advantages to undevoted men who had them all. And with good reason; for it mattered little, except in the eyes of contemporary prejudice, what the social position or even the previous history of the twelve had been, provided they were spiritually qualified for the work to which they were called. What tells ultimately is, not what is without a man, but what is within.[16]

Purposeful Association

Mark tells of a third crucial principle for disciplers: spending purposeful time with disciples. Mark 3:14 notes that Jesus "appointed twelve, that they might be with Him." He says very plainly that Jesus Christ appointed His disciples for the very purpose of being with Him. The Greek text clause, *hina ōsin meta autou*, could mean, "For the purpose" (or "so," or even "with the result") "that they be with Him." Acts 4:13 later records the fruit of the apostles' time spent with Christ: "As they [the rulers, elders and scribes] observed the confidence of Peter and John, and understood that they were uneducated and untrained men, they were marveling, and began to recognize them *as having been with Jesus*" (emphasis added). The time with Jesus was not only for the purpose of growing and learning under His teaching, but for fellowship and refreshment through His modeling and example. On one occasion, after preaching and teaching, Jesus said, " 'Come away by yourselves to a lonely place and rest awhile.' (For there were many people coming and going, and they did not even have time to eat.) And they went away in the boat to a lonely place by themselves" (Mark 6:31–32).

Any effective pastoral ministry will emphasize spending valuable, Christ-honoring time with those who will eventually follow their pastor by entering the ministry. Paul's heart for Timothy was filled with a desire to have fellowship together in the things of the Lord. He said in 1 Tim. 3:14

---

16. A. B. Bruce, *The Training of the Twelve* (reprint, Grand Rapids: Kregel, 1988), 37–38.

that he was "hoping to come to [Timothy] before long." Then in 2 Tim. 1:4, he said that he was to see Timothy and "be filled with joy." Paul pleaded with Timothy to "make every effort to come to me soon" (2 Tim. 4:9) and to "make every effort to come before winter" (v. 21). This was not simply a fellowship to meet Paul's needs, but also a time of mutual refreshment and instruction. Paul had such a bond with his disciples! The following describes the occasion after he had discipled the elders of Ephesus for some years and knew they might not see him again: "When he had said these things, he knelt down and prayed with them all. And they began to weep aloud and embraced Paul, and repeatedly kissed him, grieving especially over the word which he had spoken, that they should see his face no more" (Acts 20:36–38). What pathos between Paul and his men!

The structure of such times spent together is flexible, of course, but the point is this: One cannot truly influence those he does not spend time with. If a pastor is going to reproduce himself in the lives of others, it will result from a purposeful association of spiritual fellowship and biblical nurturing. In another context, Whitney writes,

> If you suddenly realized you had no more time, would you regret how you have spent your time in the past and how you spend it now? The way you have used your time *can* be a great comfort to you in your last hour. You may not be happy with some of the ways you used your time, but won't you be pleased then for all the times of Spirit-filled living, for all occasions when you have obeyed Christ? Won't you be glad then for those parts of your life that you spent in the Scriptures, prayer, worship, evangelism, serving, fasting, etc., for the purpose of becoming more like the One before whom you are about to stand in judgment (John 5:22–29)? What great wisdom there is in living as Jonathan Edwards resolved to live: "Resolved, that I will live so, as I shall wish I had done when I come to die."[17]

Hadidian says, "How are you going to use your time, knowledge and ability? Will you use it on that which is temporal or on that which is eternal? How satisfying it will be when we are close to death to know that we are leaving behind other people who, committed to God, His Word and His people, are carrying out the work that we have entrusted to them."[18]

---

17. Donald S. Whitney, *Spiritual Disciplines for the Christian Life* (Colorado Springs: Navpress, 1991), 132.

18. Allen Hadidian, *Successful Discipling* (Chicago: Moody, 1979), 18.

Similarly, Bounds has written,

> We are constantly on a stretch, if not on a strain, to devise new methods, new plans, new organizations to advance the Church and secure enlargement and efficiency for the gospel. This trend of the day has a tendency to lose sight of the man or sink the man in the plan or organization. God's plan is to make much of the man, far more of him than of anything else. Men are God's method. The Church is looking for better methods; God is looking for better men.[19]

The pastor who is himself spending time with Christ will have a profound discipling influence on the ones he spends time with. As he encourages them to spend time with him in the Word of God, spiritual fruit will abound. This will also result in the accrual of fruit in the people his disciples will ultimately influence. It is impossible to overemphasize the principle of purposeful association. To the degree that a leader and his prospective disciples spend time together and with Christ, he will reap a plentiful harvest of Christlikeness to the glory of God (cf. Rom. 8:29).

Powerful Proclamation

The final aspect in making disciples is powerful proclamation: "And that he might send them out to preach, and to have authority to cast out the demons" (Mark 3:14–15). As Jesus purposed to spend time with His disciples, so He also purposed for them to go out and preach with authority. The Greek construction in verse 14 (the use of a *hina* purpose clause) is similar to the previous phrase and shows distinctly that Jesus' plan was to disciple these men in order to send them out to preach the gospel with power.

The principle for contemporary application is crucial.[20] Pastors do not simply spend time with others without that association turning outward.

---

19. E. M. Bounds, *Power Through Prayer* (Grand Rapids: Zondervan, n.d.), 11.

20. We must note that the powerful proclamation of the apostles is not repeatable. Since they held a unique office, they had a supernatural power from Christ that is unavailable today. That is why the apostle Paul called their miraculous works "the signs of a true apostle" (2 Cor. 12:12). He also spoke of the apostles' uniqueness by saying that the church itself has been "built upon the foundation of the apostles and prophets, Christ Jesus Himself being the cornerstone" (Eph. 2:20). As pastors/elders in the church today, we cannot claim apostolic authority and power, but our power comes from the Holy Spirit's power working through us to preach the Word of God. Our task is not to cast out demons by supernatural strength, but to proclaim powerfully the gospel (cf. Eph. 3:20; Col. 1:29; 2 Tim. 1:7; Rom. 1:16). For a full treatment of the issue of the uniqueness of the apostles, see John MacArthur, Jr., *Charismatic Chaos* (Grand Rapids: Zondervan, 1992), 120–25, 230–35.

This ultimately is the point of discipleship: their disciples make other disciples, and so on. Discipleship reaches into the domain of darkness and brings people into the kingdom of light; this is the whole purpose of discipleship. As preachers proclaim the powerful gospel, God makes disciples who will in turn proclaim that same powerful gospel to others. The discipling chain continues unbroken until the day of Jesus Christ.

An implicit principle also emerges from the text. Jesus discipled His men to preach with authority. He purposed to teach them about how to preach (*kērussein*, to "herald" with a commission to proclaim accurately the prescribed message) and to exercise authority (*exousian*, "power") in their world. Our calling, too, is to preach and live a righteous life with power in a godless world. Our discipling, then, must include a teaching and an exemplification of how to live the truth in Jesus' name. No other means is available to manifest such a transformed, Christlike life in an un-Christlike culture. The legacy we leave in and through the lives of others we disciple will be powerful and lasting.

THE DISCIPLE-MAKING IMPERATIVE

This chapter has endeavored to show that discipleship and disciple-making are not an option; they are a clear command from Scripture. One summary of the mandate's pervasiveness is, "The consensus in the history of the church—ancient and modern—is that the concept of discipleship is apparent everywhere in the New Testament, from Matthew through Revelation."[21]

Our role as pastors also *demands* that we be disciplers. We cannot be pulpiteers who preach at our people but have no involvement in their lives. The process only *begins* with the proclamation of Scripture. It finds its real fruition across the entire spectrum of the shepherd's work—feeding, leading, cleaning, bandaging, protecting, nurturing, and every other aspect of a tender shepherd's loving care. This *is* the process of discipling.

Jesus said that every disciple, when fully trained, will be just like his teacher (Luke 6:40). That places a very heavy weight of responsibility on the discipler to be like *his* Master, Jesus Christ. We cannot demand that men and women follow us unless, like Paul, we can confidently say that we are imitators of Christ (1 Cor. 11:1). Certainly any man who falters at this point has no business in the pastorate.

---

21. Wilkins, *Following the Master*, 293.

Moreover, any pastor who is not discipling others is abdicating a primary responsibility of his calling. The pastor's calling is to preach, but he cannot be merely an orator—talking at people but never really ministering to them on a personal level. The pastor is called to exhort and instruct, but he cannot be just a professional counselor—dispensing spiritual wisdom from across a desk and apart from holding people accountable. The pastor must lead, but he cannot become a full-time administrator—bogged down with paperwork and business, forgetting that the church is *people*.

God has not called us to be professional clergymen; He has called us to be disciple-makers. Paul's mandate in 2 Tim. 2:2 extends to every leader of the *ekklēsia* of God: "The things which you have heard from me in the presence of many witnesses, these entrust to faithful men, who will be able to teach others also." That may be the best one-verse summary of the pastoral role with regard to discipling in all of Scripture.

The real test of every pastor's mettle is how he does in the arena of personal discipleship. It is there that people get to know him best and see him for who he really is. It is there that he will test his biblical knowledge most thoroughly. It is there that he is most accountable. And it is there—helping others grow more and more Christlike—that he will become more like the Master.

20

Watching and Warning

Richard L. Mayhue

Guarding Christ's flock of believers from spiritual danger is one of the most neglected pastoral duties in today's church. In addition to commissioning spiritual sentinels to watch over His flock by directing them into truth and righteousness, God has charged these sentinels to protect the flock from doctrinal error and personal sin. Ezekiel 3, 33, and Acts 20 provide clear instruction on the why's and how's of being a pastoral watchman. Undershepherds of the flock will be good servants and obedient imitators of the Chief Shepherd when they regularly watch for and warn of encroaching spiritual dangers.

"Reengineering the Church" was the theme of a recent pastoral leadership conference on how to prepare the church for the twenty-first century. As I read the conference brochure, my initial response was, "Why reengineer the church when God designed it perfectly in the beginning? Shouldn't we inspect the church first and demolish only the defective portions, so we can rebuild the demolished part according to the Builder's original plan? Who can improve on God's engineering?" The solution is not reengineering, but restoration to the perfect original specifications of the divine Designer. The goal of any changes should be a return to the church's biblical roots if she will ever regain her former glory.

An inspection of the existing church should include such questions as: Have we consulted the *Owner* (1 Cor. 3:9)? Are we dealing with the *original Builder* (Matt. 16:18)? Does the church still rest on the *beginning foundation* (1 Cor. 3:11; Eph. 2:20)? Is the *first Cornerstone* still in place (Eph. 2:20; 1 Pet. 2:4–8)? Are we using *approved building materials* (1 Pet. 2:5)? Do we employ the right *laborers* (1 Cor. 3:9)? Have we utilized the appropriate *supervisors* (Eph. 4:11–13)? Are the initial *standards of quality control* still in place (Eph. 4:13–16)? Are we continuing to work from the *original blueprint* (2 Tim. 3:16–17)?

The biblical approach to keeping the church on track during the next century requires that the role of the *construction supervisors* (i.e., God's appointed shepherds who keep watch over His flock) be one of the first areas for review. According to one biblical metaphor, the *supervisors* in the picture of the church as a building are none other than the *shepherds* of the flock according to another figure. The remainder of this discussion will use the latter terminology.[1]

Paul laid out the basic task of a shepherd with these words:

And He gave some as apostles, and some as prophets, and some as evangelists, and some as *pastors and teachers*, for the equipping of the saints for the work of service, to the building up of the body of Christ; until we all attain to the unity of the faith, and of the knowledge of the Son of God, to a mature man, to the measure of the stature which belongs to the fulness of Christ. As a result, we are no longer to be children, tossed here and there by waves, and carried about by every wind of doctrine, by the trickery of men, by craftiness in deceitful scheming; but speaking the truth in love, we are to grow up in all aspects into Him, who is the head, even Christ, from whom the whole body, being fitted and held together by that which every joint supplies, according to the proper working of each individual part, causes the growth of the body for the building up of itself in love (Eph. 4:11–16, emphasis added).

THE TRUE SHEPHERD

Scripture continually alerts its readers to watch for spiritual counterfeits.[2] Jesus warned of "false prophets, who come to you in sheep's clothing, but inwardly are ravenous wolves" (Matt. 7:15). Elsewhere He characterizes the false shepherd as "a thief and a robber" (John 10:1, see also v. 8).

Nowhere in Scripture is this more apparent than in the Old Testament prophets who incessantly warned Israel about false prophets, even rebuking the nation when they strayed by following a false leader rather than

---

1. For a succinct study of the picture of the church as a flock of sheep, see Earl D. Radmacher, *What the Church Is All About: A Biblical and Historical Study* (Chicago: Moody, 1978), 298–307.

2. The New Testament frequently exposes the false (ψευδής) such as with (1) false apostles (2 Cor. 11:13), (2) false brethren (2 Cor. 11:26; Gal. 2:4), (3) false Christs (Matt. 24:24), (4) false prophets (Matt. 24:11; 2 Pet. 2:1; 1 John 4:1), (5) false teachers (2 Pet. 2:1), and (6) false witnesses (Matt. 26:60; Acts 6:13).

a true one.[3] Though not as historically dramatic as the Old, frequently the New Testament also warns against deceiving, misleading spiritual leaders.[4] Every succeeding generation of history has proven the need for this caution. It remains a preeminent concern of God that the church be led by true shepherds.

In the 1891 Lyman Beecher lectures on preaching at Yale, James Stalker insightfully cautioned, "The higher the honour attaching to the ministerial profession, when it is worthily filled, the deeper is the abuse of which it is capable in comparison with other callings.[5] Unfortunately, the genuine attracts the uninvited clever imitation. Realistically, the true shepherd must protect the flock from the spurious. Shepherds have explicit instructions from Scripture to warn the flock that not everyone who claims to be a true shepherd is speaking the truth.

Charles Jefferson, in his classic work, *The Minister As Shepherd*, lists seven basic functions of the genuine shepherd:[6]

1.   to love the sheep

2.   to feed the sheep

3.   to rescue the sheep

4.   to attend and comfort the sheep

5.   to guide the sheep

6.   to guard and protect the sheep

7.   to watch over the sheep.

This chapter treats Jefferson's last two categories in particular—guarding and watching over the sheep. No other aspect of contemporary pastoral ministry has fallen into disuse more than the lifesaving role of a *watchman*. It is vital for effective ministry to recover the aspect of shepherdly vigilance

---

3.   For example, see Jeremiah 14, 23; Ezekiel 13, 34; Micah 3; Zechariah 11.

4.   For example, see Matthew 23; 2 Corinthians 11; 2 Timothy 3–4; Titus 1; 2 Peter 2; 1 John 4; 2 John 8–11; Jude; Revelation 2–3.

5.   James Stalker, *The Preacher and His Models* (New York: George H. Doran, 1891), 128.

6.   Charles Jefferson, *The Minister As Shepherd* (reprint, Hong Kong: Living Books, 1973), 39–66. See also John F. MacArthur, Jr., *The Master's Plan for the Church* (Chicago: Moody, 1991), 169–76.

that guards and protects the flock from preventable spiritual carnage. The true pastor will make the safety of Christ's flock a top priority. In so doing, he will also help rid the pastoral ranks of pollution brought by unauthorized look-alikes.

OVERSEEING THE FLOCK

Each of the terms *pastor*, *elder*, and *overseer* describes facets of the shepherd's role. All three appear together in Acts 20:17, 28 and 1 Pet. 5:1–2. *Elder* and *overseer* link up in Titus 1 while *overseer* and *shepherd* both describe Christ in 1 Pet. 2:25. Because of its relevance to the present subject, *overseer* will be the focus of attention in the following treatment.

Thomas Oden in a brief word captures the particular characteristic of watchfulness inherent in the term *overseer*: "Bishop translates *episkopos*, which is derived from the family of Greek words referring to guardianship, oversight, inspection—accountably looking after a complex process in a comprehensive sense. *Episkopos* implies vigilance far more than hierarchy."[7]

A shepherd's *oversight* of the flock expresses itself broadly in two ways.[8] First, shepherds provide truthful, positive direction and leadership to the flock. Second, they warn of spiritual dangers such as sin, false teaching, and false teachers, including Satan's assaults against the saints.

On one hand, the shepherd teaches truth, and on the other, he warns of sin and refutes doctrinal error. In leading the flock down the path of righteousness, the shepherd also watches for, warns, and even rescues the stray who has been enticed by false teaching and alluring sin. When shepherds exercise their oversight responsibly, they will have both a preventative and a confrontive side to their ministry. One cannot shepherd the flock with credibility unless he provides a corrective oversight of watching and warning.

---

7. Thomas C. Oden, *Pastoral Theology: Essentials of Ministry* (San Francisco: HarperCollins, 1983), 71.

8. Pastoral oversight of others assumes that the shepherd has first exercised his own "self-watch" of which C. H. Spurgeon writes in *Lectures to My Students*, series 1 (reprint, Grand Rapids: Baker, 1977), 1–17. More recently John Stott has observed, "Only if pastors first guard themselves, will they be able to guard the sheep. Only if pastors first tend their own spiritual life, will they be able to tend the flock of God" in "Ideals of Pastoral Ministry," *Bibliotheca Sacra* 146, no. 581 (January–March 1989): 11.

PASTORAL VIGILANCE

American patriot Thomas Jefferson observed that "eternal vigilance is the price of victory."[9] He spoke of political victory, but it is even more true for the church if she is to win out over false teaching and sin. W. Phillip Keller warned of *Predators in Our Pulpits* through his recent call to restore true, biblical preaching to churches around the world.[10] *Predator* might sound harsh, but it nonetheless follows the example of Christ, who rightfully called the Pharisees blind guides, serpents, and whitewashed tombs (Matthew 23). God's spiritual sentry must be forthright in his challenges and strongly confront those who would maliciously usurp the true shepherd's tasks, thereby leading Christ's flock astray.

The Shepherd of Psalm 23 comforted the sheep with His rod and staff.[11] These implements not only symbolize vigilance, but in the Shepherd's hand they are also instruments of protection and direction, which are the fruit of vigilance. The rod protected the flock against immediate, encroaching danger. The staff served to assemble the sheep, to guide them, and even to rescue them should they wander away. Likewise the shepherd of Christ's flock—the church—must be vigilant. The spiritual health and integrity of the flock depend on his devotion to this phase of his responsibility.

In his day, Charles Jefferson memorably captured the protective aspect of an ancient Near Eastern shepherd's duty. The parallels to modern-day shepherding for pastors are obvious but, unfortunately, all too often ignored.

> The Eastern shepherd was, first of all, a watchman. He had a watch tower. It was his business to keep a wide-open eye, constantly searching the horizon for the possible approach of foes. He was bound to be circumspect and attentive. Vigilance was a cardinal virtue. An alert wakefulness was for him a necessity. He could not indulge in fits of drowsiness, for the foe was always near. Only by his alertness could the enemy be circumvented. There were many kinds of enemies, all of them terrible, each in a different way. At certain seasons of the year there were floods. Streams became quickly swollen and overflowed

---

9. John Bartlett, *Familiar Quotations* (reprint, Boston: Little, Brown and Co., 1982), 397.

10. W. Phillip Keller, *Predators In Our Pulpits* (Eugene, Oreg.: Harvest House, 1988).

11. For a vivid description of the shepherd's rod and staff, see W. Phillip Keller, *A Shepherd Looks at Psalm 23* (Grand Rapids: Zondervan, 1970), 92–103,

their banks. Swift action was necessary in order to escape destruction. There were enemies of a more subtle kind—animals, rapacious and treacherous: lions, bears, hyenas, jackals, wolves. There were enemies in the air; huge birds of prey were always soaring aloft ready to swoop down upon a lamb or kid. And then, most dangerous of all, were the human birds and beasts of prey—robbers, bandits, men who made a business of robbing sheepfolds and murdering shepherds. That Eastern world was full of perils. It teemed with forces hostile to the shepherd and his flock. When Ezekiel, Jeremiah, Isaiah, and Habakkuk talk about shepherds, they call them watchmen set to warn and save.[12]

Vigilance, without question, starts in the pulpit, but it goes far beyond. Watching over the flock as a body does not preclude watching over the congregation as individuals. Strong pulpit ministry has always been the backbone of shepherding, but it does not exhaust the shepherd's responsibilities. Consider the persuasion of Charles Bridges:

> Let us not think that all our work is done in the study and in the pulpit. Preaching—the grand lever of the Ministry—derives much of its power from connexion with the Pastoral work; and its too frequent disjunction from it is a main cause of our inefficiency. The Pastor and Preacher combine to form the completeness of the sacred office, as expounded in our Ordination services and Scriptural illustrations. How little can a stated appearance in public answer to the lowest sense of such terms as Shepherd, Watchman, Overseer, Steward!—terms, which import not a mere general superintendence over the flock, charge, or household, but an acquaintance with their individual wants, and a distribution suitable to the occasion; without which, instead of "taking heed to the flock, over which the Holy Ghost hath made us overseers," we can scarcely be said to "take the oversight of it" at all.[13]

Pastoral oversight includes a strong emphasis on watching carefully for lurking spiritual danger according to the follow sampling of New Testament exhortations:

"And He was giving orders to them saying, 'Watch out! Beware of the leaven of the Pharisees and the leaven of Herod'" (Mark 8:15).

---

12. Jefferson, *The Minister*, 41–42.

13. Charles Bridges, *The Christian Minister* (reprint, Edinburgh, Scotland: Banner of Truth, 1980), 343.

"Beware of the scribes, who like to walk around in long robes, and love respectful greetings in the market places, and chief seats in the synagogues, and places of honor at banquets" (Luke 20:46).

"Beware of the dogs, beware of the evil workers, beware of the false circumcision (Phil. 3:2).

"Be of sober spirit, be on the alert. Your adversary, the devil, prowls about like a roaring lion, seeking someone to devour" (1 Pet. 5:8).

"Watch yourselves, that you might not lose what we have accomplished, but that you may receive a full reward" (2 John 8).

The early church took these biblical instructions seriously. For example, observe both the apostle John and his disciple Polycarp in action:

> The same Polycarp, coming to Rome under the episcopate of Anicetus, turned many from the aforesaid heretics to the church of God, proclaiming the one and only true faith, that he had received from the apostles, that, viz., which was delivered by the church. And there are those still living who heard him relate, that John the disciple of the Lord went into a bath at Ephesus, and seeing Cerinthus within, ran out without bathing, and exclaimed, "Let us flee lest the bath should fall in, as long as Cerinthus, that enemy of truth, is within." And the same Polycarp, once coming and meeting Marcion, who said, "acknowledge us, " he replied, "I acknowledge the first born of Satan." Such caution did the apostles and their disciples use, so as not even to have any communion, even in word with any of those that thus mutilated the truth, according to the declaration of Paul: "An heretical man after the first and second admonition avoid, knowing that such an one is perverse, and that he sins, bringing condemnation upon himself."[14]

The pattern continued to the fourth generation (Christ, John, and Polycarp being the first three) in the ministry of Irenaeus, a disciple of Polycarp:

> Inasmuch as certain men have set the truth aside, and bring in lying words and vain genealogies, which, as the apostle says, "minister questions rather than godly edifying which is in faith," and by means of

---

14. Eusebius Pamphilus, *Eusebius' Ecclesiastical History* (reprint, Grand Rapids: Guardian, 1955), 141–42.

their craftily-constructed plausibilities draw away the minds of the in-experienced and take them captive. [I have felt constrained, my dear friend, to compose the following treatise in order to expose and coun-teract their machinations.] These men falsify the oracles of God, and prove themselves evil interpreters of the good word of revelation. They also overthrow the faith of many, by drawing them away, under a pre-tence of [superior] knowledge, from Him who founded and adorned the universe; as if, forsooth, they had something more excellent and sublime to reveal, than that God who created the heaven and the earth, and all things that are therein. By means of specious and plausible words, they cunningly allure the simple-minded to inquire into their system; but they nevertheless clumsily destroy them, while they ini-tiate them into their blasphemous and impious opinions respecting the Demiurge; and these simple ones are unable, even in such a mat-ter, to distinguish falsehood from truth.[15]

More recently, in the mid-1960s, Harry Blamires has written a signifi-cant volume warning the British church of its rapid departure from truth. He has since been associated with the concept of "thinking Christianly" because of his clear call for the restoration of a Christian mind-set based on Scripture:

Our culture is bedeviled by the it's-all-a-matter-of-opinion code. In the sphere of religious and moral thinking we are rapidly heading for a state of intellectual anarchy in which the difference between truth and falsehood will no longer be recognized. Indeed it would seem pos-sible that the words *true* and *false* will eventually (and logically) be replaced by the words *likeable* and *dislikeable*. . . .

Christian truth is objective, four-square, unshakable. It is not built of men's opinions. It is not something fabricated either by scholars or by men in the street, still less something assembled from a million answers, Yes, No, and Don't know, obtained from a cross-section of the human race. Christian truth is something given, revealed, laid open to the eye of the patient, self-forgetful inquirer. You do not *make* the truth. You *reside* in the truth. A suitable image for truth would be that of a lighthouse lashed by the elemental fury of undisciplined error. Those who have come to reside in the truth must stay there. It is not their business to go back into error for the purpose of joining their drowning fellows with the pretence that, inside or outside, the conditions are pretty much the same. It is their duty to draw others

---

15. Ireneaus, *Against Heresies*, vol. 2 of *The Ante-Nicene Fathers*, ed. A. Roberts and J. Donaldson (reprint, Grand Rapids: Eerdmans, 1956), 315.

within the shelter of the truth. For truth is most certainly a shelter. And it is inviolable. If we start to dismantle it and give it away in bits to those outside, there will be nothing left to protect our own heads—and no refuge in which to receive the others, should they at length grow weary of error.[16]

What Blamires wrote to the British church of the '60s, David Wells has written to the American church in the '90s:

> The stream of historic orthodoxy that once watered the evangelical soul is now damned by a worldliness that many fail to recognize as worldliness because of the cultural innocence with which it presents itself. To be sure, this orthodoxy never was infallible, nor was it without its blemishes and foibles, but I am far from persuaded that the emancipation from its theological core that much of evangelicalism is effecting has resulted in greater biblical fidelity. In fact, the result is just the opposite. We now have less biblical fidelity, less interest in truth, less seriousness, less depth, and less capacity to speak the Word of God to our own generation in a way that offers an alternative to what it already thinks. The older orthodoxy was driven by a passion for truth, and that was why it could express itself only in theological terms. The newer evangelicalism is not driven by the same passion for truth, and that is why it is often empty of theological interest.[17]

Both Blamires and Wells stand in the long, unbroken chain of gallant men who have taken seriously the biblical injunctions to watch and warn. They serve as exemplars of shepherdly vigilance in the best tradition of the New Testament overseer.[18]

Paul wrote Titus that an overseer should hold "fast the faithful word which is in accordance with the teaching, that he may be able both to exhort in sound doctrine and to refute those who contradict" (Titus 1:9). To

---

16. Harry Blamires, *The Christian Mind* (reprint, Ann Arbor: Servant, 1978), 112-14.

17. David F. Wells, *No Place for Truth or Whatever Happened to Evangelical Theology* (Grand Rapids: Eerdmans, 1993), 11–12.

18. Doctrinal error does not always appear in its most obvious or despicable form. "Error, indeed, is never set forth in its naked deformity, lest, being thus exposed, it should at once be detected. But it is craftily decked out in an attractive dress, so as, by its outward form, to make it appear to the inexperienced (ridiculous as the expression may seem) more true than the truth itself" (Irenaeus, *Against Heresies*, 315). For a current discussion of the church's weakness in discerning truth and doctrine, see John F. MacArthur, Jr., *Reckless Faith* (Wheaton, Ill.: Crossway, 1994).

exhort only and not to refute amounts to spiritual insubordination, even gross disobedience. Certainly, it is nothing less than dereliction of duty.

John Stott recently exposed and confronted the growing negligence of late twentieth-century shepherds in their failure to watch for and confront doctrinal error:

> This emphasis is unpopular today. It is frequently said that pastors must always be positive in their teaching, never negative. But those who say this have either not read the New Testament or, having read it, they disagree with it. For the Lord Jesus and His apostles gave the example and even set forth the obligation to be negative in refuting error. Is it possible that the neglect of this ministry is one of the major causes of theological confusion in the church today? To be sure, theological controversy is distasteful to sensitive spirits and has its spiritual dangers. Woe to those who enjoy it! But it cannot conscientiously be avoided. If, when false teaching arises, Christian leaders sit idly by and do nothing or turn tail and flee, they will earn the terrible epithet "hirelings" who care nothing for Christ's flock. Is it right to abandon His sheep and leave them defenseless against the wolves to be like "sheep without a shepherd"? Is it right to be content to see the flock scattered and individual sheep torn to pieces? Is it to be said of believers today, as it was of Israel, that "they were scattered for lack of a shepherd, and they became food for every beast of the field" (Ezek. 34:5)? Today even some of the fundamental doctrines of historic Christianity are being denied by some church leaders, including the infinite personality of the living God, the eternal deity, virgin birth, atoning death, bodily resurrection of Jesus, the Trinity, and the gospel of justification by grace alone through faith alone without any meritorious works. Pastors are to protect God's flock from error and seek to establish them in the truth.[19]

Spiritual Sentinels

Any godly shepherd at the end of his ministry would like to be able to say with Paul, "I have fought the good fight, I have finished the course, I have kept the faith" (2 Tim. 4:7). Who would not want to hear the Lord's commendation, "Well done, good and faithful servant" (Matt. 25:21 NIV).

---

19. Stott, "Ideals of Pastoral Ministry," 8.

Paul told the Ephesian elders, "I am innocent of the blood of all men" (Acts 20:26). Using the imagery of Ezekiel 3:18, 20—"his blood I will require at your hand"—the apostle testified that he had delivered God's Word to both the lost and the saints. When unbelievers died in their sins, Paul had no pastoral blame since he fully discharged his duty of preaching the gospel (Acts 20:21). If believers strayed and engaged in prolonged patterns of sin, it was not because Paul did not communicate the whole purpose of God (Acts 20:27).

If today's shepherds want to finish their ministry like Paul, then they must not only be *approved workmen* (2 Tim. 2:15), but also *unashamed watchmen*. The theme of pastoral watchman is striking in Ezek. 3:16–21; 33:1–9. Later, Paul appropriately employed the same language to describe his ministry (Acts 20:17–31).

Watchman

God spoke to Ezekiel, "Son of man, I have appointed you a watchman to the house of Israel; whenever you hear a word from My mouth, warn them from Me" (Ezek. 3:17; cf. 2:7). The prophet then spoke to both the wicked (3:18–19) and the righteous (3:20–21).

Ezekiel 33:1–6 relates the duties of a military watchman to that of a shepherd. Watchmen attentively manned their post in order to warn the city of approaching danger and deliver the citizens from harm. If watchmen diligently discharge their duty, regardless of the outcome, they will be blameless (33:2–5). However, if a watchman fails to alert the city to danger, blame for the resultant destruction falls on him, as if he were the enemy and had personally attacked the city (33:6).

Twentieth-century pastoring provides appropriate parallels. The shepherd is to stand watch over the flock as the watchman did over the city. God's warnings apply to both unbelieving sheep outside the flock and believing sheep within the flock. To the degree that pastors faithfully deliver God's Word, regardless of the results, they will receive divine commendation. However, when the shepherd neglects the duties of his post, God will hold him accountable for failing to signal coming danger and judgment.

In a life-and-death situation, he must alertly tend the flock like a vigilant watchman protects his city. Thomas Oden captures the pastoral analogy:

> The image of pastor as watchman, or protective, vigilant all-night guard, was already well developed by the Hebrew prophets. Radical accountability to God was the central feature of this analogy, as dra-

matically stated by Ezekiel: "The word of the Lord came to me: . . . I have made you a watchman for the Israelites. . . . It may be that a righteous man turns away and does wrong. . . . I will hold you answerable for his death" (Ezek. 3:16–21). Such injunctions for prophetic accountability have often been transferred by analogy to the Christian office of elder.

Listen to the analogy: The watchman over a city is responsible for the whole city, not just one street of it. If the watchman sleeps through an attack, the whole resultant damage is his responsibility. This was the covenantal analogy later applied repeatedly to the pastor, who was charged with nothing less than caring for the souls of an analogous small city, the *ekklēsia*. If the congregation falls prey to seductive teaching or forgetfulness, whose responsibility can it be but that of the presbuteros, the guiding elder?[20]

Workmen

Paul's address to the elders of the Ephesian church comprises the most explicit and complete instruction on spiritual leadership given to a New Testament church. He relies heavily on the imagery and ideas of Ezekiel 3 and 33.[21] The watchman theme extended itself far beyond Ezekiel's personal ministry. Not only did Paul serve as a vigilant sentinel, but he commands the elders of Ephesus to do likewise.

At least five features attest to the close parallel between Ezekiel 3, 33, and Acts 20. First, both Ezekiel and the Ephesian elders were appointed by God. "I have appointed you a watchman" (Ezek. 3:17). "The Holy Spirit has made you overseers" (Acts 20:28). The commission in both instances resulted from God's direct call to ministry.

Second, the task assigned to both essentially involved vigilant oversight. The Hebrew צוֹפֶה (*sôpeh*), translated "watchman" in Ezek. 3:16, is

---

20. Oden, *Pastoral Theology*, 70. Great church reformers of the past like John Knox (*The First Blast of the Trumpet*, in *On Rebellion*, ed. Roger A. Mason [Cambridge, England: Cambridge University, 1994], 7–8) and Martin Luther (*Luther's Works*, vol. 39, ed. by Eric W. Gritch [Philadelphia: Fortress, 1957], 249–50) clearly sensed the watchman analogy in Ezekiel 3, 33—a factor that strongly influenced their ministries.

21. See F. F. Bruce, *The Book of Acts*, in NICNT (Grand Rapids: Eerdmans, 1980), 415; Charles Lee Feinberg, *The Prophecy of Ezekiel* (Chicago: Moody, 1969), 29; Everett F. Harrison, *Acts* (Chicago: Moody, 1975), 315; Evald Lövestam, "Paul's Address at Miletus," *Studia Theologica* 41 (1987): 1–10; Walter R. Roehrs, "Watchmen in Israel: Pastoral Guidelines from Ezekiel 1–3," *Concordia Journal* 16, no. 1 (January 1990): 6–17; Stott, "Ideals of Pastoral Ministry," 6–7.

rendered σκοπός (*skopos*) in the Greek LXX version.[22] Compare this to ἐπίσκοπος (*episkopos*), translated "overseer," in Acts 20:28.[23] Both prophet and shepherd are accountable to God as a spiritual sentry responsible to warn of impending danger. Paul warned the Ephesian elders,

> Be on guard for yourselves and for all the flock, among which the Holy Spirit has made you overseers, to shepherd the church of God which He purchased with His own blood. I know that after my departure savage wolves will come in among you, not sparing the flock; and from among your own selves men will arise, speaking perverse things, to draw away the disciples after them. Therefore be on the alert, remembering that night and day for a period of three years I did not cease to admonish each one with tears (Acts 20:28–31).

Third, in both passages the watchman is assigned to deliver God's Word as His warning. What proved true of Ezekiel (2:7, 3:17, 33:7) also marked Paul's ministry (Acts 20:20–21, 27). They both delivered the Word of God without compromise. That is why the apostle commended the elders to the Word of God's grace, which would be their message likewise (Acts 20:32).

Fourth, the watchman had a word for both the unrighteous (Ezek. 3:18–19; 33:8–9) and the righteous (Ezek. 3:20–21). Paul preached repentance to both Jew and Gentile (Acts 20:21) and the whole purpose of God to the church (Acts 20:20, 27). This twofold responsibility to reach the lost with the gospel and to watch over the saints continues to the present.

Fifth, both Ezekiel and Paul considered their watchman/oversight duties to be issues of highest importance—a matter of life and death. When Ezekiel carried out his task, regardless of the outcome, he had delivered himself from any spiritual liability (3:19, 21). On the other hand, if he failed to sound the warning, God promised, "His blood I will require at your

---

22. A watchman is "fully aware of a situation in order to gain some advantage or keep from being surprised by the enemy" (*The Wordbook of the Old Testament*, vol. 2, ed. R. Laird Harris, et al. [Chicago: Moody, 1980], 773). "Watchman" is used in a true military sense in 1 Sam. 14:16; 2 Sam. 18:24; 2 Kgs. 9:17–20; Isa. 21:6. Watching in a spiritual sense also appears in Jer. 6:17; Hab. 2:1.

23. John Calvin, *Commentaries on Ezekiel*, vol. 1 (reprint, Grand Rapids: Eerdmans, n.d.), 148–49, commented, "For we know that the word Bishop means the same as watchman." The related verb σκοπέω (*skopeō*) is used in the New Testament of both watching for the positive (Phil. 3:17) and for the dangerous (Rom. 16:17).

hand" (3:18, 20; 33:8). Paul reported, "I am innocent of the blood of all men" (Acts 20:26).

The concept of blood being on your head or hands originated in Gen. 9:5–6, which articulates the judicial principle of capital punishment. This idea finds application in three categories of life.

1. Actual death, whether intentional (Josh. 2:19, 1 Kings. 2:33; Matt. 27:25; Acts 5:28) or accidental (Exod. 22:2; Deut. 22:8).

2. Heinous crimes not involving death but deserving of death as punishment (Lev. 20:9, 11–13, 16, 27).

3. Spiritual matters of life and death proportion (Ezek. 3:18, 20; 33:4, 6, 8; Acts 18:6; 20:26).

When the shepherd's responsibility as taught in Ezekiel 3, 33, and Acts 20 gets our attention, we will understand increasingly why Paul exclaimed, "For woe is me if I do not preach the gospel" (1 Cor. 9:16). The apostle fully understood the serious responsibility given to him by God as a preacher of the gospel. He would incur the displeasure of God should he do anything less. Watching and warning are duties in preaching the gospel that are required, not optional or left to a specialist.

Ezekiel and Paul also shed light on Heb. 13:17. The biblical writer succinctly cites the implication of being a faithful overseer, one who watches over the flock and will one day give an account for his labors: "Obey your leaders, and submit to them; for they keep watch over your souls, as those who will give an account. Let them do this with joy and not with grief, for this would be unprofitable for you." Pastors will give an account to God for watching and warning the flock in spiritual matters. Vigilance plays a vital part in the ministry entrusted by God to His pastoral servants.

A GOOD SERVANT OF JESUS CHRIST

"In pointing out these things to the brethren, you will be a good servant of Christ Jesus, constantly nourished on the words of the faith and of the sound doctrine which you have been following" (1 Tim. 4:6). For the spiritual good of the Ephesian church, Paul insisted that Timothy point out "these things," referring back to the false doctrine exposed in 4:1–3 and truth taught in 4:4–5. "A good servant of Jesus Christ" points them out to the flock by way of warning and instruction.[24] Failure to warn invites a spiritual Chernobyl, because real danger still exists even though the sheep are unaware. Ultimately, they will suffer harm through the negligence of a shepherd to sound a timely warning.

As a former naval officer, I have stood many four-hour watches on the bridge of a destroyer at sea. During the watch I had responsibility for the operation and safety of the ship. If a dangerous situation appeared, I had to warn both the captain and the crew. They depended on my alertness in carrying out my assigned task. Failure to function would have amounted to gross negligence on my part, possible damage to the ship or loss of life, and the dishonorable end of my naval career. Just as a good naval officer warns when danger lurks nearby, so must a good servant of Jesus Christ.

Be assured that it is good to protect the flock from false teachers, untrue doctrine, and personal sin.[25] They will find comfort in your diligent protection (Ps. 23:4). If you begin by preaching the whole of Scripture, then the process of watching and warning will take place in the normal course of ministry, because His saints receive warnings through the truth of God's Word (Ps. 19:11).

Paul, the courageous shepherd, had only a few fears. This is one of them: "But I am afraid, lest as the serpent deceived Eve by his craftiness, your minds should be led astray from the simplicity and purity of devotion to Christ" (2 Cor. 11:3).

As good servants of Jesus Christ we will share this fear with Paul, not as a sign of weakness or cowardice, but as a significant demonstration of spiritual strength coupled with a clear sense of spiritual reality. To do less would result in hollow ministry, invite Christ's displeasure with our service, and endanger the spiritual health of the flock. Their blood would be on our hands. Because the flock is so susceptible to deception, shepherds must be ever vigilant.

Jesus Christ stands as the ultimate Shepherd and Guardian of our souls (1 Pet. 2:25). Today's undershepherds could do no better than to follow His example of watching and warning. To do less would be biblically unthinkable and spiritually unconscionable.

---

24. C. H. Spurgeon proved to be a classic watchman in the nineteenth century in such writings as "How to Meet the Evils of the Age" and "The Evils of the Present Time" (in *An All-Round Ministry* [reprint, Pasadena, Tex.: Pilgrim, 1983], 89–127, 282–314).

25. For helpful material on church discipline as a means of dealing with and prayfully restoring a sinning believer, see J. Carl Laney, *A Guide to Church Discipline* (Minneapolis: Bethany, 1985) and John MacArthur, Jr., *Matthew 16–23* (Chicago: Moody, 1988), 123–39.

21

Observing Ordinances

John MacArthur, Jr.

Communion and baptism are the two ordinances instituted by Christ for observance by the church. Communion grew out of the last Passover of Christ with His disciples before His crucifixion. Later, Paul corrected the Corinthian church because they had perverted the commemoration through their selfish conduct. The purpose of Communion is to proclaim the death of Christ symbolically. It behooves each Christian to prepare himself carefully each time he celebrates the Lord's Supper. Also, Christians should view the ordinance of baptism with the utmost seriousness. This means that no one who professes faith in Christ should remain unbaptized. Baptism portrays a believer's identification with Christ in His death, burial, and resurrection. Jesus personally submitted to the baptism of John before beginning to baptize people Himself. While baptism plays no part in one's personal salvation, it is a nonoptional act of obedience to Christ (Matt. 28.19).

Communion—also referred to as the Lord's Table or the Lord's Supper—and baptism are the two significant ordinances within Protestant Christianity. The reason the church attaches so much significance to them is that the Lord Jesus Christ instituted and commanded both. I believe so strongly in a Christian's obedience to those two practices that I think a Christian should question his own commitment to Christ if he does not observe them. Sometimes we struggle to know exactly what God's will is on a certain issue, but these ordinances are Christ's clear commands and, thus, are a vital part of Christian experience. They should not be taken lightly and certainly should not be ignored.

Communion

The Historical Context

On the night before His death, our Lord Jesus Christ gathered with His disciples in the Upper Room to eat the Passover meal. Every year the Jewish people met together to celebrate the Passover, which was a special meal designed by God to commemorate the deliverance of Israel from Egypt. He brought upon Egypt a series of plagues designed to free the Israelites from Pharaoh's clutches. It was only after the last plague—the death of the firstborn throughout the land of Egypt—that Pharaoh finally agreed to let the people go. The Israelites protected themselves from the plague against the firstborn by taking the blood of a slain lamb and applying it to the doorposts and lintels of their homes. Then they ate the roasted lamb along with some unleavened bread and bitter herbs, a meal that became known as the Passover meal because the angel of death passed over them.

Whenever an Israelite participated in the annual Passover feast, he would remember that God delivered his nation out of bondage in Egypt. The Passover celebrated today still recalls that great historic deliverance but tragically misses the greater deliverance that it foreshadowed: the cross of Christ.

Jesus took that ancient feast and transformed it into a meal with new meaning when He instructed His disciples to drink the cup and eat the bread in remembrance of His death on their behalf. Calvary supersedes the Exodus from Egypt as the greatest redemptive event in history. Christians do not recall the blood on the doorposts and lintels but the blood shed at the cross. The Lord's Supper is a memorial that Christ Himself instituted. He became the ultimate fulfillment of deliverance from sin and death when He shed His blood and died on the cross.

Mark 14:22–25 records the account of the Passover meal known as the Last Supper of the Lord:

> While they were eating, He took some bread, and after a blessing He broke it; and gave it to them, and said, "Take it; this is My body." And when He had taken a cup, and given thanks, He gave it to them; and they all drank from it. And He said to them, "This is My blood of the covenant, which is poured out for many. Truly I say to you, I shall never again drink of the fruit of the vine until that day when I drink it new in the kingdom of God."

Matt. 26:26–29 and Luke 22:17–20 also record that incident. John 13:12–30 alludes to it, and Paul comments on it in 1 Cor. 11:23–34. It is that commentary on which we focus our attention below.

The Lord's Supper became the normal celebration of the early church. Acts 2:42 says, "They were continually devoting themselves to the apostles' teaching and to fellowship, to the breaking of bread and to prayer." The expression "breaking of bread" became synonymous with a fellowship meal, with believers incorporating the Communion established by Jesus into the end of their meals together. Eventually that combination of a fellowship meal and Communion became known as the love feast (Jude 12).

The early church attached Communion to a meal not only because the Lord Jesus had done so, but because the Jewish people had always associated the Passover with a meal. The Gentiles likewise included a potluck meal with their religious festivals.

Apparently the early church celebrated the Lord's Supper on a daily basis (Acts 2:46). Perhaps they had Communion with every meal they ate. It was common in biblical times for fellowship to revolve around a table as people ate together. The host simply sat down, took a piece of bread, broke it, and that act initiated the meal.

Later in the life of the church, the frequency of sharing a meal along with Communion was reduced to a weekly pattern (Acts 20:7). Since the Bible does not make a specific point about how often we should observe the Lord's Supper, it would be acceptable to observe it after any meal, whether at home or at church. The important point is obeying what the Lord says and exercising the wonderful privilege of commemorating His death and anticipating His return.

The Literary Context

In 1 Corinthians 11, the Apostle Paul writes to correct abuses that had occurred within the Corinthian church in connection with the Lord's Supper. The Corinthian situation is marvelously instructive and applicable to the present day.

The perversion that had taken place. Christianity had broken down socioeconomic barriers, yet within twenty years of Jesus' ascension, the Corinthians were starting to erect them again. The well-to-do were supposed to bring food to the fellowship meal and share it with the poor, but the rich would arrive early and eat all their food in their own exclusive groups before the poor arrived. The latter group then went home hungry (1 Cor. 11:33–34). Such an abuse of Christian love and unity made participating in the Lord's Table a mockery.

Paul begins his discussion of this problem by saying, "You come together not for the better but for the worse" (v. 17). It is sad to say, but that condemnation probably applies to many churches today, because either the people do not hear or apply the truth, or else they wrangle over personal preferences or trivial theological issues. When a church gets to the place where its meetings are for the worse, it is in trouble.

The Corinthians may have thought they were observing the Lord's Supper by breaking some bread, passing a cup, and saying some of Jesus' words, but those actions did not make up for the spirit in which they conducted Communion. Their divisive and selfish hearts produced only a superficial ceremony.

Everyone knows you do not come to a potluck and sit in a corner, eating your own food. But that is what the Corinthians were doing. The rich were gorging themselves and even getting drunk (v. 21), while the poor had nothing to eat and remained hungry. That defeated the very purpose of the love feast, which was to meet the needs of the less fortunate in a harmonious way and to remember the great sacrifice that made them one. Selfish insensitivity to the needs of others had replaced the intended unity.

The church is one place—possibly the only place—where rich and poor can commune together in mutual love and respect (John 13:34–35; James 2:1–9; 1 Pet. 4:8–10; 1 John 3:16–18). Unity through ministry to diverse groups in need became the pattern for the new church as they shared all things together (Acts 4:32–37). Racial, social, or economic separations between believers has no place in the church.

The purpose behind the ceremony. The Lord's Supper is a memorial to the One who lived and died for us, a time of communion with Him, a proclamation of the meaning of His death, and a sign of our anticipation of His return. The sacred and comprehensive nature of Communion behooves us to treat it with the dignity it deserves. That is precisely what the Corinthians did not do. They had turned the Lord's Supper into a mockery.

To get them back on track, Paul now gives a beautiful presentation of the meaning of the Lord's Supper. Amidst the shameful situation in Corinth, these verses are like a diamond dropped on a muddy road:

> I received from the Lord that which I also delivered to you, that the Lord Jesus in the night in which He was betrayed took bread; and when He had given thanks, He broke it, and said, "This is My body, which is for you; do this in remembrance of Me." In the same way He took the cup also, after supper, saying, "This cup is the new covenant

in My blood; do this, as often as you drink it, in remembrance of Me." For as often as you eat this bread and drink the cup, you proclaim the Lord's death until He comes (1 Cor. 11:23–26).

What Paul said was not his own opinion. It was not a tradition handed down from person to person; it was special revelation he received directly from the Lord Jesus Christ. Most conservative Bible scholars agree that 1 Corinthians was probably written before any of the four Gospels, which would make this passage the first written revelation regarding the Lord's Supper.

The night Jesus instituted the Lord's Supper was not an ordinary night. It had special significance since it was the Passover. And that particular Passover was significant because the crucifixion of Jesus came the next day while Passover was still being observed. As the Lamb of God, Jesus was the ultimate Passover sacrifice (John 1:29; 1 Cor. 5:7).

The Passover meal was structured around sharing four cups of wine at different intervals during the meal:

- **The First Cup**: The Passover began when the host pronounced a blessing over the first cup, which was filled with red wine, symbolic of the blood of the lamb at the Passover in Egypt. That was followed by bitter herbs, which symbolized the bitterness of the Israelites' bondage and an explanation of the meaning of the Passover. The participants then sang Psalms 113 and 114 from a grouping of psalms called the *Hallel* (the Hebrew word for "praise").

- **The Second Cup**: After this cup the host would break unleavened bread, dip it into the bitter herbs and a fruit sauce called *haroseth*, and share it with the participants in the meal. The unleavened bread symbolized the haste with which Israel left Egypt. Then the roasted lamb was brought out.

- **The Third Cup**: When the Passover meal was finished, the host prayed and then took the third cup. At this point the participants sang the rest of the *Hallel* (Psalms 115–118). It was this third cup that Jesus blessed and transformed into a part of the Lord's Supper. Rather than remembering the physical deliverance of the Israelites from Egypt, participants in Communion are to remember Christ's death and the deliverance it provided.

- **The Fourth Cup**: The fourth and final cup celebrated the coming kingdom. After drinking it, the participants in the Passover feast sang a closing hymn, a tradition mentioned in Scripture: "After singing a hymn, [Jesus and His disciples] went out to the Mount of Olives" (Mark 14:26).

The Lord Jesus initiated the Lord's Supper by taking "bread; and when He had given thanks, He broke it, and said, 'This is My body, which is for you; do this in remembrance of Me.' In the same way He took the cup also, after supper, saying, 'This cup is the new covenant in My blood; do this, as often as you drink it, in remembrance of Me' " (1 Cor. 11:23–25). "He had given thanks" is from the Greek verb *eucharisteō*. The English adaption, *Eucharist*, is a name some people use to refer to the Lord's Supper.

Some have misunderstood Jesus' identification of the bread and wine with His body and blood as a literal reference to His physical body and blood. The verb *estin*, "is," frequently means "represents." Jesus was saying that the bread and wine of that particular Passover meal *represented* His body and blood. The wine was not literally His blood—is blood was still in His veins when He said that. And the bread was not His body—His body was still physically present at the supper for all to behold.

Jesus often spoke in figurative language. When He said, "I am the door" (John 10:9), He meant He is the channel through which people enter into eternal life. He is not literally a door. The parables He told are examples of common things He pointed to as illustrations of spiritual realities. The failure of some of His followers to understand the figurative or metaphorical sense in which Jesus spoke of His body and blood caused them to stop following Him (John 6:53–66).

The bread that had represented the Exodus now came to represent the body of the Lord. According to Jewish thought, the body represented the whole person, so this reference to Christ's body can be seen as symbolizing the entire period of His incarnation from His birth to His resurrection. Christ was born, crucified, and resurrected as a sacrificial gift given to mankind.

The cup that Jesus took was the third cup of the Passover meal, the one immediately following dinner. Jesus stated that the cup of wine represented the promise of the New Covenant that would soon be ratified by His blood. The Old Covenant was ratified by the blood of animals, but the New Covenant was ratified by the blood of Christ. In the same way that a signature ratifies a contract or promise today, shedding the blood of a sacrificial animal accomplished the same thing in Old Testament times. The foremost example, of course, is God's promise not to take the lives of the Israelites' firstborn if they would agree to sign on the dotted line, so to speak, with the blood of a lamb smeared on the doorposts and lintels of their homes.

Whereas the Old Covenant required continual animal sacrifices, the New Covenant, represented by the cup of Communion, was fulfilled by the once-for-all sacrifice of the Lamb of God (Heb. 9:28). It was as if on the cross Jesus was taking His blood and signing on the dotted line. The blood of the cross has replaced the blood of the Passover.

In response to all He has done for us, Christ asks us to remember Him and what He has accomplished. To the Hebrew mind the concept of remembering meant more than simply recalling something that happened in the past. It meant recapturing as much as possible the reality and significance of a person or situation in one's conscious mind. Jesus was requesting that all Christians of all times ponder the meaning of His life and death on their behalf. A person can participate in Communion, but if his mind is a million miles away, he has not truly remembered the Lord.

We proclaim the death of Christ every time we remember Him in Communion (1 Cor. 11:26). This is a reminder to the world that God became man and died a substitutionary, sin-atoning death for all mankind (1 John 2:2). We also look forward to the day of His second advent when we all will commune with Him in His presence.

The preparation required before partaking. The Lord's Table is a comprehensive ordinance. We remember what Christ has done, we refresh our commitment to Him, we commune with Him, we proclaim the gospel, and we anticipate His return. That is why we must observe it with the right attitude.

The Corinthian church participated in Communion in an unworthy manner (1 Cor. 11:27). We also can be guilty of this in any of several ways:

- **By ignoring it rather than obeying it**: If we say Communion is irrelevant and unimportant, we are observing it unworthily.

- **By failing to observe it meaningfully**: We can be concerned with going through the ritualistic motions without understanding the reason for observing it. Superficial ceremony and irreverence can prevent us from personally communing with Christ.

- **By assuming it can save**: Taking Communion does not impart saving grace. It is the privilege of those who are already saved to confront their sin and renew their fellowship with Christ.

- **By refusing to confess and repent from sin:** We should never participate in the Lord's Supper if we have known, unconfessed sin in our lives.

- **By having a lack of respect and love for God or His people.**

Those who do such things "shall be guilty of the body and blood of the Lord" (1 Cor. 11:27). That is to treat Christ's unique life and death as something common and insignificant. A man who tramples on his nation's flag is not merely trampling on a piece of cloth; he is guilty of dishonoring his country. Communion is a real encounter with the Lord Jesus Christ. It is so real that failing to acknowledge the reality behind it brings judgment (1 Cor. 11:29).

To avoid judgment, each participant should "examine himself, and so let him eat of the bread and drink of the cup" (1 Cor. 11:28). The Greek word translated "examine" conveys the idea of a rigorous self-examination. Check out your life—your motives and your attitudes toward the Lord, His Supper, and other Christians. Once you have done that and have dealt with any sin or improper motive, then you are ready to share in the bread and the cup.

He who participates in Communion without having done that "eats and drinks judgment to himself, if he does not judge the body rightly" (v. 29). The word translated "judgment" (*krima*) is better translated "chastisement." It refers to the Lord's chastisement of believers, not the damnation of unbelievers, which is referred to in verse 32 with the term *katakrinō*. Such a person has not discerned the meaning and significance of the Lord's body. Although this may be a reference to the corporate body of Christ, the church, the context supports a reference to the Lord Himself.

The Lord disciplined the Corinthians for their abuse of the Lord's Supper by causing some to be sick and taking the lives of others (v. 30). In a similar way, God put to death Ananias and Sapphira for lying to the Holy Spirit (Acts 5:1–11). Such stark reminders of God's holiness and man's sinfulness show what everyone deserves and what some actually receive. Some Christians today may have become sick or die from observing Communion improperly.

Although that is true, God does not want believers to be overly fearful of celebrating the Lord's Supper. Paul assures us that though we might be disciplined by the Lord, we will not be damned with the world (1 Cor. 11:32). No Christian under any circumstance will ever be damned. God disciplines His children not to punish them, but to correct their sinful behavior and to direct them in paths of righteousness. Heb. 12:6 says, "Those whom the Lord loves He disciplines, and He scourges every son whom He receives." We never have to fear losing our salvation and being eternally damned. God will intervene with His chastening hand before that can happen.

Paul concludes his discourse on Communion by saying, "So then, my brethren, when you come together to eat, wait for one another. If anyone is hungry, let him eat at home, so that you may not come together for judgment" (1 Cor. 11:33–34). The Corinthians were to wait for each other when they gathered for a fellowship meal rather than selfishly gorge themselves before everyone else arrived. Those who attended just to satisfy their physical hunger were to eat at home. Otherwise they would pervert the purpose of Communion and be subject to divine chastening.

The Lord is very serious about how the ordinance of Communion is to be treated. We must never overlook its significance or fail to evaluate our hearts before we partake of it.[1]

BAPTISM

As noted previously, the Lord has left only two ordinances for the church: Communion and baptism. We teach much about the Lord's Table because we celebrate it, as commanded, on a regular basis. The subject of baptism, however, seems to be somewhat of a nonissue in the church today. We hear little about it. It has been years since anyone has written a book emphasizing baptism. Religious programming gives practically no thought to baptism. To my knowledge, "Grace to You"—our daily radio program—is the only radio program in America that puts baptismal services on the air. Such a wide diversity of opinion exists about what baptism means and how important it is that most believers have relegated it to the level of an antiquated ecclesiastical discussion. They have little concern for its spiritual importance. At best, baptism has become a secondary matter.

I believe this failure to take baptism seriously is at the root of the most serious problems in today's church because it betrays an unfaithfulness to the simple and direct commands of the Lord. Baptism is central to Jesus' Great Commission to the church: "Go . . . and make disciples of all the nations, baptizing them in the name of the Father and the Son and the Holy Spirit" (Matt. 28:19). The command "repent, and . . . be baptized" (Acts 2:38) is as applicable to each believer today as when it was first uttered on the Day of

---

1. I have not addressed some of the secondary questions often raised concerning the Lord's Table, e.g., how frequently a church observes communion, grape juice versus real wine, and unleavened or leavened bread. Since the Bible does not address these issues, I assume there is some liberty regarding them.

Pentecost. When all three thousand who believed that day were immediately baptized, they set the example for the church of all time.

Why Would Someone Who Professes Christ Not Be Baptized?

Several reasons may lie behind the failure of some professing Christians to be baptized.

Ignorance—Such a person has been ill-taught about baptism or has not been taught at all.

Pride—Some people choose not to be baptized as a matter of spiritual pride. For them to go a long time without a proper New Testament baptism and then be baptized would be a public confession of a long period of disobedience or ignorance.

Indifference—Other people just can't be bothered. They understand the New Testament teaching about baptism and are not against it. They may even believe in it, but never get around to applying it, because they obviously don't think it is very important.

Defiance—These people flatly refuse to be baptized. Most often it is because they are courting sin in their lives, and they are not about to get up in front of a congregation of people and publicly acknowledge their submission to the lordship of Jesus Christ and their joy in knowing Him.

Lack of regeneration—This last category describes people who are not really Christians, so they have no inner prompting by the Spirit of God compelling them toward obedience. They enjoy the blessings of being around the church but have no desire to make a public confession.

What Is Baptism?

From a physical viewpoint, baptism is a ceremony by which a person is immersed, dunked, or submerged into water. There are two verbs in the New Testament describing this reality: *baptō* and *baptizō*. *Bapto* occurs only four times. It always means to dip, as in dipping a piece of cloth into dye. *Baptizō* is an intensive form of *baptō*. It is used many times in the New Testament and always means "to dip completely" or even "to drown."

Another important technical note is that *baptō* and *baptizō* are never used in the passive sense. Water is never said to be baptized on someone—i.e., sprinkled or dabbed onto someone's head. Always someone is baptized into water. That is clear in the New Testament from its very outset.

Matthew 3 begins by describing the ministry of John the Baptist. Verse 6 notes that people were coming out to him and being baptized by him in the Jordan River. Obviously, if they were baptized in the river, they had to be immersed. You do not need a river if you are just going to dab a dot of water on someone's forehead.

John 3:23 says that "John was also baptizing in Aenon near Salim, because there was much water there." Why did he need much water? Because he had multitudes of people who needed to be submerged into water.

The familiar account of Philip and the Ethiopian eunuch is in Acts 8. Philip preached Christ and the eunuch believed. As a result of his faith he said, "Look! Water! What prevents me from begin baptized?" (v. 36). Therefore "they both went down into the water" (v. 38).

Only immersion can accurately portray the reality that baptism is meant to picture: The believer at salvation is united with Christ in His death, burial, and resurrection. Going into the water symbolizes death and burial; coming out symbolizes new life. As any student of the Old and New Testaments knows, God likes to teach with symbols, pictures, illustrations, parables, and analogies. Baptism is one of His finest.

What Is the History of Baptism?

Where did it originate? How did we get it? Where did it start? It began back in Old Testament times. The people of Israel had received God's law, promises, prophets, and covenants. They worshiped the true God. Some of the peoples from other nations, called Gentile nations, recognized that and wanted to identify with Israel so they could worship the true God in the true way. They wanted to become Jews—not racially, for that is impossible—but religiously or spiritually. The system for their doing so was called proselyte induction. It had three parts: circumcision, animal sacrifice, and baptism.

The baptism part involved being immersed in water. It represented the Gentile as dying to the Gentile world and then rising in a new life as a member of a new family in a new relationship to God. It was in proselyte Gentile immersion that baptism first appeared in redemptive history.

Now skip ahead to the ministry of John the Baptist. His job as Christ's forerunner was to prepare people for the coming of Christ. How did he attempt to do that? He knew Christ would be holy and demand righteousness, so he preached repentance from sin and turning toward God. Then he baptized the people as a visible symbol of that inward turning.

On a special day in the midst of his ministry, a marvelous thing happened: "Then Jesus arrived from Galilee at the Jordan coming to John, to be baptized by him. But John tried to prevent Him, saying, 'I have need to be baptized by You, and do You come to me?' But Jesus answering said to him, 'Permit it at this time; for in this way it is fitting for us to fulfill all righteousness.' Then he permitted Him" (Matt. 3:13–15).

How did Jesus fulfill the righteousness of God? By dying on a cross. Whatever Jesus' baptism means, it is somehow connected to the time when God in His righteous indignation poured out vengeance on the Lord Jesus Christ, the perfect sacrifice. All righteousness was then fulfilled, and a righteous God was satisfied and able to impute righteousness to believing people.

In Luke 12:50 Jesus says, "I have a baptism to undergo, and how distressed I am until it is accomplished!" Notice He did not say, "I have a death or crucifixion to undergo." He viewed His death as an immersion, which gave a hint of the resurrection or rising to come. This was all beautifully prefigured in His own baptism.

When James and John asked to sit on Jesus' right and left in the kingdom, Jesus responded, "You do not know what you are asking for. Are you able to drink the cup that I drink, or to be baptized with the baptism with which I am baptized?" (Mark 10:38). I believe that when Jesus looked at His baptism and said it was to fulfill all righteousness, He was saying, "My death and resurrection will fulfill all righteousness, and I will give a symbolic demonstration of that great baptism yet to come."

What followed after the baptism of Jesus? Jesus Himself began to baptize. According to John 4:1, the Lord was making and baptizing more disciples than John the Baptist. It signified that sinners who believed in Him were affirming their need to die and be buried to the old and to rise in newness of life. After Jesus Himself died and rose again, He gave the command to go into all the world and make disciples, baptizing them.

When the church was born, three thousand believed and three thousand were baptized. There's absolute continuity in the historical record of baptism as symbolizing the death of the old and the resurrection of the new. It finds its ultimate fulfillment in the death, burial, and resurrection of Jesus Christ.

What Is the Theological Significance of Baptism?

What is the spiritual significance of Christian baptism? What is it really depicting? When you as a believer are baptized by immersion into water, you are demonstrating not just the death, burial, and resurrection of Christ, but also *your union with Christ* in that death, burial, and resurrection.

For whom did Christ die? You. Whose sins did He bear? Yours. For whom did He rise? You. The Apostle Paul expressed that reality by saying, "I have been crucified with Christ; and it is no longer I who live, but Christ lives in me; and the life which I now live in the flesh I live by faith in the Son of God, who loved me, and delivered Himself up for me" (Gal. 2:20). Through a sovereign, spiritual miracle at the moment of salvation, God puts you in Christ. It is as if you died when He died on the cross, and you rose again when He did.

The New Testament sometimes uses the word *baptism* to speak of that spiritual union only, not of water baptism. Gal. 3:27 says, "All of you who were baptized into Christ have clothed yourselves with Christ." Col. 2:12 says, "Having been buried with Him in baptism, . . . you were also raised up." And perhaps the most explicit passage of all on our union with Christ reads, "Do you not know that all of us who have been baptized into Christ have been baptized into His death?" (Rom. 6:3).

Although those passages are not referring to water, it is water baptism that symbolizes our spiritual union with Christ. Notice how the apostle Peter made that distinction: "Baptism now saves you—not the removal of dirt from the flesh, but an appeal to God for a good conscience—through the resurrection of Jesus Christ" (1 Pet. 3:21). What saves is not water baptism but our spiritual union with Christ, also spoken of as the washing of regeneration in Titus 3:5 and the washing away of sins in Acts 22:16. But water baptism is the symbol of what saves.

What Is the Relation of Immersion to Salvation?

Some people say you have to be baptized to be a Christian, and if you are not baptized, you are not saved. They are confusing the relationship of water baptism to salvation, which is akin to the relationship of obedience to salvation. Having been saved, we enter into obedience. In the New Testament we see baptism as the immediate and inseparable indicator of salvation. On the day of Pentecost three thousand believed, three thousand were baptized, and three thousand continued in the Apostles' doctrine, prayer, fellowship, and the breaking of bread. No loss. That's God's standard. The Apostles insisted on it.

Typically today you may hear someone say, "We had a great evangelistic rally: three thousand were saved, forty-two were baptized, and ten integrated themselves into local churches." What a difference! The cost of baptism was very high in New Testament times—ostracism from one's culture, persecution, and sometimes even death. Only those who were serious in their commitment to Christ would pay the price. Baptism was, therefore, the inseparable token of salvation, as it should be today.

In Acts 2:38 Peter says, "Repent, and . . . be baptized . . . for the forgiveness of your sins." Does that mean water is needed to wash away sin? No, but the act of baptism is what demonstrates to others that one's sins have been remitted or forgiven.

People often ask, "Do you have to be baptized to get into heaven?" The thief on the cross did not (Luke 23:39–43). There may be exigencies that preclude baptism, but if someone is reluctant to be baptized, it may be a sign of a heart that is unwilling to obey. And a disobedient heart is a sign of an unregenerate person, for as Jesus said, "If you love Me, you will keep My commandments" (John 14:15), and "Why do you call Me, `Lord, Lord,' and do not do what I say?" (Luke 6:46).

Why Is There So Much Confusion Regarding Baptism?

Is the Bible's discussion of baptism confusing? No, but there are a lot of confused Christians, nonetheless. One of Satan's main objectives in the life of a believer is to shatter any pattern of obedience—and the sooner the better. If he can make baptism so confusing that one ignores it, then he has started the believer on the path of indifference and disobedience. And Satan has been working overtime to confuse churches throughout the centuries.

The confusion of churches. The Salvation Army, the Quakers (otherwise known as the Friends Church), and the ultradispensationalists (who follow the teachings of E. W. Bullinger) all deny that baptism has a place in the believer's life today. On the other hand, the Churches of Christ say that baptism saves you. They think that if you believe but do not get baptized, you will go to hell. One extreme errs on the side of grace, and the other on the side of law. One ignores the command to obedience; the other ignores that salvation is by faith.

Outside orthodox Christianity, the Mormon church practices proxy baptism for the dead. It sanctions the heretical concept of being baptized vicariously for another to assure him or her a place in heaven. It is not uncommon in one year alone for the Mormons to have three million proxy baptisms for three million dead people. This is clearly an unbiblical practice.

The error of infant baptism. The Roman Catholic Church instituted infant baptism as a ritual of regeneration. The Catholic Church officially teaches that water cleanses a baby from original sin and results in salvation. Until the Middle Ages they immersed all the babies, and then they started sprinkling them after that.

Roman Catholic theology asserts that a baby who dies without being christened or baptized goes to "the Limbo of the Innocent." That is supposedly a place where babies live forever enjoying some kind of natural bliss, but without any vision of God. A baptized infant who dies, however, is said to avert that second-class status by going to another place that does have the vision of God.

That notion is patently unbiblical, but it has pervaded many churches beyond just the Roman Church. For example, Martin Luther—initiator of the Protestant Reformation and, therefore, the father of many churches— never disentangled himself from Roman infant baptism. In fact, he wrote the manual that the Lutheran Church uses for infant baptism. He believed that baptism cleansed a baby from sin. When asked, "How can you affirm that if you believe in justification by faith alone?" he replied, "Well, somehow a baby must be able to believe." There is nothing in the New Testament about babies being baptized or about salvation apart from personal faith in the Lord Jesus Christ, which can come only to one who understands the meaning of the gospel.

Why did the practice of infant baptism get started? Early on, the Roman Catholic Church did it to secure everyone into the system. By making everyone from birth a "Christian," they made sure they belonged to the church and were therefore under its control.

Reformed or Reformation-based churches unfortunately adopted— instead of jettisoning—the long-standing practice of infant baptism, but in time varied it a little. They teach that when Christian parents have their baby baptized, that baby automatically becomes a little member of God's covenant people. They say that reality is confirmed when the child is old enough to recite the church's catechism properly—a rite known as Confirmation.

A threat to both the Roman and Reformed churches was a group of people who arose and said, "This is all wrong: Baptism is only for people who consciously put their faith in Jesus Christ. Infant baptism means nothing in God's eyes." They faithfully preached the gospel, and many people became converted as a result of their ministry. These infant-baptized converts proved the reality of their conversion by being rebaptized as believers. The bold preachers who led them to do that were known historically as Anabaptists, *ana* being the Greek word for "again." Both Catholic and Protestant churches persecuted them severely, because they viewed them as a threat to their power base. That is one of the greatest tragedies of church history, because the Anabaptists were upholding the teaching of God's Word.

People often ask, "Should I be rebaptized?" If a person was not baptized according to the New Testament—not immersed in water after a conscious commitment of one's life to Jesus Christ—then he or she needs to be baptized. Any other baptism experienced, either wittingly or unwittingly, means nothing. Baptism is only for believers, and it should be done as soon as possible following conversion (Matt. 28:18–19).

22

Answering Frequently Asked Questions

John MacArthur, Jr.

John MacArthur's thoughts about miscellaneous phases of pastoral ministry do not fit under any main heading of Rediscovering Pastoral Ministry, *but have come in response to questions asked him in pastors' conferences and chapels at The Master's Seminary. The current discussion reproduces his brief but suggestive answers to these questions. As it progresses, the discussion falls into four main categories: beginning a pastoral ministry, personal support, ministry threats, and sustaining a pastoral ministry.*

BEGINNING A PASTORAL MINISTRY

What are the components of a successful first-time pastor? Or put another way—if you were to start all over again, what things would you emphasize?

I'm not sure I would change a lot. I know so much more now, but I don't think I would do anything very differently. I started immediately teaching the Word. I wanted to teach the books of the Bible that would exalt Christ, so we would have a Christ-centered church. I wanted to teach on spiritual gifts, so we would have people who were working and serving and using their gifts. I wanted to disciple men so we could build up leadership. I emphasized evangelism.

If there is anything I would do differently, I would be less concerned about structure. A temptation when you are young is always organization and structure. You think you have found a great new concept, a new flow chart, a new way to organize, but that rarely is crucial to effective ministry. You don't want to spend very much time on that; you want to spend most of your time on the dynamics of ministry, on building your people spiritually. I would again raise my own staff from within the church, from those who are effective in ministry and in teaching. I do regret that I did not listen and pray more. But from the very start I have believed that God was leading, so I wouldn't want to second-guess Him or go back and redo what He has done.

What one overarching word of wisdom would you give to new pastors just starting out?

Paul said it when he told the Philippians, "This one thing I do, pursue Christ" (see Phil 3:13–14). Pursue the knowledge of Christ, the person of Christ, study the Bible to know Him. I never studied to make a sermon—I studied to know Him. The more you know Him, the more you know the standard you have to live by.

Build your ministry around the Scriptures. Relentlessly force your ministry to conform to the Word of God and that's how you put yourself in the place of preeminent blessing. Do ministry biblically—nothing less and nothing more. Make friends with people who will challenge you, stimulate you, question you, make you defend what you do. Draw around you the best people who best handle the Scripture, who live the purest lives, and who don't stop studying. Stay fresh for your sake as well as for the church.

PERSONAL SUPPORT

To whom does a pastor look as his own pastor? Where do you look for shepherding in your own life?

I look to my staff, and since I am always the preacher and I don't hear another preacher, I depend on reading books and occasionally listening to tapes. When you talk about "your pastor," you are talking about somebody who is an example of spiritual leadership to you, someone who has a high spiritual standard to maintain and uphold in his life. It is just like people in the congregation looking at their pastor. They watch his life, they watch his character, and they watch his family—and he sets an example for them. I have men near me who work with me every day and who do the same for me. They are men I look to as examples and spiritual friends.

I have other pastor friends outside our church, though I don't have the opportunity to be with them nearly as much as with my own co-pastors. I also need to add that I am frequently pastored by the books and the writers I have grown to know and appreciate. Biographies of noble and sacrificial ministers also provide strong motivation for my own devotion to Christ.

Is there one particular person to whom you would go when you need personal advice on a tough subject?

My personal approach would be to go to certain men with whom I work nearly every day. The truest and purest environment for me to get help is right with my own fellow pastors. I trust I have allowed those men to rise to the highest level of their own development doctrinally, biblically, and practically, not by telling them what to believe but by leading them toward a body of convictions that has become their own. Then when it comes to the point where I cannot resolve something and need help, I go back to them, because they are going to have some answers for me. That's where I would go first of all. It would be rare for me to go beyond these men to someone outside that circle, since they have proven to be such a blessing to me.

Over the years, who have been the people who have influenced you the most?

First, my father. He is still influencing me and still faithful. He is eighty and still preaches the Word, loves to read, and loves to study.

When I studied under Dr. Charles Feinberg, then Dean of Talbot Seminary, he also greatly impacted me because of his commitment to know the truths of Scripture and his unabashed devotion to its inerrancy. Also, the unflagging discipline in his life affected me in setting a standard for me to try to live up to.

Ralph Keiper, one-time researcher for Donald Grey Barnhouse, affected me dramatically in my preaching by challenging me to explain one Scripture by means of another one, which is basically what I do in almost all of my sermons.

Although I never met him, D. Martin Lloyd-Jones has impacted me. I know his family and have read his books. He would explain and then theologize the text, and he would take firm biblical stands without sacrificing the grace of godliness. He would take a stand, where the Scripture took a stand, even if everybody else in his whole city , whole country, wherever, went another way—he would stand on what the Scripture taught. He would not equivocate.

Years ago, I started reading the Puritans, which I have found to be a rich resource. There are a number of other writers and personal friends who have influenced me. My wife, Patricia, has influenced me with her intense devotion to what is right and honoring to God.

How does a pastor stay accountable?

He must have an accountability first to God. I love the Lord and I don't want to do what dishonors Him; that is the most intimate aspect of my accountability and the highest point, because that's a twenty-four hour a day relationship through all of life. Next, I have a point of accountability at home with my wife and my children. I want to lead them to love God and serve Him, and I don't want to disappoint them or lead them astray. I don't want to lead them to distrust my devotion to Christ, and thereby cheapen their understanding of Christian faith and commitment. Too much is at stake in their lives and the lives of their families. Third, I have personal accountability to men who labor with me and are my friends.

Fourth, I have an accountability to preach several times every week of my life. That throws me into the Word. If pastors, when they are young, will establish a standard of diligent study and excellent preaching, then they will have to spend the rest of their lives living up to it. If early in your ministry you establish a low standard, a standard of sloppiness and of minimum study, you have nothing to live up to. If young men give the first five to ten years of ministry to diligent and deep study of God's Word, they set a standard for themselves that pleases the Lord and that demands faithfulness. This, then, becomes the standard they will gladly spend the rest of their life living up to, rejoicing in its fruit. That forces you into the Word at a depth where you really commune with God and come to know His heart.

Finally, build around you godly, devout men who have very high expectations of you. Don't hide your life. You need an accountability to your fellow leaders and pastors. Let them argue, let them debate; don't just get to the place where they do whatever you say. You don't want yes-men. You want friends who will question when they need to question and ask you why you are doing something that isn't clear. That's a very important accountability. It keeps you from making foolish, unwise, and hasty decisions. It keeps you from being blindsided by your own ignorance or your own will, or becoming habitually less than God desires and spiritual excellence requires.

MINISTRY THREATS

What do you see as the greatest threats that may undermine a man's ministry today?

One threat is laziness. We live in a really busy and fast-paced culture. Many men run fast, but I'm not sure they go very deep. By that I mean it is easy to be busy with the short and easier tasks but leave the long, hard jobs undone. We are raising a culture, for example, that does not do the manual labor, at least in the major cities. You hire people to do that. It's a service-oriented culture in America, it's moving away from farming and manufacturing, and it's all automated. Many men do not know how to work hard, especially those who have been in school for a long time. They know how to stay busy doing a number of little things, but they do not know how to focus with discipline on the main thing—diligence and discipline in the Scripture. The result is often a failure to attend to the priorities and a resultant superficiality in the ministry. A lot of activity happens at a shallow level, but the hard work of ministry—the things that take time and prayer and intense study of the Word—are often not done well.

Second, there are constant threats in the area of personal purity. We all have to guard our hearts and strengthen the inner man to remain pure, devoted to Christ, and dedicated to things that are holy.

Third, one of the chief problems that tears men down in the ministry is poor judgment in building a ministry team. Whether it is elders, staff pastors, lay elders, or friendships, we need to pursue those who are faithful to the highest level of spiritual excellence. We need the kind of people whose virtue, wisdom, and faithfulness to the work will force us to think and justify everything we do biblically. They are not going to roll over because we want to do something. I think that kind of accountability is really important.

A fourth threat to undermine a man's ministry is a nonsupportive wife. It could also extend to the children, but particularly a nonsupportive wife, one who nags and battles a pastor as he tries to be faithful and loyal to the Lord and the church. If she is negative on the church or the people in it, or if she is spiritually out of sorts or materialistic and self-indulgent or a little too controlling, she will cease to be that support that her husband so desperately needs to serve his people with joy. A fully supportive, loving, trusting wife who will be honest but who will stand with her husband to the very end frees a man up to do with all his heart what God has called him to do.

Every church and pastor has his critics. How do you live with your critics?

First of all, I check my life to see if the criticism is valid. If not, I affirm that I am privileged to render my service to the Lord, not men. I have to live in 1 Corinthians 4 where Paul said in effect, "It's a small thing what men say of me." He was criticized mercilessly, particularly by the people in Corinth, yet he could respond by saying, "I don't really care what they say about me. I do care what they say about my Lord and about His truth—but it's a small thing what men say of me." He also affirmed that he was the chief sinner.

I try to follow that pattern and say, "It really doesn't matter what people think, and I'm certainly not worth defending. I may have been accused falsely of something, but there certainly has been sin in my life somewhere that my accusers didn't even know about."

We have to wait and let the Lord judge us. I have to be faithful to the Lord and not worry about reputation, and not take criticism personally—getting my ego involved. I have learned that whenever an unjust criticism comes, I thank the Lord for using it to humble and refine me. I commit myself to the faithful care of my Creator as Jesus committed Himself to His Father. Let God defend me if I'm worthy of defending. I will defend the truth, I will defend Christ, I will defend the Bible, but I am not going to defend John MacArthur. When someone criticizes me, I would just rather say, "Pray for me. Thank you for caring enough to share your concern. I want to be all that God wants me to be."

Sustaining a Pastoral Ministry

Church Growth

How do you react to the perceived dichotomy of a big church versus a small church?

Size may relate to different cultures and demographics. It is true that some are smaller than they should be because of sin or unfaithfulness—some are larger than they should be because of compromise. But God obviously has sovereign purposes for big ones as he has purposes for small ones. They are all just pieces of the one Body of Christ on earth—size is not the issue. Scriptural integrity and faithfulness to God are the only issues.

In England during the Puritan era, those profound men were preaching to 150 to 300 people in towns and villages. Later, C. H. Spurgeon preached to 4,000 in London. God has His reasons for what He does and what He allows in a given place and time. But God is always building His church sovereignly—and all the elect will be gathered in. God has not stopped the fragmentation of the church into so many denominations and congregations, but it is probably true that if all the little churches in certain areas came together to begin one large church, they would have a greater impact, more exhilarating worship, and less trouble trying to find leaders, since it would only take one gifted preacher to feed them all. Personal ministry and small groups could still develop. Nevertheless, God measures the success of each local church, not by its size or reputation, but by its devotion to truth and to purity.

What is the right balance between church growth that is energized by the Spirit and the human effort we put into church growth?

I think that when church growth is accomplished by the Word and the Spirit of God on a sound spiritual level, it is wonderful. The Lord will grow His church. It is a travesty when growth is engineered by unbiblical means of human technique involving manipulation, psychology, or gimmickry and becomes humanly engineered, not emphasizing the Scripture or following the priorities or the theology God has given in Scripture. For example, whatever creative things we do to evangelize, we have to remember that man is totally depraved.

Therefore, we understand that for him to be saved, God has to work in his heart and totally change him. That is a work of God, not a work of man. If we do not understand the theology regarding man's nature, then we might think that we could manipulate His will by our clever words, music, or programs.

I think much of the church growth movement of today involves human manipulation. There are a lot of techniques that do not build on the Word of God or a truly spiritual basis. When the technique tries to manipulate the heart of man, does not recognize salvation as all of God, or downplays the Word of God to make Christianity more palatable, then it is unbiblical and unacceptable to the Lord.

The terms seeker service, user-friendly church, and churching the unchurched all have a high profile in our day. How do you react to them?

First of all, no man seeks after God, but God does seek true worshipers. So there's one seeker in the church that we should be most concerned about—God, who seeks true worshipers. Only those God has sought first will seek Him. The church should be user-friendly to believers who are living in righteousness and gather to worship. It will be unfriendly to sinners who reject the Lord.

Churching the unchurched is an absolute fallacy—it is like purposing to let the tares in. It is absolutely bizarre to want to make unsaved people feel comfortable in a church. The church is not a building—the church is a group of worshiping, redeemed, and sanctified people among whom an unbeliever should feel either miserable, convicted, and drawn to Christ, or else alienated and isolated. Only if the church hides its message and ceases to be what God designed the church to be, can it make an unbeliever comfortable. The people of the church must be friendly and loving toward the unsaved and sinful who attend, but even in evangelism they must never hedge on confronting sin and proclaiming the offense of the gospel.

You have survived a number of building programs at Grace Church. What is the secret?

The secret for me was to let the lay leaders guide such projects and to stay out of them myself. I do not think I can remember attending more than five meetings about new buildings in twenty-five years. We never had trouble with raising money to build, because we never built a building until the need was so pressing that we were just crying "uncle" out of desperation. We never built an edifice or monument to the church or to ourselves.

At one point we were so crowded that we had three worship services every Sunday morning—people were sitting outside and listening to a loudspeaker, and we had to turn kids away from Sunday school and children from the nursery. In other words, we were at the wall and our people saw it and understood the pressing need.

We always built frugally, as inexpensively and yet with as much quality as we could. We always had the full and unanimous support of our elders so that we could go back to our people and tell them we want their support in this because we *all* believe it is God's will. Their trust in the spiritual wisdom of their leaders and the obvious need always made them willing followers.

If there were features in the building relating to my particular functions, they asked me what I wanted—things such as what kind of pulpit, platform, congregational configuration, baptistry, office setup, etc. It has been important for our church that no egos have been involved, that we are doing it frugally, and that we have only minimal borrowing after raising most, if not all, of the money up-front.

We have a philosophy to raise as much of that money as possible on one Sunday rather than spending weeks and months of a campaign that usually eats away at the general giving. We have targeted one Sunday, months in advance, and set our focus on that. The people then take months to accumulate or pray for money to be able to give on that one Lord's Day. It makes for a great time of joy because the sum is so large and the people all share in the joy together.

Since you believe so strongly in the sovereignty of God, does human creativity have any place in the church?

Of course, God has given us creative gifts, and He uses every believer in unique ways. God is sovereign in salvation, but not apart from human faith, not apart from the will to respond and obey. God is sovereign in sanctification, but not apart from obedience. And He is sovereign in the building of the church, but not apart from spiritual gifts and devoted service and fellowship. God has designed the ends but also the means to the ends.

God has given us fertile minds. The apostle Paul had a well-thought-out strategy. Upon entering a new city, he went to the synagogues first and tried to win Jews to Christ. When he had a group of converts from the synagogue, he would go on to evangelize the Gentiles. He knew the reverse would not work. If he went to the Gentiles first, the Jews would be very reluctant even to hear him, let alone accept his message.

You must think through careful strategies; you do anything you can to enhance every opportunity to present the gospel and bring out spiritual development. Believers and church leaders should be as creative as they possibly can be without violating divine priorities or principles.

It is amazing what the prophets did in getting the attention of the people. Sometimes putting on some rather bizarre demonstrations to draw a crowd. God has used a myriad means. Even our Lord Jesus used miracles as a means to collect a crowd. On the day of Pentecost, God used the speaking of languages to collect a crowd—a very creative way to get their attention. I think the Lord expects us to do appropriate things, but obviously within a framework of what is mandated in Scripture.

Staff Development and Relationships

What advice would you give to pastors on the hiring and discipling of church staff and moving them on when they are ready for greater responsibilities?
In 1 Tim. 3:6 Paul tells us not to lift up a novice. Before elevating any individual to this role, his giftedness, his capabilities, and his track record need to be thoroughly familiar. The man himself must be known. As the apostle Paul organized young churches, he selected men whom he knew. As I grew up, I watched my dad experience heartache because staff came in from outside and were not in tune with what was going on. I decided I would look inside to a very small circle of people whom I had known and discipled to staff the church. Whenever I brought somebody in cold turkey from the outside, with few exceptions, it was a bad experience.

Discipling a new staff member means spending time with him, taking him on trips, sharing conferences, etc. In the early years, when we had a smaller staff than we do now, I would meet with them every week. I would stop by their offices. I think that discipling is mostly informal. It must be more than just "they work for me and I give them things to do." It must be a relationship-building process. Occasionally, I have given fellow pastors theological assignments to do, just to sharpen them in some area. I encourage them to share with me what they are doing, in an unofficial and friendly way. It is essential to pull them to your heart, because generally, if you are the senior pastor, they are pouring their life into you and your ministry. You are the one who rides the crest, and you are the one who has unique joys if the church grows. Since these faithful staff are not going to get the accolades that you get, they need to have a heart of real love and loyalty toward their senior pastor. They should know that, as much as they serve you, you also serve them.

With regard to staff pastors moving on, you have to remain sensitive to their growth, interest, and developing gifts. At times there may be internal movement. For example, men will start out in youth ministry, and after some years, they do not want to do that anymore, so you look at their gifts. If it is the kind of man you want to keep on the team, see what other areas of ministry open up. If it is time for him to go to another church to preach or to the mission field, stay close to him and help him through the process so that as he leaves, a bridge is built over which continued support may flow and on which he may return. Most pastors just let men go and do not sustain that friendship bridge, so they sever good relationships. It is important to sustain relationships so that when they go, the relationship is Christ-honoring. You have to be there to assist them and to demonstrate concern and commitment to them beyond their time with you and on through their life and ministry.

Over the years, how have you structured the most effective staff meetings?

That changes from time to time, but I look at staff meetings as primarily relationship-building. A minor component of a staff meeting is to talk over informational things and resolve issues. Having a special service, facing low offerings, or difficulty in the children's division, should not be the main focus. Staff meetings center on building relationships. You need to be informal, warm, enthusiastic, and affirming.

I think there ought to be a sort of leveling of everybody so that the senior man does not come in with a personal agenda and dump it on everybody. It should be a time of fellowship, a time of prayer, a time to talk about marriage and family life, the joys of ministry, and the difficulties in ministry. And no one is in charge; rather, it is a time of common sharing. I lead only by wisdom in the discussion or by interpreting Scripture. There are times for giving strong directives about issues, but rarely in staff meetings do those occur. More often such issues were dealt with one-to-one.

By building strong and firm relationships, you sustain loyalty and faithfulness. If you treat your staff like functionaries who have a job to do, they will do it with a dutiful sort of mentality, but if they sense love for one another, they will work with a completely different motivation.

Second, it is a time to reinforce and settle issues of doctrine or to re-affirm or clarify principles of ministry that keep the work on a biblical course. It should be open to the point where everyone has the right to speak and nobody really dominates by force or position. Staff meeting is a team-building time, and I think the men need that fellowship every week.

What kind of relationship do you try to build with staff pastors?

You are asking these men to come alongside you, undergird you, help you, strengthen your ministry, pray for you, and do the work you do not have time to do. You cannot visit everybody, plan every event, and oversee every ministry, so you are asking them to come alongside and do that for you. The least you can do is build your heart into them.

It is obvious you cannot do that equally with all your men, if you have a large group as is the case in our church. There are men who are higher on the leadership chart with whom I work more closely and with whom I spend more intimate time. And some men need more attention in their development. The policy I have had with the others is that I am always available—any time they would ever need me.

Although Jesus had twelve apostles, even He had an inner circle (Peter, James, and John). The one thing that allowed the rest of the men to know His heart, even though He did not always call them into the inner circle, was that He always responded when they called Him.

That is the key. I think at the elders' meetings I need to bare my heart—to be open and transparent about what moves me. That builds relationships. I don't pontificate. I don't want to dominate these meetings; I want to be one of many. I don't want them to think I'm their boss; I want to be their guide, their shepherd, and their teacher. I want to help them to clarify doctrine, verify principles, and resolve issues by leading them through the process that is necessary to know the will of the Spirit.

What are your thoughts on the role of the church secretary and the pastor's relationship to her?

Finding the right secretary is critical. She must be one who has been under your ministry for some time and has had some spiritual development and growth in your philosophy of ministry and teaching. She must be a person who is secure and does not need constant building up and affirmation. She needs to be smart and have extremely good people skills, since her kindness, wisdom, and understanding reflect the attitude of the pastor. Technical skills are necessary, but what really makes or breaks your office is the treatment people receive when they make contact with it. Very often they are not going to reach you personally; they are going to reach your secretary. Her sensitivity and love toward them, her depth of spirituality, her trustworthiness, and her character—along with her skills for managing many details with grace—are crucial.

I also think she needs a great memory. So much data channels through that office that her memory is really critical. Sometimes the issues are matters of life and death; sometimes people's heavy burdens, important mail, calls that must be handled promptly—things easily lost in the distractions of a busy office. She must be able to manage all of that. She needs to be very organized.

In my own situation, it is my secretary who makes my very busy ministry work as smoothly as it does. Apart from her devotion and skill, my office would be chaotic. Since her working should entail no sacrifice in the home, a secretary should be an older woman, a woman with no children, or a single woman. Sometimes even a young man can be an excellent secretary.

Your secretary must be someone who is your wife's friend and whom your wife appreciates and trusts, someone who can totally control her tongue and respect the trust of inside information. The highest level of integrity is essential. A lot of private information flows through your office about people's lives, and you want to make sure not to betray their confidence.

Church Nurture

How do you keep the church from being culturalized like the Corinthians?
It is really very simple—you have to stay in the Word. The Scripture is a very old book written in a completely different culture, yet it is relevant to all. Culture may appear to change dramatically from time to time and place to place, but it only changes in a superficial sense. In reality, it does not change at all. The heart of man is the same as it has always been. His spiritual needs are the same as they have always been. If you just stay with the Word, you won't become culturalized.

That has never really been a problem for us. I can honestly say that we have not had to battle the encroachment of culture into the frame or format of our ministry. I am sure there is some of that, like musical styles or certain expectations of soft seats, good P. A. system, or air conditioning, or a good parking lot. But I don't see those as the satanic system. I don't see those as part of the philosophical, antichrist spiritual culture. They are external things. You may have to adjust to those kinds of things to some degree because people in our society are not going to sit on a three-inch-wide wooden bench in a rainstorm and listen to you preach with a megaphone. But at the same time, it does not have to affect your theology.

It may affect some of the outward accouterments, but we are still called to preach an unchanging word to people with unchanging spiritual needs.

What role do worship and music play in the church?

The Father seeks true worshipers, and His church is that group of true worshipers. We were redeemed to worship God. That is ultimately why we were saved, that we might be part of a redeemed and glorified humanity whose eternal purpose is worship. Worship, then, is the priority; it is the ultimate priority. Music is a God-given gift to allow spiritual expression to the Spirit-filled, worshiping heart. We are to worship in spirit and in truth. Truth has to do with the mind; spirit has to do with the passion, the emotion, the heart.

Music is a tremendous help in both those areas, since it speaks truth in the lyrics and provides emotion in the tune. The Scripture even says we are to speak to ourselves in psalms and hymns and spiritual songs. Music is a wonderful gift whereby emotion can express what our mind knows is true. It's cathartic. It's cleansing. It's affirming. It's instructive. Music that speaks the truth of divine revelation will honor the Lord when presented by people whose hearts are right before Him. I thank God for the lyrics that I could never write that give expression to what I feel. I thank God for melodies I could never score that give emotional expression to what I believe to be true. When the church comes together, that kind of expression is important; it gives the soul freedom to express its emotions. Music is also instructive because the lyrics rhyme and allow one to remember truths easier. In the worship service music also teaches and instructs to prepare the heart to receive the Word of God. There is no place in worship for a show or something that is intended to be entertainment. The music of the church is for the saints, not to be directed at unbelievers.

What are the secrets of staying power for a pastor who has been in the same church for twenty-six years?

At the heart of endurance is one's relationship to the Lord and the belief that you are in the place of His will. Then comes family support. It would cut my heart out if my family lost heart for the church. If they love my church and ministry, then they keep my heart loving it. A lot of times family members, even a wife, will turn a man's heart away from his beloved church because she is unhappy with certain things. Another source of enduring is having really strong friendships with your fellow pastors and the people who are in your church.

Seeing the hand of God on your ministry also helps immensely. If I did not experience the power of God and did not see blessing and spiritual growth, I would probably be feeling the need to go and let somebody else come in. I have been blessed with people who are thrilled with the Scriptures and who are growing and bringing others to Christ.

I am to the point where I have done the foundational work already, like when building a house. The tough work was digging the hole, pouring the concrete, laying the foundation, and building on it. Now I have the joy of leading the family that lives in the house. I am talking about more than building structures. If I were to go somewhere else, then I may have to do all the building over again. I couldn't just step in and preach, teach, and write as I do now. But, in the end, I have stayed because God has never given me a sense of release.

Church Outreach

What role, if any, should the pastor play in evangelism in the local church?

As is the case in every aspect of spiritual leadership, the pastor is in a modeling role. I have always felt that I needed to be God's instrument to lead others to Christ in my personal life as well as preaching the gospel. My world is not full of unbelievers, it is full of believers. But I endeavor to take those opportunities when God gives them to lead people to Christ. When you have such a privilege, let people know, so that they see you are committed to that enterprise.

It is also crucial to emphasize in preaching the priority of evangelism. Personally, I think, in the pattern of Ephesians 4:11, a church needs a teaching pastor and then it needs an evangelist who can mobilize the congregation to evangelism. The reason the Lord left His church on earth is evangelism. If all we were saved to do was worship, then we would go to heaven where worship is perfect. If we are saved to serve God, let's go to glory where we can serve Him with glorified bodies. If we are saved for praise, let's go where praise is perfect. But we are left here for the purpose of being His instruments to gather the remaining elect. I don't think we have to be in a panic about that, but rather, we need to be available with an open heart so when God brings somebody across your path you are ready with a presentation of the gospel.

The people need to understand the condition of the lost; they need to know the reality of hell and judgement. That is part of what you preach and teach. While having a holy hatred of sin and sinners, they need to have a tender heart towards unbelievers. They need to feel responsible to reach out to them.

As I have said through the years, the church gathers to be edified, but it scatters to evangelize. Having leaders to oversee that whole area of evangelism, who mobilize people and provide various forms of training, is essential. We have always had evangelism training courses of several different natures in the church so that we can capture people at different points in their Christian development and train them how to evangelize effectively in their sphere of influence.

What is your view on church planting?

Well, I am certainly glad some folks followed the Lord's leading and planted Grace Community Church. Generally, my view is that there are probably too many churches—about 350,000 in America. There are not enough gifted pastors to go around. I wish that we could move back toward a New Testament model where you had one city and one church. You might need more than that, of course, in large population centers. The idea of starting churches because there is one little nuance of doctrinal uniqueness or a different style is foolish. Churches should be planted in places where Christ is not named, by preaching the gospel and winning people to Christ. I admit there are places where a lot of churches exist, but none of them is faithful to the Word of God. Such a place may call for a church to be started by another strong church, which takes the oversight and helps support that new work.

How should the local church relate to the body of Christ worldwide?

We want to maintain the unity of the faith in the bond of peace. We want to pursue fellowship with those of like precious faith. We want to support other churches that are faithful to the Word. We want to send missionaries to various parts of the world. The first and primary thing is our Jerusalem—where we are. The other has to be an overflow of a dynamic, Spirit-led local ministry. A strong base is the key to everything. After all, that is where God has put the church, and that is where the priority of its ministry is.

Ministry Perspective

In your opinion, why is Grace Church so blessed?

Our blessing has come simply from the grace of our sovereign Lord. If Paul could say "I'm the chief of sinners," I don't know where that puts me. So it isn't because of me that God has blessed Grace Church. But I do believe that what we have done through the years, very simply, is try to follow the New Testament teaching about what the church is to be. And that is the richness of our church; not the size, or programs, or influence. The size has to do with God's purposes. The blessing, the joy, and the fervency of the ministries at Grace Church have come because we are so serious about the Scripture. There is pervasive devotion and dedication to the Word of God and whatever it says. We want to preach it and teach it and live it. I know God blesses His truth; it is not our great ideas, but faithfulness to the Word. I never wanted to have to ask myself if I built the church or if Jesus was building His church, so we worked hard to just do biblical ministry biblically. The biggest challenge, as in preaching, is getting out of the way of the Word and the Spirit so God can speak and move.

After twenty-six years of pastoring the same church, what is your perspective on ministry?

It is so simple. My goal is to walk right before the Lord and pour my life into my wife and family so that we may establish, by God's grace, a godly home. Then I preach and teach the Word as faithfully as I can, build up faithful men who can multiply themselves in the other men and women of the congregation, and then minister on a personal level as I am able.

Everything is built on what we understand Scripture to teach and the pattern for ministry it clearly lays out: edifying, leading people to the Lord's Table, baptizing, discipling, training, evangelizing locally, and sending to the fields of the world. All such efforts are led by a plurality of godly men who are devoted to the Word of God and who will faithfully teach, preach, and apply it to the people. I also think it's crucial for them to lead the people in the confrontation of sin, calling them to holy living, and being involved in the refuting of doctrinal error. We have to do the warning side of ministry, too.

As you look forward to the next twenty-five years of ministry, what challenges excite you?

My church still excites me and is still a tremendous challenge. I am challenged because Los Angeles is the most racially mixed city in America. I am challenged because there are vast millions of people pouring into our city who need to hear the gospel. I could never go to all places they come from, but they are coming to us. I am challenged to see young people educated and young men go into ministry. The Master's College and Seminary provides the most unique opportunity for that to occur. I am challenged to continue to preach the Word to a new generation. I am excited to speak to church members for the strengthening of their knowledge of truth, for their holiness, and for their purity in doctrine.

In the twenty-six years I have been in the church I have seen a lot of faces come and go through our doors. Some of the people who were there long ago are gone, and brand new people have replaced them. It keeps changing—ebbing and flowing. In many ways Grace Church is as fresh and as new a church now as it was at any point in the twenty-five years I have served there, because there are so many new people. I see our congregation getting younger, which means it is a dynamic ministry in the lives of the new generation, especially young couples.

I also want to continue writing. That challenges me. The issues that face the church just continue to mount and it is exciting to address those and help people see their way through them biblically.

My life is in God's hand, and I serve Him first—that is always challenging. In fact, the unending challenge for me is to become like Christ.

Additional Reading[1]

Jay E. Adams. *Shepherding God's Flock.* Grand Rapids: Zondervan, 1974.

Robert C. Anderson. *The Effective Pastor.* Chicago: Moody, 1985.

Richard Baxter. *The Reformed Pastor.* Reprint, Edinburgh: Banner of Truth, 1979.

Charles Bridges. *The Christian Ministry.* Reprint, Edinburgh: Banner of Truth, 1980.

Harvie M. Conn, ed. *Practical Theology and the Ministry of the Church.* Phillipsburg, N.J.: Presbyterian and Reformed, 1990.

Os Guinness and John Seel, eds. *No God But God.* Chicago: Moody, 1992.

Michael Horton, ed. *Power Religion.* Chicago: Moody, 1992.

Kent and Barbara Hughes. *Liberating Ministry from the Success Syndrome.* Wheaton: Tyndale, 1987.

Bill Hull. *Can We Save the Evangelical Church?* Grand Rapids: Baker, 1993.

Charles Jefferson. *The Building of the Church.* Reprint, Grand Rapids: Baker, 1969.

———. *The Minister As Shepherd.* Reprint, Hong Kong: Living Books, 1973.

H. B. London, Jr. and Neil B. Wiseman. *Pastors At Risk.* Wheaton: Victor, 1993.

John MacArthur, Jr. *Ashamed of the Gospel: When the Church Becomes Like the World.* Westchester, Ill.: Crossway, 1993.

---

1. The following pastoral resources represent some of the more notable contributions of the nineteenth and early twentieth centuries, which today are either unavailable and/or out of date: Charles R. Erdman, *The Work of the Pastor* (Philadelphia: Westminster, 1928); Patrick Fairbairn, *Pastoral Theology* (reprint, Audubon, N.J.: Old Paths, 1992); Washington Gladden, *The Christian Pastor and the Working Church* (New York: Scribner's Sons, 1907); James M. Hoppin, *Pastoral Theology* (New York: Funk & Wagnalls, 1895); Daniel P. Kidder, *The Christian Pastorate: Its Character, Responsibilities, and Duties* (New York: Methodist Book Concern, 1871); J. H. Jowett, *The Preacher: His Life and Work* (London: Hodder and Stoughton, 1912); William G. T. Shedd, *Homiletics and Pastoral Theology* (reprint, London: Banner of Truth, 1965).

For a comprehensive bibliography of volumes relating to pastoral ministry through about 1980 see Thomas C. Oden, *Pastoral Theology* (San Francisco: HarperCollins, 1983), 321–54.

————. *The Master's Plan for the Church*. Chicago: Moody, 1991.

John MacArthur, Jr. et al. *Rediscovering Expository Preaching*. Dallas: Word, 1992.

John MacArthur, Jr. and Wayne A. Mack et al. *Introduction to Biblical Counseling*. Dallas: Word, 1994.

James E. Means. *Effective Pastors for a New Century*. Grand Rapids: Baker, 1993.

A. T. Robertson. *The Glory of the Ministry*. Reprint, Grand Rapids: Baker, 1979.

Darius Salter. *What Really Matters in Ministry*. Grand Rapids: Baker, 1990.

J. Oswald Sanders. *Spiritual Leadership*. Rev. ed., Chicago: Moody, 1980.

John Seel. *The Evangelical Forfeit*. Grand Rapids: Baker, 1993.

Charles Haddon Spurgeon. *An All-Round Ministry*. Reprint, Pasadena, Tex.: Pilgrim, 1983.

————. *Lectures to My Students*. Reprint, Grand Rapids: Baker, 1977.

John Stott. *The Preacher's Portrait*. Grand Rapids: Eerdmans, 1961.

Howard F. Sugden and Warren W. Wiersbe. *Confident Pastoral Leadership*. 2d ed. Grand Rapids: Baker, 1993.

W. H. Griffith Thomas. *Ministerial Life and Walk*. Reprint, Grand Rapids: Baker, 1974.

David F. Wells. *God in the Wasteland: the Reality of Truth in a World of Fading Dreams*. Grand Rapids: Eerdmans, 1994.

————. *No Place for Truth or Whatever Happened to Evangelical Theology*. Grand Rapids: Eerdmans, 1993.

Warren W. Wiersbe and David Wiersbe. *Making Sense of the Ministry*. 2d ed. Grand Rapids: Baker, 1989.

Appendix 1

Affirmation of Doctrinal Convictions

Check the appropriate space and provide additional information if applicable.

❏ 1. I have carefully read *What We Teach* and affirm without reservation that I am in total agreement with the Elders of Grace Community Church.

❏ 2. I have carefully read *What We Teach* but have reservations about the following areas because I have not yet had the time or opportunity to study them fully for myself.

    a. _____

    b. _____

    c. _____

    d. _____

❏ 3. I have carefully read *What We Teach* and after careful personal study of the subjects still have strong reservations about the following areas:

    a. _____

    b. _____

    c. _____

    d. _____

_____
Applicant's Signature

_____
Date

(Grace Community Church grants permission for this form to be quoted, reprinted, or adapted without prior written permission.)

Appendix 2

Ordination Applicant Profile

Please answer the following questions thoroughly and objectively. If you have already graduated, answer only those questions that apply.

Please type.

Date _____

Name _____

Address _____

City, State, Zip code _____

Home Phone Number _____

Work Phone Number _____

Age _____ Birthdate _____ Seminary Student ❑ Yes ❑ No

❑ Married   ❑ Single   ❑ Divorced (explain circumstances)

_____

_____

_____

Children:

Name	Age	Birthdate

1. When did you come to know the Lord? (Give full testimony on a separate sheet) _____

2. How long have you been at Grace? _____

3. How many units have you completed? _____

4. What is your expected graduation date? _____

5. What is your anticipated schedule for the next semester? _____
   Number of work hours per week _____
   Number of units _____

6. Explain your understanding of a "call to ministry." What confirms that call to you? _____
   _____

7. Why did you choose to go to seminary? Do those who know you support your desire to attend seminary? _____
   _____

8. What is your major? _____
   Why was this your choice? _____

9. What are your short- and long-range goals? (Include in your answer specific areas of future ministry: pastorate, C.E. director, chaplain, etc.)
   _____
   _____

10. Is your spouse enthusiastic about your goals? Explain._____
    _____

11. In what ways do you see that your spouse can contribute to your ministry? _____

12. If your spouse asked you to take a break from your seminary training, what would you do? _____
    _____

13. What would happen if your wife became pregnant while you were in Seminary? How would this affect your further education?_____
    _____

14. Are you willing to submit the direction of your future ministry to the guidance and wisdom of the elders of Grace Community Church? Are you willing to receive counsel that would lead you in a direction other than seminary? _____

15. What role and responsibility would you like the elders to assume in the direction of your present and future ministry? Be specific.
    _____
    _____

16. What are your spiritual gifts? _____
    _____

17. How have your gifts manifested themselves in the body of Christ? Explain. _____

18. How have others counseled you as to your gifts and the particular type of ministry you should consider? Explain. _____

_____

19. List your previous and present ministries. With what pastor are you working closest? _____

_____

20. What are your strengths and weaknesses? Be objective. _____

_____

21. If the pastors and elders of Grace Church were to examine your current ministry, what "fruit" would they find? _____

_____

22. How will you order your priorities in the areas of seminary, ministry, and home?_____

23. How would you define a leader? Would you consider yourself a leader? If yes, explain your experience in this capacity. _____

_____

24. Is there anything in your life (since conversion) that you feel might or would disqualify you from future ministry? _____

_____

_____

(Grace Community Church grants permission for this questionnaire to be quoted, reprinted, or adapted without prior written permission.)

Appendix 3

Ordination
Comprehensive Questions

The Ordination Comprehensive comprises three areas in which ordination candidates will be required to demonstrate proficiency. These areas are systematic theology, general Bible knowledge, and practical theology. You are expected to be knowledgeable in every topic specified.

Ordination is conditioned on satisfactorily answering a minimum of seventy percent of all questions presented.

Recommendations for your preparation:

Systematic and Practical Theology

1. Be concise and to the point.

2. Cover what you believe are the essential points.

3. Outline your answer with verses (i.e., quote a verse, explain it; quote a verse, explain it; etc.)

General Bible Knowledge

1. Work with a top-down approach (book themes, outlines, chapters, passages, dates, people, verses).

2. Be sure to have someone quiz you periodically.

I. **Systematic Theology Comprehensive**

In systematic theology, the candidate shall be required to commence all answers by quoting a biblical reference(s) followed with an explanation of the text. The candidate must not proof-text his answers but must demonstrate a systematized theology based upon biblical exegesis.

A. *What We Teach*

The candidate must be able to articulate any doctrinal truth found in *What We Teach* with supporting Scripture.

B.   *Topical*

In addition, the candidate must be able to demonstrate a thorough knowledge of biblical systematics in the following areas.

1.   Bibliology

    a.   Scripture

        (1)   Theme
        (2)   Purpose

    b.   Revelation

        (1)   General
        (2)   Specific

    c.   Inspiration

        (1)   Method
        (2)   Verbal
        (3)   Plenary

    d.   Authority of Scripture

        (1)   Inerrancy
        (2)   Infallibility

    e.   Illumination

        (1)   Saved
        (2)   Unsaved

    f.   Canonicity

        (1)   Internal testimony
        (2)   External testimony

    g.   Theology Proper

        (1)   Proof of God
        (2)   Cosmological
        (3)   Teleological
        (4)   Anthropological
        (5)   Ontological
        (6)   Biblical

    h.   Attributes of God

        (1)   Communicable

(2) Incommunicable

i. Divine Decrees

(1) Problem of sin
(2) Providence

j. Trinity

(1) Unity
(2) Plurality

k. God the Father

l. God the Son

(1) Names
(2) Prerogatives
(3) Preexistence
(4) Theophanies
(5) Incarnation
(6) The kenosis
(7) Hypostatic union
(8) Humanity
(9) Temptation and impeccability
(10) Transfiguration
(11) Teachings

(a) Sermon on the Mount
(b) Olivet Discourse
(c) Upper Room Discourse

(12) Miracles
(13) Resurrection and ascension
(14) Glorification
(15) Mediatorial work
(16) Second Coming

m. God the Holy Spirit

(1) Baptism
(2) Filling
(3) Indwelling
(4) Sealing
(5) Ministry to believers
(6) Spiritual gifts
(7) Ministry in Old Testament versus New Testament

2.   Anthropology

    a.   Origin and nature of man
    b.   State of innocence
    c.   Original sin
    d.   The Fall
    e.   Personal sin
    f.   Punishment

3.   Soteriology

    a.   The Savior

        (1)   Offices
        (2)   Sufferings
        (3)   First and second Adam
        (4)   Work of Christ

    b.   Terminology

        (1)   Atonement
        (2)   Depravity
        (3)   Expiation
        (4)   Forgiveness
        (5)   Grace
        (6)   Guilt
        (7)   Imputation
        (8)   Justification
        (9)   Propitiation
        (10)   Reconciliation
        (11)   Redemption; ransom
        (12)   Regeneration
        (13)   Sacrifice
        (14)   Vicarious substitution

    c.   Election

        (1)   Predestination
        (2)   Man's free will
        (3)   Limited/unlimited atonement
        (4)   Convicting work of the Spirit
        (5)   Terms

            (a)   Calling
            (b)   Drawing
            (c)   Foreknowledge

            (d)   Foreordination
            (e)   Chosen

    d.   Conditions of salvation

        (1)   Old Testament versus New Testament
        (2)   Terminology

            (a)   Believe
            (b)   Repent
            (c)   Confess
            (d)   Surrender
            (e)   Lordship of Christ

    e.   Sanctification

        (1)   New birth/new creature
        (2)   Joint heirs with Christ
        (3)   Position versus practice
        (4)   Eternal security
        (5)   Ultimate glorification

    f.   Grace versus law
    g.   Heaven versus hell
    h.   Calvin's Tulip

4.   Ecclesiology

    a.   Christ and the church
    b.   Church government (see practical theology for additional subject matter)

5.   Eschatology

    a.   Covenants

        (1)   Abrahamic
        (2)   Mosaic
        (3)   Davidic
        (4)   New

    b.   Daniel's seventy weeks
    c.   Church and Israel
    d.   Advents of Christ
    e.   Rapture
    f.   Tribulation
    g.   Jacob's trouble
    h.   The Antichrist

        i.   The Beast
        j.   Marriage of the Lamb
        k.   Armageddon
        l.   The Kingdom
       m. Resurrection of the dead
       n.   Bema seat
       o.   Great white throne judgment
       p.   New Jerusalem
       q.   Hell and heaven
       r.   Eschatological chronology
       s.   Millennial views

  6. Angelology

        a.   Classification of angels
        b.   Angels and free will
        c.   Satan

             (1) Satan's sin
             (2) Career
             (3) Character
             (4) Methods
             (5) Future

        d.   Fallen angels
        e.   Ministry of angels

C. Apologetics

The candidate must be able to give a brief apologetic in the following areas:

  1. Historicity of the Bible

  2. Sudden Creationism (six days)

  3. Deity of Christ

  4. Problem of evil

  5. Existence of God

  6. Resurrection of Christ

  7. Virgin birth

II. General Bible Knowledge-Comprehensive

The candidate must be able to demonstrate breadth and depth in general Bible knowledge.

A.   General

   1.   Order of the sixty-six books

   2.   Old Testament and New Testament divisions

   3.   Contribution of each book to the whole

   4.   History, prophecy, poetry

   5.   Chronology of Israel (give dates for the following persons or events)

      a.   Abraham
      b.   Jacob
      c.   Joseph
      d.   Exodus
      e.   Judges
      f.   Saul, David, Solomon
      g.   Division of kingdom
      h.   Assyrian captivity
      i.   Babylonian captivity

         (1)   Phase 1 (Daniel)
         (2)   Phase 2 (Ezekiel)
         (3)   Phase 3 (Jeremiah)

      j.   Return under Zerubbabel
      k.   Major and minor prophets
      l.   Intertestamental period
      m.   Birth of Christ
      n.   Death of Christ
      o.   Jerusalem Council
      p.   Paul's first, second, and third missionary journeys
      q.   Destruction of Temple

   6.   Date of creation and flood

   7.   Religious Sects of Israel (date, theology, politics)

      a.   Pharisees
      b.   Sadducees
      c.   Essenes
      d.   Zealots

B.   Old Testament

   1.   General theme, date, and outline of each Old Testament book

2. Theme/importance of key Old Testament chapters

    a. Genesis 1, 2, 3, 4, 6–8, 9, 11, 12, 18–19, 22, 32, 37, 49

    b. Exodus 3–4, 7–11, 12, 14, 18, 19, 20, 32, 40

    c. Leviticus 1–7, 10, 16, 18, 23, 25, 26

    d. Numbers 6, 11, 12, 13, 22–25

    e. Deuteronomy 5, 6, 18, 28, 32, 34

    f. Joshua 1, 2, 6, 7, 9, 13–19, 20

    g. Judges 5, 6–8, 13–16

    h. Ruth 4

    i. 1 Samuel 1–4, 8–10, 13, 15, 16, 17, 18, 24, 25, 28, 31

    j. 2 Samuel 5, 6, 7, 11, 12, 13–20, 24

    k. 1 Kings 1, 2, 3, 8, 9, 11, 17, 18, 19, 21

    l. 2 Kings 2, 4, 5, 6, 17, 18, 22–23, 24–25

    m. 1 and 2 Chronicles. What is the chief feature that distinguishes Kings from Chronicles?

    n. Ezra 1, 3, 7–9, 10

    o. Nehemiah 1–2, 3–7

    p. Esther 3, 6–7, 9

    q. Job 1–2, 3–37, 38–41, 42

    r. Psalms 1, 2, 8, 15, 16, 19, 22, 23, 32, 42, 51, 73, 90, 100, 119, 127, 139, 150

    s. Proverbs 3, 31

    t. Isaiah 6, 13, 24, 36–37, 40–48, 53, 66

    u. Jeremiah 1, 23, 25, 30, 31–32, 34–44, 52

    v. Ezekiel 1, 8–11, 36–37, 38–39, 40–48

    w. Daniel 1, 2, 3, 4, 5, 6, 7, 8, 9, 10, 11, 12

    x. Hosea 1–3, 11–14

    y. Jonah 1, 2, 3, 4

    z. Haggai 1

3. Meaning/significance of key Old Testament passages

    a. Genesis 1:24–27, 31; 2:24; 3:15; 6:1–4; 12:1–3; 35:9–12; 50:20

    b. Exodus 3:13–15; 4:11; 15:26; 19:5–6; 20:1–17; 21:22–24

    c. Leviticus 17:11; 19:2; 20:6–8

    d. Numbers 16:31–35; 21:4–9

    e. Deuteronomy 4:2; 6:4–9; 13:1–5; 21:18–21; 22:28–29; 24:1–4; 29:29; 32:39

    f. Joshua 1:7–9; 10:12–15; 24:14–15

    g. Judges 11:34–40; 17:6 (21:25)

h.   Ruth 4:18–22

i.   1 Samuel 15:20–23; 16:7

j.   2 Samuel 7:8–16; 12:23; 24:24

k.   1 Kings 13:2

l.   2 Kings 4:18–28; 6:1–7

m.   1 Chronicles 11:2; 17:11–14

n.   Ezra 4:3; 10:9–15

o.   Nehemiah 8:4–8

p.   Esther 4:14

q.   Job 14:14; 19:25–26; 23:10–12; 26:7; 42:12–13

r.   Proverbs 3:5–8; 5:15–23; 6:16–19; 10:18–20; 16:18–19; 19:17; 22:6; 25:21–22; 27:17

s.   Ecclesiastes 1:2; 12:11–14

t.   Song of Solomon 8:6–7

u.   Isaiah 7:14; 9:6; 11:1–5; 53:4–6; 64:6

v.   Jeremiah 1:4–10; 29:10

w.   Lamentations 3:22–23

x.   Ezekiel 36:24–27

y.   Daniel 2:44–45; 7:13–4; 9:24–27; 12:1–2

z.   Hosea 4:6; 6:6; 11:1

aa.   Joel 2:28–32; 3:9–15

bb.   Amos 9:8, 13–15

cc.   Jonah 2:8–9; 4:2

dd.   Micah 4:3; 5:2; 6:8

ee.   Habakkuk 2:4

ff.   Zephaniah 1:14–8

gg.   Haggai 2:20–23

hh.   Zechariah 4:6; 12:10; 14:9–11

ii.   Malachi 1:6–14; 2:15–16; 3:8–10

C.   New Testament

1.   General theme, date, and outline of each New Testament book

2.   Theme/importance of key New Testament chapters

a.   Matthew 4, 5–7, 10, 13, 18, 23, 24–25

b.   John 2, 3, 4, 10, 13, 14, 15, 16, 17

c.   Acts 1, 2, 5, 6, 7, 9, 10, 13–14, 15, 27–28

d.   Romans (entire book by chapter)

e.   1 Corinthians (entire book by chapter)

f.   2 Corinthians 3, 5, 8–9, 11

g.   Galatians 2, 5
h.   Ephesians (entire book by chapter)
i.   Philippians 2, 3, 4
j.   Colossians 1, 3, 4
k.   1 Thessalonians 4
l.   2 Thessalonians 2, 3
m.   1 Timothy 2, 3, 4, 5
n.   2 Timothy 2, 3
o.   Hebrews (entire book by chapter)
p.   Revelation 1, 2–3, 4–5, 6, 8–9, 11, 12, 17–18, 19, 20, 21–22

3.   Meaning/significance of key New Testament passages

a.   Matthew 1:1–17, 23; 2:15; 5:1–11, 17–20, 31–32; 7:21–23; 13 (parables); 18:3–5; 28:18–20
b.   Mark 10:45
c.   Luke 18:31–33
d.   John 1:1; 3:5; 3:16; 10:30; 20:31
e.   Acts 1:8; 2:38; 4:12; 5:29; 8:15–17; 10:44–46; 16:31; 19:1–7
f.   Romans 1:18–32; 2:4–10; 3:21–28; 5:1–10; 7:15–25; 8:1–4, 28; 9:6, 19–24; 11:13–32
g.   1 Corinthians 2:12–16; 3:1–3; 5:1–13; 6:9–11; 7:1–7, 12–16; 11:4–10, 17–34; 12:13; 13:8–12
h.   2 Corinthians 9:6–5
i.   Galatians 5:16–6
j.   Ephesians 1:3–14; 2:1–10; 4:11–16; 5:22–23, 25; 6:10–17
k.   Philippians 2:5–8; 4:12–13, 19
l.   Colossians 1:15; 2:16–17
m.   1 Thessalonians 4:3–, 13–8; 5:1–3
n.   2 Thessalonians 2:1–12
o.   1 Timothy 2:9–15; 3:1–7, 8–13; 5:9–16, 17–25
p.   2 Timothy 2:1–9; 3:16; 4:1–6
q.   Titus 1:5–9; 2:3–5, 11–13
r.   Hebrews 2:17–18; 3:7–19; 4:15; 6:1–8; 9:11–15; 10:26–29; 12:4–11; 13:7, 17
s.   1 Peter 1:23; 2:2, 18–25; 3:7–9, 21; 5:1–3
t.   2 Peter 1:20–21
u.   1 John 1:5–10; 5:16–17
v.   Revelation 3:10; 12:1–4; 20:4

D.   Identify key Bible characters

Aaron	Elisha	Joshua the High Priest
Abednego	Elizabeth	Josiah
Abel	Enoch	Lazarus
Abihu	Epaphroditus	Leah
Abraham	Esau	Lois
Absalom	Esther	Lo-ammi
Achan	Eunice	Lo-ruhamah
Adam	Eutychus	Lot
Agrippa	Eve	Luke
Ahasuerus	Ezekiel	Mary
Ahithophel	Ezra	Mary and Martha
Alexander	False Prophet	Mary Magdalene
Ananias	Felix	Matthew
Andrew	Festus	Matthias
Annas	Gabriel	Melchizedek
Apollos	Gamaliel	Mephibosheth
Aquila	Gideon	Meshach
Artaxerxes	Haman	Michael
Balaam	Hannah	Miriam
Barak	Herod	Mordecai
Barnabas	Isaac	Moses
Beast	Isaiah	Naaman
Belshazzar	Jacob	Nabal
Bildad	James	Nadab
Boaz	James (Jesus' brother)	Nathanael
Caiaphas	Jephthah	Nebuchadnezzar
Cain	Jeremiah	Nehemiah
Cornelius	Jeroboam	Nicodemus
Cyrus	Jethro	Nimrod
Daniel	Jezebel	Noah
Darius	Joab	Onesimus
David	Job	Onesiphorus
Deborah	Jonah	Paul
Demas	Jonathan	Peter
Demetrius	John	Philemon
Eli	John the Baptist	Philip
Elihu	John Mark	Pilate
Elijah	Joseph	Priscilla
Eliphaz	Joshua	Rachel

Rahab	Shimei
Rebekah	Silas
Rehoboam	Simeon
Rhoda	Simon of Cyrene
Ruth	Simon Magus
Samson	Solomon
Samuel	Stephen
Sanballat	Thomas
Sapphira	Terah
Sarah	Timothy
Satan	Zaccheus
Saul	Zacharias
Shadrach	Zipporah
Shem	Zophar

III.   Practical Theology-Comprehensive

A.   General

The candidate must be able to discuss effectively, with biblical references, the following areas.

1.   Church government

    a.   Plurality of elders
    b.   Deacons
    c.   Deaconesses

2.   Principles of biblical decision making

3.   Role of women in the church

4.   Pastoral ministry priorities

5.   Expository preaching

    a.   Eisegesis versus exegesis
    b.   Whole counsel of God

6.   Biblical hermeneutics

7.   Church discipline

8.   Biblical ordinances

9.   Baby dedications

10.   Leadership development

11.   Biblical concept of missions

      a.   Local and foreign
      b.   Sending process
      c.   Evangelism
      d.   Parachurch versus local church

12. Stewardship

      a.   Loans
      b.   Giving

13. Lawsuits

14. Biblical basis of marriage and remarriage

15. Biblical basis for divorce

16. Manifestations of salvation

17. Progressive sanctification

      a.   Prayer
      b.   Personal Bible study tools/methods
      c.   Confession of sin
      d.   Worship
      e.   Fellowship

18. Social issues

      a.   Abortion
      b.   Politics
      c.   Homosexuality

19. Church's responsibilities to widows, orphans, and the poor

20. Demon possession/oppression

B. Situations

In addition, the candidate must have studied the following situations and be able to provide proper biblical counsel. The actual ordination questions need not be limited to the cases presented.

1.   Deacon/Elder responsibilities

      a.   Among the people you are called to shepherd is a man who is very analytical. He wants to understand just what deacons are supposed to do according to the Bible. What Scriptures would you use in helping him discern what the ministry of deacons should include?

b.   Someone from another church states that their church's position is that the pastor is the only elder and that he and his Board of Deacons form the ruling body of the church, but even their decisions are subject to congregational approval. He then challenges you to show him if you think there is a more biblical pattern for church rule. If you disagree with him, what form of church order and rule would you advocate? What line of scriptural evidence would you use to prove your position?

c.   A man comes to you and says he would like to be an elder in the church. He has served faithfully as a deacon for a number of years and now feels he is ready to serve as an elder. He asks you to tell him how he can become an elder. What would you say to him as far as what a faithful deacon should do and be in order to become an elder?

d.   An argument has occurred over whether 1 Tim. 3:11 refers to wives of deacons or whether it provides for an office in the church for women deacons. What would you state as your position on this issue, and how would you defend it?

e.   An elder in your church has a grown son who has recently deserted his wife and children and joined a cult. This elder has served faithfully for many years and is above reproach in the eyes of the people. Do you think he is still qualified to serve as an elder? If so, explain why, and if not, give your biblical reasons for thinking he should step down.

f.   Two leaders from a newly formed church come to you with an issue that has divided the leadership. Some of the leadership feel that a simple majority is reasonable, while others feel that leadership decisions should be made on a unanimous basis. Which do you believe is the biblical pattern for decision making, and what kind of biblical reasoning would you take them through to prove your point?

g.   The pastor and some of his leaders from a congregationally ruled church come to you and tell you that they are convinced that a plurality of elders is the biblical pattern for rule in the church. If you disagree with them, show what you believe is the biblical argument for your position. If you agree with them, show them a way to move the church from congregational to elder rule with the greatest possibility of maintaining church harmony in the process.

h. An elder, because of an indiscretion on his part, has stained his reputation and is no longer "above reproach." Because you are his close friend, you are asked to lead in dealing with him and his position as an elder. Describe step-by-step how you would handle the situation, taking it to the point of what you would do if he rejected counsel. What Scripture would you use to support your approach?

i. A man in your church has been suggested for the office of elder, and for the five years he has been in the church he and his family have led exemplary lives. His personal life in business, sports, and church has been above reproach. However, you know that he has been divorced in the past. You have talked with him and found that he was a Christian at the time of his divorce. However, his wife was unfaithful and she divorced him, even though he told her he was willing to forgive her and try to rebuild the marriage. In trying to determine how you would stand on his becoming an elder, what else might you want to know about him before you decided? Also, if another elder pointed out that he feels that 1 Tim. 3:2 ("husband of one wife") prohibits the man from ever being an elder, would you accept that as a valid reason for rejecting him? If not, why not?

2. Church leadership

a. To what Scripture passages would you refer to find the personal characteristics that God considers essential in calling men to the leadership of His people? What are the key qualities that you find in these passages? Are these qualities the kind of things that can be developed in a person, or are they a part of a person's innate nature?

b.   A deacon comes to you and asks you for some things he can say and do in the following situations: What would you say to help him prepare for each of these possible situations?

(1)   Visiting someone in the hospital who is very ill.

(2)   Someone whose spouse has just died.

(3)   Someone whose child has just died accidentally.

(4)   Someone who has just lost a job he's had for thirty years.

(5)   Someone who has just discovered he (she, his wife, parent, child) has a fatal disease.

3.   Discipling

a.   One of the young men you are shepherding has a genuine desire for spiritual growth, and he has come to you with a request that you disciple him. Under what circumstances would you be available to help him in his Christian walk? What is the first thing that you would tell him to do?

b.   A young man you are shepherding comes to you and asks if you will disciple him. He, however, is not sure what that means and asks you to tell him what the process of discipling includes. What would you tell him? List at least three things you think the process of discipling should include.

c.   A group of men in your fold asks you to teach them how to disciple other men. Outline or list what you would teach them, including philosophy, goals, bibliography, tools, materials, and methods.

d.   A man in your fold comes to you and says he is discipling someone who is most anxious to get on with using his spiritual gifts for the welfare of the body. He asks you how to help the young man identify his spiritual gifts. What would you tell him about spiritual gifts versus natural talents and how he could lead the young man to discover his gifts and implement them in the body?

e.   A young man you are shepherding is active in the youth ministry at the church, but he seems not to be doing well in gaining credibility with the youth, and he is unable to teach and lead them effectively. He is beginning to get very discouraged and is wondering if his spiritual gifts and natural talents really equip him for that ministry. How would you help him?

4.   Counseling situations

a.   One of the couples you have been shepherding has been anxiously awaiting the birth of their first child. You get a phone call from the new father telling you that the baby has been born with a serious physical handicap. His wife is in a semihysterical state. He wants you to come over. What will you tell him? How will you comfort her?

b.   A man who is the husband of one of the ladies in your fold calls you and in a desperate voice tells you his wife is packing her bags and preparing to leave him. He wants you to come over and talk her into staying. He admits that he has been unfaithful and he does, on occasion, drink too much and beat her. Now he realizes how much he loves her and needs her. What will you say? How will you deal with each of them?

c.   The doctor of a thirty-nine-year-old man you know very well calls to tell you that the man has terminal cancer and has less than a year to live. The doctor has just told him this, and he asked the doctor to call you and ask you to come to the hospital. He is married and has three children ranging from four to thirteen years old. What will you say to him? What will you say to his wife and children?

d.   You get a call from a crying mother and a distraught father. You have been shepherding their family, and they have just discovered that their fourteen-year-old daughter has been using drugs. Not only that, but she has been sexually involved with her boyfriend and is pregnant. She says she loves him. They want you to come over and talk to the four of them. How will you handle this?

e.   You discover that a woman you have been shepherding is in a deep state of depression over the recent death of her husband of over forty years. She has lost all her desire to live. She is not eating, and she appears to be willing to die herself. How would you deal with her?

f.   You have just been asked to come to the home of a couple in your fold whose seven-year-old son was hit by a car and killed. What will you say to them?

g.   A dear woman in the church whose husband has been painfully ill for an extended period of time calls you and tells you that her husband has just committed suicide. How will you comfort her? What would you say to her if her husband was not a believer?

h.   While passing the men's room late in the evening when everyone appears to be gone, you hear two familiar voices. Because there is stress in the voices, you stop and discover that one is asking the other to continue in a homosexual relationship. The other indicates that he thinks that what they've been doing is wrong, but the first voice continues to plead for one more sexual episode. By now you realize that both men are members of your church. What would you do?

i.   One of the men you have been shepherding is proving to be a very godly man and an exceptionally capable leader. You and he have developed a very close friendship. He requests your help in making a decision about a job opportunity. He has a good job where he is, but it has limited opportunities for advancement. He has been offered a job in another state with a lower starting salary but excellent prospects for advancement. His family has left the decision up to him and he wants to do whatever God directs.

He is having trouble making the decision and has come to you for help. What will you say?

j. A lady in your fold has been seeing a psychiatrist for some strange fears she has developed. Just recently she has become a Christian and believes that Christ can deal with the problem more adequately. There is no outwardly apparent reason for her fears. They seem to come on her without any connection to fearful events. How would you treat this problem using the Word?

k. The teenage son of one of the couples you shepherd has a problem with a compulsive desire to steal. He knows it is wrong, and he has the desire under control most of the time. His frustrated parents have taken him to a psychologist, who suggests long months of expensive counseling for their kleptomaniac son. You sense that there is more to this than simply the obvious sin of stealing. How would you diagnose this problem and attempt to help them deal with it?

l. A man comes to you with a tremendous burden for his wife who constantly nags him. He indicates to you that the only way he can have peace is for his wife to somehow change. He is desperate for her to change and wants your help. He intimates that he would like you to talk with her about this. What would you tell him?

m. A teenager in your shepherding area comes to you and pours out his heart about his poor self-image. He says that this has been a problem since early childhood. There are no obvious sin issues that you can discern. In fact, he is one of the exemplary young men in the church youth group. He confides that in the last month or so the problem has surfaced again with some intensity. How would you deal with this problem?

n. One of the women in your fold confides with you that she is being abused by her husband, who is not a church attender. He has made it clear to her that he wants nothing to do with her religion. As far as you are able to tell, there has been no sexual immorality, and you cannot discern any scriptural grounds for divorce. What would you advise her to do?

o.   "I'm terribly afraid that I'm going to hurt one of my children." The frustrated voice is from one of the new members of your fold. She confides that in the last month she has exploded at the slightest disobedience of her two preschool children. It is not that their behavior is out of the ordinary, but her reactions are sometimes violent. Just today she knocked one child across the room with a violent attack. In despair over her own uncharacteristic violence, she has called you for help to understand what her root problem is. What would you look for in your effort to help her?

p.   A father cannot understand why he clashes with his second son when his oldest son's antics do not seem to bother him half as much. You are asked to help him understand why he reacts this way. What would you tell him?

q.   One of the young people who has grown up in the church is doubting his salvation. He has been plagued with this for almost a year. You know that he knows all the verses that would give him assurance. In fact, you have discipled him personally. How would you help him understand the reason for his lack of assurance? What Scripture passages would you use?

r.   A woman in your fold comes to you very concerned about a decision she must make. It seems that her son has asked permission to drive a carload of other young people to a church retreat. She sees the value in his driving, since it would be a boost to his confidence. Still, she is unsure about the wisdom of it. In the course of the conversation you learn that she has not discussed this problem with her husband because she is the one to whom the children have always come. What would you advise her to do?

s.   An active couple in the church has a boy who is a terror. They have tried just about everything they can think of to deal with him, but he seems to be getting worse. Even their stern discipline is often ineffective. In fact, he almost seems to enjoy it. What Scriptures would give you insight into the cause and cure for this situation? How would you advise them?

t.   "We're having a communication problem in our marriage," confides a couple in your fold. They have tried to work it out, but they have come to an impasse. Their greatest frustration is that they do not even know why the problem exists. There is no outwardly sinful behavior in either of their lives. They have simply lost the desire to communicate with each other. How would you help them discern the root problem and deal with it?

5.   Church discipline

a.   A man you are shepherding comes to you and asks you to help him deal with a situation in which he feels he must admonish a fellow believer. A friend of his has taken the first step into a sinful situation, and he needs to confront him. What Scriptures would you share with him to inform him of how to admonish a sinning brother? Be sure to include the whole process so that he knows how to carry it through to the end, regardless of his friend's response.

b.   You have received second-hand information that one of the men in your fold has been coming home very late at night on several occasions recently, which is highly unusual for him since he works nearby and has always come home right after work. You were also told that his car has been noticed parked in front of a bar in the next town. What is the first thing that you would do? Would you confront him with this information yourself?

c.   A man who is a member of your fold has left his wife and family and is living with another woman. He has rejected your admonishment and also that of

412 Rediscovering Pastoral Ministry

the two others who went with you the second time. It is now time to "tell it to the church." You want to let him know that you are going to do that at the next communion service, but he has made himself unavailable to either personal contact or phone calls. You know where he is staying, so you are writing a letter to send to him by registered mail. What would you say in the letter? What would you do if before the communion service you received a letter or phone call from him resigning his membership in the church? In "telling it to the church," if you were asked to make the statement in regard to what he had done, what exactly would you say?

d. In regard to the preceding situation, what would be the church's obligation to this disobedient member's wife and family? What information would you have to collect and to what extent should the church help them financially and otherwise?

e. A woman in the church was asked to separate herself from the fellowship because she persisted in pursuing a divorce from her husband on unbiblical grounds. In spite of numerous efforts by her husband, her friends, and the elders of the church, she refused to change her mind and turned away from everyone close to her. Six months later she fell in love with another man and was soon remarried. Two years after the second marriage she contacts you in a very humble and repentant attitude. She knows she has offended her family, her friends, the church, and God Himself. She is deeply sorry and says that she wants to "make things right." She and her new husband both want to join the church. What would you tell her to do? What biblical guidance would you give her? Under what circumstances do you think she should be allowed to join the church again?

f. A deacon is dealing with a man in the church who has fallen into a sinful behavior pattern. The man has rejected the deacon's admonition on several occasions when they have talked privately. This time the deacon wants you to go along with him to be a witness to this confrontation. You have no firsthand knowledge of the matter, but you agree to serve as a witness to the man's response. What will you do to prepare your own heart and mind for this meeting? What Scripture passages will you review ahead of time? How will you pray for your own attitude? How will you pray for the others involved in this situation?

6. Apologetics

   a. A new neighbor catches you out in the yard and says he has heard that you are a Christian. He asks what it means to be a Christian. He says he has to leave in a few minutes so he would like you to give him as short an answer as possible. What would you include in your short answer?

   b. A new person at work is assigned to work with you. The second day on the job he says to you, "Hey, I understand you're a Christian, too. I'm a Mormon, what are you?" How would you reply? Describe what strategy you would use, knowing that you are going to be working next to each other.

   c. An acquaintance who has recently seen her baby die asks you how a loving God could allow innocent babies to die or be born deformed, people to suffer incurable illnesses, and others to be killed in accidents, war, or plagues. What kind of biblical defense would you give?

   d. You are visiting a new Christian who has just been assigned to you to shepherd. When you call upon her, her non-Christian husband challenges you with the following question: "How could a God of justice condemn people to everlasting hell just because they did not believe in Christ? How could He condemn those who have not heard the gospel and have never heard of Jesus?" How would you respond to his question?

   e. A woman who is new to the church and has just been assigned to you to shepherd says that she considers herself to be a "Christian feminist." She states that Paul was wrong to bar women from being elders in the church. What scriptural arguments would you use to refute her position?

f. If a person from any of the following groups were to challenge you to show them at least three major differences between what you believe and what they believe, what major differences would you delineate?

Jehovah's Witnesses	Liberal Christianity
Mormonism	Charismatics
Catholicism	Occultism
Christian Science	Eastern Mysticism
Scientology	Hinduism
New Age Movement	Buddhism

Index of Authors

Index of Scriptures

Index of Subjects

In this index, Greek and Hebrew words and phrases are transliterated and rendered in italics. References to books of the Apocrypha are also listed in this index.

The Master's Seminary Contributors

Irvin A. Busenitz, Th.D.
   Dean of Academic Administration,
   Professor of Old Testament

David C. Deuel, Th.M., Ph.D.
   Associate Professor of Old Testament

James M. George, Th.M.
   Associate Dean of Admissions and Placement,
   Assistant Professor of Pastoral Ministries

John MacArthur, Jr., D.D., Litt.D.
   President,
   Professor of Pastoral Ministries

Richard L. Mayhue, Th.D.
   Senior Vice President and Dean,
   Professor of Pastoral Ministries

Donald G. McDougall, Th.M.
   Associate Professor of New Testament

Alex D. Montoya, Th.M.
   Associate Professor of Pastoral Ministries

S. Lance Quinn, Th.M.
   Faculty Associate—Pastoral Ministries

James E. Rosscup, Th.D., Ph.D.
   Professor of Bible Exposition

James F. Stitzinger, Th.M., M.S.L.S., Ph.D. (A.B.D.)
   Director of Library Services,
   Associate Professor of Historical Theology

Robert L. Thomas, Th.D.
   Professor of New Testament

George J. Zemek, Th.D.
   Faculty Associate—Theology